p-Bits and q-Bits

Probabilistic and Quantum Computing

New Era Electronics: A Lecture Notes Series

Series Editors: Vijay Raghunathan *(Purdue University, USA)*
Muhammad Ashraf Alam *(Purdue University, USA)*
Mark S Lundstrom *(Purdue University, USA)*

Published

Vol. 3 *p-Bits and q-Bits*
Probabilistic and Quantum Computing
by Supriyo Datta

Vol. 2 *Quantum Communication:*
The Physical Layer of Future Optical Networks
by Mahdi Hosseini

Vol. 1 *Transistors!*
by Mark S Lundstrom

New Era Electronics: a Lecture Notes Series ▪ Volume 3

p-Bits and q-Bits

Probabilistic and Quantum Computing

Supriyo Datta
Purdue University, USA

World Scientific

NEW JERSEY · LONDON · SINGAPORE · BEIJING · SHANGHAI · HONG KONG · TAIPEI · CHENNAI · TOKYO

Published by

World Scientific Publishing Co. Pte. Ltd.
5 Toh Tuck Link, Singapore 596224
USA office: 27 Warren Street, Suite 401-402, Hackensack, NJ 07601
UK office: 57 Shelton Street, Covent Garden, London WC2H 9HE

Library of Congress Control Number: 2024941790

British Library Cataloguing-in-Publication Data
A catalogue record for this book is available from the British Library.

New Era Electronics: A Lecture Notes Series — Vol. 3
P-BITS AND Q-BITS
Probabilistic and Quantum Computing

ISBN 978-981-12-9449-5 (hardcover)
ISBN 978-981-12-9461-7 (paperback)
ISBN 978-981-12-9450-1 (ebook for institutions)
ISBN 978-981-12-9451-8 (ebook for individuals)

For any available supplementary material, please visit
https://www.worldscientific.com/worldscibooks/10.1142/13877#t=suppl

Desk Editor: Joseph Ang

Typeset by Stallion Press
Email: enquiries@stallionpress.com

To Anuradha

Tumi rabe nirabe …

Contents

Acknowledgements

I am indebted to Soumitra Choudhury and Shuvro Chowdhury who created the starting draft for these lecture notes from the slides and transcripts of video lectures for the online course that we have offered since Fall 2020.

I am grateful to Rishi Jaiswal and our Purdue online team, Lynn Hegewald, Leslie Schumacher, Joe Cychosz and Rick DeSutter for producing the course, especially under the pandemic conditions in 2020.

These lecture notes reflect the research in our group over the last decade and I thank Behtash Behin-Aein, Kerem Camsari and Brian Sutton for launching us on this path. I am also indebted to many other past and present group members who have taught me much of what is described here. This includes Rafatul Faria, Pervaiz Zeeshan Ahmed, Orchi Hassan, Jan Kaiser, Shuvro Chowdhury, Lakshmi Anirudh Ghantasala, Rishi Jaiswal, Sagnik Banerjee, Angik Sarkar, Vinh Quong Diep, Samiran Ganguly, Seokmin Hong, Shehrin Sayed.

I have also learnt much from outstanding collaborators including Joerg Appenzeller, Zhihong Chen, Pramey Upadhyaya, Shreyas Sen at Purdue, Sayeef Salahuddin at Berkeley and Drew Borders, Shunsuke Fukami, Hideo Ohno of Tohoku University.

A special thanks to the series editors Mark Lundstrom, Ashraf Alam and Vijay Raghunathan for their encouragement throughout this work. And finally I am thankful for my very supportive immediate and extended family: you know who you are :-)

A Note to Readers

These lecture notes are based on an online course *Boltzmann Law: Physics to Computing* which has been offered since Fall 2020 on nanoHUB and edX.

Like our previous courses *Fundamentals of Current Flow* (nanoHUB, edX) and *Introduction to Quantum Transport* (nanoHUB, edX), this course also deals with fairly advanced topics assuming no background beyond differential equations and linear algebra.

But unlike our previous courses this is a work in progress. We are publishing it in the spirit of the lecture note series which is to make cutting edge topics accessible as early as possible. With your feedback we eventually hope to create a more complete textbook.

There are NO displayed equations. All we have is a sequence of figures that are created from the slides used in the video lectures for the online course which has been offered since Fall 2020 on nanoHUB and edX.

The text is rather colloquial since it is an edited version of the transcripts for the video lectures and just tries to talk through the figures. The quiz questions are few in number and generally elementary.

No references to the original literature have been included. Hopefully readers can easily use modern search engines to look them up as needed. We cover three distinct fields, statistical mechanics, machine learning and quantum computing, each with a rich literature of its own.

What could these topics have in common to merit a course like this, one that cannot possibly do justice to any of the topics individually? I try to explain my rationale in the **Prologue:** *Please be sure not to skip it.*

Chapter 1

Prologue

Welcome to our course Boltzmann Law: Physics to Computing. We normally cover this course in 5 weeks: Week 1 on statistical mechanics, Weeks 2-3 on topics that you might see in a course on machine learning and finally weeks 4-5 on topics that you might see in a course on quantum computing. That is quite a spectrum of topics each of which is usually taught over multiple semesters in distinct academic communities. What could they have in common to merit a course like this, one that cannot possibly do justice to any of the topics individually?

1.1 Fig. 1.1: n versus 2^n

n	2^n	
1	2	
2	4	
10	1024	10^3
20	1 *million*	10^6
40	1 *trillion*	10^{12}

Fig. 1.1 n versus 2^n.

The short answer is that if we are talking about a system with n bits, then all these topics require us to visualize and work in a space with 2^n components as opposed to our familiar space with n components. Those two numbers are vastly different as you can see. An n of just 40 leads to $2^n \sim 10^{12}$! The computing paradigms we will talk about derive their power from being able to manipulate a system of n bits to control a response in a space with 2^n components.[1]

Now for a long answer, hope you don't find it too long :-)

[1]We will talk in terms of binary units or bits (d=2), but one could generalize to units with d states leading to a space with d^n components.

1.2 Figs. 1.2-1.3: Spintronics

We are all familiar with the wonders of modern electronics made possible by the high-speed operation of billions of transistors all integrated into a single chip. Information is stored and manipulated using bits or binary units each of which has two states that can be used to represent a 0 or a 1. This has proved to be a powerful paradigm which has continued the triumphant march of Moore's law decade after decade with no end in sight, though there is talk of slowing down. There is, however, extensive interest in an alternative paradigm generally referred to as quantum computing based on the use of *q-bits*. How are *q-bits* different from *bits*?

1.2.0.1 *Fig. 1.2*

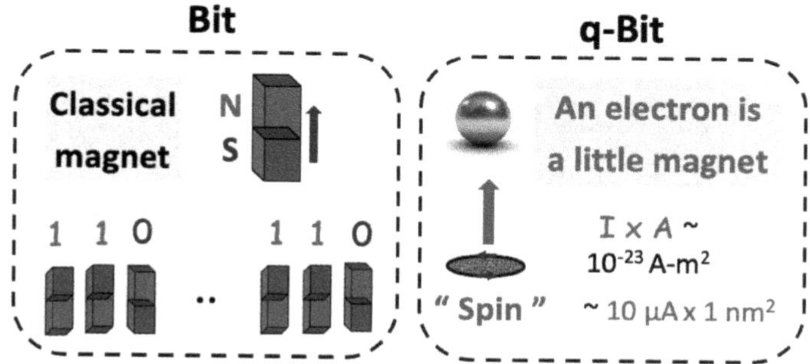

Fig. 1.2 One of the many possible physical representations of a *bit* and a *q-bit*.

One way to understand the difference between *q-bits* and *bits* is to consider a specific physical representation. A *bit* could be represented using small magnets or *nanomagnets* whose magnetization can be reversed as in MRAM[2] technology. The nice thing about this representation is that it connects smoothly with a representation for q-bits based on elemental *quantum magnets*.

Everyone knows that an electron carries an elemental charge, q. What is less-well known is that an electron is also an elemental magnet carrying a magnetic moment of $q\hbar/2m \sim 10^{-23} A\text{-}m^2$. It is as if the electronic charge is *spin*ning to give rise to a current, generating a magnetic moment whose

[2]Magnetoresistive Random Access Memory.

magnitude is roughly what would be created by a loop of area 1 nm^2 carrying a current of 10 μA. This elemental magnet or *spin* is the prototypical *q-bit*. How is it different from a classical magnet which is a prototypical *bit*?

1.2.0.2 *Fig. 1.3*

The difference can be understood by considering an experiment that took the scientific world by storm when first performed a hundred years ago. Suppose we come in with a beam of nanomagnets that have been passed through a strong magnetic field B along $\hat{z}$, such that their magnetic moments are all aligned in that direction. They are passed through a detector that separates magnetic particles based on their magnetic moment along a specific direction $\hat{n}$ that makes an angle θ with $\hat{z}$. The classical magnets all bend by the same amount determined by *cos* θ producing a *single spot* on the screen.

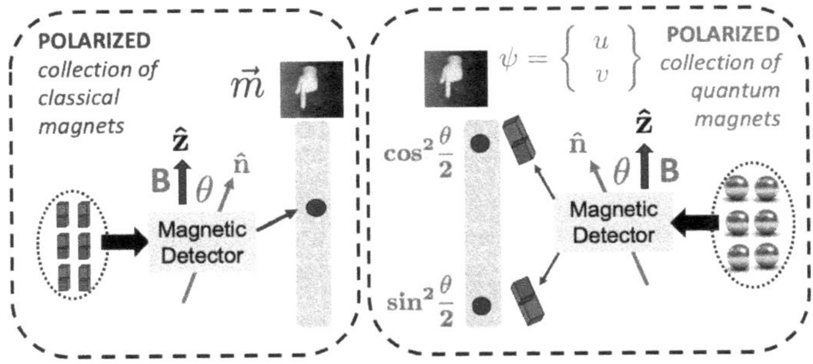

Fig. 1.3 Classical magnet versus quantum magnet, polarized collection.

Experimentally it is found that the quantum magnets produce *two spots*, but not equally strong. A fraction $cos^2(\theta/2)$ produce the spot corresponding to $+\mu_B\hat{z}$ while a fraction $sin^2(\theta/2)$ produce the spot corresponding to $-\mu_B\hat{z}$, giving an *average* magnetic moment of $cos^2(\theta/2)$ - $sin^2(\theta/2)$ = *cos* θ.[3] The two spots suggest that each quantum magnet has a magnetic

[3]Note that similar experiments can be done with polarized photons instead of spin-polarized electrons but the spots then have strengths $\sim cos^2\theta$ and $\sim sin^2\theta$. Mathematically the difference comes from the use of *vectors* for photon polarizations as opposed to *spinors* for electron spin polarizations. In these notes we will focus on the latter.

moment $\sim +\hat{n}$ or $\sim -\hat{n}$, with the degree of bending indicating a magnitude of $\mu_B = q\hbar/2m \sim 10^{-23} A\text{-}m^2$ for the associated magnetic moment.[4]

These observations may defy "common sense", but those are the facts and a straightforward mathematical framework has been developed to describe them. We say that quantum magnets do not have a magnetic moment $\vec{m}$, only a 2-component probability amplitude $\psi(\vec{m}) = \{u \quad v\}^T$. Any property S, like the *x-component* of spin, has an associated 2×2 matrix S_{op}: the average value of repeated measurements will be given by $\psi^T S_{op} \psi$. There is thus a major conceptual jump from a classical magnet to a quantum magnet, replacing a moment $\hat{m}$ with a complex probability amplitude $\psi(\vec{m})$, which can be used to tell the probability of measuring one of the two possible outcomes for any measurement.

These results were originally discovered through experiments conducted in vacuum with atoms, but have subsequently been exploited in devices as well leading to the term *spintronics*. Such spin-related effects are routinely included in the description of electronic devices, as some of you may remember from our course on quantum transport.[5] In short quantum effects *per se* are not new to device physicists. But then, what distinguishes *q-bits* and quantum computing from these "everyday" quantum effects?

1.3 Fig. 1.4: It's the correlations!

The key distinction is that *q-bits* and quantum computing require *strong correlations* among the quantum magnets, while the usual design of everyday devices rely on the correlations being weak. To understand this we can consider a toy device with just two *q-bits*, one of which shows has a 70-30 probability of being 0 or 1, while the other has a 30-70 probability. What is the composite probability of the collection being 00, 01, 10, 11?

The answer may seem simple: Probability of {00} equals 70% × 30% = 21%, that of {01} equals 70% × 70% = 49%, and so on. This should be accurate if the two are uncorrelated or only weakly correlated as we assume in our usual devices. But if they are *strongly correlated* then the composite probability is not the product of the components. For example if the two are perfectly anti-correlated then we may not have any 00 or 11,

[4]Although an electron is a quantum magnet it is difficult to do this experiment with electrons because they are charged particles with strong repulsive forces that will mask what we are looking for. Instead the experiments are done with neutral atoms having a net magnetic moment coming from unpaired electrons.

[5]On nanoHUB, on edX.

only 01 and 10 with probabilities 70-30 as shown. This is consistent with the individual p_1, p_2 shown, but it is not unique. We could come up with other composite probabilities that are intermediate between the fully correlated and un-correlated limits shown.

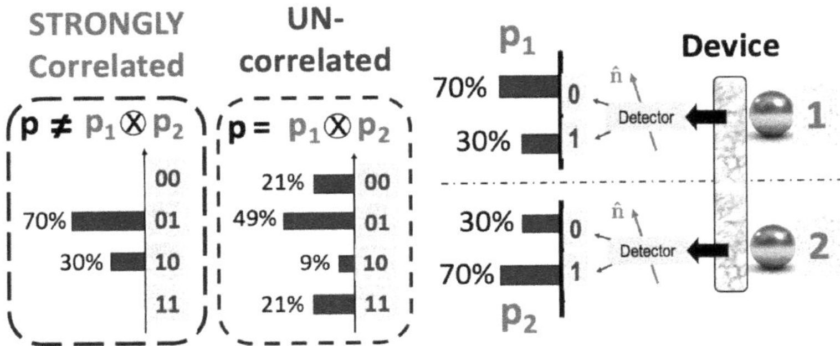

Fig. 1.4 Composite probability distribution cannot be obtained from the product of individual distributions *if they are strongly correlated.*

In more general terms, we can say that in the uncorrelated case the composite p with 2^n components is *factorizable*, that is, it can be written as the Kronecker product of the n individual p_i's each having 2 components. This means we can specify a distribution with $\sim n$ parameters. By contrast, to specify a distribution with strong correlations, we need $\sim 2^n$ parameters, making it much richer in the amount of embedded information. And as we noted at the outset (Fig. 1.1) there is an enormous difference between the two: An n of 40 corresponds to a 2^n of $\sim 10^{12}$! And this exponential advantage is what quantum computing seeks to harness.

1.4 Figs. 1.5-1.6: q-bits versus p-bits

1.4.0.1 *Fig. 1.5: q-bits*

A gated quantum computer (GQC) consists of a system of n *q-bits* that are operated on sequentially by a set of quantum gates to put them into a strongly correlated state such that if we measure the output repeatedly we will get a specific probability distribution whose peaks will solve some practical problem for us. The challenge of course is to construct gates operating in n*-space* for times of order n, that will give us a desired response

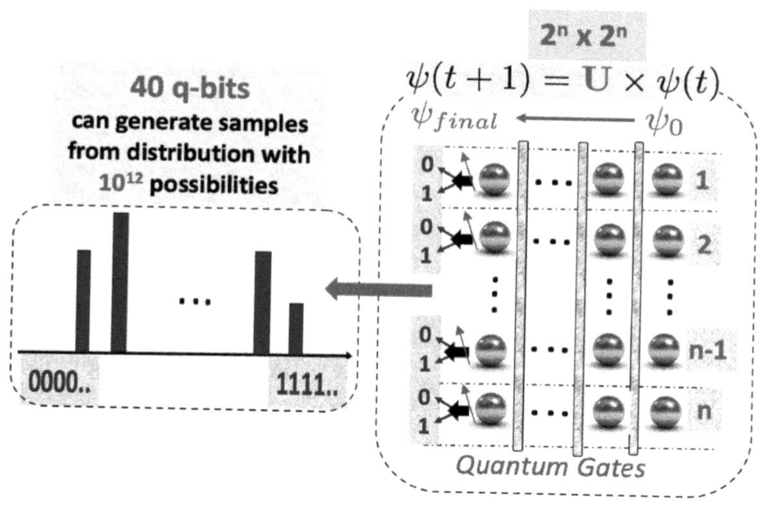

Fig. 1.5 A system of n *q-bits* can be correlated through a sequence of quantum gates to generate samples according to a desired distribution with 2^n components.

in 2^n-space. Grover search and Shor's algorithm[6] are two celebrated algorithms that you may have heard of in this context.

1.4.0.2 *Fig. 1.6: p-bits*

If the 2^n advantage we are talking about comes from *strong correlations* then perhaps a classical probabilistic system could also do something similar, namely prepare a strongly correlated classical state with 2^n components? The answer is kind of, but not exactly.

How could we construct the probabilistic version of the GQC sketched in Fig. 1.5 which operates on a set of 'n' *q-bits* with coherent quantum gates to transform its 2^n component complex wavefunction from $\psi(t)$ into $\psi(t+1)$? Answer: By replacing the quantum magnets in Fig. 1.5 with classical magnets as in Fig. 1.6, and using classical gates to transform its 2^n component real non-negative probability distribution function $p(t)$ into $p(t+1)$.

Could such a *p-computer* be useful? The reader may have heard of deep belief networks (DBN) used in the field of machine learning (ML) which

[6]These are discussed in Sections 6.3 and 6.4 respectively.

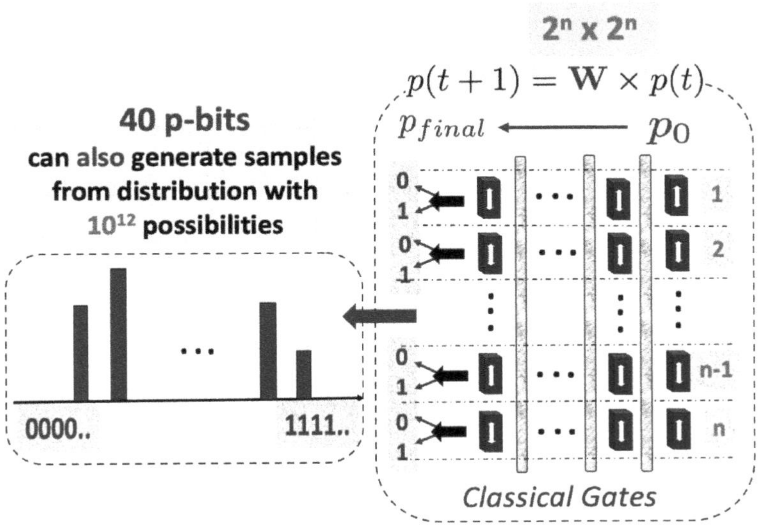

Fig. 1.6 A system of n *p-bits* can also be correlated through a sequence of classical gates to generate samples according to a desired distribution with 2^n components.

are essentially the *p-computer* sketched in Fig. 1.6. Each *p-bit* takes on one of two values 0 and 1 with probabilities determined by the weighted sum of the current values of all *p-bits*. In the ML literature these elements are known as binary stochastic neurons (BSN). The weights used in this summation can be *trained* to provide a desired response in 2^n-space. We could view the DBN sketched in Fig. 1.6 as the classical analog of the GQC sketched in Fig. 1.5.

I should note that in this course we will focus on the use of binary units or *p-bits* to correspond to standard *q-bits*. More generally we could think of d-valued units[7] or even continuous valued units. The latter are used in deep neural networks (DNN) based on *neurons* whose output takes on continuous analog values determined by applying a non-linear activation function to the weighted sum. The basic principle is that of interconnecting 'n' units to obtain a desired response in an exponentially larger space, in a manner that some readers may find reminiscent of Koopman operators.

[7]In quantum computing d-valued units are sometimes referred to as qudits.

1.5 Figs. 1.7-1.8: The key difference

1.5.0.1 *Fig. 1.7*

So what distinguishes the *q-circuit* from the *p-circuit*?

As we will see, their mathematics look similar

q-bits: $\psi(t+1) = \mathbf{U} \times \psi(t)$ **U**: Unitary matrix (Chapter 6)

p-bits: $p(t+1) = \mathbf{W} \times p(t)$ **W**: Stochastic matrix (Chapter 4)

But there is at least one *fundamental* difference: **U** is a unitary matrix with complex components while **W** is a stochastic matrix with real non-negative real components. In his seminal 1982 paper that inspired much of quantum computing, Feynman referred to this as the *only difference*.

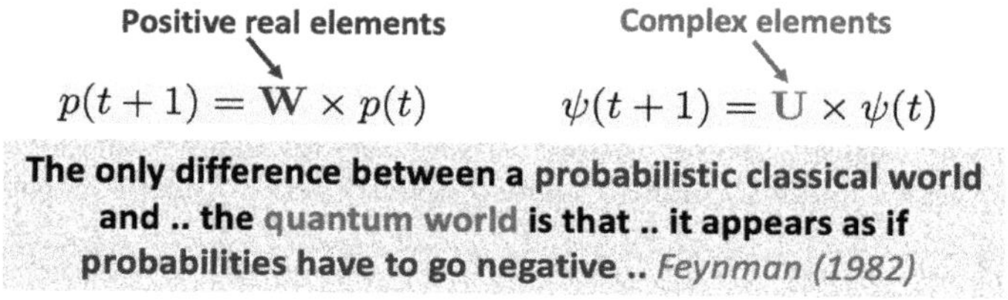

Positive real elements

$p(t+1) = \mathbf{W} \times p(t)$

Complex elements

$\psi(t+1) = \mathbf{U} \times \psi(t)$

The only difference between a probabilistic classical world and .. the quantum world is that .. it appears as if probabilities have to go negative .. *Feynman (1982)*

Fig. 1.7 The key distinction between quantum hardware and classical probabilistic hardware arises from the complex elements of the **U** matrix in place of the non-negative real components of **W**.

1.5.0.2 *Fig. 1.8*

To understand this key difference, it may be helpful to compare two toy examples one representing a 2 *p-bit circuit* and the other a 2 *q-bit circuit*. Each one has four states labeled $\{00\ 01\ 10\ 11\}$ and each circuit converts an evenly distributed probability into one that is peaked at $\{00\}$.

The *p-circuit* achieves this conversion with classical gates that effectively multiply the initial distribution with a stochastic matrix **W** having real non-negative components, while the *q-circuit* achieves this conversion with quantum gates that effectively multiply the initial distribution with a unitary matrix **U** having complex components,

In the first case, the only way to get 0 at the output is by making the entire row zero, since all elements are positive. But in the second case

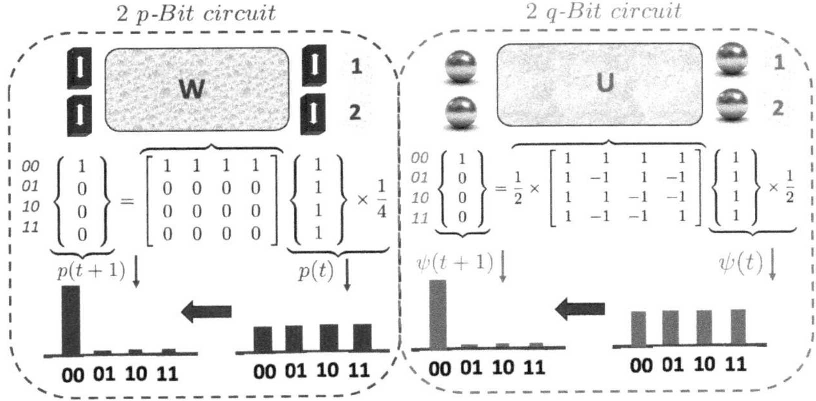

Fig. 1.8 A *p-circuit* and a *q-circuit* each of which converts a probability evenly spread among four states {00 01 10 11} into one peaked at {00}.

there are positive and negative elements[8] which can cancel each other out to produce a net zero output. But this added flexibility comes with the need to control each of the elements accurately so that the positives and negatives indeed cancel out to produce zero.

Note that with *q-circuits* the ψ represents a complex probability amplitude whose squared magnitude is a non-negative number that gives us the actual probability of a particular observation. All components of the probability function $p(t)$ add up to one, while it is the the squared magnitudes of the components of the wavefunction $\psi(t)$ that add up to one.

In the classical case when the probability distribution $p(t)$ is not factorizable, the system is said to be **correlated**. In the quantum case when the complex wavefunction $\psi(t)$ is not factorizable, the system is said to be **entangled**.

1.6 Fig. 1.9: Hardware acceleration

Both probabilistic circuits (Chapters 3, 4) and quantum circuits (Chapters 5, 6) have to be designed to control the interactions among n elements to control the response in 2^n-space. Their key difference is the nature of the $2^n \times 2^n$ matrices, **W** and **U** operating on the probability distribution $p(t)$ and the wavefunction $\psi(t)$ respectively. One has real non-negative

[8]More generally, complex elements.

elements describing classically understood behavior, while the other has complex elements that can enable non-classical behavior, some of which can be very intriguing like the EPR experiment discussed in Section 5.6.

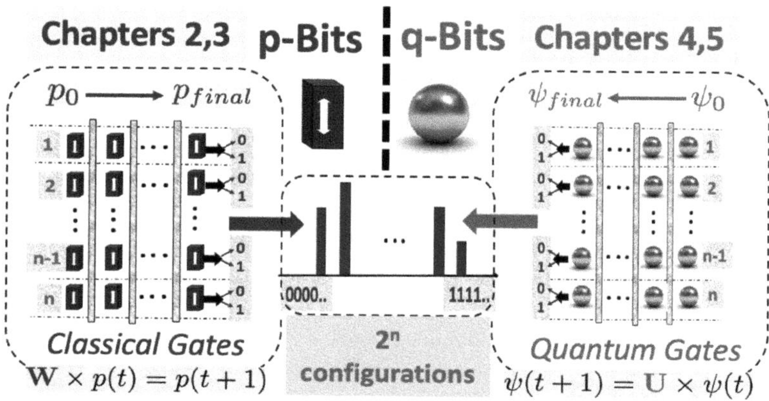

Fig. 1.9 Both *p-* and *q-circuits* are designed in n-space to control the response in 2^n-space. But their key difference is the nature of the matrices $\mathbf{W}$ and $\mathbf{U}$. One has real non-negative elements, the other has complex elements that can enable non-intuitive behavior like the EPR experiment discussed in Section 5.6.

Note that if we are actually multiplying matrices then it is not too much more difficult to handle complex matrices relative to real matrices. But these matrices are $2^n \times 2^n$ which can be enormous even for modest values of n. And so in practice, one uses powerful Monte Carlo sampling techniques which can often provide sufficiently accurate approximate results, not unlike the way a well-designed *exit poll* of a few thousand people can predict the results of a full election with millions of voters.

The sampling technique often works well for *p-circuits* with non-negative probabilities, but are less effective for *q-circuits* with complex probabilities that show large degrees of cancellation.[9] Indeed this is the chief rationale behind building *q-circuits* that can sum up the complex probabilities through its *intrinsic quantum physics.*

For problems that only involve non-negative probabilities, *p-circuits* can be just as effective as the corresponding *q-circuits*, provided the *p-circuit* is implemented using the natural physics of *p-bits* and classical circuits. Usually the sampling algorithms are implemented by writing a code in

[9]This so-called sign problem is discussed in Section 6.5.3.

a high level language, making it versatile but inefficient. Much can be gained simply by replacing software with specialized hardware, and such improvements should be distinguished from those that come from exploiting the magic of quantum physics through the cancellation properties of the complex wavefunction ψ.

This is why we find it instructive to use *p-circuits* as a counterpoint to clarify what is unique about a specific *q-circuit*. Both have to design the interactions among n bits and implement them in hardware, so as to generate desired samples form a vast repertoire with 2^n possibilities. One has the added power that comes from the use of complex probability amplitudes, but which also comes with stringent demands on the phase.

1.7 Statistical mechanics

Hope you see my rationale for looking at both probabilistic (Chapters 3 and 4) and quantum (Chapters 5 and 6) generative models in the same course. But why Chapter 2 on statistical mechanics?

It reviews seminal concepts like the Boltzmann law, entropy and free energy that were developed in the 19th century to understand macroscopic properties in terms of the atoms at the microscopic level. This may sound very different, but this too is about relating interactions in n-space with response in 2^n-space. Their motivation, however, is reversed from ours. We want a response in 2^n-space and train our gates in n-space to provide the necessary interactions. By contrast, they took the "gates" provided by Nature in n-space and wanted to calculate the resulting properties in 2^n-space. But their insights can be useful to us, an example of which is the *diffusion model* in machine learning.

It is time to get started :-)

Chapter 2

Statistical Mechanics

2.1 State Space

Welcome to our course, *Boltzmann Law: Physics to Computing.* This is Lecture 2.1: Watch youtube video

2.1.1 *Fig. 2.1: Fermi function*

Let me start with something that probably most of you have seen before. Whenever we talk about any material like an atom or a molecule or a solid, we draw a set of energy levels which the electrons in that material can occupy (Fig. 2.1a). And usually left to itself at equilibrium, the electrons all want to go to the lowest energy levels.

Now, why don't they all crowd into the same level? Well, that's where we invoke the exclusion principle and say that each level can at most accommodate one electron. And so the lowest levels are usually filled and the high upper levels are empty. At low temperatures, there's a nice clean dividing line between them, which we call the electrochemical potential or μ.

But as you raise the temperature, that dividing line becomes more diffuse, and we have something called the *Fermi function* (see Fig. 2.1(b)). This Fermi function is plotted here on the horizontal axis, whereas on the vertical axis, I have this dimensionless quantity which tells you how far the level is from the electrochemical potential, normalized to the thermal energy, kT. k is Boltzmann's constant and T is the absolute temperature.

When you consider levels that are way above the electrochemical potential, the Fermi function is 0, indicating that the level is surely empty. When you're down way below the electrochemical potential, that's when the Fermi function is 1 indicating that the level is surely full. And in between,

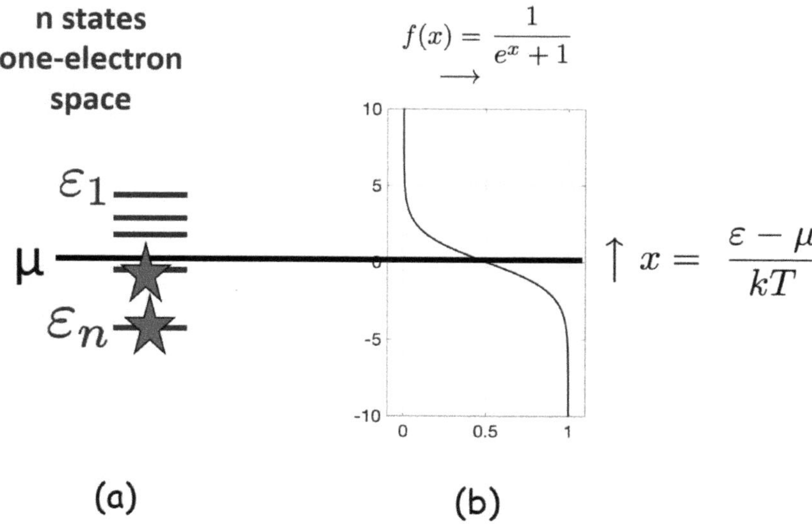

Fig. 2.1 Fermi function.

it changes from 0 to 1. Right at $\varepsilon = \mu$ it's 0.5. What does that mean? Well, not that there's half an electron there. What it means is that levels there are sometimes full and sometimes empty, and the average occupation is 0.5. Anyway, this is the Fermi function that you have probably seen before.

But what I really want to talk about is a much more general law, *Boltzmann law*. The Fermi function can be obtained from it. You may have heard of the *Bose-Einstein distribution* that's obeyed by photons. Well, that too can be obtained from the Boltzmann law, although we won't be talking about it. The *Boltzmann law* applies to all systems in equilibrium. It doesn't matter how complicated or simple it is.

2.1.2 *Fig. 2.2: Boltzmann law*

Now, in order to explain the Boltzmann law, I need to introduce the concept of *state space* which is a very important concept in this entire course. The idea is that each of our one electron levels (see Fig. 2.2(a)) can be in one of two possible states. It can be either full or empty, that's a 0 state or a 1 state. So when you want to describe the states of the entire system, then you have to write a binary number, something like this

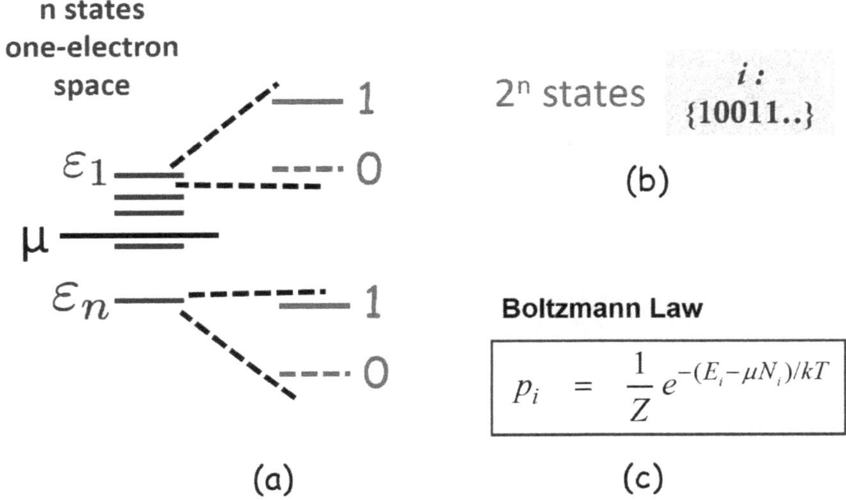

Fig. 2.2 State space and Boltzmann law.

(see Fig. 2.2(b)): {10011}, meaning the first state is full. The second state is empty. The third state is empty. Fourth state is full. Fifth state is full, and so on.

So how many such states are possible in state space? The answer is 2^n, because you see, there are n of these digits and each one can be 0 or 1: Overall you can think of 2^n combinations. And that's the state space as opposed to the one electron space, which has only n levels.

Now, the *Boltzmann law* is stated in this state space (see Fig. 2.2(c)) and what it says is that the probability for the system to be in the i-th state, depends on the exponential of the negative of this quantity $((E_i - \mu N_i)/kT)$. What is this quantity? It involves the energy E_i of the ith state and the number N_i of electrons in the ith state, and the thermal energy, as in the Fermi function, the same kT.

And what's this constant $(1/Z)$ in front? Well, that constant should be chosen so that all the probabilities add up to 1, because the system must be in one state or another. What I'll show you next is how from this general law you can obtain the Fermi function. Because as I said, this is the most general law that applies to anything. Doesn't matter how complicated or simple, okay?

2.1.3 *Figs. 2.3-2.4: Fermi function from Boltzmann law*

2.1.3.1 *Fig. 2.3*

Let's take the simplest thing, a system with just one level (see Fig. 2.3(a)). So in the one electron space, there's just one state. Now, how many states are there in state space? Well, 2^1, which is to say that you have a zero state and a one state. And to write down the Boltzmann law, I need the energy and the number of electrons for each one of those.

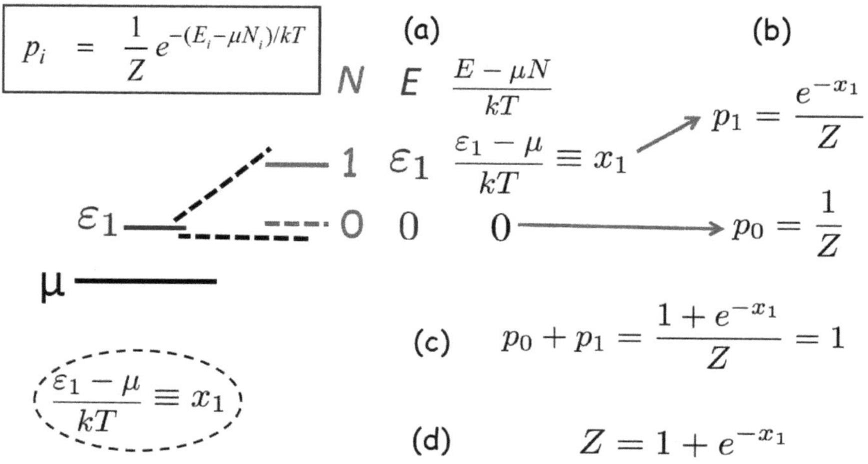

Fig. 2.3 System with one energy level.

The number of electrons is (a) 0 for the zero state and (b) 1 for the one state. The energy is (a) 0 for the zero state and (b) equal to whatever the energy level is ϵ_1 for the one state. So we can now write down the $(E - \mu N)/kT$ as (a) 0 for the zero state and $(\epsilon_1 - \mu)/kT$ for the one state.

Now we are ready to write down the probabilities (see Fig. 2.3(b)). The probability of the zero state is $1/Z$, because e^0 is 1. The probability of the one state, well that's e^{-x_1}/Z, where we define this dimensionless quantity x_1, as $(\epsilon_1 - \mu)/kT$.

Well, then how do I find Z? The idea is that the two probabilities must add up to one because this system has only two possibilities (see Fig. 2.3(c)). And so $p_0 + p_1 = 1 + \exp(-x_1)$ divided by Z must equal one, which tells me that Z must be $1 + \exp(-x_1)$.

2.1.3.2 *Fig. 2.4: Boltzmann Law is NOT the Boltzmann approximation*

So now we can take this Z and substitute it back to write p_1 as $\exp(-x_1)$ divided by $1 + \exp(-x_1)$ (see Fig. 2.4(a)). And with a little bit of algebra, you can write it in a form, that you will recognize as the Fermi function that I've stated before. So what I've shown you then is that starting from Boltzmann law when I apply to a simple system, I get the Fermi function.

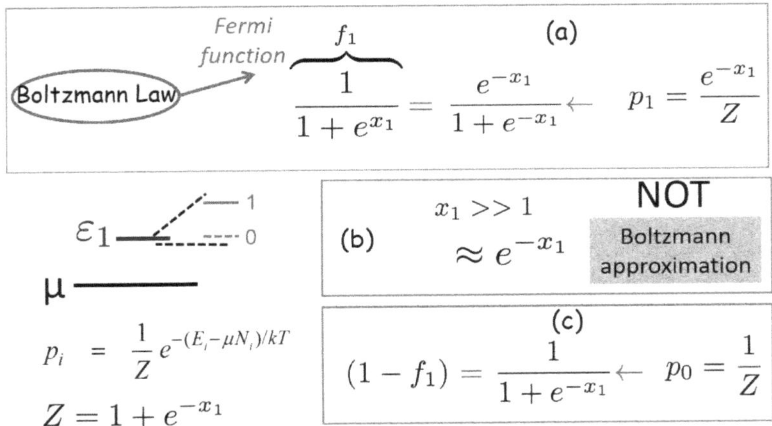

Fig. 2.4 Fermi function from Boltzmann law.

Sometimes people approximate the Fermi function with $\exp(-x_1)$. They say, well if $x \gg 1$, then I can drop the one and then this will become $\exp(-x_1)$. And that's often referred to as the Boltzmann approximation (see Fig. 2.4(b)). And if you have taken courses in semiconductor devices, you've probably seen it and used it extensively.

But I want to stress again, that the Boltzmann law we are going to talk about in this course, is not this Boltzmann approximation. What we are talking about is the Boltzmann law which is far more general than the Fermi function, and certainly not an approximation to it.

Finally, just as we wrote down the Fermi function f_1 describing the probability for the system to be in state 1, we could also write down the probability for the system to be in state 0 (see Fig. 2.4(c)). And that, as you might expect will be $1 - f_1$ so that the two probabilities add up to one. All this follows straight from the Boltzmann law applied to a one level system.

2.1.4 *Figs. 2.5-2.7: Two non-interacting energy levels*

2.1.4.1 *Fig. 2.5*

Let me now go through a little more complicated example involving two energy levels in the one-electron space, each of which can be 0 or 1.

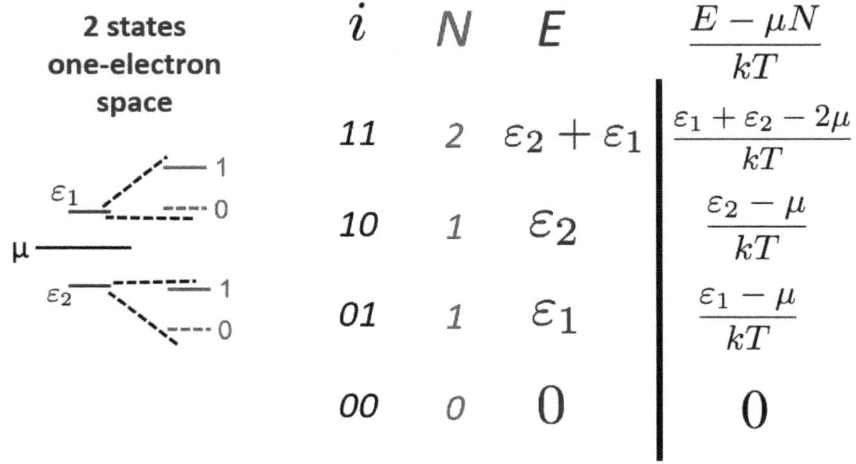

Fig. 2.5 System with two energy levels.

In this system then, I could label all the different states as {00}, {01}, {10}, and {11}. {00}, means both are empty. {01} means first one's empty. second one's full. {10} is first one's full. second one's empty. {11} is where both are full.

Now, to apply the Boltzmann law, I need to write down $(E - \mu N)/kT$ for each one of these possibilities. So let's first write down the number of electrons. For {00} there are no electrons, so $N_i = 0$. For {01} or {10}, there's one electron, so $N_i = 1$. For {11}, then there are two electrons because both are full and $N_i = 2$.

What about the energy? {00} has no electrons and the energy $E_i = 0$. For {01}, then then energy $E_i = \epsilon_1$. For {10} energy is $E_i = \epsilon_2$. And for {11}, then $E_i = \epsilon_1 + \epsilon_2$.

So now you can fill out $(E_i - \mu N_i)/kT$ for each of the four possibilities as shown. For {00}, $(E_i - \mu N_i)/kT$ is just 0. For {01} it is $(\epsilon_1 - \mu)/kT$. For {10} it is $(\epsilon_2 - \mu)/kT)$. And finally for {11}, it is $(\epsilon_1 + \epsilon_2 - 2\mu)/kT$.

2.1.4.2 *Fig. 2.6:* $E - \mu N$

Now I can fill out the probabilities as shown in Fig. 2.6(a)).

$$p_i = \frac{1}{Z} e^{-(E_i - \mu N_i)/kT}$$

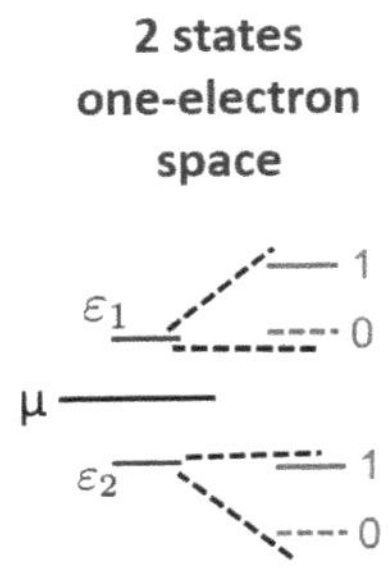

2 states one-electron space

ε_1 — 1, 0; μ; ε_2 — 1, 0

i	p_i	$\frac{E-\mu N}{kT}$	
11	$p_{11} = \frac{e^{-x_2}e^{-x_1}}{Z}$	$\frac{\varepsilon_1 + \varepsilon_2 - 2\mu}{kT}$	$= x_1 + x_2$
10	$p_{10} = \frac{e^{-x_2}}{Z}$	$\frac{\varepsilon_2 - \mu}{kT}$	$= x_2$
01	$p_{01} = \frac{e^{-x_1}}{Z}$	$\frac{\varepsilon_1 - \mu}{kT}$	$= x_1$
00	$p_{00} = \frac{1}{Z}$	0	

(a)

(b) $$Z = 1 + \underbrace{e^{-x_1}}_{y_1} + \underbrace{e^{-x_2}}_{y_2} + \underbrace{e^{-x_2}e^{-x_1}}_{y_2 \times y_1} = (1 + y_2)(1 + y_1)$$

Fig. 2.6 State space probabilities of a system with two levels.

What's the next step? Well, now I have to find Z. For this I require all probabilities to add up to 1 (see Fig. 2.6(a)). So, I have to add all four probabilities, and the answer should be 1. Which means just like before, Z should be equal to the sum of the numerators, which is $1 + \exp(-x_1) + \exp(-x_2) + \exp(-x_2)\exp(-x_1)$.

Just to simplify the algebra a little, I've given names to two of these terms. This exponential of $-x_1$, I call it y_1, and $\exp(-x_2)$, well that's y_2. And $\exp(-x_2)\exp(-x_1)$? Well, that's y_2 times y_1. Now, I can easily factorize this and I can write it as $(1 + y_2)(1 + y_1)$. You can see that when you multiply that out, you'll get $1 + y_2 + y_1 + y_2 y_1$.

2.1.4.3 *Fig. 2.7: Probabilities*

So now I put Z back into the probability expressions (see Fig. 2.7), and with a little algebra I find that p_{11} is basically just f_1 times f_2, which is what you might have guessed if you note that f_1 is the probability one level is full and f_2 is the probability the other one is full. So the probability that both are full is $f_1 f_2$. But it comes straight out of the Boltzmann law.

$$
\begin{array}{cccc|cc}
 & & & p_i & \dfrac{E-\mu N}{kT} & \\
\overbrace{\dfrac{e^{-x_2}}{1+e^{-x_2}}}^{f_2} & \overbrace{\dfrac{e^{-x_1}}{1+e^{-x_1}}}^{f_1} & = & p_{11} = \dfrac{e^{-x_2}e^{-x_1}}{Z} & \dfrac{\varepsilon_1+\varepsilon_2-2\mu}{kT} & = x_1 + x_2 \\
 & & & p_{10} = \dfrac{e^{-x_2}}{Z} & \dfrac{\varepsilon_2-\mu}{kT} & = x_2 \\
\underbrace{\dfrac{1}{1+e^{-x_2}}}_{1-f_2} & \underbrace{\dfrac{e^{-x_1}}{1+e^{-x_1}}}_{f_1} & = & p_{01} = \dfrac{e^{-x_1}}{Z} & \dfrac{\varepsilon_1-\mu}{kT} & = x_1 \\
 & & & p_{00} = \dfrac{1}{Z} & 0 &
\end{array}
$$

$$
\boxed{p_i = \frac{1}{Z}\, e^{-(E_i-\mu N_i)/kT}}
$$

Fig. 2.7 State space probabilities of a system with two levels (contd.).

Now, if we want to write say p_{01}, it'll be similar, look much the same, except that now the numerator only has $\exp(-x_1)$. So I don't have the $\exp(-x_2)$ anymore. And so I have two factors where the first one f_1, is the same Fermi function. But the other factor instead of being f_2, what I really got now is $1 - f_2$. It's a little algebra, you can check that this is indeed 1 minus that quantity. And again, the result makes good sense if you consider what's p_{01}?

You're asking what is the probability that one level is full and the other one is empty? Well, the chance that the first level is full, that's f_1. The chance that the second level is empty, well, that's $1-f_2$. So the probability of finding the system in state $\{01\}$ is $(1-f_2)f_1$. And you could go ahead and look at p_{10} and p_{00} as well and you'd get the answers you expected.

2.1.5 *Fig. 2.8: Two levels with interaction*

Now what you might say is okay, but then why am I bothering with the Boltzmann law? Because all the information is there in the Fermi functions, and I could have written these down anyway without using the general law.

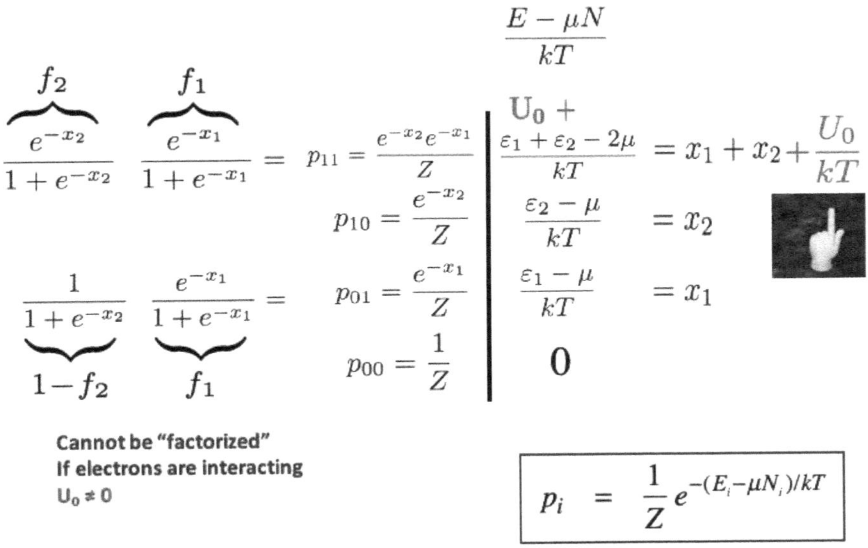

$$\frac{E-\mu N}{kT}$$

$$\overbrace{\frac{e^{-x_2}}{1+e^{-x_2}}}^{f_2}\;\overbrace{\frac{e^{-x_1}}{1+e^{-x_1}}}^{f_1} = p_{11} = \frac{e^{-x_2}e^{-x_1}}{Z} \qquad U_0 + \frac{\varepsilon_1+\varepsilon_2-2\mu}{kT} = x_1 + x_2 + \frac{U_0}{kT}$$

$$p_{10} = \frac{e^{-x_2}}{Z} \qquad \frac{\varepsilon_2-\mu}{kT} = x_2$$

$$\underbrace{\frac{1}{1+e^{-x_2}}}_{1-f_2}\;\underbrace{\frac{e^{-x_1}}{1+e^{-x_1}}}_{f_1} = p_{01} = \frac{e^{-x_1}}{Z} \qquad \frac{\varepsilon_1-\mu}{kT} = x_1$$

$$p_{00} = \frac{1}{Z} \qquad 0$$

Cannot be "factorized"
If electrons are interacting
$U_0 \neq 0$

$$p_i = \frac{1}{Z}e^{-(E_i-\mu N_i)/kT}$$

Fig. 2.8 State space probabilities of a system with two levels (contd.).

Well, the answer is that that's only true because we have assumed that the electrons are not interacting. And so when you have two electrons, the energy is really just the sum of what you get for one electron. And that is what allows you to nicely factorize all the probabilities into separate Fermi functions.

But if they were interacting, then you'd have an extra term here (see Fig. 2.8), something that would denote the interaction energy between a pair of electrons. That's this U_0. And then you wouldn't be able to factorize it so nicely. So you wouldn't be able to write your answers in terms of Fermi functions, but you'd still be able to use the Boltzmann law.

This general law which applies to, as I said, all systems, whether they're interacting or not interacting, whether they're simple or complicated. But it's only for the special case of non-interacting electrons that you can factorize it nicely into Fermi functions.

But you might say, when I took my courses on solid state devices or solid state physics we always used the Fermi functions but electrons are interactive. So how did we get away with it? Well, the answer is that the way people use the Fermi functions in this one electron space is using something called the *mean field theory*. And this is something we'll come back to in the last lecture of this week. We'll come back and connect up to this and explain how that mean field theory works.

But right now the main point I wanted to make is that the Boltzmann law is the general law that applies to any system. And everything else kind of follows from it. This is really the central principle of equilibrium statistical mechanics. And that's this Boltzmann law, which we just introduced. In the next lecture I'll try to explain where it comes from.

2.1.6 *Quiz*

2.1.6.1 *Question 1*

With 8 one-electron energy levels, what is the number of levels in state space?[1]

2.1.6.2 *Question 2*

If we have two one-electron energy levels with NO interactions, what is the probability that they will both be empty? The answer should be in terms of the Fermi functions, f_1 and f_2 corresponding to each of the two levels.[2]

2.1.6.3 *Question 3*

At what value of the energy ε is the Fermi function equal to 0.5? The answer should be in terms of the electrochemical potential μ?[3]

[1] 256.

[2] $(1 - f_1)(1 - f_2)$.

[3] μ.

2.2 Boltzmann Law

This is Lecture 2.2: Watch youtube video
In Lecture 2.1, we introduced the Boltzmann law. This is the central principle of equilibrium statistical mechanics which says that in equilibrium, the probabilities of the different states are given by the p_i shown in Fig. 2.9d. In this lecture, I'll try to justify it.

In the last lecture, I introduced the notion of state space, which is kind of fundamental to much of what we'll be discussing in this course. The Boltzmann law applies to the state space. I took an example of a problem where you had two one electron levels, and which gave rise to 2^2 or 4 states in state space.

Now more generally, you could of course have an arbitrary number of states in state space and for this discussion now, we'll just say they are labeled as 1, 2, 3, 4, etc. and each state is characterized by a certain number of electrons and a certain total energy. What we want to show is why the probability that the system is in one of these states should be given by the Boltzmann law.

2.2.1 *Fig. 2.9: System and reservoir*

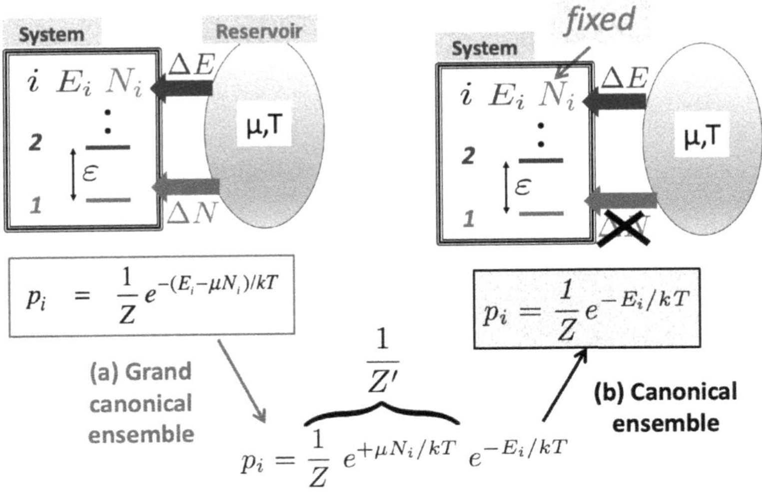

Fig. 2.9 System exchanging energy and particle with "reservoir".

Now, in order to discuss this point, the first thing to note is that our system is continually exchanging energy as well as particles, meaning electrons in this case, with the surroundings, which we call the reservoir (see Fig. 2.9), something big, with lots of energy and particles available. You see if our system were isolated then E and N couldn't change and if you started off with some E, N it would kind of stay that way. In in order to be able to change states within the system, you need to be able to exchange E and/or N with some reservoir which is characterized by an electrochemical potential μ and a temperature T. What these words actually mean will hopefully get a little clearer as we go further in this lecture.

In some cases you might have a system that can only exchange energy but cannot exchange particles, as shown in Fig. 2.9b. Because you cannot exchange particles, the N_i would be fixed, in other words, the system would always be in states which have all the same N_i, because after all, the particles have nowhere to go. So if you're in a two electron state you stay in a two electron state.

Now in that case, you see this Boltzmann law, we have these two terms in the exponent, you can separate them out and write it as shown at the bottom in Fig. 2.9). And you see if the N_i is fixed, then $exp(\mu N_i/kT)$ is also kind of part of the constant. Remember we have this constant in front, to make sure all probabilities add up to one. So we could take $exp(\mu N_i/kT)$ as part of that constant and then you'd have a probability that could be written like Fig. 2.9b, that does not mention the N_i explicitly.

So sometimes depending on the problem at hand, one might be using this expression (see Fig. 2.9b) rather than the other one. This is the case that is generally referred to as a *canonical ensemble*, which means that you have an ensemble of systems, that exchange only energy with the reservoir. If it is exchanging both energy and particles then you call it a *grand canonical ensemble* and use the expression in Fig. 2.9a. So those are the technical names that you'd see if you'd look at a book in statistical physics.

2.2.2 *Figs. 2.10-2.13: Justifying the law*

Now for this discussion, let us first focus on the canonical ensemble, where it's only exchanging energy. So the expression we're trying to understand or justify is the one shown in Fig. 2.9b without the μ and the N appearing explicitly. Now, as I mentioned before, it is connected to this reservoir with which it is exchanging energy, okay.

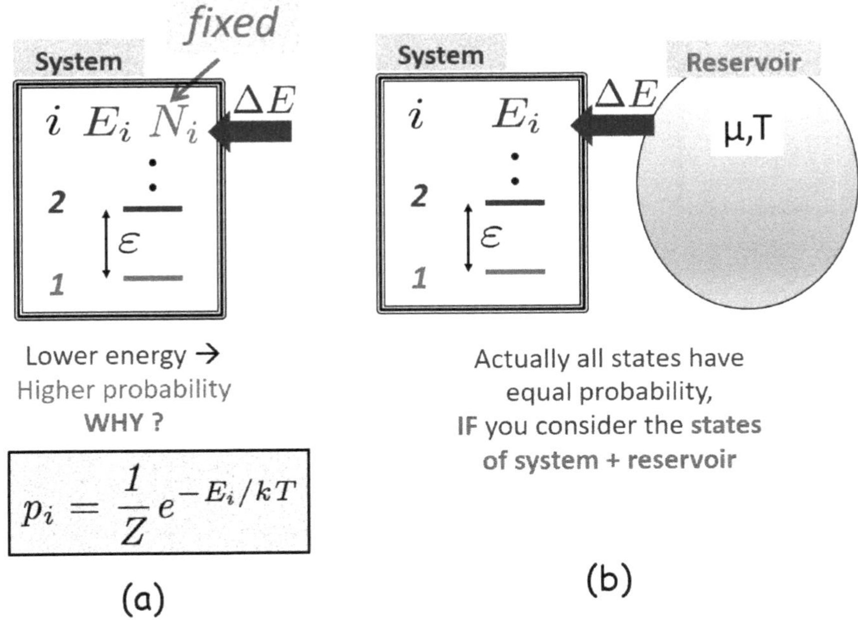

Fig. 2.10 Justifying Boltzmann law in canonical ensemble.

2.2.2.1 *Fig. 2.11*

The Boltzmann law says, that the more the energy, lower the probability. Why is that you might ask (see Fig. 2.10a)? If I have a thing sitting by itself, one might have expected all states to be equally probable. Why is it that lower energy has higher probability?

The answer is that you see, you have to consider the states of the entire system, meaning, system plus reservoir (see Fig. 2.10b) and the whole thing does fluctuate around all the different available states with equal probability for each *composite* state. But that does not correspond to equal probability for all the *system* states. If the system is say in state, 1, then corresponding to that the reservoir has let's say, a certain number of states, W_1 (see Fig. 2.11a). Similarly, if the system is in state 2, the reservoir has W_2 number of states, and the point is that W_1 is larger than W_2.

Why is that? Well, because you see, when the system has a lower energy, the reservoir has a higher energy (see Fig. 2.11b) since together, they have

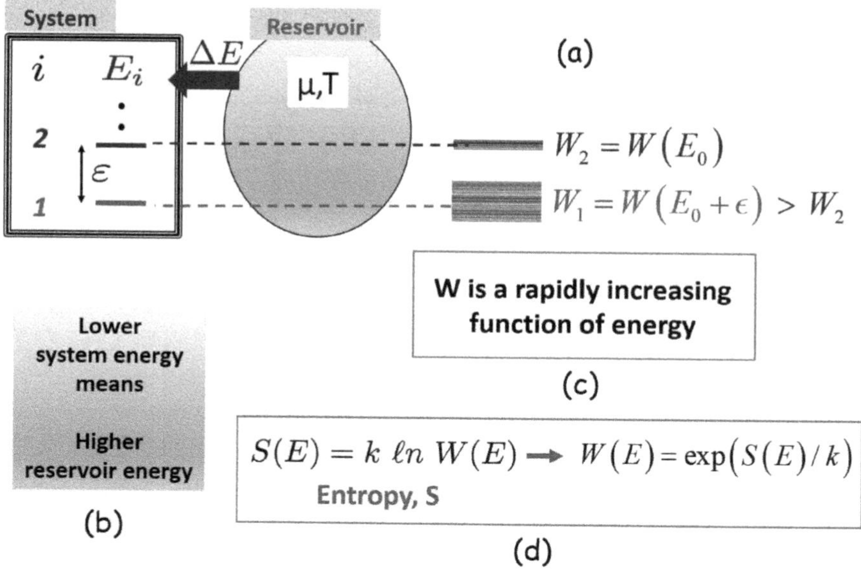

Fig. 2.11 Introducing entropy, S.

a *fixed* energy $E_0 + \varepsilon$. So when the system gets a little more energy, it means that the reservoir has a little less energy. That is the first point: lower system energy means higher reservoir energy.

The second point is that if the reservoir has more energy then it will also have more states that it can access (see Fig. 2.11c). Those are the two key points. Remember what we are trying to understand is, why the system has a higher probability for being in a lower energy state. The answer is, if the system has lower energy then the reservoir has higher energy, and if it has higher energy, it can access a lot more states.

Now, if I want to know the probability that the system will be in state 1, as opposed to in state 2, that ratio will be proportional to the number of states of the reservoir that correspond to it (see Fig. 2.12a) . So $p_1/p_2 = W_1/W_2$. Let's say there are 100 states of the reservoir for W_1 and only 10 for W_2. Then $p_1/p_2 = 100/10$, because state 1 of the system looks like 100 states for the composite thing, while state 2 looks like 10 states for the composite thing. Naturally the composite thing is more likely to be in the 100 states than in the 10 states. That's the essential point.

This leads us to define something called entropy S (see Fig. 2.11d) which is one of the very deep seminal concepts in statistical mechanics. This S is proportional to the logarithm of the number of states available to the reservoir $S(E) = k \ln W(E)$). More the energy E, the more the number of states available, so bigger the W and bigger the entropy. We can start from $S = k \ln W$ and turn it around to write $W = \exp(S/k)$.

2.2.2.2 *Fig. 2.12*

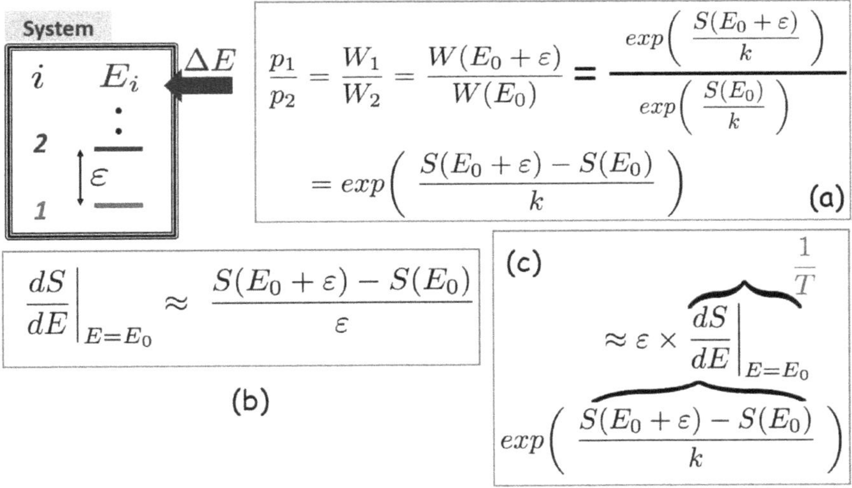

Fig. 2.12 Defining temperature T from entropy S.

So now we'll do a little algebra and go on from here and obtain the Boltzmann law. We start from $p_1/p_2 = W_1/W_2$, where W_1 is the value of this function W, for $E = E_0 + \varepsilon$ ($W_1 = W(E_0 + \varepsilon)$), while W_2 corresponds to the energy E_0 ($W_2 = W(E_0)$). Now we replace W in terms of entropy. This gives us a ratio of exponentials like this $(\exp(S(E_0 + \varepsilon)/k)/\exp(S(E_0)/k))$ which we can write it as the difference between the two $(\exp(S(E_0 + \varepsilon) - S(E_0))/k)$.

Now this difference is something I will now approximate, using the fact that the reservoir is a huge thing with a lot of energy and this ε is a small change in its energy. And so, we can write the derivative of the entropy of the reservoir with respect to energy, in this form, $(S(E_0 + \varepsilon) - S(E_0)/\varepsilon)$.

As you know when you first learn about derivatives in college, they define it this way, in the limit as ε tends to 0. And in this case, we would argue that ε being the energy of this little system, it is kind of 0 in the context of the huge reservoir energy. So you could write the derivative in this form (see Fig. 2.12b). What that means is, I could write this difference as ε times the derivative. So that's what I've done here. And then the key point is that this derivative is what is defined as the inverse temperature of the reservoir, that's what is called $1/T$ (see Fig. 2.12c). And so now you can put it all together, we have this epsilon over T, and then there's the k here, which brings us to ε/kT.

2.2.2.3 *Fig. 2.13*

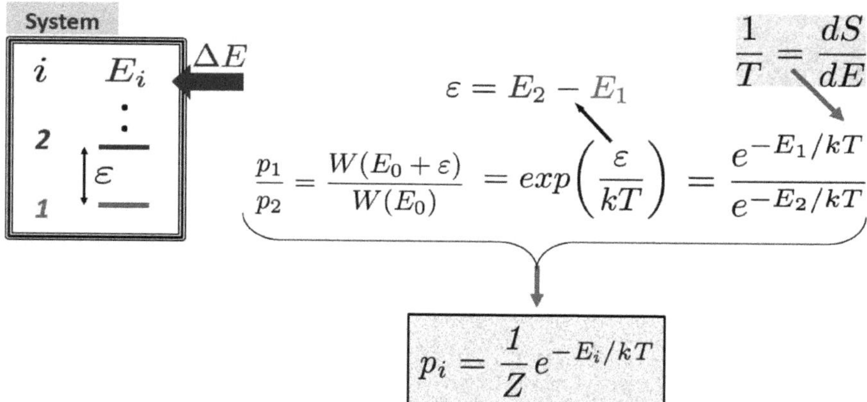

Fig. 2.13 Obtaining Boltzmann law for canonical ensemble.

So basically it says that the ratio of $p_1/p_2 = \exp(\varepsilon/kT)$. And since $\varepsilon = E_2 - E_1$ (see Fig. 2.13), what we are saying is that $p_1/p_2 = (\exp(-E_1/kT)/\exp(-E_2/kT))$, which you can see is consistent with the Boltzmann law. Boltzmann law says that the probability of any state i, is proportional to $\exp(-E_i/kT)$. And what we showed in the last few slides is that if I consider any 2 states of our system, 1 and 2, the ratio of their probabilities will be the ratio of these exponentials. Which is consistent with exactly what the Boltzmann law states.

2.2.3 *Fig. 2.14: Canonical ensemble*

Recapping what we did, we're trying to figure out the probabilities for the system. So we say that consider the entire system plus reservoir and together the composite system will spend equal time in all possible states. And so, the ratio of p_1/p_2, is proportional to the ratio of the corresponding states of the reservoir. Which then can be written as $\exp(\varepsilon/kT)$, where this inverse temperature is defined in terms of the energy derivative of the entropy function, $1/T = \mathrm{d}S/\mathrm{d}E$.

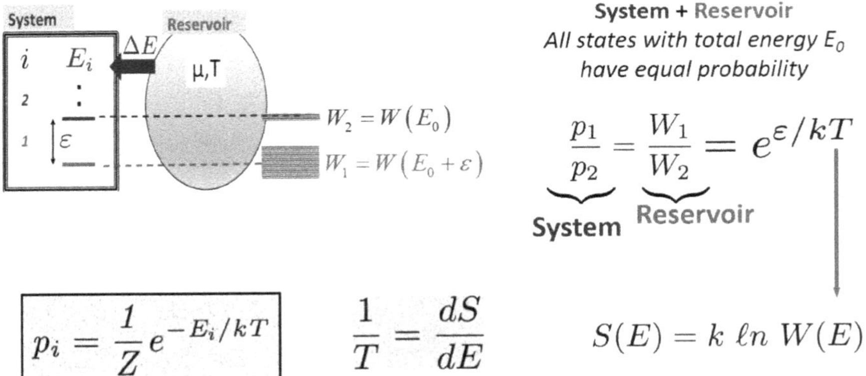

Fig. 2.14 Summary: Only energy exchange is involved (canonical ensemble).

So that's what we have done. And the next few slides, let me just show how this derivation is extended to the grand canonical ensemble, namely the case where you are also exchanging particles because remember, I kind of simplified things a little by saying let's assume particles are not exchanged only energy is. So when you exchange particles as I mentioned before, the more general Boltzmann law would not have just E_i but would have $E_i - \mu N_i$. And what I had argued before was that if N_i were fixed, then you could essentially write it this way $p_i = (1/Z)\exp(-E_i/kT)$, and that's the canonical ensemble. Well, if you want to include the variations in particles, then what would happen is p_1/p_2 would still be equal to this W_1/W_2, but now, W would be a function of both E and N.

2.2.4 *Fig. 2.15: Grand canonical ensemble*

When they exchange particles, the total number of particles stays constant. So the one that has a lower number of particles, would correspond to a higher number for the reservoir. So just as we had argued, if the reservoir had energy E_0 corresponding to p_2, then it would have energy $E_0 + \varepsilon$ corresponding to p_1, where ε is the energy difference.

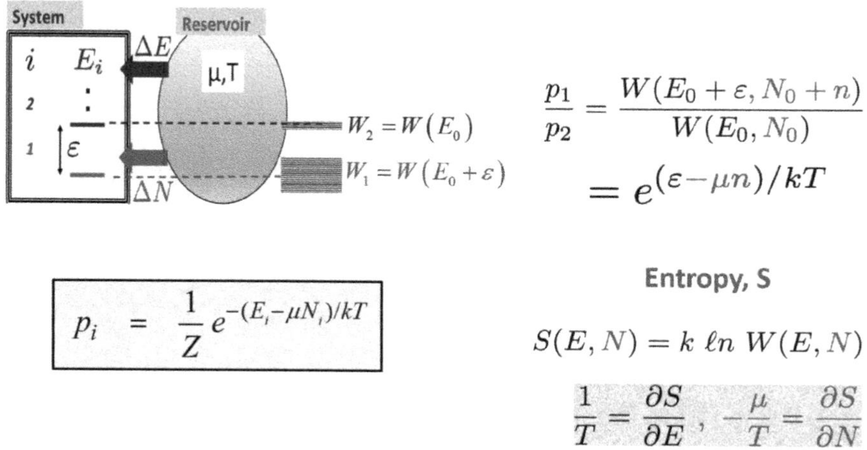

Fig. 2.15 Summary: Both energy and particle exchanges are involved (grand canonical ensemble).

Similarly, if the reservoir has N_0 particles corresponding to p_2, then it would have $N_0 + n$ particles corresponding to p_1, where this small n represents the difference in the number of particles. And what you can show is that this too can be written as $\exp((\varepsilon - \mu n)/kT)$, where this extra factor this $-\mu/T$ now, is defined in terms of the derivative of the entropy function with respect to N, $-\mu/T = \partial S/\partial N$. You see, previously we wrote derivative of the entropy function with respect to energy as $1/T$. Now we are writing derivative of the entropy function with respect to the number of particles as $-\mu/T$. And when you put that in there, you will get this relation $\exp((\varepsilon - \mu n)/kT)$, which is consistent with the Boltzmann law as stated for the Grand canonical ensemble. So, that kind of completes the overall derivation here.

What needs more discussion is why we can define the temperature in terms of $\partial S/\partial E$, *irrespective of the details of the reservoir.* You see what I said earlier is that Boltzmann law applies to everything. It doesn't matter how complicated your system is, it could be something complicated like including superconducting elements for example. It could be a strongly interacting system, or it could be something really simple, like just a single level. It doesn't matter how complicated or simple it is, the law is the same.

Now why is the law the same for all systems, irrespective of its details? The answer is, well, it's because this is a property not of the system but of the reservoir. And what it really reflects is the non-obvious fact, that all normal reservoirs irrespective of details kind of have this property. That if you look at the number of states available the W and define the entropy function in this way, $S(E, N) = k \ln W(E, N)$ then, this $\partial S/\partial E$ would be $1/T$, while $\partial S/\partial N$ would be $-\mu/T$ and this is irrespective of exactly what the reservoir is comprised of. And that is not really obvious, but in the next lecture, we'll try to clarify this point a little when we talk more about this concept of entropy.

2.2.5 *Quiz*

2.2.5.1 *Question 1*

Why does the Boltzmann law $p_i = (1/Z)e^{-(E_i - \mu N_i)/kT}$ apply to all systems irrespective of its details?[4]

2.2.5.2 *Question 2*

At equilibrium, why are states with less energy more probable?[5]

2.2.5.3 *Question 3*

What is the Boltzmann law corresponding to systems that exchange BOTH energy and particles with the reservoir?[6]

[4] Because this law reflects a property of the reservoir, not the system.

[5] Because the reservoir then has more energy and hence more available states.

[6] $p_i = (1/Z) \times e^{(E_i - \mu N_i)/kT}$.

2.3 Entropy

This is Lecture 2.3: Watch youtube video

As you may recall, in the first lecture, we stated the Boltzmann law $p_i = (1/Z)\exp(-(E_i - \mu N_i)/kT)$, which gives us the probability that a system will be in a certain state in the state space. In the second lecture, we went a little deeper and recognized that what makes the law applicable to all systems is that it is a property of the reservoir, and all normal reservoirs shared a certain non-obvious property. In the process, we introduced the concept of entropy, $S(E,N) = k\ln(W(E,N))$, whose derivatives give you the two parameters μ and T that enter the equilibrium law. Now what we'll be doing in this lecture is to introduce a model for this reservoir and use it to calculate quantities like $W(E,N)$ so that we get a little more insight into how $\partial S/\partial E$ and $\partial S/\partial N$ help define μ and T.

2.3.1 *Figs. 2.16-2.18: Entropy from reservoir model*

2.3.1.1 *Fig. 2.16: Model for reservoir*

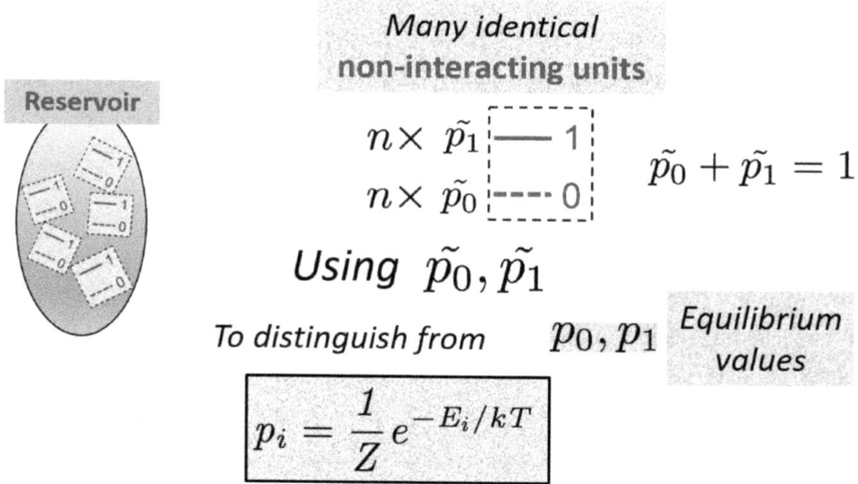

Fig. 2.16 Model for reservoir as a collection of identical 2-level units.

Let me introduce a simple model for the *reservoir* that's also composed of these little two level systems, 0 and 1, and there are many of them, that's the small n, and they are all non-interacting (see Fig. 2.16). Notice that

I'm using $\widetilde{p}_i$, to distinguish it from the equilibrium probabilities p_i. Of course, the reservoir could also be in equilibrium, in which case these probabilities would be given by p's without the tilde. But just to keep it general we have the tilde.

2.3.1.2 *Fig. 2.17*

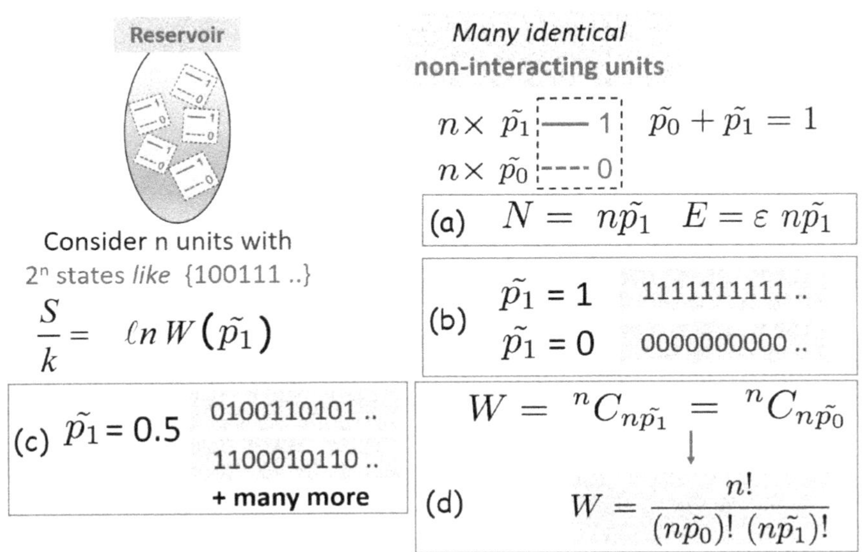

Fig. 2.17 Entropy from reservoir model.

Now, consider n units, so there will be 2^n states, each one could be described by a string of 1's and 0's (see Fig. 2.17a). And the number of units that will be in state 1 will be $N = n\widetilde{p}_1$, the total number times $\widetilde{p}_1$. The energy will be $E = \varepsilon n\widetilde{p}_1$, where ε is the energy corresponding to 1, relative to the zero.

Now, we write the entropy, that's this $k \ln W$, k being the Boltzmann constant, and W is the number of different states that correspond to that particular, for a given $\widetilde{p}_1$, the number of different states that correspond to it.

Now let me explain what I mean by that. Supposing $\widetilde{p}_1$ were 1 (see Fig. 2.17b), then there's only one state that one could write down, that's all 1s, or if the $\widetilde{p}_1$ were 0, it would be all 0's and so W would be 1, and the entropy would be 0. On the other hand, if the probability is, say, 50%, (0.5) (see Fig. 2.17c), that means half are 0 and half are 1, and then you will see there are many ways of writing that, and so there will be lots of states, W will be a big number, and the corresponding entropy would also be big.

Now, mathematically, I could write W as ${}^{n}C_{n\widetilde{p}_1}$ (see Fig. 2.17d): The idea is, I've got n units, in how many ways can I choose $n\widetilde{p}_1$ units that will be 1. And this is also equal to $W = {}^{n}C_{n\widetilde{p}_0}$: In how many ways can I choose $n\widetilde{p}_0$ units, that will be 0. And those are mathematically the same thing: $W = (n!)/((n\widetilde{p}_0)!(n\widetilde{p}_1)!)$. This is the elementary combinatorial law that you have probably seen, if not, you could look it up easily.

2.3.1.3 *Fig. 2.18*

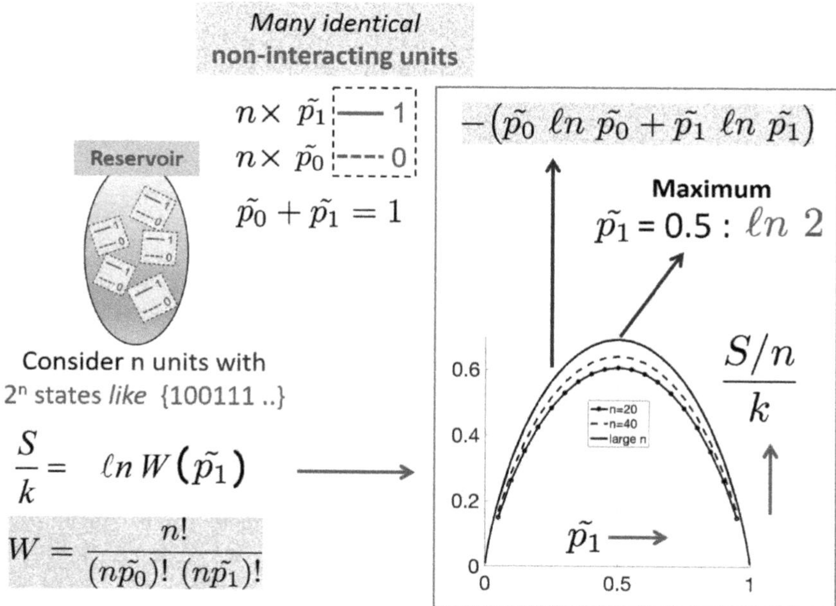

Fig. 2.18 Plot of entropy versus $\widetilde{p}_1$ for different number of units, n.

Now, if we take $W = (n!)/((n\widetilde{p}_0)!(n\widetilde{p}_1)!)$ and plot it as a function of $\widetilde{p}_1$, you'll get a curve looking like this (see Fig. 2.18). When $\widetilde{p}_1$ is zero at that end, as we discussed, there is only one state possible. When $\widetilde{p}_1$ is 1, again, only one state is possible. So at either of those ends, the entropy is 0, in the middle, when it's 0.5, that's when the entropy is the maximum and if you plot it for different values of n, n, meaning the total number of units. As you increase n it converges to a particular curve. So, once you get to, say, 1000, it really doesn't matter whether n is 1000 or 10,000, you get much the same curve.

And this curve has a maximum of $\ln(2)$, and actually, there is a simple expression that describes this limiting curve, the one that you get when n tends to infinity. Now, what we'll be showing is that starting from this combinatorial expression, $W = (n!)/((n\widetilde{p}_0)!(n\widetilde{p}_1)!)$ and $S = k\ln(W(\widetilde{p}_1)$, how you get to this relatively simple expression, $S/n = -k(\widetilde{p}_0 \ln \widetilde{p}_0 + \widetilde{p}_1 \ln \widetilde{p}_1)$.

2.3.2 *Figs. 2.19-2.20: Thermodynamic versus information entropy*

2.3.2.1 *Fig. 2.19*

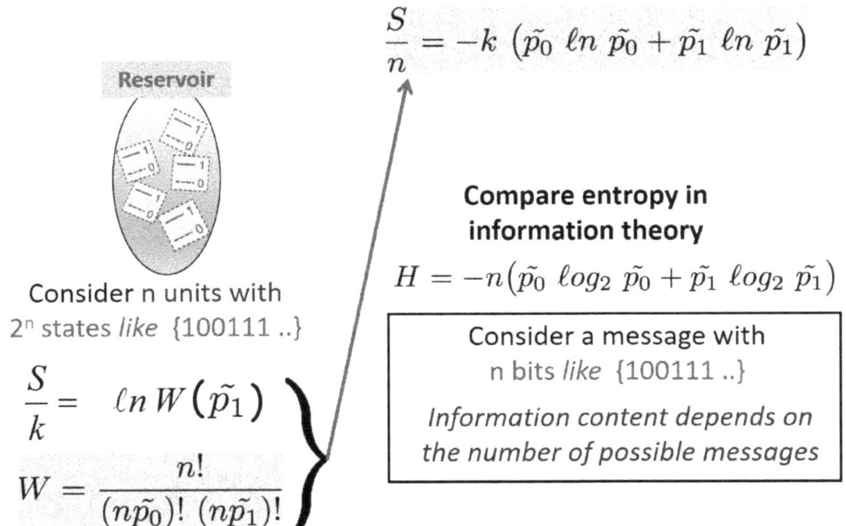

Fig. 2.19 Similarity in expressions between thermodynamic entropy and the Shannon entropy used in information theory.

But before we go on, let me just mention that there is a similar expression you may have seen if you have taken a course in information theory, because in information theory the way you think is, supposing I send a message with n bits that looks like this, 100111. What is the information content? The argument is that if there were, let's say 100 possibilities, then when I send you one particular message, the information content is $\ln(100)$. So, that is how you define the information content and in information theory, entropy is a *dimensionless* number, whereas, in what we are doing, we're coming at it from the point of view of thermodynamics, and the thermodynamic entropy is a *dimensionful* number. It has the same units as the *Boltzmann constant*, k. And if you Google it, you'll see lots of discussions about the relationship between the thermodynamic entropy and the information entropy. Some believe there is a deep relation, some don't and there's a lot of arguments about that.

2.3.2.2 *Fig. 2.20: Expression for entropy*

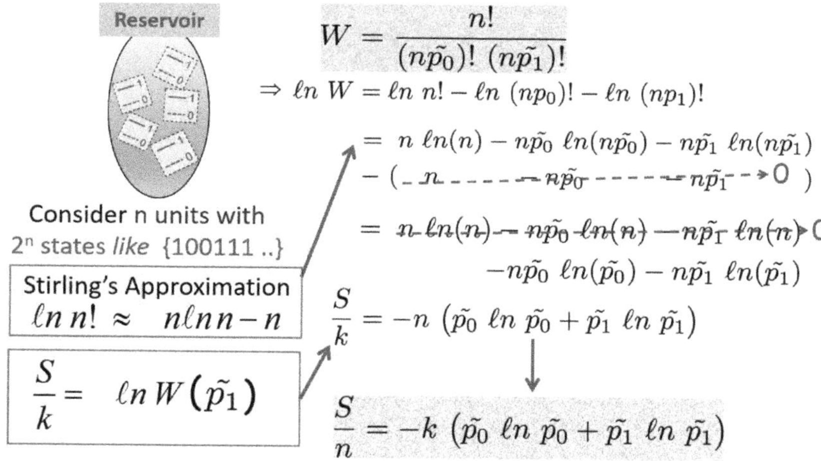

Fig. 2.20 Deriving the expression for entropy.

Now, we'll go through a little bit of algebra to show how you get from this combinatorial expression to a relatively simple expression (see Fig. 2.20). So the first step is, you take the logarithm of both sides, because you want $\ln W$, and $\ln W = \ln(n!) - \ln(n\tilde{p}_0)! - \ln(n\tilde{p}_1)!$. Now, next what we use is something called the *Stirling's Approximation*, which is that when n is large, remember, this equivalence we are trying to prove only applies for large n. So when n is large, you can write the $\ln(n!)$ as $n\ln(n) - n$. So instead of $\ln(n!)$, we can write $n\ln(n) - n$. Similarly, instead of $\ln(n\tilde{p}_0)!$, we can write $n\tilde{p}_0 \ln(n\tilde{p}_0) - n\tilde{p}_0$. Similarly, $\ln(n\tilde{p}_1)!$ becomes $n\tilde{p}_1 \ln(n\tilde{p}_1) - n\tilde{p}_1$. So, we are applying this *Stirling's Approximation* to each of the three things. Now, you'll notice that, what's in here, $n\ -n\tilde{p}_0\ -n\tilde{p}_1$, that just cancels out. Why? Because, remember, $\tilde{p}_0$ plus $\tilde{p}_1$ is equal to 1 and so we are left with the top-line $n\ln(n) - n\tilde{p}_0 \ln(n\tilde{p}_0) - n\tilde{p}_1 \ln(n\tilde{p}_1)$.

Next what we do is, we expand it a little in the sense that when you have $\ln(n\tilde{p}_0)$, that's like $\ln(n)+\ln(\tilde{p}_0)$. Similarly, $\ln(n\tilde{p}_1)$ is $\ln(n)+\ln(\tilde{p}_1)$. So from here, we get this $n\ln(n) - n\tilde{p}_0 \ln(n) - n\tilde{p}_1 \ln(n) - n\tilde{p}_0 \ln(\tilde{p}_0) - n\tilde{p}_1 \ln(\tilde{p}_1)$. We have broken up each of these two terms into these two each, so now we have five terms there and here again, what I'd argue is that this top line cancels out, because $n\tilde{p}_0 + n\tilde{p}_1 = n$. So everything in that top line cancels out and so we are now left with just this, $-n\tilde{p}_0 \ln(\tilde{p}_0) - n\tilde{p}_1 \ln(\tilde{p}_1)$, which is what I've written here, $S/k = -n(\tilde{p}_0 \ln(\tilde{p}_0) + \tilde{p}_1 \ln(\tilde{p}_1))$. And that's basically what we set out to prove, $S/n = -k(\tilde{p}_0 \ln(\tilde{p}_0) + \tilde{p}_1 \ln(\tilde{p}_1))$. So that's all the algebraic steps, getting from the original combinatorial expression to the relatively simpler expression at the end.

2.3.3 *Figs. 2.21-2.22: Reservoir model with d-level units*

2.3.3.1 *Fig. 2.21*

So this is the result when the reservoir is composed of little two-level systems, 0 and 1. Now, if the reservoir is composed of, say d level systems, you have lots of levels from 0 to d, d could be 10, could be 4, whatever it is. Once again, we have n number of units but if you have multi levels like this, then the generalization is, instead of $\tilde{p}_0 \ln(\tilde{p}_0) + \tilde{p}_1 \ln(\tilde{p}_1)$, you get a sum over all of these. So, we'll have $\tilde{p}_0 \ln(\tilde{p}_0) + \tilde{p}_1 \ln(\tilde{p}_1) + \tilde{p}_2 \ln(\tilde{p}_2) + \tilde{p}_3 \ln(\tilde{p}_3)$, and so on. So, that's what this summation is $S/n = -k\sum_{i=0}^{d-1} \tilde{p}_i \ln(\tilde{p}_i)$. It says go and sum them all up. So that's the general expression for the entropy. Finally to complete the story, we can also generalize expressions for the energy and the number of particles: $E/n = \sum_{i=0}^{d-1} \tilde{p}_i E_i$ and $N/n = \sum_{i=0}^{d-1} \tilde{p}_i N_i$.

2.3.3.2 *Fig. 2.22*

In deriving expressions for S, E, N we started from a model with n *identical* units, n being a large number, 1000 of them, for example. But another way to think about it is that we have only one unit which is continually jumping around and you can average over time. So, instead of writing the total entropy of n units, you could take the entropy per unit and think of it as the entropy of one unit, but when averaged over time. Alternatively

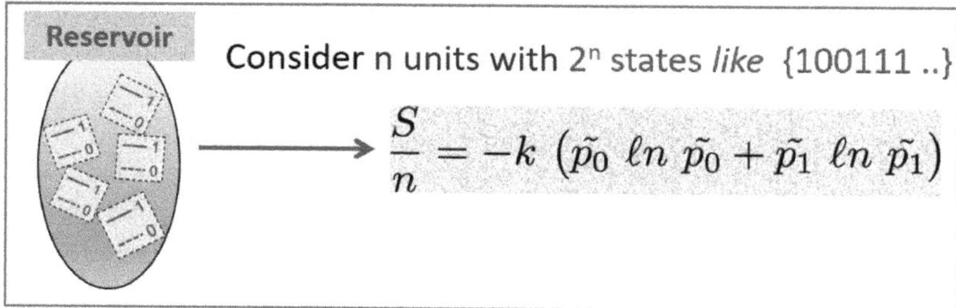

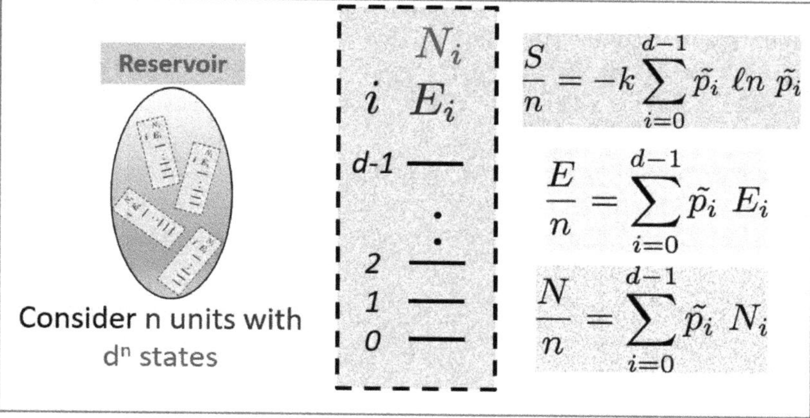

Fig. 2.21 Generalization from 2-level to d-level units.

you could interpret it as an ensemble average, averaged over an ensemble of n, identical units (Fig. 2.22).

2.3.4 *Fig. 2.23: μ, T from entropy S*

In the last lecture we said that T is related to the derivative of entropy with respect to energy, whereas the μ/T is related to the derivative of S with respect to N (see Fig. 2.23b). We could combine the two expressions and write it this way, $\mathrm{d}S = (\mathrm{d}E/T) - (\mu\mathrm{d}N/T)$ (see Fig. 2.23c). Is this relation satisfied by the explicit expressions for S, E and N that we have obtained from an explicit model?

The answer is *not* always, but only if $\widetilde{p}_i = p_i$. Meaning, if we assume that this reservoir that we are talking about is actually in equilibrium, which is often the case for reservoirs. But we may want to apply these expressions to other things which are out of equilibrium and we could still

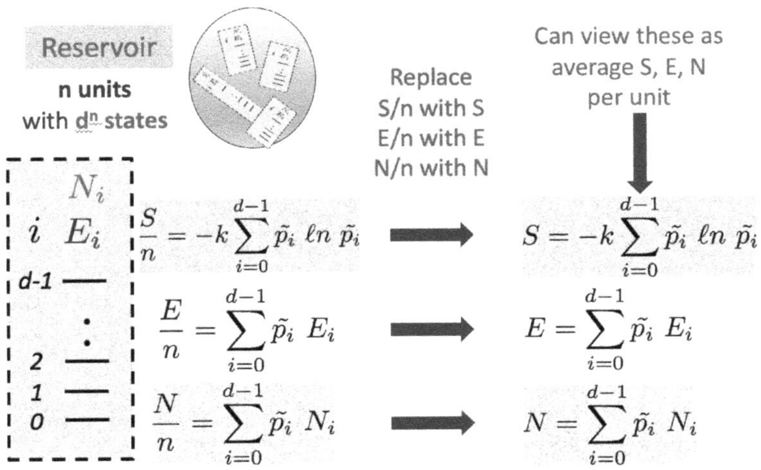

Fig. 2.22 Expressions for S, E, N per unit.

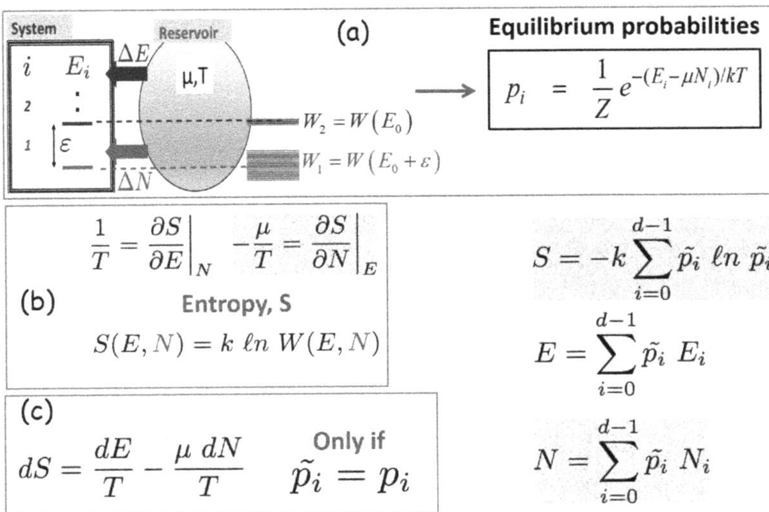

System
Reservoir
(a)
Equilibrium probabilities
i E_i
2
1
ε
ΔE
ΔN
μ,T
$W_2 = W(E_0)$
$W_1 = W(E_0 + \varepsilon)$
$p_i = \frac{1}{Z} e^{-(E_i - \mu N_i)/kT}$
(b)
$\frac{1}{T} = \left.\frac{\partial S}{\partial E}\right|_N \quad -\frac{\mu}{T} = \left.\frac{\partial S}{\partial N}\right|_E$
Entropy, S
$S(E,N) = k \, \ell n \, W(E,N)$
(c)
$dS = \frac{dE}{T} - \frac{\mu \, dN}{T}$
Only if
$\tilde{p}_i = p_i$
$S = -k \sum_{i=0}^{d-1} \tilde{p}_i \, \ell n \, \tilde{p}_i$
$E = \sum_{i=0}^{d-1} \tilde{p}_i \, E_i$
$N = \sum_{i=0}^{d-1} \tilde{p}_i \, N_i$

Fig. 2.23 Connecting entropy, S back to the concepts of electrochemical potential, μ and temperature, T.

use these expressions. That is why I went to the trouble of putting a tilde on top of p, $(\widetilde{p}_i)$, to make it clear that the expressions we're obtaining are valid in general. But if the entity is in equilibrium, so that the $\widetilde{p}$'s happen to equal the $p's$ then you'd have this interesting relation $\mathrm{d}S = (\mathrm{d}E/T) - (\mu \mathrm{d}N/T)$. We will pick this up in the next lecture.

2.3.5 *Quiz*

2.3.5.1 *Question 1*

What is the entropy of a collection of 8 one-electron levels that are all full?[7]

2.3.5.2 *Question 2*

What is the entropy of a collection of n identical units, EACH having 3 levels that are all equally probable.[8]

2.3.5.3 *Question 3*

What is the entropy of a collection of 8 one-electron levels each have a probability of 0.5 of being full?[9]

---

[7] 0.

[8] $nk\ \ell n3$.

[9] $8k\ \ell n2$.

2.4 Free Energy

This is Lecture 2.4: Watch youtube video

As you may recall we started by introducing the Boltzmann law for the equilibrium probabilities p_i. In general of course a system need not be in equilibrium and the probabilities could be something very different, $\widetilde{p}_i$. In this lecture we will introduce the concept of free energy $F = E - \mu N - TS$ and show that it has a *minimum* value at *equilibrium* when all the $\widetilde{p}_i = p_i$. This property of F leads to the *equilibrium* relation $\mathrm{d}S = (\mathrm{d}E/T) - (\mu \mathrm{d}N/T)$ that I stated at the end of the last lecture.

2.4.1 *Fig. 2.24: Free energy, F*

Now, to start with we'll be doing a bit of algebra, starting from the expression for the free energy $F = E - \mu N - TS$ (Fig. 2.24).

Step 1: Substitute for E,N and S from the expressions that we obtained in the last lecture (see Fig. 2.24, lower right): $S = -k\sum_{i=0}^{d-1} \widetilde{p}_i \ln \widetilde{p}_i$, $E = \sum_{i=0}^{d-1} \widetilde{p}_i E_i$ and $N = \sum_{i=0}^{d-1} \widetilde{p}_i N_i$. This takes us to $F = kT\sum_i \widetilde{p}_i((E_i - \mu N_i)/kT) + \ell n \widetilde{p}_i)$.

$$F = E - \mu N - TS$$
$$= \sum_i \tilde{p}_i (E_i - \mu N_i + kT \ \ell n \ \tilde{p}_i)$$
$$= kT \sum_i \tilde{p}_i \left(\underbrace{\frac{E_i - \mu N_i}{kT}}_{-\ell n \ Z - \ell n \ p_i} + \ell n \ \tilde{p}_i \right)$$
$$= -kT \sum_i \tilde{p}_i \ \ell n Z + kT \sum_i \tilde{p}_i (\ell n \ \tilde{p}_i - \ell n \ p_i)$$
$$= -kT \ \ell n Z + kT \sum_i \tilde{p}_i \left(\ell n \ \frac{\tilde{p}_i}{p_i} \right)$$

Equilibrium probabilities
$$p_i = \frac{1}{Z} e^{-(E_i - \mu N_i)/kT}$$

$$\ell n \ p_i = -\ell n \ Z - \frac{E_i - \mu N_i}{kT}$$

$$\frac{E_i - \mu N_i}{kT} = -\ \ell n \ Z - \ \ell n \ p_i$$

if $\tilde{p}_i = p_i$

$$F = -kT \ \ell n Z$$

$$S = -k \sum_{i=0}^{d-1} \tilde{p}_i \ \ell n \ \tilde{p}_i$$
$$E = \sum_{i=0}^{d-1} \tilde{p}_i \ E_i \quad N = \sum_{i=0}^{d-1} \tilde{p}_i \ N_i$$

N_i i E_i d-1 2 1 0

Fig. 2.24 Deriving an expression for free energy.

Step 2: Use equilibrium probabilities $p_i = (1/Z)\exp\left(-(E_i - \mu N_i)/kT\right)$, to replace the term $(E_i - \mu N_i)/kT$ with $-\ell n Z - \ell n p_i$ to obtain $F = -kT\ell nZ + kT\sum_i \widetilde{p}_i \ell n(\widetilde{p}_i/p_i)$.

Now, you'll notice that if the probabilities of your system, are actually equal to the equilibrium probabilities, then you see, $\ell n(\widetilde{p}_i/p_i) = \ell n(1) = 0$, and so the term $kT\sum_i \widetilde{p}_i \ell n(\widetilde{p}_i/p_i)$ drops out giving us just $F = -kT\ell nZ$.

2.4.2 *Fig. 2.25: Gibbs' inequality*

Now, what's not so clear is that when you're off equilibrium, so that these $\widetilde{p}_i$, are a little different from the equilibrium ones, p_i, the term $kT\sum_i \widetilde{p}_i \ell n(\widetilde{p}_i/p_i)$ *will always be positive*, it will never be negative (see Fig. 2.25). This means that the free energy is equal to $-kT\ell nZ$, plus a quantity that's always positive. So, at equilibrium, when the $\widetilde{p}_i$ is equal to the equilibrium p_i, you get a minimum value for the free energy. Any other distribution will give you something bigger.

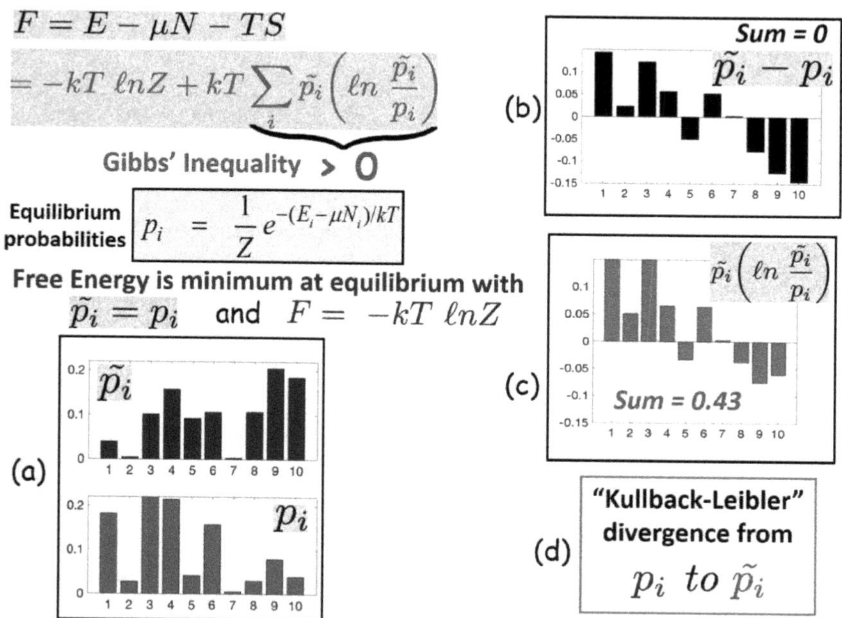

$F = E - \mu N - TS$
$= -kT\ \ell n Z + kT \sum_i \widetilde{p}_i \left(\ell n \frac{\widetilde{p}_i}{p_i}\right)$
Gibbs' Inequality > 0
Equilibrium probabilities
$p_i = \frac{1}{Z} e^{-(E_i - \mu N_i)/kT}$
Free Energy is minimum at equilibrium with
$\widetilde{p}_i = p_i$ and $F = -kT\ \ell n Z$
(a)
$\widetilde{p}_i$
p_i
(b)
Sum = 0
$\widetilde{p}_i - p_i$
(c)
$\widetilde{p}_i \left(\ell n \frac{\widetilde{p}_i}{p_i}\right)$
Sum = 0.43
(d)
"Kullback-Leibler" divergence from
p_i to $\widetilde{p}_i$

Fig. 2.25 Illustrating Gibbs' inequality from the expression for free energy.

Let me give you an example, to show how this works. I ran on MATLAB® you could do it also, and check it out (see Fig. 2.25a). With 10 states, I have chosen two probability distributions, $\widetilde{p}_i$ and p_i. They're both just selected at random, so if you look at the difference (see Fig. 2.25b), some will be positive, some will be negative, but if you add them all up, it will be 0. Why? Because the sum of all the $\widetilde{p}_i$ is equal to 1, and sum of all the p_i is also equal to 1, both being probability distributions. So if we look at the difference and sum it, that must be 0, since the sum of each one is 1. That's exactly what you'll find.

But if you plot this quantity, $\widetilde{p}_i \ell n(\widetilde{p}_i/p_i)$ (see Fig. 2.25c), then you will find that the positives are a little bigger than the negatives and overall it always comes out positive. This is the *Gibbs' inequality*, something you can prove mathematically. In statistics, people often compare two distributions: one is a reference distribution, the p_i, just like our equilibrium distribution and the other is some other distribution like our non-equilibrium one. To quantify how far one is from the other, one measure people use is the *Kullback-Leibler divergence* (see Fig. 2.25d) and that's exactly the expression that came up from our free energy expression. When the distributions $\widetilde{p}_i$ and p_i match, you get zero. When the distributions don't match, we get some positive number.

2.4.3 *Fig. 2.26: Equilibrium free energy*

So when you're at equilibrium, we have $F = -kT \ln Z$ (see Fig. 2.26) and this represents a *minimum* value. If you change the probabilities a little bit, the energy E or the number of particles N or the entropy S might all change, but $F = E - \mu N - TS$ won't change because it's a minimum where the derivative is zero.

The result is that $\mathrm{d}F = 0$ when you make small changes in your probabilities. Since $\mathrm{d}F = \mathrm{d}E - \mu \mathrm{d}N - T\mathrm{d}S$, with a little algebra, you can write $\mathrm{d}S = (\mathrm{d}E/T) - (\mu \mathrm{d}N/T)$. And this is the expression that I had stated before: remember that $1/T$ was defined as the derivative of S with respect to E and $-\mu/T$ was the derivative of S with respect to N. But these relations all hold ONLY when you're really close to equilibrium. Away from equilibrium the free energy is something bigger given by $F = -kT \ln Z + kT \sum_i \widetilde{p}_i \ln(\widetilde{p}_i/p_i)$ and $\mathrm{d}F \neq 0$ so that $\mathrm{d}S \neq (\mathrm{d}E/T) - (\mu \mathrm{d}N/T)$.

$$F = E - \mu N - TS$$
$$= -kT\ \ell n Z + kT \sum_i \tilde{p}_i \left(\ell n\ \frac{\tilde{p}_i}{p_i} \right)$$

$$\boxed{\textit{if}\ \tilde{p}_i = p_i\ \text{then}\ F = -kT\ \ell n Z}$$

$$\mathbf{dF = 0} \rightarrow dE - \mu\ dN - T\ dS = 0$$

$$dS = \frac{dE}{T} - \frac{\mu\ dN}{T}$$

Equilibrium probabilities

$$p_i = \frac{1}{Z} e^{-(E_i - \mu N_i)/kT}$$

$$\sum_i p_i = 1$$

$$Z = \sum_i e^{-(E_i - \mu N_i)/kT}$$

$$S = -k \sum_{i=0}^{d-1} \tilde{p}_i\ \ell n\ \tilde{p}_i \quad E = \sum_{i=0}^{d-1} \tilde{p}_i\ E_i \quad N = \sum_{i=0}^{d-1} \tilde{p}_i\ N_i$$

Fig. 2.26 Properties of free energy at equilibrium.

2.4.4 *Figs. 2.27-2.28: Entropy drives flow*

2.4.4.1 *Fig. 2.27*

Now, in the next few slides I'd like to explain how a lot of flow that we see in the real world is driven by *entropy*. This is kind of important because we often tend to ascribe all flow to mechanical or electrical forces.

You see in physics there are two big branches, one is mechanics and the other is thermodynamics: Mechanics started with Newton's laws that explained planetary motion for example. A few hundred years later came heat engines and that's when the science of thermodynamics started. People recognized that heat was a form of energy, but it was very different from mechanical or electrical energy. Mechanics is usually driven by force but heat is driven by entropy and what I'd like to give you is a few examples of entropy driven processes.

Suppose I have a system (see Fig. 2.27), which is away from equilibrium and is exchanging energy and particles with some reservoir, which is close to equilibrium. Now, when this energy and particles are exchanged, the free energy change of the reservoir will be zero because it's close to equilibrium, but for the system, what will happen is, the free energy will always go down because to start with you're not at equilibrium so F is $-kT\ell nZ$ *plus* some positive quantity and then as you get to equilibrium, this second term goes away and you get $-kT\ell nZ$.

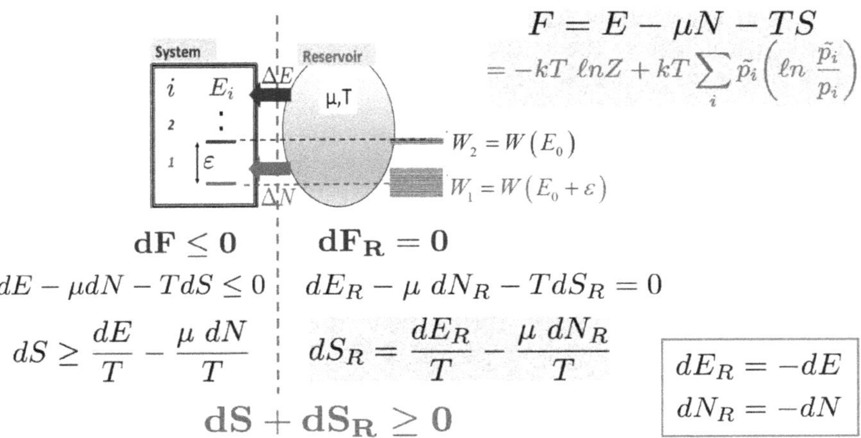

System
Reservoir
i E_i
2
1
ε
ΔE
ΔN
μ,T
$W_2 = W(E_0)$
$W_1 = W(E_0 + \varepsilon)$
$F = E - \mu N - TS$
$= -kT\,\ell n Z + kT \sum_i \tilde{p}_i \left(\ell n\,\frac{\tilde{p}_i}{p_i}\right)$
$\mathbf{dF \le 0}$
$dE - \mu dN - TdS \le 0$
$dS \ge \frac{dE}{T} - \frac{\mu\, dN}{T}$
$\mathbf{dF_R = 0}$
$dE_R - \mu\, dN_R - TdS_R = 0$
$dS_R = \frac{dE_R}{T} - \frac{\mu\, dN_R}{T}$
$\mathbf{dS + dS_R \ge 0}$
$dE_R = -dE$
$dN_R = -dN$

Fig. 2.27 Total entropy increases when an out-of-equilibrium system interacts with a reservoir.

So, what that means is, $\mathrm{d}F = \mathrm{d}E - \mu \mathrm{d}N - T\mathrm{d}S \geq 0$ but $\mathrm{d}F_R = \mathrm{d}E_R - \mu \mathrm{d}N_R - T\mathrm{d}S_R = 0$. With a little algebra, if you turn it around, you'd see that the entropy change of the reservoir, $\mathrm{d}S_R = (\mathrm{d}E_R/T) - (\mu \mathrm{d}N_R/T)$ while the entropy change of the system, $\mathrm{d}S > (\mathrm{d}E/T) - (\mu \mathrm{d}N/T)$ and this difference is because the reservoir is close to equilibrium, while the system is *not*.

Next we note that because the overall energy stays the same, we must have $\mathrm{d}E + \mathrm{d}E_R = 0$. If $\mathrm{d}E$ is positive, then $\mathrm{d}E_R$ must be negative so that they add up to zero. Similarly the overall number of particles stays the same, we must have $\mathrm{d}N + \mathrm{d}N_R = 0$. This means that $\mathrm{d}S + \mathrm{d}S_R \geq 0$. In words, this means that the flow will occur in such a way that the *overall entropy of the system plus the entropy of the reservoir will go up.*

This can be understood by noting that entropy is a measure of the number of states that are available and generally speaking, all flow occurs in such a way that things spread out in terms of available states. If only certain states are filled to start with, then as you let it evolve, it will tend to fill all accessible states, and so the entropy will increase.

Note that if both sides are at equilibrium to start with, then energy and/or particle exchange does not result in change of entropy, since we have an equality for both system and reservoir: $\mathrm{d}S_R = (\mathrm{d}E_R/T) - (\mu \mathrm{d}N_R/T)$, $\mathrm{d}S = (\mathrm{d}E/T) - (\mu \mathrm{d}N/T)$. Adding the two we get $\mathrm{d}S_R + \mathrm{d}S = 0$, noting the conservation of the total energy and particle number: $\mathrm{d}E + \mathrm{d}E_R = 0$, $\mathrm{d}N + \mathrm{d}N_R = 0$.

2.4.4.2 *Fig. 2.28: Flow driven by temperature*

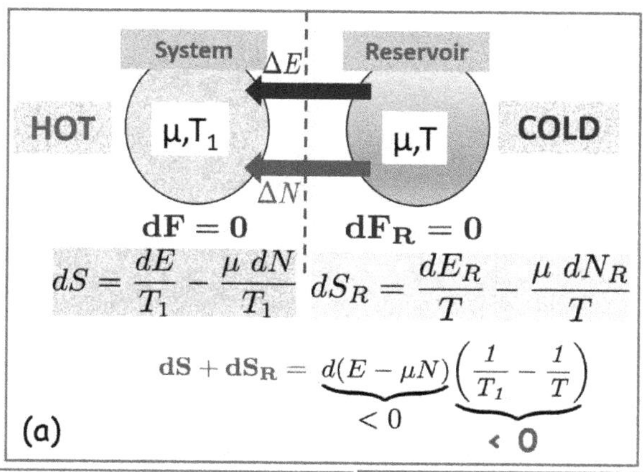

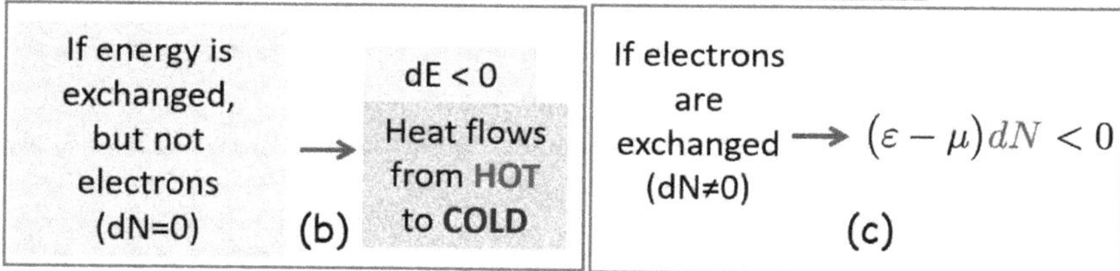

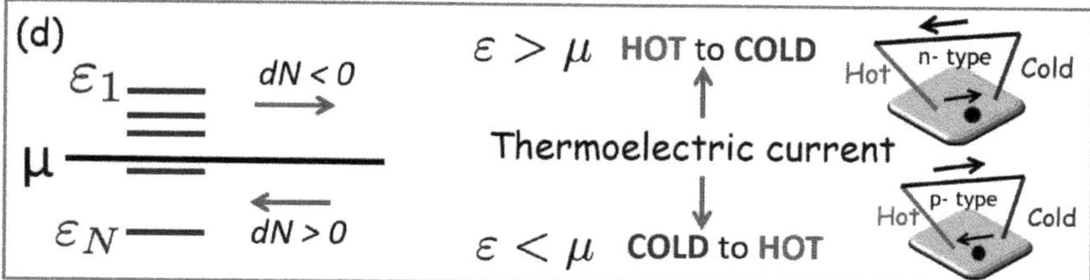

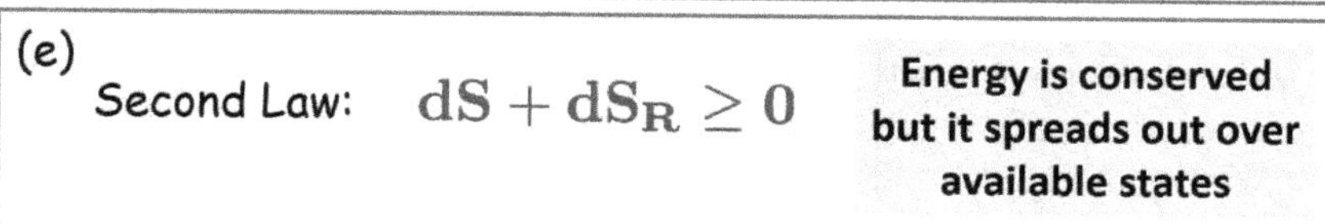

(e)
Second Law: $\mathbf{dS + dS_R \geq 0}$
Energy is conserved but it spreads out over available states

Fig. 2.28 Heat flow between two systems at different temperatures.

Now one interesting condition is when both are in equilibrium but with different temperatures (see Fig. 2.28a), like one of them is hot and the other is cold and we bring them together. The question is, which way will the energy flow and which way will the particles flow?

Okay, this time we can write the changes in the entropy for system and reservoir as $\mathrm{d}S = (\mathrm{d}E/T_1) - (\mu \mathrm{d}N/T_1)$ and $\mathrm{d}S_R = (\mathrm{d}E_R/T) - (\mu \mathrm{d}N_R/T)$. Both are locally in equilibrium, so we have an equality for both. But the temperatures are different, so they don't cancel when we add them, even though E,N are still conserved: $\mathrm{d}E + \mathrm{d}E_R = 0$, $\mathrm{d}N + \mathrm{d}N_R = 0$. Instead we get $\mathrm{d}S + \mathrm{d}S_R = d(E - \mu N) \times (1/T_1 - 1/T)$.

Now the question is, which way will energy/particles flow? Answer: In such a way as to make the total change in entropy, $\mathrm{d}S + \mathrm{d}S_R \geq 0$.

Say the system is hot and the reservoir is cold, meaning $T_1 > T$. That means this $1/T_1 < 1/T$ making this $(1/T_1 - 1/T)$ quantity negative. Hence to make the overall entropy change positive, the flow will occur in a way so as to make the quantity $\mathrm{d}(E - \mu N)$ negative. Let us now look separately at dE and dN, the energy flow and the particle flow.

Exchange of energy only, no particles: Since $dN = 0$, the flow will be such as to make $dE < 0$, meaning that the system will *lose* energy. Total energy is conserved, so this means $dE_R > 0$ indicating that the reservoir *gains* energy. This should come as no surprise, since we all know that heat flows from *hot to cold*, which in this case means *system to reservoir*. But it provides us with a nice *reality check*.

Exchange of particles: Now let us look at something for which the answer is a little less well-known. Suppose electrons are exchanged (see Fig. 2.28c) so that $\mathrm{d}N \neq 0$. There is also an associated change in energy which is $\varepsilon \mathrm{d}N$ if each electron or particle carries an energy ε. So $\mathrm{d}(E - \mu N)$ now looks like $(\varepsilon - \mu)\mathrm{d}N$ and this quantity must be less than 0.

So which way will the particles flow? Well, it depends on whether you're talking of energy levels above μ or below μ (see Fig. 2.28d), because if you are above μ, then you see $(\varepsilon - \mu)$ is a positive quantity and then $\mathrm{d}N$ must be negative. What that means is that the flow must be from system to reservoir, from hot to cold. On the other hand, if you look below μ, then $(\varepsilon - \mu)$ is negative, and so $\mathrm{d}N$ must be positive. And that means they'll flow from cold to hot.

So in other words, for energy levels above μ, electrons will flow from hot to cold, below μ, they'll flow from cold to hot and this is actually a very well known phenomenon in the field of *thermoelectricity*. There are two types of solids: (a) n-type where there are more states above μ than below, and so when you put a hot probe and a cold probe, the net electron flow is from *hot to cold*, (b) p-type where there are more states below μ than above, and in that case electrons flow from *cold to hot*. Once again, a well known phenomena, but what we're trying to show here is that everything follows from this principle of increasing entropy which is what is known as the second law of thermodynamics (see Fig. 2.28e).

You see, everybody has heard of the first law of thermodynamics which says that energy is conserved. But the *second law* is relatively less appreciated. It says that, yes, energy is conserved but it continually spreads out over the available states. So if it is originally in one particular state, it will want to spread out over everything that is available to it, making the overall entropy increase continually.

2.4.5 *Quiz*

2.4.5.1 *Question 1*

Consider an out-of-equilibrium system that exchanges energy and particles with a reservoir as it comes to equilibrium. In this process what happens to the (a) free energy of the system, (b) overall entropy of the system + reservoir.[10]

2.4.5.2 *Question 2*

Consider contacts 1 and 2 held at the same temperature T, but at two different electrochemical potentials $\mu_1 > \mu_2$. If a number of electrons ΔN is transferred from 1 to 2, what is the overall increase in entropy in terms of $\mu_1, \mu_2, \Delta N$.[11]

2.4.5.3 *Question 3*

Consider contacts 1 and 2 held at two different temperatures $T_1 > T_2$. If an energy ΔE is transferred from 1 to 2, what is the overall increase in entropy in terms of T_1, T_2, ΔE.[12]

---

[10](a) Free energy goes down, (b) overall entropy of system + reservoir goes up.
[11]$\Delta N(\mu_1 - \mu_2)/T$.
[12]$\Delta E(1/T_2 - 1/T_1)$.

2.5 Self-Consistent Field

This is Lecture 2.5: Watch youtube video

2.5.1 *Figs. 2.29-2.32: The exponential problem*

2.5.1.1 *Figs. 2.29*

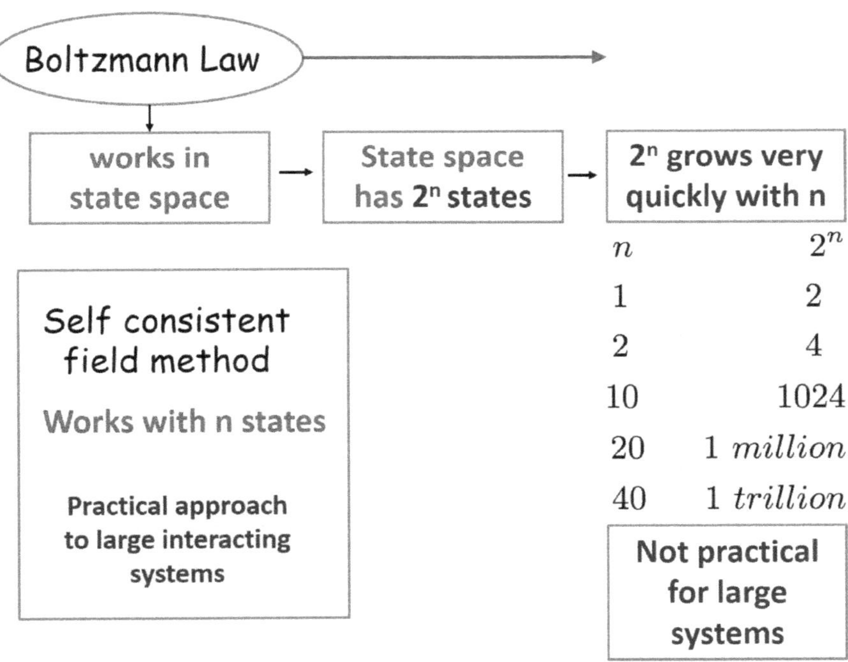

Fig. 2.29 Need for the self-consistent field method to handle large systems.

In the last four lectures we have tried to summarize some of the seminal concepts of statistical mechanics like the Boltzmann law, entropy and free energy. Now this Boltzmann law is very general, it applies to any system but one thing about it is that it operates in a space with 2^n states which is so large that it is often impractical to use. As n increases, this 2^n actually increases very rapidly, that is exponentially. Just to appreciate this point, I've put together a little table here, when n is 1 well 2^n is 2, if n is 10, 2^n is about 1000. Now, from 10 to 20 point is 1000 becomes a million, because it gets squared, it being in the exponent. Going from 20 to 40, that gets squared and so it becomes enormous like in a hurry. And so once you have a reasonable number of states, working in state space, although conceptually very sound, is often not practical.

What I'll be describing to you is a method that is widely used everywhere, in condensed matter physics, semiconductor devices, everywhere we are always using this method to describe electron electron interactions. It allows you to do your calculations in this other space, the space of n states, which is much more manageable. This will also lead us into the rest of the course where we'll be talking about neural networks and quantum computing.

2.5.1.2 *Fig. 2.30: Toy example*

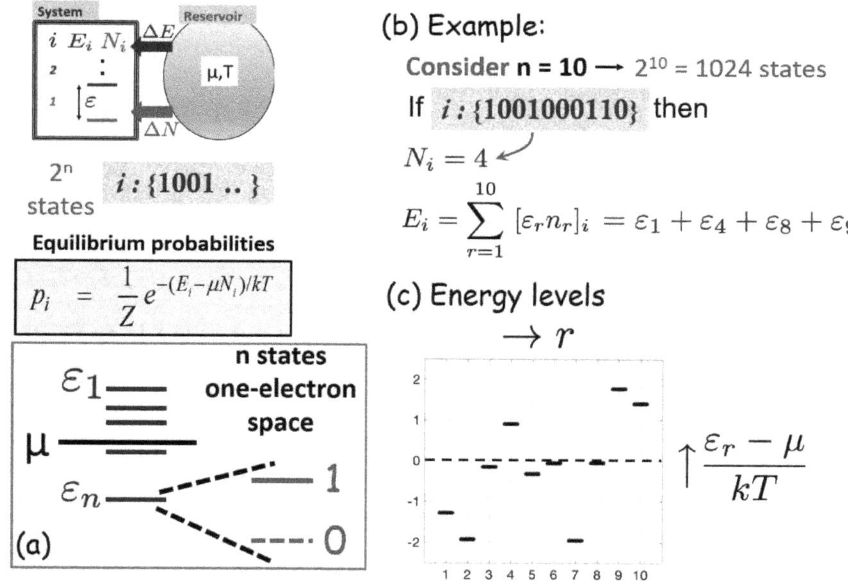

Fig. 2.30 Toy example to illustrate the direct Boltzmann law approach.

To understand this practical approach then, let's start with a toy example and first see how we would apply the Boltzmann law to it. If you've got a bunch of one electron levels (see Fig. 2.30a), each level can be occupied or unoccupied. And so in the state space, you have states that are described by these binary numbers, like $1001\cdots$. Now, if you have say 10 states (see Fig. 2.30b), then there will be 1,024 states in state space. So these 10 states have different energies, which I've shown here (see Fig. 2.30c).

So what is the occupation of these states? Now, Boltzmann law tells us how they're occupied at equilibrium but the Boltzmann law applies to the state space, which is not the $n = 10$ space but rather the 2^{10} space. The way you would apply the Boltzmann law is to say that, okay, let's consider a particular state, say 1001000110, and we want to know its probability. So to apply the Boltzmann law, I first need to know the energy and the number of electrons involved in that state. Now, the number of electrons is the number of ones, which is four. What is the energy? Well, all of these are empty except for those four, so the total energy is $E_i = \varepsilon_1 + \varepsilon_4 + \varepsilon_8 + \varepsilon_9$.

2.5.1.3 *Fig. 2.31*

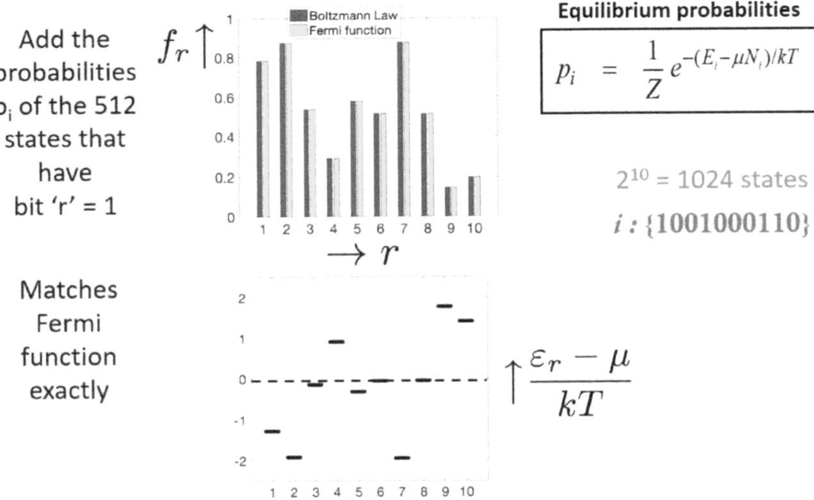

Fig. 2.31 Occupation factors of different energy levels for the example considered of Fig. 2.30.

Now, what you could do then is write down the probabilities of all these types (see Fig. 2.31), so this one has a certain probability from Boltzmann law, next one has a certain probability and then you add up the probabilities of all the 512 states that have $r = 1$. So supposing I want to know, well what is the occupation of the fourth state? Well when I write down all of these 1024 states, half of them will have 1 in the fourth state and half of them will have 0. So, what you do is that, consider the half that have one, add up their probabilities, and that will then tell you how many electrons are there in the fourth state. So that's how you could do this if you are starting from the Boltzmann law. Of course, it forces you to work in the 2^{10} space.

But in this case though, if you just applied the *Fermi function* to each of these ten levels, you would have come up with exactly the same answer that you get from this much more elaborate procedure using Boltzmann law. You can see I've compared the Boltzmann law to the *Fermi function*, they match each other perfectly. The Fermi function of course you can understand easily. You see, those levels that are above the equilibrium chemical potential, like this one, they are weakly occupied, that's why the *Fermi function* is relatively low. Whereas the ones that are way below the equilibrium chemical potential, that's where the Fermi function is higher, it is more occupied. So in this case you could do it either way and you'll get the same answer. Then you would say, well why am I even wasting my time with this 2^{10} thing? Let's just work with the $n = 10$ space.

2.5.1.4 *Fig. 2.32*

But the problem is that as soon as you include interactions (see Fig. 2.32), the answers you will actually get from Boltzmann law, that's these blue ones, are very different from the answer that you'd get if we just applied the *Fermi function*, and see, they don't match at all in this case. We have assumed that there is some interaction energy in this case, and that's why they don't match. If it was completely non-interacting, then it would have matched.

Now how do you include the interactions? Well in terms of Boltzmann law, the point is that when you evaluate the energies you not only add up the energies of all these levels, like I had done, but you also add the interaction energy. Let's say U is the interaction energy per pair of electrons, so the overall interaction energy will be U times the number of pairs, which is what I've written here mathematically: $U \times \sum_{r<q} \sum_{q=1}^{10} [n_r n_q]_i$.

Consider for example the state {1001000110} having four electrons. What is the interaction energy? Answer: U times the number of pairs. How many pairs? How many ways can you choose 2 electrons out of 4? Answer: ${}^4C_2 = 6$. You could write them out explicitly if you like. Levels 1, 4, 8, and 9 are occupied by electrons and the six possible pairs are (1-4),

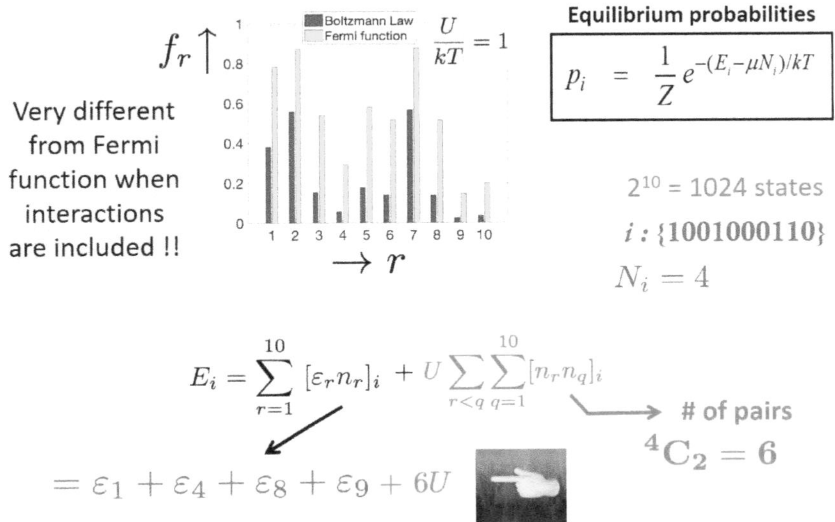

Fig. 2.32 Boltzmann law and Fermi function produce different results when interactions are included.

(1-8), (1-9), (4-8), (4-9), and (8-9). Those are the pairs, and there's 6 of them, so the energy is $6U$. So this way you have to take into account the energies of all the 2^{10} states and then use the Boltzmann law the same way we did the non-interacting problem. That's how you get this blue curve and the point is it wouldn't match the *Fermi function* at all.

2.5.2 *Figs. 2.33-2.36: SCF method*

So when I have an interacting system, how would we actually get the correct answers? You might say well apply Boltzmann law. Yes, but then that requires us to work in this 2^{10} space and as I mentioned at the outset, that's a problem. Okay, thousand is not too big, but if instead of 2^{10}, we had 2^{20}, that would be a million and if it is, like 2^{40}, it would be like a trillion. So this is the number that goes up in a hurry. So we need a method for dealing with interacting systems, a practical method, and that's what we'll be describing now, what's called the self consistent field method. It works reasonably well for weakly interacting systems and is widely used.

So how does this work? Well, if there were no interactions, then we would look at these energy levels ε_r (see Fig. 2.33, right hand side), calculate this dimensionless quantity, x_r and then find the *Fermi function*, which

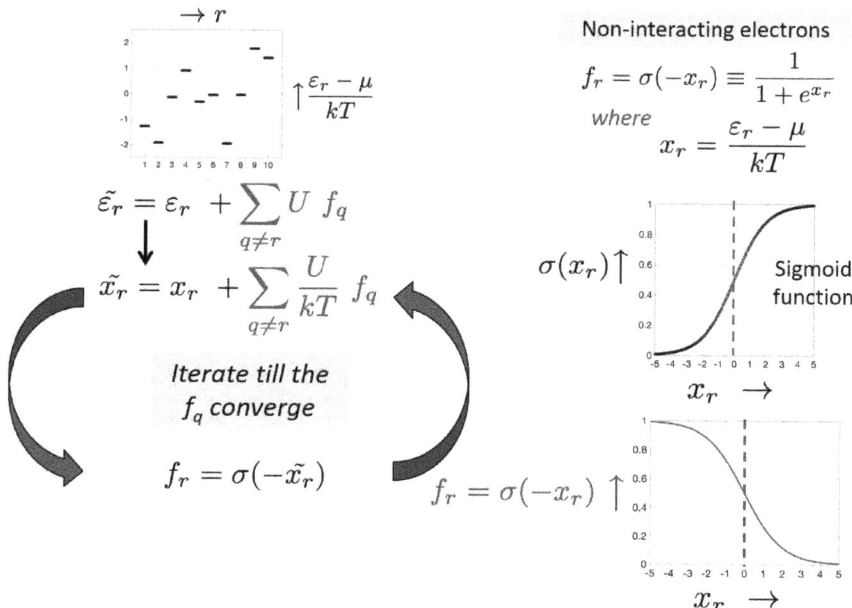

Fig. 2.33 Outline of the self-consistent field method.

is the mirror image of the sigmoid function, $f_r = \sigma(-x_r) \equiv 1/(1 + e^{x_r})$. The self consistent field method defines an *interacting energy level* $\tilde{\varepsilon}_r$, as if each of the bare energy levels ε_r gets raised by an amount that depends on how many levels are filled and then proceeds as before applying the *Fermi function* to the interacting levels $\tilde{\varepsilon}_r$.

How do we calculate the $\tilde{\varepsilon}_r$? The idea is that every time there is an electron in some level q, it gives rise to an interaction energy U with the rth level. So what you have to do is to add up these effects of all the occupied levels, except for itself because no electron affects itself, only the others. So,the new levels are given by $[\tilde{\varepsilon}_r = \varepsilon_r + \sum_{q \neq r} U f_q]$.

So that's the idea. It sounds almost as simple as doing the non-interacting case, but not quite, it's actually a little more complicated and the reason is this. You see, when we didn't have this interaction term, $[\tilde{x}_r = x_r + \sum_{q \neq r} (U/kT) f_q]$, it was straightforward. You calculate x_r, find the $f_r = \sigma(-\tilde{x}_r)$ and you have your answer. Now you see I can't calculate $\tilde{x}_r$ till I know f_r. So what I have to do is I assume some x_r and use it to calculate the f_r, but then I use that f_r to recalculate the x_r and of course, it won't match what I had started with, so what I do is, I take it, feed it back again, again calculate f_r and keep iterating till the result converges to a self-consistent answer. So that's what is called the Self Consistent Field Method which is widely used everywhere in condensed matter physics and in device physics.

2.5.2.1 *Fig. 2.34*

Now, this actually works quite well if the interaction isn't too large (Fig. 2.34). So for example, I mentioned earlier that when $U/(kT) = 1$ I showed you results that the Boltzmann and the *Fermi function* were not matching at all, but once you do the self consistent method, they match reasonably well.

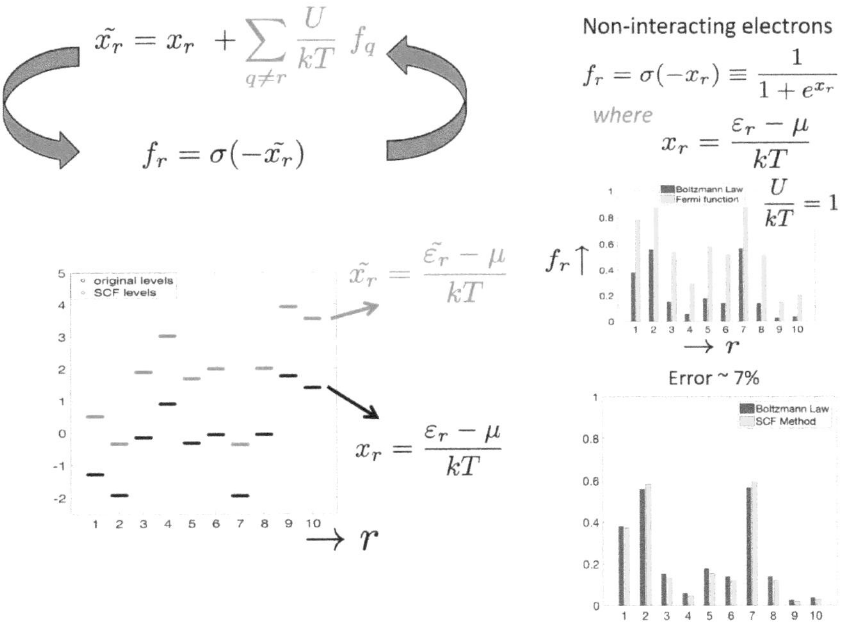

Fig. 2.34 Occupation factors and energy levels obtained from SCF method for the problem considered in Fig. 2.30.

You'll notice it's not exact and actually numerically if you check the difference between these two distributions (see Fig. 2.34), there's about a 7% difference, so it hasn't matched very well and if U were bigger, actually the discrepancy would also get bigger. But for relatively small U it works quite well and is, as I said, widely used in this field.

2.5.2.2 *Fig. 2.35*

Now, if you plot these $\widetilde{x}_r s$ then you'll get these red levels the ones have shown here. So you might ask then well, in practice when people draw energy levels, which ones do they really mean? Do they mean the red ones or the black ones? The answer is that it's really the red ones that you are drawing as if the interactions have already been considered.

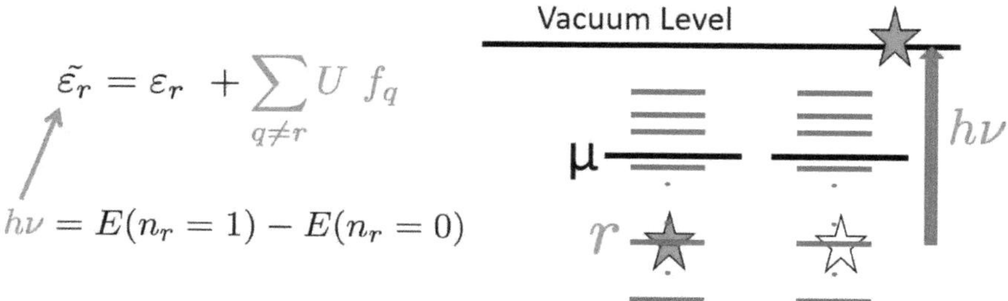

Fig. 2.35 Illustration of photo-emission method to determine energy levels.

Now, how do we know that? Well consider how you actually measure the one electron energy levels that we commonly use? You do what's called a photo emission experiment (see Fig. 2.35). You hit it with light and see what photon energy is needed to knock the electron out. The photon energy we need is the difference in the energy between two configurations that are basically identical, except that in one case the r-th level is filled and in the other case the r-th level is empty.

What is the difference? It is equal not to the bare ε_r, but to the interacting $\widetilde{\varepsilon}_r$. When I take out an electron, I've also removed its interaction with all the other electrons. So the difference bewteen the final and the initial energy which the photon has to supply, is not just the bare level, but also includes the interaction term, $\widetilde{\varepsilon}_r = \varepsilon_r + \sum_{q \neq r} U f_q$.

2.5.2.3 *Fig. 2.36*

Now another way to think about it is well, what would you have expected from Boltzmann law? Consider the same two configurations which are identical except that in one case one r is not occupied, which we call state 0, and in the other case r is occupied, which we call state 1. The ratio of their probabilities should equal $(1 - f_r)/f_r$.

Boltzmann law gives the ratio of their probabilities as $exp(-(E_0 - \mu N_0)/kT)$ divided by $exp(-(E_1 - \mu N_1)/kT)$ which we have inverted and switched the minus to a plus to write as $exp(+(E_1 - \mu N_1)/kT)$ divided by $exp((E_0 - \mu N_0)/kT)$. Now $N_1 - N_0 = 1$, and we saw earlier that $E_1 - E_0 = \tilde{\varepsilon}_r$. Hence the probability ratio from Boltzmann ratio is $exp((\tilde{\varepsilon}_r - \mu)/kT) = exp(\tilde{x}_r)$.

Equating the Boltzmann ratio $exp(\tilde{x}_r)$ to $(1 - f_r)/f_r$, a little algebra tells us that $f_r = 1/(1 + exp(\tilde{x}_r))$, which is also the sigmoid function of the negative, okay. So, Boltzmann law also kind of leads you to the same idea that basically what you have are these interacting energy levels and then you have to apply the Fermi function to the interacting levels.

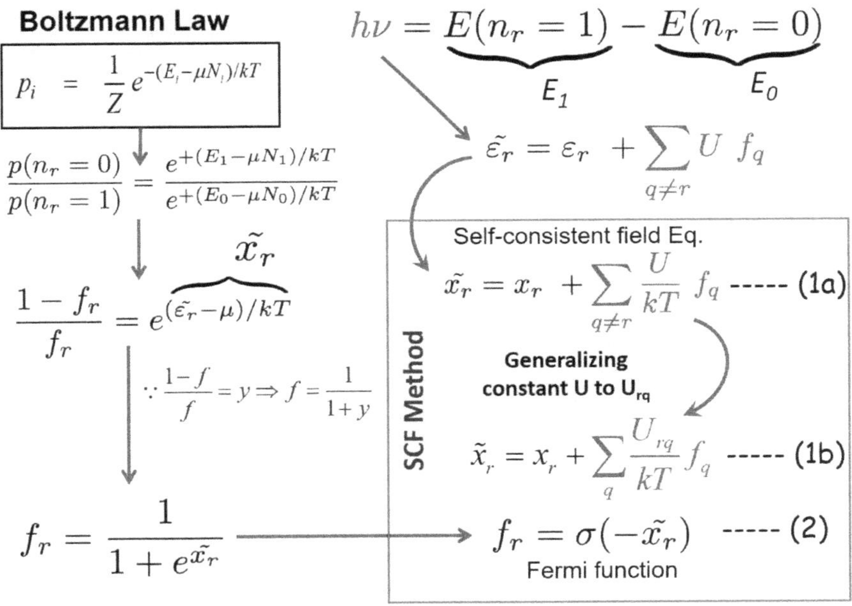

Fig. 2.36 Interacting energy levels from Boltzmann law.

Finally one little thing: I assumed that the interaction between the q-th electron and the r-th electron is aconstant U. In general, what could happen is you could have different interactions between them because levels r and q may be right next to each other, in which case the interaction will be large, or they could be far away in which case it would be small. So you can generalize it to put U_{rq} instead of just constant U as shown on the lower right in Fig. 2.36.

2.5.3 *Fig. 2.37: SCF and neural networks*

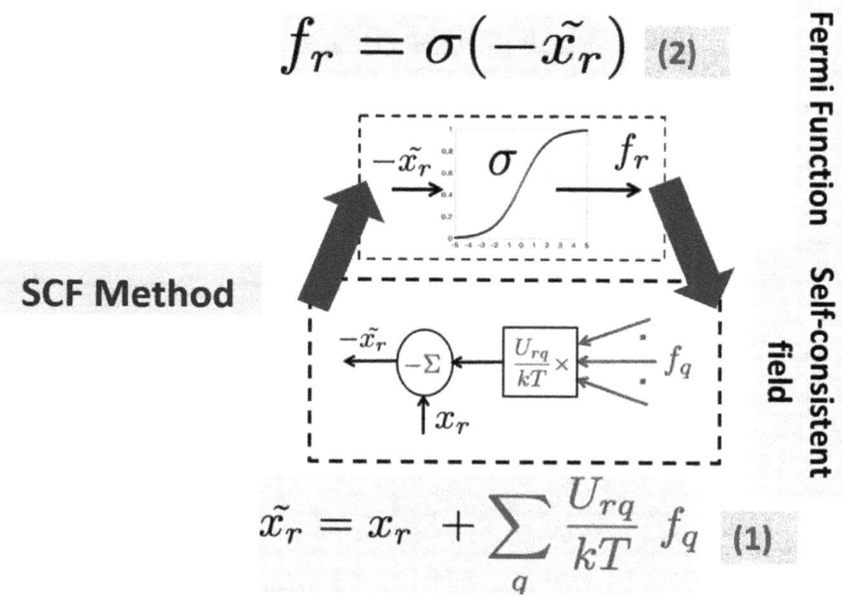

Fig. 2.37 Similarity in expressions between SCF method and neural-networks.

Fig. 2.37 shows our SCF equations in pictorial form: Top one is the sigmoid function and the bottom one is the summation. The reason I'm drawing it this way is that we'll next be talking about Boltzmann machines which are one kind of stochastic neural networks. In the context of neural networks, you often see pictures just like this. The sigmoid function is called the *neuron* while the summation is called the *synapse*.

But there is a **subtle difference**. Remember that the Fermi function f_r is a number between 0 and 1 which gives us the average occupation of a level, not the actual occupation which can only be either 0 or 1. The SCF method treats f_r as the actual occupation and does not do justice to this point.

By contrast, in Boltzmann machines, the output of the neuron is not f_r, but a binary number which is 0 with probability $1 - f_r$ and is 1 with probability f_r, just like the number of electrons in an energy level. This extension of the SCF method leads us to the concept of Gibbs sampling which we will see a lot of in the coming lectures. But I am getting ahead of myself. Let us pick this up in Lecture 3.1.

2.5.4 *Quiz*

2.5.4.1 *Question 1*

Consider a collection of 10 one-electron energy levels whose occupation we can calculate in two ways: (1) using the general Boltzmann law and (2) using the self-consistent field method. How many probabilities do we have to evealuate in each case?[13]

2.5.4.2 *Question 2*

Consider four one-electron energy levels each of energy ε having an interaction U for every pair of electrons. What is the total energy of the state $\{0110\}$?[14]

2.5.4.3 *Question 3*

Consider four one-electron energy levels each of energy ε having an interaction U for every pair of electrons. What is the total energy of the state $\{0111\}$?[15]

---

[13]Method 1 requires us to evaluate 2^{10} probabilities, while Method 2 requires us to evaluate 10 probabilities.

[14]$2\varepsilon + U$.

[15]$3\varepsilon + 3U$.

2.6 Fig. 2.38: 5-minute Summary

This is Chapter 2 summary: Watch youtube video
Welcome to a "five minute" summary of the last five lectures.

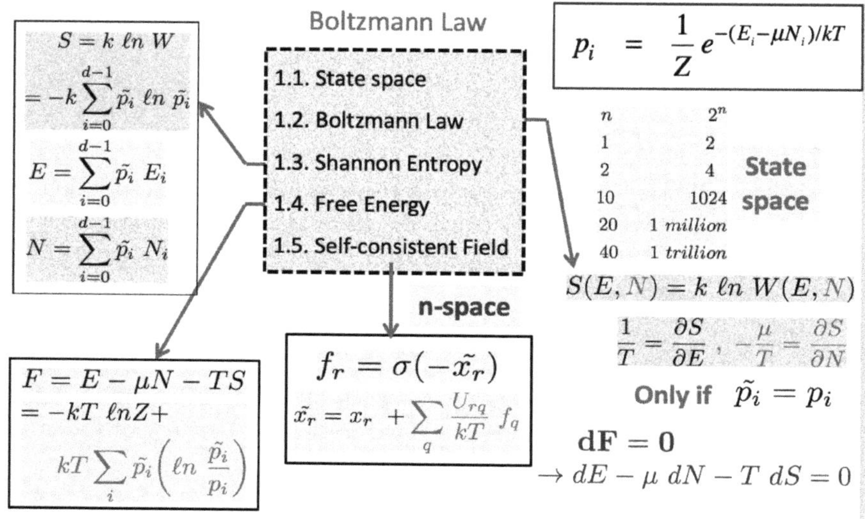

Fig. 2.38 Summary of Lectures 2.1-2.5.

Well, we started in Lecture 2.1 by introducing the state space. You see, usually we always draw this one electron space, but if you have n states here, in state space you have 2^n states, which can be labeled with binary numbers like this $[i : 1001\cdots]$, where each digit tells you whether one of these is occupied or empty. It's very important to be clear about which space we are talking about, the n space or the 2^n space. Boltzmann law is stated in terms of the latter. It is the central law of equilibrium statistical mechanics, not to be confused with the Boltzmann approximation to the Fermi function that you may have seen in semiconductor courses.

In Lecture 2.2 we try to explain why this law is so general that it applies to any system irrespective of its details. The reason is that the law comes from a property of the reservoir, not the system. If the system is in a lower energy state, then the reservoir has higher energy, and because it has higher energy, it has many more states that are accessible to it. So the chances of finding the system in a lower energy is high because corresponding to it there are many more states of the reservoir. This is the aspect that is captured through this function $W(E, N)$, which tells you how many states are accessible, and the logarithm of that is what's called the entropy, $S(E, N) = k \ln W(E, N)$.

In Lecture 2.3 explicitly evaluated the entropy (S), energy (E) and the number of particles (N) in terms of the probabilities of occupation of its different states represented by $\widetilde{p}_i$, where we have introduced the *tilde* to distinguish from the equilibrium probabilities p_i given by the Boltzmann law. So the expressions we obtain are quite general, they apply to the system whether it's close to equilibrium, at equilibrium, or totally out of equilibrium. But at equilibrium with $\widetilde{p}_i = p_i$ we can relate the derivatives of the entropy to the temperature T and the electrochemical potential μ.

To show this in Lecture 2.4, we introduced the concept of free energy, which has a *minimum* value of $-kT \ln Z$ at equilibrium, when the probabilities $\widetilde{p}_i$ are actually equal to the equilibrium probabilities p_i. A system not in equilibrium has a higher free energy which it will lower as it comes to equilibrium. This also corresponds to an increase in the total entropy of the system plus reservoir.

And finally in Lecture 2.5, we talked about something different, namely this self consistent field (SCF) method, which is widely used in condensed matter physics and device physics. Boltzmann law works in this 2^n space, which gets to be huge in a hurry. So it's important in practical problems, to have a method that can be applied in n space, like the SCF method. But the real reason I have introduced it is that an extension of this method leads us to the concept of Gibbs sampling that we'll see much more of in the coming lectures when we get into neural networks.

Chapter 3

Boltzmann Machines

3.1 Sampling

This is Lecture 3.1: Watch youtube video

3.1.1 *Figs. 3.1-3.4: From f to n*

3.1.1.1 *Fig. 3.1: Recap*

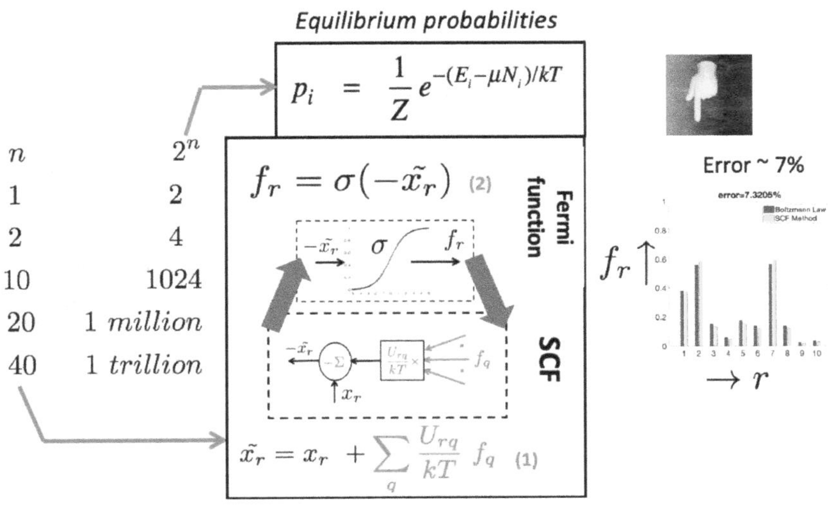

Fig. 3.1 Boltzmann law and the self-consistent field method.

Now, in Chapter 2, as you may recall (see Fig. 3.1), we were generally talking about the basic principles of equilibrium statistical mechanics starting from the Boltzmann law: $p_i = (1/Z)\exp(-(E_i - \mu N_i)/kT)$. We noted that this law operates in the space with 2^n states, which increases exponentially with n often making it impractical to use.

At the end in Lecture 2.5 we introduced what's called the self consistent field (**SCF**)method, where you have these two equations, $f_r = \sigma(-\widetilde{x}_r)$ and $\widetilde{x}_r = x_r + \sum_q (U_{rq}/kT)f_q$, that you can solve self consistently to obtain the equilibrium probabilities. This self consistent field method operates in the n space, which is a much smaller space and hence much more practical. However, it is kind of approximate. I gave you an example where the error was 7%, and it could be less or more depending on the parameters in the problem.

3.1.1.2 *Fig. 3.2: Replace f with n*

Now what I'll be describing to you in this lecture may look like a minor modification of the self-consistent field method, but it goes way beyond that, the full significance of which will only be evident after we talk about Markov chain Monte Carlo and transition matrices in Chapter 4. For the moment let me just say that the Boltzmann result can be written as a sum over an exponentially large number of *'Feynman paths'*. An exact evaluation is impractical, but depending on the problem at hand it is often possible to obtain accurate results with far fewer paths sampled using appropriate sampling algorithms. The basic idea is not unlike that of predicting an election from an exit poll of only a few voters sampled from a much larger population. But as we know, from time to time such predictions fail badly too!

Interestingly the "minor" modification I am talking about leads to a very popular sampling algorithm known as Gibbs sampling. The modification involves replacing the Fermi function f with a binary variable n (see Fig. 3.2), which we could view as the number of electrons, that can only be 0 or 1: you can't really have half an electron. What the Fermi function tells us is the probability that it's 1.

To obtain n we can use a random number generator to generate a random number, $R_{0,1}$, uniformly distributed in the window between 0 and 1. If that random number happens to be less than f, that's to the left, then we choose $n_r = 1$. Otherwise we choose $n = 0$. That way, the probability of n being 1 is proportional to f_r whereas the probability of n_r being 0 is proportional to $1 - f_r$.

Mathematically we can write $n_r = \vartheta(f_r - R_{0,1})$. Suppose f_r is 0.5, then $f_r - R_{0,1}$ will be positive 50% of the time, so that the step function ϑ gives 1 for n_r. The other 50% of samples will give $n_r = 0$ since $f_r - R_{0,1}$ will be negative. So we have a sequence of roughly equal number of 0's and 1's. But if $f_r = 0.9$ then $f_r - R_{0,1}$ will be positive 90% of the time making $n_r = 1$. n_r will be zero only 10% of the time as shown.

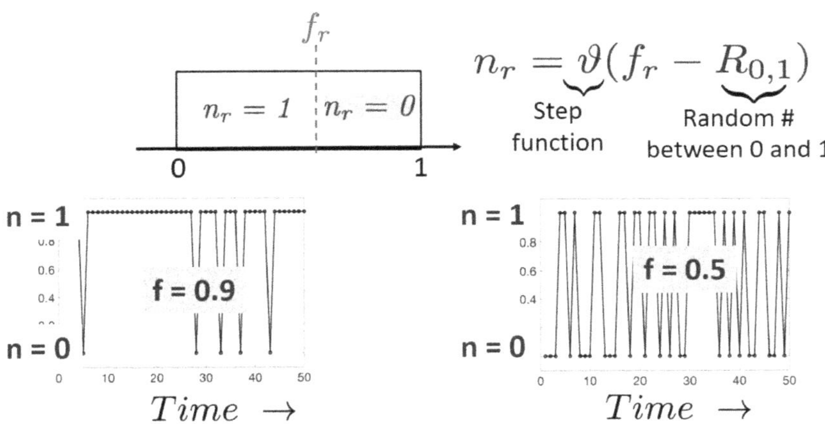

Fig. 3.2 From f to n.

3.1.1.3 *Fig. 3.3*

What we are going to do then is to take the self consistent field from Chapter 2 and replace the f's with n's (see Fig. 3.3). We'll add this equation $n_r = \vartheta(f_r - R_{0,1})$ which chooses the binary variable n_r according to the Fermi function $f_r = \sigma(-\widetilde{x}_r)$. That's what is called a **binary stochastic neuron** in the machine learning literature. We will generally refer to it as a probabilistic or a **p-bit** to contrast it with the qubits of quantum computing to be discussed in Chapters 5 and 6.

For the self consistent field equation, $\widetilde{x}_r = x_r + \sum_q (U_{rq}/kT) f_q$, we replace f_q with n_q. We also replace U_{rq}/kT with a dimensionless number w_{rq} since we will not be modeling physical systems with interaction energy and thermal energy any more. Just an abstract system with a weight logic w_{rq} that defines what is called the *synapse* $\widetilde{x}_r = x_r + \sum_q w_{rq} n_q$ in the machine learning literature.

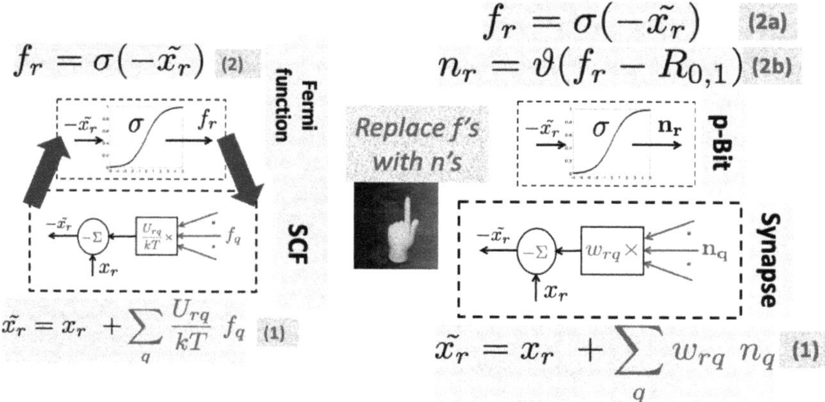

Fig. 3.3 Replace f with n.

3.1.1.4 *Fig. 3.4: Generating samples*

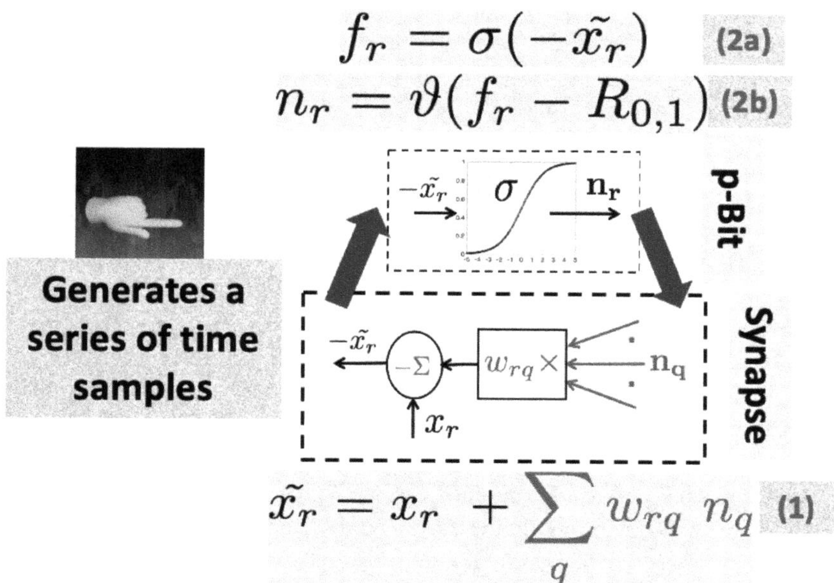

Fig. 3.4 Generating samples.

With this replacement then our self consistent field method morphs into a sampling method (see Fig. 3.4). We start with a set of initial samples n_r, representing the state of all the neurons, calculate x, then use that x to generate this Fermi function $f_r = \sigma(-\widetilde{x}_r)$, which is then used to update all neurons giving us a new set of samples. Keep doing this and thereby you'd be generating a entire series of samples of the states of the neurons. If you use those time samples to generate a histogram, then you get the Boltzmann probabilities that you're looking for.

3.1.2 *Figs. 3.5-3.8: Synapse from interaction energy*

3.1.2.1 *Fig. 3.5*

As you may recall, the synapse function $\widetilde{x}_r = x_r + \sum_q w_{rq} n_q$ (see Fig. 3.5) came from the interaction energy. So the idea was that these electrons had a pairwise interaction energy of U_{rq} between the electron, r, and the electron, q and this w is that interaction energy normalized to kT. Let us try to get a deeper understanding of the synaptic function by delving a little more into this connection with the interaction energy.

3.1.2.2 *Fig. 3.6*

I'd mentioned earlier that one way of thinking of this self consistent potential (see Fig. 3.6), is to consider how much the normalized interaction energy ($\widetilde{E} \equiv E/kT$) would change if n_r were to change from 1 to 0: $\widetilde{x}_r = \widetilde{E}(n_r = 1) - \widetilde{E}(n_r = 0)$, which you could write as $\partial \widetilde{E}/\partial n_r$.

That's not generally true though, but it's true if it's a linear function like say $\widetilde{E} = 10n_r$. Now the thing is, in this context, we'll always be dealing with linear functions. Why is that? Well, because n_r is a binary variable, it's either 0 or 1. And as such it has the property that you can raise it to any power, and it's basically the same variable since $0^2 = 0$, $1^2 = 1$. So basically, n_r^k is really the same as n_r, k being any real number.

One other point, that in our discussions last week we had often made the distinction between E and $E - \mu N$, but going forwards, we'll just write this normalized quantity, as $\widetilde{E}$, and we won't make these distinctions anymore.

3.1.2.3 *Fig. 3.7*

Now, often the interactions are what you might call quadratic (see Fig. 3.7), in the sense you have pairwise interactions, that is between n_r and n_q. In that case, when you take the derivative, the synapse function will be linear.

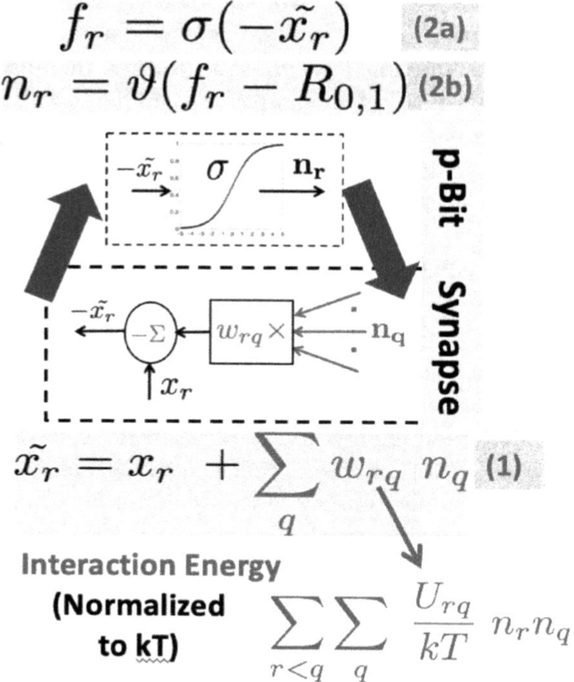

$f_r = \sigma(-\tilde{x}_r)$ (2a)
$n_r = \vartheta(f_r - R_{0,1})$ (2b)
p-Bit
Synapse
$\tilde{x}_r = x_r + \sum_q w_{rq} n_q$ (1)
Interaction Energy
(Normalized
to kT)
$\sum_{r<q} \sum_q \frac{U_{rq}}{kT} n_r n_q$

Fig. 3.5 Synapse from interactions.

On the other end in general, you could have higher order interactions. You could have a three body interactions, involving n_r, n_q, n_s. In which case the synapse function would involve quadratic terms, but most of the time people deal with this quadratic interactions and linear synapses. So we often write the linear version $\tilde{x}_r = x_r + \sum_q w_{rq} n_q$, but more generally, of course, you could have a more higher order interactions and in that case, you should find the synapse from the derivative.

3.1.2.4 *Fig. 3.8: A simple code*

Okay, next, if you actually want to solve a particular problem and generate these samples (see Fig. 3.8), it is relatively easy to write down a code. Here's a MATLAB® code that will do exactly what is stated on the right hand side. I have also tried to write down the Python version of the same code. If you want to try out on your own, you could do that.

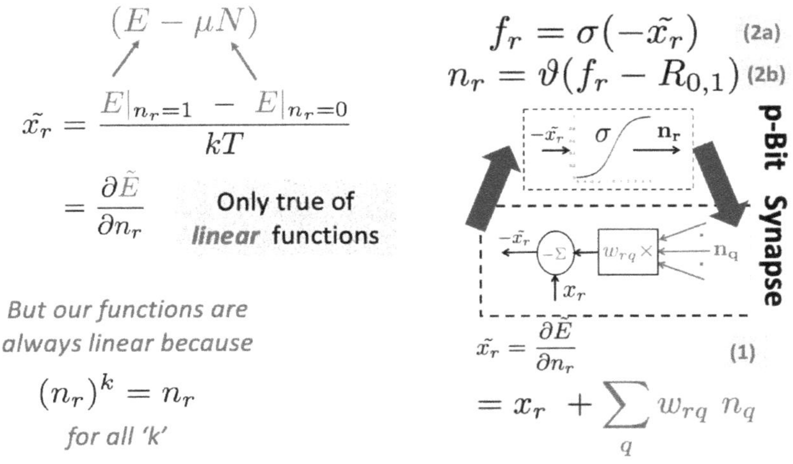

$$(E - \mu N)$$

$$\tilde{x_r} = \frac{E|_{n_r=1} - E|_{n_r=0}}{kT}$$

$$= \frac{\partial \tilde{E}}{\partial n_r}$$

Only true of *linear* functions

But our functions are always linear because

$$(n_r)^k = n_r$$

for all 'k'

$$f_r = \sigma(-\tilde{x_r}) \quad \text{(2a)}$$

$$n_r = \vartheta(f_r - R_{0,1}) \quad \text{(2b)}$$

p-Bit Synapse

$$\tilde{x_r} = \frac{\partial \tilde{E}}{\partial n_r} \quad \text{(1)}$$

$$= x_r + \sum_q w_{rq}\, n_q$$

Fig. 3.6 Synapse from interactions (contd.).

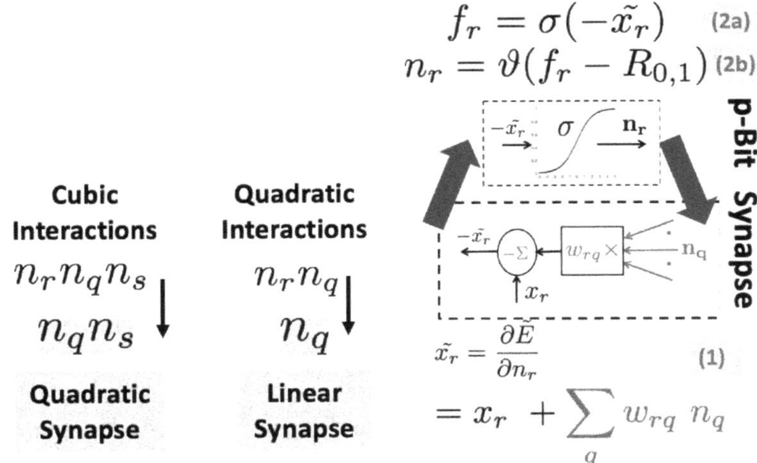

Fig. 3.7 Synapse from interactions (contd.).

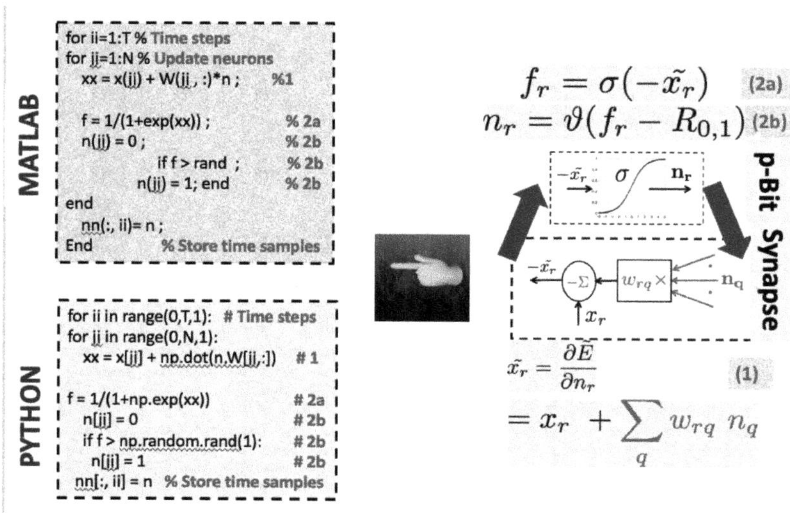

MATLAB
for ii=1:T % Time steps
for jj=1:N % Update neurons
xx = x(jj) + W(jj, :)*n ; %1
f = 1/(1+exp(xx)) ; % 2a
n(jj) = 0 ; % 2b
if f > rand ; % 2b
n(jj) = 1; end % 2b
end
nn(:, ii)= n ;
End % Store time samples
PYTHON
for ii in range(0,T,1): # Time steps
for jj in range(0,N,1):
xx = x[jj] + np.dot(n,W[jj,:]) # 1
f = 1/(1+np.exp(xx)) # 2a
n[jj] = 0 # 2b
if f > np.random.rand(1): # 2b
n[jj] = 1 # 2b
nn[:, ii] = n % Store time samples
$f_r = \sigma(-\tilde{x}_r)$ (2a)
$n_r = \vartheta(f_r - R_{0,1})$ (2b)
p-Bit
Synapse
$w_{rq}\times$
$\tilde{x}_r = \frac{\partial E}{\partial n_r}$ (1)
$= x_r + \sum_q w_{rq}\, n_q$

Fig. 3.8 Codes.

3.1.3 *Figs. 3.9-3.15: Toy example*

3.1.3.1 *Fig. 3.9: Solution, the Boltzmann way*

μ

ε 1 2 ↕1

$$\tilde{E} = -n_1 - n_2 + 2n_1n_2$$

n_1	n_2	E	
0	0	0	
0	1	−1	
1	0	−1	
1	1	−2	+2

$$p_i = \frac{1}{Z} e^{\overbrace{-(E_i - \mu N_i)/kT}^{\tilde{E}_i}}$$

n_1	n_2	E_i	e^{-E_i}
0	0	0	1
0	1	−1	2.7
1	0	−1	2.7
1	1	0	1

Fig. 3.9 Toy example.

Now what we'll do in the rest of this lecture is to go through what you might call a toy example (see Fig. 3.9). So we don't really need a computer to do this, we could just do it on paper, as we'll be doing in the next few slides. So consider a problem with two neurons or two energy levels, 1 and 2, and whose energy levels are below their chemical potentials. So, $E - \mu$ is, like -1 and so our energy function is $-n_1 - n_2$. So you could make up the set of energies for all the state space levels. The state space, it could be $\{00\}$, $\{01\}$, $\{10\}$, and $\{11\}$ and corresponding to that, the energies would be 0, -1, -1 and -2 and we can now use this to find the probabilities using the general Boltzmann law. Now, if we add interactions, so supposing there is a term that's like $2n_1n_2$, that's an interaction term. So, how will that change this table of energies? Well, the first three are not affected at all because n_1n_2 is 0. Only the last one changes, where we add a $+2$ and so these two add to give me 0. So finally we get a table like this, where $\{00\}$ and $\{11\}$, both have an energy of 0 whereas $\{01\}$, and $\{10\}$, have a lower energy, which is -1.

3.1.3.2 *Fig. 3.10*

So Boltzmann law, then tells me that the probabilities will be proportional to $e^0 = 1$, $e^0 = 1$, and then $e^1 = 2.7$, $e^1 = 2.7$. So the probabilities of the system being in these four states is proportional to [1 1 2.7 2.7] respectively. The actual probabilities are obtained by normalizing them such that they add up to 1: [1 1 2.7 2.7]./7.4 (see Fig. 3.10).

Moving on, if let's say we multiply this energy function by a factor of 10. Well, then what happens is that the 0's still remain 0's, but the -1's now become -10. And so now when we look at the probabilities. What we'll find is that, $\{01\}$ and $\{10\}$ have a much bigger probability proportional to e^{10}. If you now draw the histogram, you'd see just two peaks with the other two strongly suppressed. In physical systems the normalized energy function $\widetilde{E} = E/kT$ increases when we lower the temperature and this is just what you see: at higher temperatures things tend to be relatively, uniformly distributed probability wise. At lower temperatures they tend to lock into the lowest energy states.

3.1.3.3 *Fig. 3.11: How NOT to sample*

Now in the next few slides, I just want to explain how you'd get the same answers from the sampling method (see Fig. 3.11). First let us look at a sampling method that does not work.

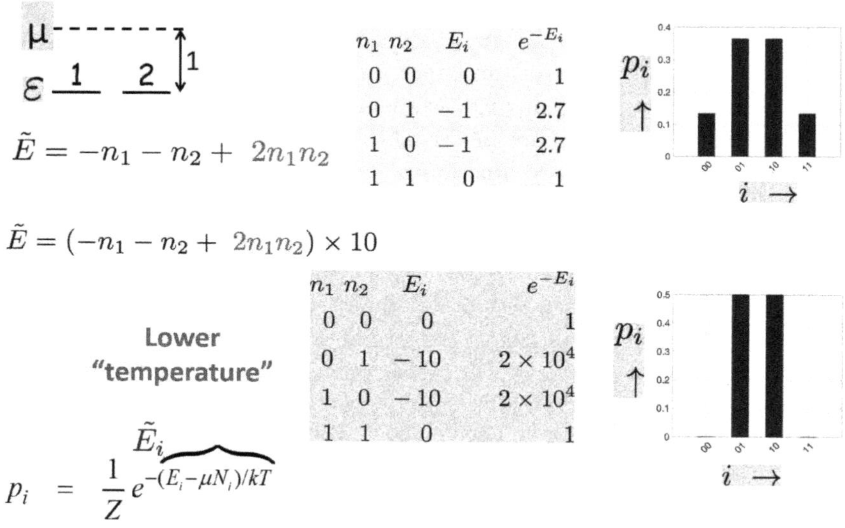

μ - - - - - - 1

ε 1 2

$$\tilde{E} = -n_1 - n_2 + 2n_1 n_2$$

n_1	n_2	E_i	e^{-E_i}
0	0	0	1
0	1	−1	2.7
1	0	−1	2.7
1	1	0	1

$p_i \uparrow$

$i \rightarrow$

$$\tilde{E} = (-n_1 - n_2 + 2n_1 n_2) \times 10$$

Lower "temperature"

n_1	n_2	E_i	e^{-E_i}
0	0	0	1
0	1	−10	2×10^4
1	0	−10	2×10^4
1	1	0	1

$p_i \uparrow$

$i \rightarrow$

$$p_i = \frac{1}{Z} e^{-\overbrace{(E_i - \mu N_i)}^{\tilde{E}_i}/kT}$$

Fig. 3.10 Toy example.

Say we start with both states empty, at {00}. Okay, so next we calculate this synaptic function, and we get −10 for each one. Okay, so now if it's −10, then when we calculate the Fermi function, it tells us that both states must be occupied, so we fill them both up to get {11}. But once both are occupied, with $n_1 = 1$ and $n_2 = 1$, the synaptic functions are +10 and +10, which then tells you that both states must be unoccupied, taking us back to {00}. Now if you try again, you're back to the old situation, so now you again predict that the next state should be {11}. So this clearly isn't working because from Boltzmann, you expect {01} and {10} to be high probability, while this seems to be just oscillating between {00} and {11}.

3.1.3.4 *Fig. 3.12: Solution by sampling*

Where did we go wrong? We were updating both *p-bits* simultaneously. What you need to do is update them one by one (see Fig. 3.12), and then it will work. So the way it would work then is, start with {00} so it tells you that they should both be filled, but we don't fill both of them, we just do one of them. update the synaptic function, and then go to the next *p-bit*.

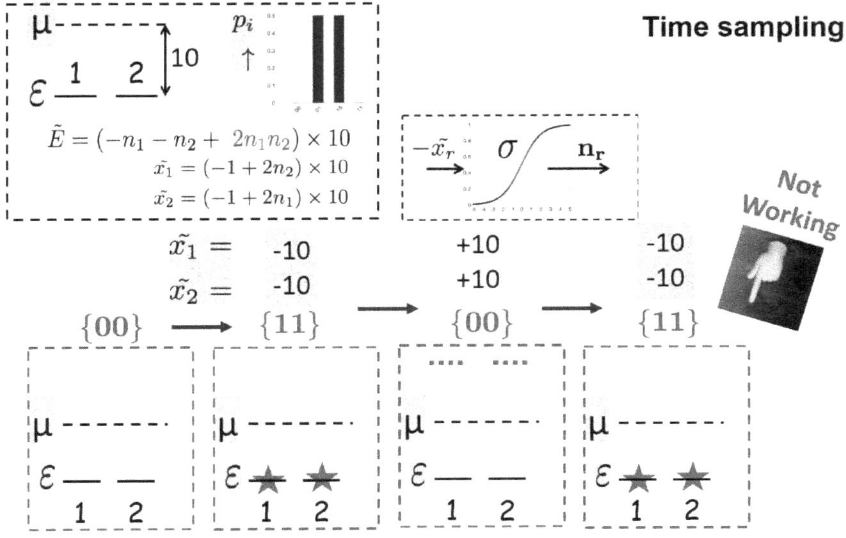

Fig. 3.11 How NOT to sample.

So let's say we update only the first *p-bit* to get {10} instead of {11}. Then when we recalculate the synaptic functions, $\widetilde{x}_2$ goes from -10 to $+10$, telling me to keep *p-bit* 2 at 0. On the other hand, $\widetilde{x}_1$ remains -10 because I've only changed n_1, I have not changed n_2, telling me to keep *p-bit* 1 at 1. So the system gets stuck in {10} thereafter.

If we go back to our physical picture with electrons occupying two levels, it is as if the presence of an electron in level 1 has raised level 2 way up making it empty. But level 1 itself hasn't changed because the electron doesn't feel anything due to itself. And so it stays full and {10} represents a self-consistent state that the system locks into.

3.1.3.5 *Fig. 3.13*

But wait a minute. Why did the system lock into {10} and not {01}. That too would be a self-consistent state with level 2 filled ($n_2 = 1$) and level 1 empty ($n_1 = 0$). Well if we had updated neuron 2 first the system would indeed have locked into {01} instead of {10} as shown in Fig. 3.13.

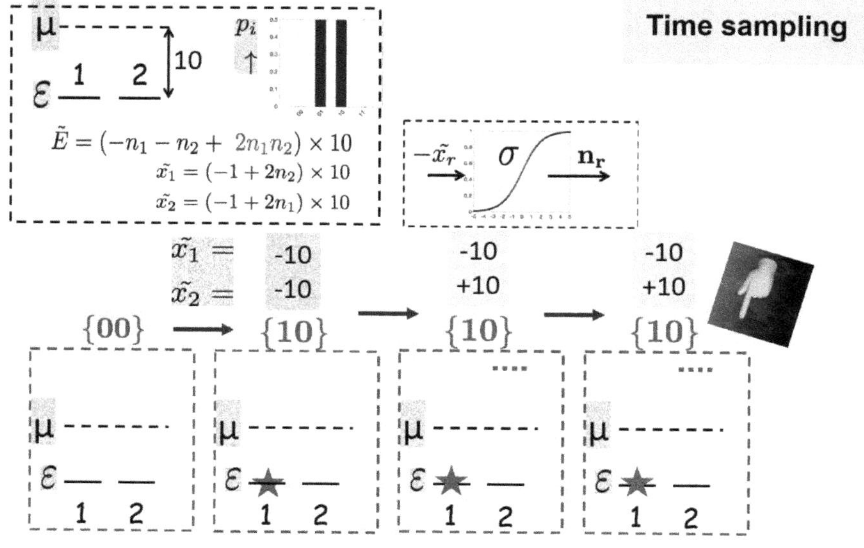

Fig. 3.12 How to sample.

3.1.3.6 *Fig. 3.14*

So the bottom line is that simultaneously updating two *p-bits* that are interconnected synaptically does not work. But if you update sequentially, what you'd find is that the system locks into one of two *self-replicating* states (see Fig. 3.14). That is once you get into one of them, you just stay there, you don't move and that's why when you create a histogram, you'll see large peaks corresponding to these $\{10\}$ and $\{01\}$. Whereas if you start in any of the other ones like $\{00\}$ or $\{11\}$, you get out of it right away.

But why do I see two peaks? Shouldn't we see one or the other? Indeed that is true if E_0 is large making the synaptic functions like ± 10 as we assumed in our discussion. In practice you don't want this E_0 to be too big, you want it something intermediate, so that the synaptic functions are smaller like say ± 2. In that case neither $\{10\}$ nor $\{01\}$ is firmly locked in, and each has a reasonable chance to go over to one of the low probability states $\{00\}$ or $\{11\}$ and then transition over to the other high probability state. That way, you can pick up both peaks as you draw more and more samples.

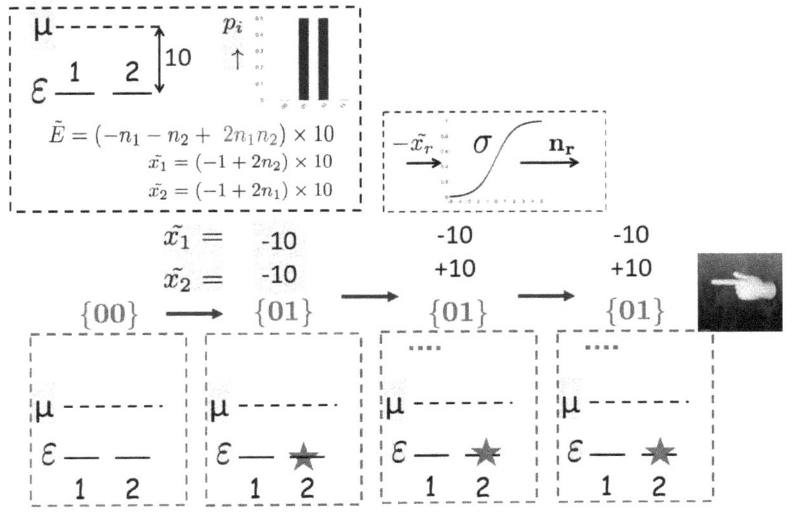

Fig. 3.13 How to sample.

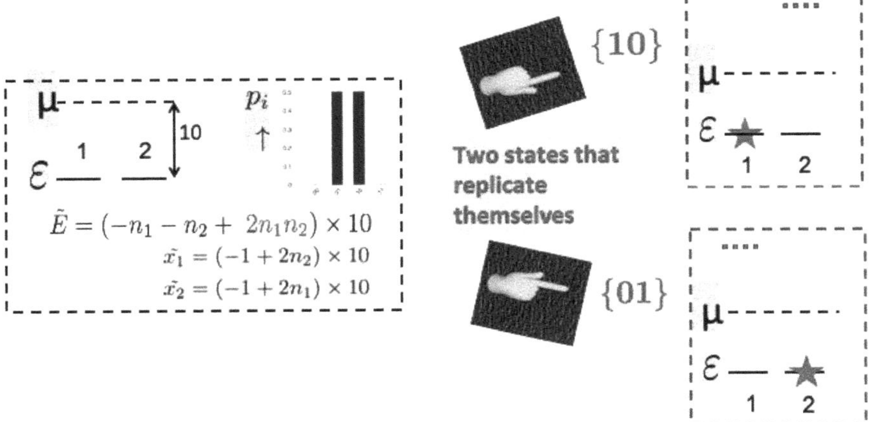

Fig. 3.14 Self-replicating states.

3.1.3.7 *Fig. 3.15: Sampling method, key points*

Fig. 3.15 tries to summarize our discussion regarding the sampling method. The key message is that this method will reproduce the Boltzmann law (see Fig. 3.15), as long as you update *synaptically connected p-bits* sequentially, and not simultaneously. It is also important to avoid large values of E_0 which could lock the system into a subset of all the states.

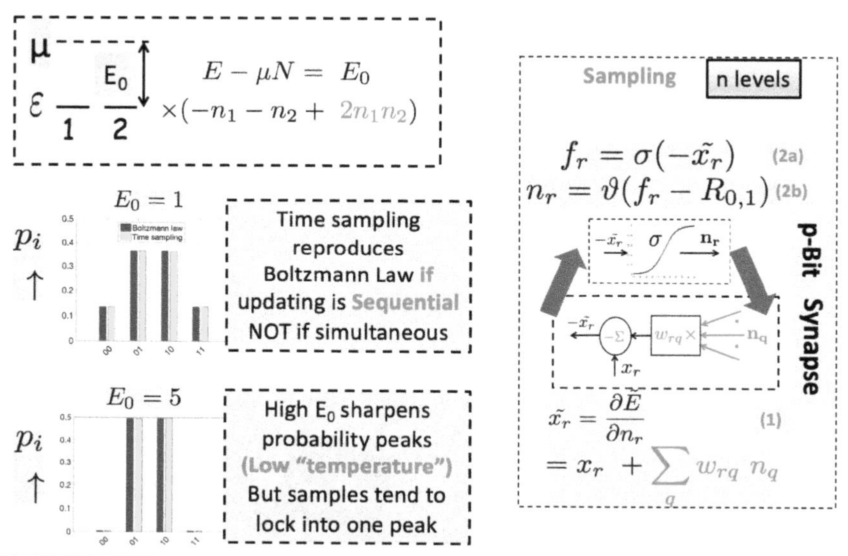

Fig. 3.15 Sampling method, key points.

3.1.4 *Quiz*

3.1.4.1 *Question 1*

What is the relation between the Fermi function f_r and the electron number n_r?[1]

3.1.4.2 *Question 2*

If the energy of a system of three levels is given by $\widetilde{E} = x_3 n_3 + n_1 n_2 n_3$ what is the the synaptic output driving level 3?[2]

3.1.4.3 *Question 3*

If the energy of a system with two levels is given by $\widetilde{E} = 2n_1 n_2 - n_1 - n_2$ which states have the highest probability?[3]

---

[1] n_r takes on the value 1 with probability f_r, and the value 0 with probability $1 - f_r$.
[2] $\widetilde{x_3} = x_3 + n_1 n_2$.
[3] $\{01\}$ and $\{10\}$.

3.2 Orchestrating Interactions

This is Lecture 3.2: Watch youtube video

As you may recall, in the last lecture, we introduced the sampling method which works in n space, but it allows us to analyze the response in the huge 2^n space. Now, just to remind you what I mean by n space and 2^n space: n represents the number of binary stochastic neurons or *p-bits*, and 2^n tells you, how many configurations they represent and the Boltzmann law, gives us the probability of each configuration in this 2^n space. But 2^n, can be a huge number and so the sampling method is really very attractive since it allows us to work in the n space and yet give accurate results for the probability distribution, in the 2^n space.

As an example we had talked about a system with just two *p-bits*. And that means, $n = 2$, $2^n = 4$ which is no big deal. This was meant to be toy example, to just illustrate the principles. Now, what we will do first is to generalize this a little bit. Then we will try to get a feeling for how the interactions in n space affect and control the probability response in 2^n space.

3.2.1 *Figs. 3.16-3.20: Generalizing the toy model*

3.2.1.1 *Fig. 3.16*

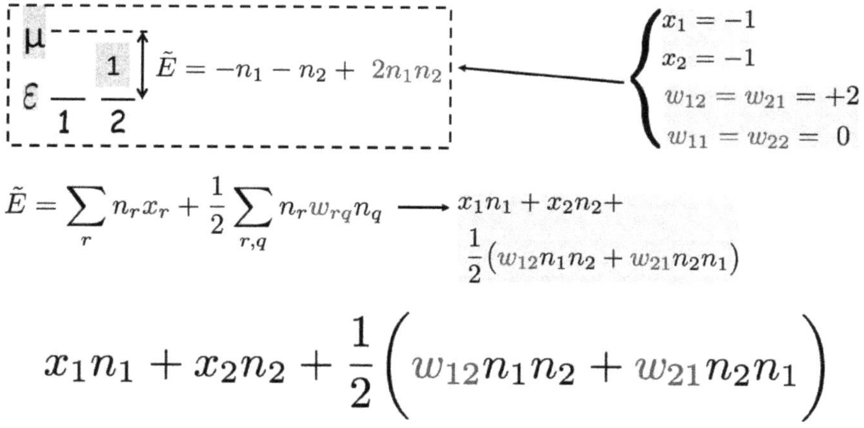

μ

ε

1 2

1

$$\tilde{E} = -n_1 - n_2 + 2n_1n_2$$

$$x_1 = -1$$
$$x_2 = -1$$
$$w_{12} = w_{21} = +2$$
$$w_{11} = w_{22} = 0$$

$$\tilde{E} = \sum_r n_r x_r + \frac{1}{2}\sum_{r,q} n_r w_{rq} n_q \longrightarrow x_1n_1 + x_2n_2 + \frac{1}{2}\left(w_{12}n_1n_2 + w_{21}n_2n_1\right)$$

$$x_1n_1 + x_2n_2 + \frac{1}{2}\left(w_{12}n_1n_2 + w_{21}n_2n_1\right)$$

Fig. 3.16 Generalizing the two *p-bit* energy expression to arbitrary number of *p-bits*.

Earlier we had just two *p-bits*, so it was easy to write out the energy expression. There were just a few terms in there. But in general, if we had say 10 *p-bits* then we would be just writing forever. So to write it in a compact way, what you could do is use these summations $\widetilde{E} = \sum_r n_r x_r + \sum_{r,q} n_r w_{rq} n_q$. So for example, what I've written here, $\widetilde{E} = \sum_r n_r x_r + \sum_{r,q} n_r w_{rq} n_q$, is a generalization of what was done earlier for just two *p-bits*. To see this you can write out all the terms in the summation, assuming that there are only two *p-bits* so that the indices r and q each take on just two values 1 and 2. You can see that we get our old expression $\widetilde{E} = -n_1 - n_2 + 2n_1 n_2$ if we set $x_1 = 1$, $x_2 = 1$ and $w_{11} = 0$, $w_{12} = +2$, $w_{21} = +2$, $w_{22} = 0$.

3.2.1.2 *Fig. 3.17*

Now, what we'll do is describe to you something that's even more compact using matrix notation as shown in Fig. 3.17. So the idea is that we could write $\sum_r n_r x_r$ in the form of a row vector $\{n_1\ n_2\ \cdots\}$ times a column vector $\{x_1\ x_2\ \cdots\}^T$, which in matrix notation becomes $n^T x$. Similarly the term $\sum_{r,q} n_r w_{rq} n_q$ in matrix notation becomes $n^T w n$ as shown.

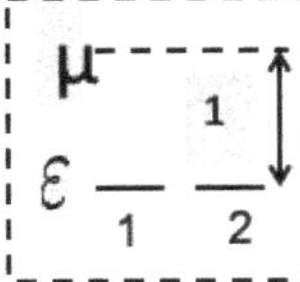

μ, 1, ε, 1, 2

$$\tilde{E} = -n_1 - n_2 + 2n_1 n_2$$

$$x_1 = -1,\quad x_2 = -1,\quad W_{12} = W_{21} = +2,\quad W_{11} = W_{22} = 0$$

$$\tilde{E} = \sum_r n_r x_r + \frac{1}{2}\sum_{r,q} n_r w_{rq} n_q \longrightarrow x_1 n_1 + x_2 n_2 + \frac{1}{2}\left(w_{12} n_1 n_2 + w_{21} n_2 n_1\right)$$

$$= \{n_1\ n_2\}\begin{Bmatrix} x_1 \\ x_2 \end{Bmatrix} + \frac{1}{2}\underbrace{\{n_1\ n_2\}\begin{bmatrix} 0 & w_{12} \\ w_{21} & 0 \end{bmatrix}}_{=\{w_{21} n_2\ \ w_{12} n_1\}}\begin{Bmatrix} n_1 \\ n_2 \end{Bmatrix}$$

$$= n^T x + \frac{1}{2}\, n^T w n$$

Fig. 3.17 Matrix notation.

3.2.1.3 *Fig. 3.18: Four level example*

In general, the energy function $\widetilde{E} = n^T x + (1/2) n^T w n$ is defined by two parameters x and w: x is a column vector, sometimes called the bias, and w is what's called the weight matrix.

So for example (see Fig. 3.18), if you had four *p-bits*, then x would be a 4×1 column vector and w would be a 4×4 matrix. So what would the response look like? I have plotted it in Fig. 3.18 with two *p-bits* on one axis, and the other two on another axis. And we plot the probability along the vertical axis, the third one. Of course we could have just written all four neurons in one line, but then we'd have 16 points along that line. Instead we have written it in a two dimensional matrix, 4 of them on one side, and 4 on the other side.

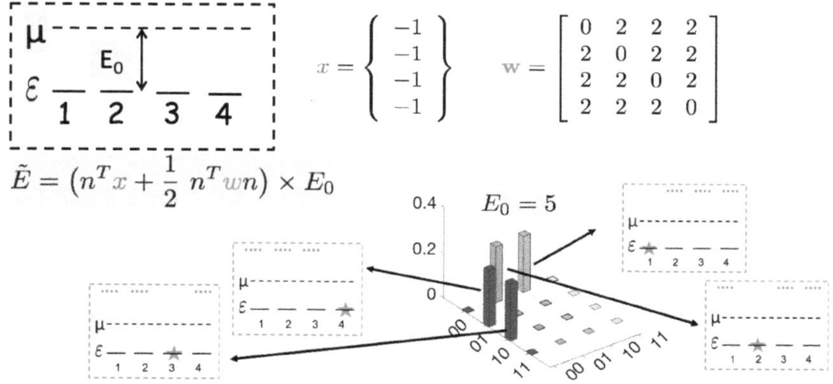

Fig. 3.18 Four levels with all-to-all interactions.

Now, if we actually put down those numbers and solve it, what you'd see is four peaks, corresponding to the lowest energy states. Which ones are they? As you can see from the plot they are {0010}, {0001}, {0100}, and {1000}. In terms of our physical picture of energy levels filled with electrons, these all represent states having just one electron, so that only one of the four is 1, rest are zero. Why don't we have states with two, three or four electrons? Because of this strong interaction term, w, what happens is if you try to put more than one electron the energy becomes too high because of the interaction. Why not eliminate electrons altogether and go to the {0000} state? Then you do not take advantage of the bias

$x_r = -1$. Anytime you put in an electron, there's an energy term like an n_1x_1 or an n_2x_2, which are negative, so they give rise to a lower energy. So finally, the lowest energy states are those which have one electron, but that one electron could be in any one of the levels.

3.2.1.4 *Fig. 3.19*

Now, what happens if I, let's say (see Fig. 3.19), only keep nearest neighbor interactions? So what I've done is taken out the 2's from the intercation matrix $[w]$, when they're far from the diagonal, and I'm only keeping the upper diagonal and the lower diagonal, rest are all set to zero. And physically that would correspond to, electrons only interacting with electrons next to them, but not if they're far away.

Now the lowest energy states are those having two electrons but not in contiguous levels. There are three such configurations: $\{1001\}$, $\{0101\}$ and $\{1010\}$.

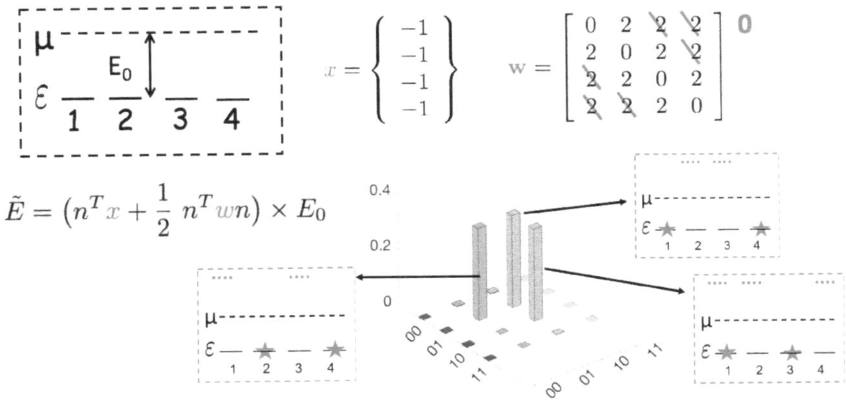

Fig. 3.19 Four levels with nearest neighbor interactions.

Now, what would happen if I take off one of the bias terms, namely the one for Level 2, so that $x = \{-1\ 0\ -1\ -1\}^T$? One of the three peaks in Fig. 3.19 would be eliminated, namely the one having an electron in Level 2. That would leave only two peaks: $\{1001\}$ and $\{1010\}$.

3.2.1.5 *Fig. 3.20*

Fig. 3.20a summarizes the four combinations of different x's and w's that we just discussed. My main point is that the parameters $\{x\}$ and $[w]$ in n space control the response in the 2^n state space. In these simple examples you can understand the results in terms of a physical picture that views *p-bits* as energy levels that can be full (1) or empty (0).

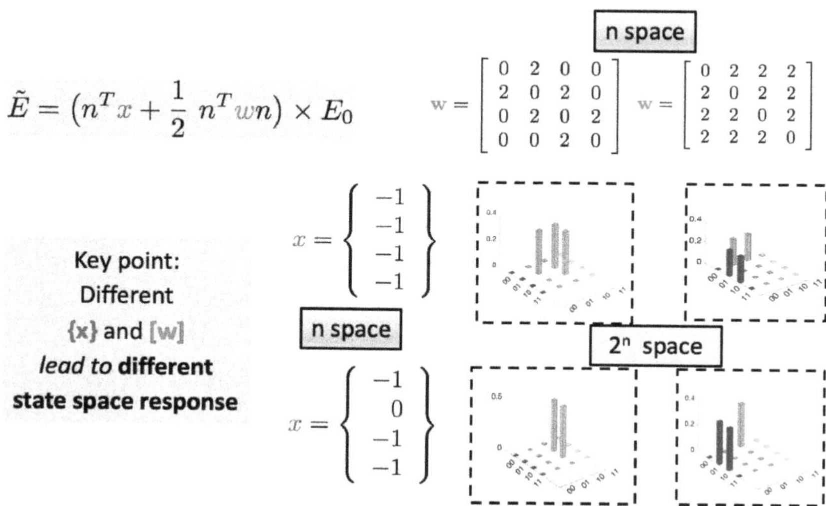

Fig. 3.20 Four Levels: Summary.

3.2.2 *Figs. 3.21-3.23: From natural to orchestrated interactions*

3.2.2.1 *Fig. 3.21*

Next what we want to do is kind of change our approach a little bit. You see, so far, as you know, we are coming from this Boltzmann law and equilibrium statistical mechanics where the objective is to understand nature, and nature gave us certain x's and w's with the interaction coming from *Coulomb interaction* between electrons. So it's the natural interaction that dictates it and the objective was, well, how do I analyze the state space response that I get?

Going forward (see Fig. 3.21), we will want a particular state space response, in order to solve a certain problem. There is some application that requires us to solve some problem, and that's what the state space response is supposed to do for us. Now the question is what kind of x and w will get us there? So x and w are no longer things that nature gives us. It's something that we have to figure out so that it gives us a particular state space response. So a complete reversal of which comes first and which comes next.

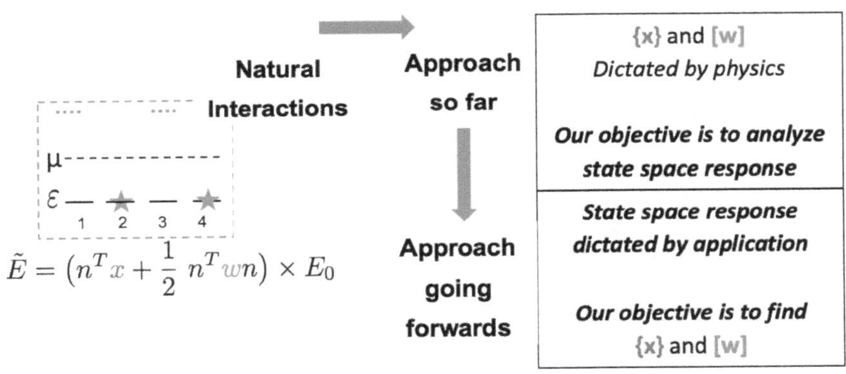

Fig. 3.21 Change in approach.

3.2.2.2 *Fig. 3.22: Software implementation*

But then you might ask, well, supposing I figured out x and w? How will I implement them? The answer is straightforward if you're doing all this in software: we can implement any x and w. For example (see Fig. 3.22), as I mentioned in this method, you could write a MATLAB® code or a Python code to simulate all this. So there will be a line which says okay, this is how you find these x's. You use the x and w to figure out the next state of the neurons. Then you can put in any x and any w you want, we are not restricted by the physics of anything.

3.2.2.3 *Fig. 3.23*

So in this approach, in software, we view n as just a binary variable. And just to keep this in mind (see Fig. 3.23), what I'll do going forwards is

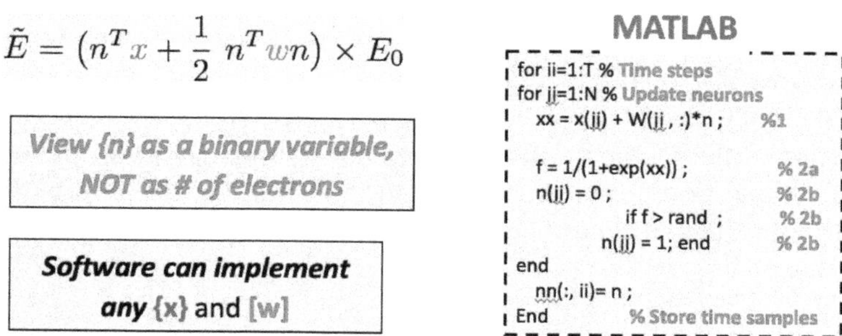

Fig. 3.22 Software implementation.

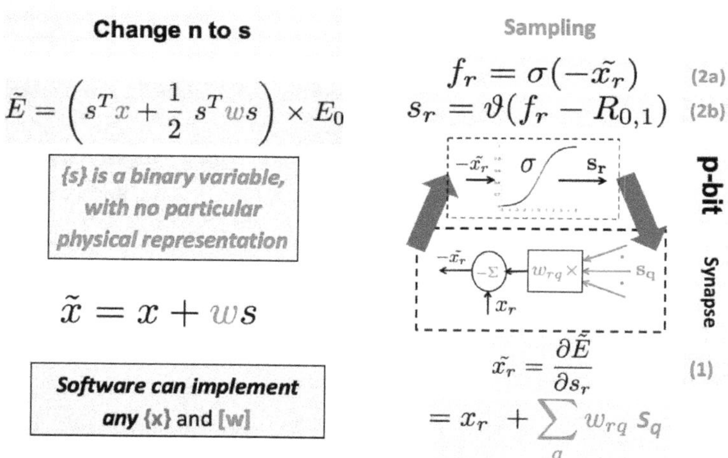

Fig. 3.23 Changing n to s.

instead of n I'll write s, just a change in symbol. I mean, n had two values, 0 and 1, same is true for s, it also has two values, 0 and 1. That's it. It's just that n has this connotation of being the number of electrons in a particular level which I'd used to motivate it when we got started, but going forwards we'll just write as it as a binary variable it s. So the equations are exactly what I had before, but now instead of n I've written s, that's all, $\widetilde{E} = (s^{\mathrm{T}}x + (1/2)s^{\mathrm{T}}ws)E_0$.

3.2.3 *Figs. 3.24-3.25: p-bits and q-bits*

3.2.3.1 *Fig. 3.24*

One more thought before we move on. We started with the electron number n to motivate the concept of a *binary stochastic neuron* or a *p-bit* and then replaced it with a binary variable s not tied to any specific physical representation, noting that we will be implementing all in software anyway. The strength of a software implementation is its generality, it can implement any $\{x\}$, $[w]$ and even more complicated energy functions that may not have simple analytical expressions.

On the other hand there is a lot of interest in *hardware accelerators* that take advantage of appropriate hardware to implement computational steps in a fast and energy-efficient manner. And so it is of practical interest to ask what physical hardware could represent a *p-bit*. In any case physical representations can be useful in providing intuitive physical pictures.

We have already seen one physical representation for *p-bits*, namely an energy level that can be filled (1) or empty (0). Another possibility is the basis of MRAM[4] technology, namely nanomagnets which represent 1 or 0 depending on whether the north pole is upwards or downwards. For memory devices stable magnets are desirable, magnets that stay 1 or 0 for a very long time. But a well-known problem with nanomagnets is that as you make them smaller they become unstable and tend to fluctuate between 0 and 1. This is bad for memory applications, but perfect for implementing a *p-bit*.

However, in order to be useful as a hardware accelerators, the challenge is to design a complete device that can take an analog input $\widetilde{x}$ as input and produce a binary output which is 1 with probability $\sigma(-\widetilde{x})$.

3.2.3.2 *Fig. 3.25*

Now this nanomagnet representation for a *p-bit* is kind of nice because it naturally morphs over into a *q-bits* which we will talk about in the quantum part of this course (see Fig. 3.25). You see nanomagnets are actually composed of lots of elemental magnets which have all lined up because of certain internal interactions. Now, what are these elementary magnets?

The basic elemental magnet is the electron itself. We all know that an electron carries a charge, but it also carries a magnetic moment and often pictorially you think of it as spinning, as if you have a spinning charge which

[4] Magnetoresistive Random Access Memory.

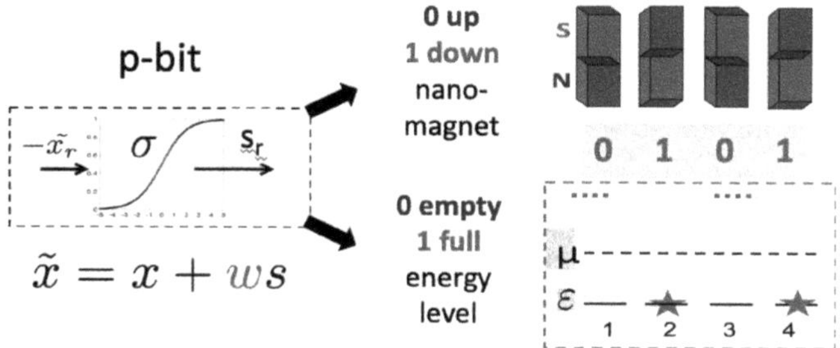

Fig. 3.24 Physical representation of *p-bits*.

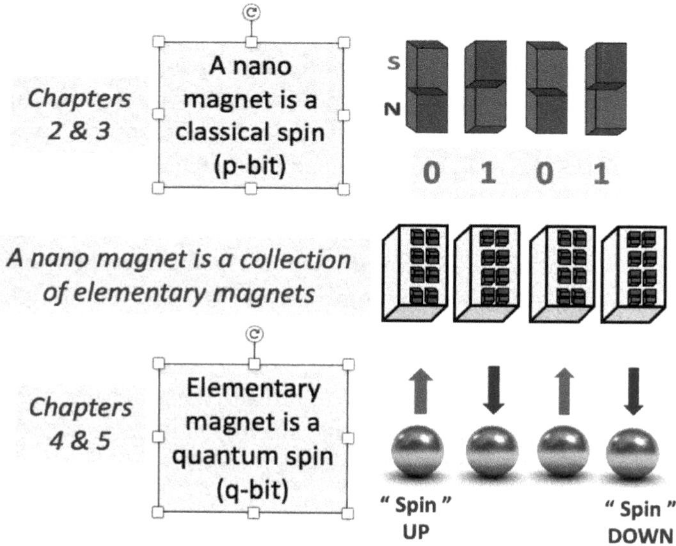

Fig. 3.25 *p-bits* and q-bits.

gives rise to a circulating current that is giving you a magnetic field. However, these electrons, this elemental magnet is actually a quantum magnet and that requires a conceptual change from where we are, that's what we'll try to do in the last two chapters.

But for the moment, we will stick to classical spins that you could visualize as classical magnets and try to understand the behavior of *p-bit* networks. We believe this provides a perfect backdrop for understanding q-bit networks. Indeed that is why we use the word *p-bit* to contrast with *q-bits* that are the building blocks of quantum hardware.

3.2.4 *Quiz*

If the energy of a system of four levels is given by $\widetilde{E} = \left(n^T x + 0.5\, n^T w n\right) \times E_0$ where $x = \begin{Bmatrix} -1 \\ -1 \\ -1 \\ -1 \end{Bmatrix}$ and $w = \begin{bmatrix} 0 & 2 & 0 & 0 \\ 2 & 0 & 2 & 0 \\ 0 & 2 & 0 & 2 \\ 0 & 0 & 2 & 0 \end{bmatrix}$.

3.2.4.1 *Question 1*

What is the synaptic output driving level 4?[5]

3.2.4.2 *Question 2*

What are the states with the highest probability?[6]

---

[5] $\widetilde{x}_4 = -1 + 2n_3$.

[6] {0101}, {1010}, {1001}.

3.3 Optimization

This is Lecture 3.3: Watch youtube video

In the last lecture we showed that the $n \times 1$ bias vector $\{x\}$ and the $n \times n$ weight matrix $[w]$ control the response in 2^n state space. In this lecture we will see how we can design $\{x\}$ and $[w]$ so that the state space response actually does something useful for us. The problem we'll consider (see Fig. 3.26), graph partitioning, is an example of a very broad class of problems that you could call constrained optimization.

3.3.1 *Figs. 3.26-3.27: Graph partitioning*

3.3.1.1 *Fig. 3.26*

Let's say there are six nodes, having some connections between them described by the connection matrix $[C]$. The connections are bi-directional in the sense that C_{12} is the same as C_{21}.

Now the min-cut problem would be, how do I take these six nodes and break it up into two groups so that they are as weakly connected as possible between the two groups? So the groups may have internal connections, but there should be very little connection between one group and the other. The reverse problem, that's your max-cut problem, that is how do you divide them so that the connections are as strong as possible.

3.3.1.2 *Fig. 3.27*

With the given connection matrix $[C]$, the answer to the mincut problem is kind of obvious because of the way I chose the connections here is that 1, 2, and 5 have connections and 3, 4, and 6 have connections. So you obviously break it up as $\{1\ 2\ 5\}$ and $\{3\ 4\ 6\}$.

The answer to the max-cut problem, is not immediately obvious. It seems that well, you should take 1, 2, and maybe another from the other group. Or maybe one and two more from the other groups. So there are many possibilities and it's not immediately obvious which one will be the maximum. Now the method we'll describe to you kind of allows you to solve both these problems.

$$\mathbf{C} = \begin{bmatrix} 0 & 12 & 0 & 0 & 3 & 0 \\ 12 & 0 & 0 & 0 & 5 & 0 \\ 0 & 0 & 0 & 6 & 0 & 8 \\ 0 & 0 & 6 & 0 & 0 & 14 \\ 3 & 5 & 0 & 0 & 0 & 0 \\ 0 & 0 & 8 & 14 & 0 & 0 \end{bmatrix}$$

Connection Matrix

In this lecture we will discuss how [x}, [w] can be designed so that peaks in state space response indicate the *optimal solution to a problem*

$$\tilde{E} = \left(s^T x + \frac{1}{2}\, s^T w s \right) \times E_0$$

Graph Partitioning

Min-cut

Divide into two equal groups so that they are as weakly connected as possible

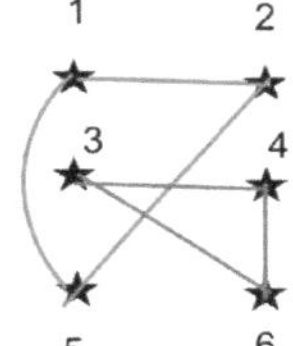

Max-cut

Divide into two equal groups so that they are as strongly connected as possible

Fig. 3.26 Graph partitioning.

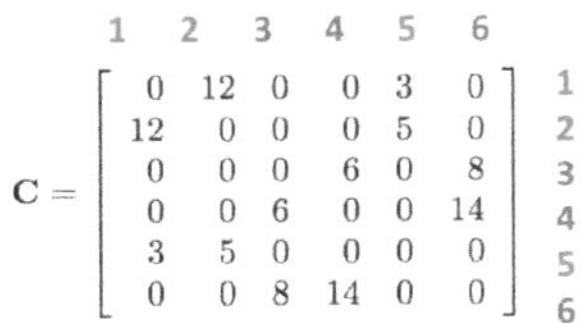

$$\mathbf{C} = \begin{bmatrix} 0 & 12 & 0 & 0 & 3 & 0 \\ 12 & 0 & 0 & 0 & 5 & 0 \\ 0 & 0 & 0 & 6 & 0 & 8 \\ 0 & 0 & 6 & 0 & 0 & 14 \\ 3 & 5 & 0 & 0 & 0 & 0 \\ 0 & 0 & 8 & 14 & 0 & 0 \end{bmatrix}$$

In this lecture we will discuss how [x}, [w] can be designed so that peaks in state space response indicate the *optimal solution to a problem*

$$\tilde{E} = \left(s^T x + \frac{1}{2}\, s^T w s \right) \times E_0$$

{1 1 0 0 1 0}

{0 0 1 1 0 1}

0.6
0.4
0.2
0

000 001 010 011 100 101 110 111

1 2 3 4 5 6

Answer obvious

Min-cut

Divide into two equal groups so that they are as weakly connected as possible

Fig. 3.27 Mincut problem.

3.3.2 *Figs. 3.28-3.31: Defining energy*

3.3.2.1 *Fig. 3.28*

Now, the question is (see Fig. 3.28), how do I choose my energy function $\widetilde{E}$ in terms of x and w, so that the peaks tell me the answer. For example if the peak occurs at {110010} then the 1's will define one group, namely {1 2 5} and the 0's will define the other group, namely {3 4 6}.

First we write $\widetilde{E} = \sum_{r,q} C_{rq}F_{rq}$ What is F_{rq}? Well, the idea is that if r and q both belong to the same group, which means if both are 0 or if both are 1, then it doesn't contribute to the energy, that's 0. On the other hand, if one is 0 and the other is 1, that means you're kind of cutting across from one group to the other and in that case, the F_{rq} is 1. This way, when I add them all up, we will basically add up the value of C for all those connections between the two separate groups[7]. So when I minimize the energy, it will tend to minimize it such that the C's are as small as possible between the two groups.

So how do I write this ? Well, one way to write it is $(S_r - S_q)^2$, well, why? Because while you see the two are equal, I get 0. If the two are not equal, one is 1, and the other is 0, I get 1, that's it. So, this is it really.

3.3.2.2 *Fig. 3.29*

So once you have written this energy, the point is the energy is a minimum when you have this min cut condition is satisfied. So whatever I'll do for the next few slides is work on this a little bit algebraically, so that I can come out with the x and w matrices, that I need in order to do my time sampling.

So first thing is I squared this, so $(a - b)^2$ is, $a^2 + b^2 - 2ab$, so we get $s_r^2 + s_q^2 - 2s_r s_{rq}$. I then note that you see s being this binary variable 0 or 1, s^2 is really equal to s, so I dropped the squares. So then basically $\widetilde{E} = \sum_{r,q} C_{rq}(s_r + s_q - 2s_r s_q)$.

3.3.2.3 *Figs. 3.30-3.31: Finding x,w*

Now, what I want to do is take this $\widetilde{E} = \sum_{r,q} C_{rq}(s_r + s_q - 2s_r s_q)$ and put it in our canonical form $\widetilde{E} = \sum_r s_r x_r + (1/2)\sum_{r,q} s_r w_{r,q} s_q$. There is

[7]Note that the $[C]$ matrix elements are all positive numbers.

$$\mathbf{C} = \begin{bmatrix} 0 & 12 & 0 & 0 & 3 & 0 \\ 12 & 0 & 0 & 0 & 5 & 0 \\ 0 & 0 & 0 & 6 & 0 & 8 \\ 0 & 0 & 6 & 0 & 0 & 14 \\ 3 & 5 & 0 & 0 & 0 & 0 \\ 0 & 0 & 8 & 14 & 0 & 0 \end{bmatrix}$$

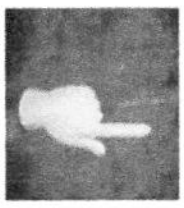

$$\tilde{E} = \sum_{r,q} C_{rq} F_{rq}$$

where

$$F_{qr} = 1, \ \textit{if } s_q \neq s_r$$
$$= 0, \ \textit{if } s_q = s_r$$
$$= \left(s_r - s_q\right)^2$$

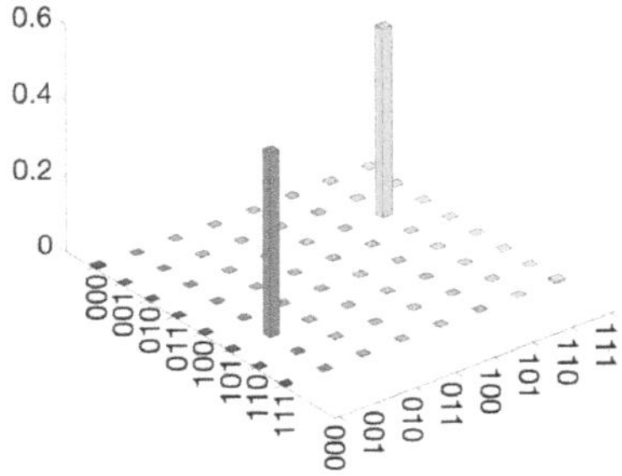

Fig. 3.28 Defining the energy function for the mincut problem.

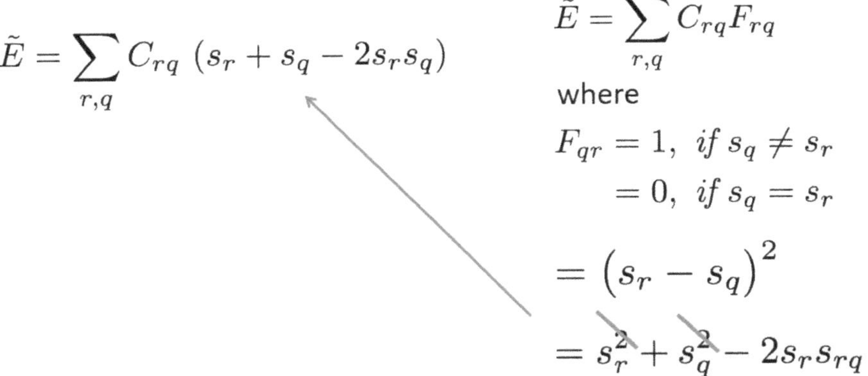
$\tilde{E} = \sum_{r,q} C_{rq} \left(s_r + s_q - 2 s_r s_q\right)$
$\tilde{E} = \sum_{r,q} C_{rq} F_{rq}$
where
$F_{qr} = 1, \ \textit{if } s_q \neq s_r$
$= 0, \ \textit{if } s_q = s_r$
$= \left(s_r - s_q\right)^2$
$= s_r^2 + s_q^2 - 2 s_r s_{rq}$

Fig. 3.29 Simplifying the energy function.

a term that's linear, which is what you often called the bias term and then there's a term that's quadratic, which you call the weight term. So, what I want to do is fool around with this $\tilde{E} = \sum_{r,q} C_{rq}(s_r + s_q - 2 s_r s_q)$

$$\tilde{E} = \sum_{r,q} C_{rq}\,(s_r + s_q - 2s_r s_q)$$

$$= \sum_r s_r \left[\sum_q C_{rq}\right] + \sum_q s_q \left[\sum_r C_{rq}\right] - 2\sum_{r,q} C_{rq} s_r s_q$$

$$\tilde{E} = \sum_r s_r \left[\sum_q C_{rq}\right] + \sum_r s_r \left[\sum_q C_{qr}\right] - 2\sum_{r,q} C_{rq} s_r s_q$$

Compare $\quad \tilde{E} = \sum_r s_r x_r + \frac{1}{2}\sum_{r,q} s_r w_{rq} s_q$

Fig. 3.30 Identifying $\{x\}$, $[w]$ from the energy function.

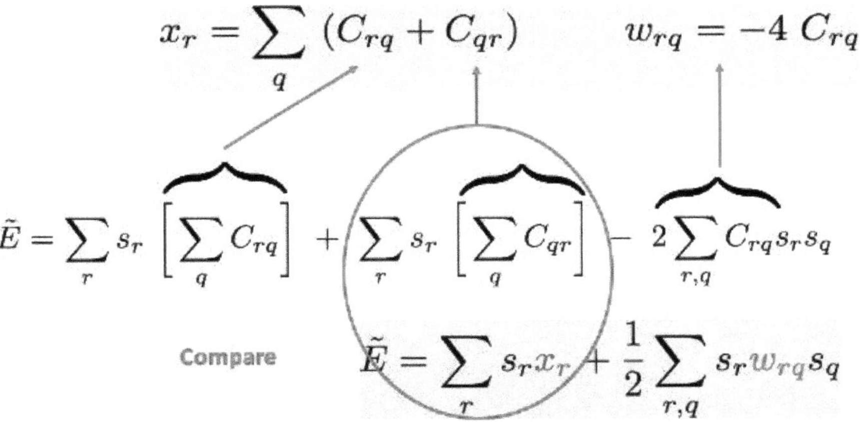
$x_r = \sum_q (C_{rq} + C_{qr})$
$w_{rq} = -4\, C_{rq}$
$\tilde{E} = \sum_r s_r \left[\sum_q C_{rq}\right] + \sum_r s_r \left[\sum_q C_{qr}\right] - 2\sum_{r,q} C_{rq} s_r s_q$
Compare
$\tilde{E} = \sum_r s_r x_r + \frac{1}{2}\sum_{r,q} s_r w_{rq} s_q$

Fig. 3.31 Identifying $\{x\}$, $[w]$ from the energy function (contd.).

a little bit, manipulate it, so that I can write it in the form $\widetilde{E} = \sum_r s_r x_r + (1/2)\sum_{r,q} s_r w_{r,q} s_q$. The algebra is spelt out in Figs. 3.30 and 3.31. The end result is $x_r = \sum_q (C_{rq} + C_{qr})$, and $w_{rq} = -4C_{rq}$.

3.3.3 *Figs. 3.32-3.38: Imposing constraints*

3.3.3.1 *Fig. 3.32: State space response*

Now that we have x, w we can just simulate this system the system of six *p-bits* generating a sequence of samples and it will do automatically is select out the lowest energy states, and those lowest energy states would be the solutions to my min cut problem.

Now if we do that (see Fig. 3.32), actually, so this is relatively straightforward. You could do it numerically or actually if you want to write out all the energies, you can, in this case, you see you don't really need to do the sampling method, you could just do it the Boltzmann way. Which means write out the energy of all the 64 states and calculate their probabilities and see which ones are highest.

Anyways, so if you do all that, you will see that you actually get the peaks that we talked about. These were the correct solutions, remember, but you also get two additional solutions here. One, that's all 0 and the other that's all 1, why? Because you see both of them satisfied the condition we imposed. We say that, if a for any bond, any connection that goes between a 1 and a 0 should be as small as possible, well, here they're all 1s, so there are no bonds between 1 and 0, and the same here. So these kind of satisfy the condition we imposed, and so it's not surprising that these solutions also came up. But of course, it's not the solution we want, because the original problem said, take your six neurons, six nodes and break it up into two equal groups, put three in one and three in the other. So here we have taken all six and put them in one group, then the same here, so that's not what you're looking for.

3.3.3.2 *Figs. 3.33-3.35: Constraints through energy*

So, that is where we have to put in a constraint into the problem. We have to figure out a way so that whenever the number in the two groups, when the number of 1s is not equal to the number of 0s, there is a large energy cost to it. Remember, in all optimization problems there is a cost function, you see what the problem does is try to minimize that cost. Of course, in these Boltzmann circuits, in these things what is minimized is the energy, so energy is the cost function. So the way you do it is (see Fig. 3.33), I could add a term like this $(\sum_r s_r - (n/2))^2$ to the energy. Now I already have something and I'm going to add another term, and what is this term? It says that well, when I add up the values of all the spins, the answer

$$x_r = \sum_q (C_{rq} + C_{qr}) \qquad w_{rq} = -4\ C_{rq}$$

Have to enforce equal number of 0's and 1's

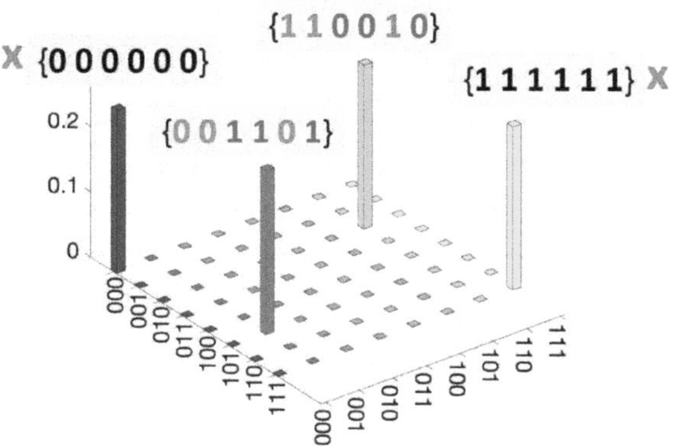

Fig. 3.32 State space response.

$$x_r = \sum_q (C_{rq} + C_{qr}) \qquad w_{rq} = -4\ C_{rq}$$

Add another term to Energy

$$\begin{aligned}
\tilde{E} &= \left(\sum_r s_r - \frac{n}{2}\right)^2 \\
&= \frac{n^2}{4} - n\sum_r s_r + \sum_r s_r \sum_q s_q \\
&= \frac{n^2}{4} - n\sum_r s_r + \sum_{r,q} s_r s_q \\
&= \frac{n^2}{4} - n\sum_r s_r + \overbrace{\sum_r s_r^2 + \sum_{r \neq q} s_r s_q}
\end{aligned}$$

Fig. 3.33 Imposing constraint through energy.

$$x_r = \sum_q (C_{rq} + C_{qr}) \qquad w_{rq} = -4\, C_{rq}$$

$$\tilde{E} = \left(\sum_r s_r - \frac{n}{2}\right)^2$$

Add another term to Energy

$$= \frac{n^2}{4} - (n-1)\sum_r s_r + \sum_{r \neq q} s_r s_q$$

$$= \frac{n^2}{4} - n\sum_r s_r + \sum_r s_r^2 + \sum_{r \neq q} s_r s_q$$

Fig. 3.34 Imposing constraint through energy.

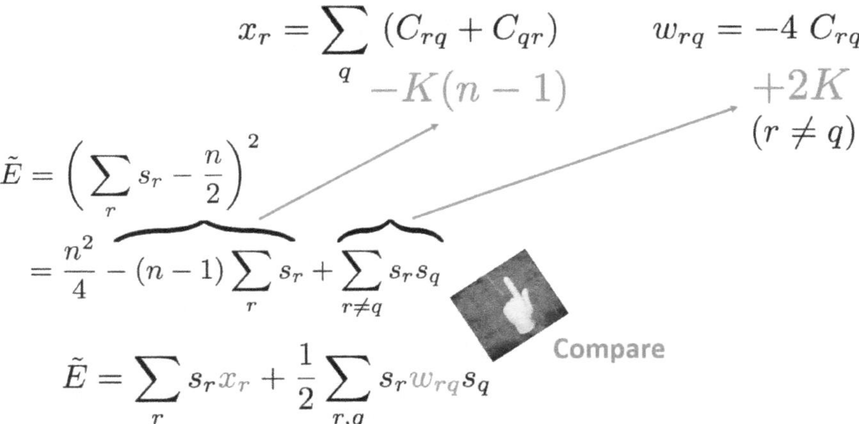
$x_r = \sum_q (C_{rq} + C_{qr})$
$w_{rq} = -4\, C_{rq}$
$-K(n-1)$
$+2K$
$(r \neq q)$
$\tilde{E} = \left(\sum_r s_r - \frac{n}{2}\right)^2$
$= \frac{n^2}{4} - (n-1)\sum_r s_r + \sum_{r \neq q} s_r s_q$
$\tilde{E} = \sum_r s_r x_r + \frac{1}{2}\sum_{r,q} s_r w_{rq} s_q$
Compare

Fig. 3.35 Imposing constraint through energy.

should be equal to half the total number, so if I add 6, the answer should be 3. Then you can see that these, {110010} and {001101}, when I add them all up, I get 3. But these ones, {000000} and {111111}, when I add them up, I get 0 here, {000000}, and I get six there, {111111}, so those are not acceptable,

If I add a term like this $(\sum_r s_r - (n/2))^2$ to the energy, it will discriminate against those solutions. So again, we want to get it back into this canonical form. The algebra is shown in Figs. 3.33, 3.34 and 3.35.

3.3.3.3 *Fig. 3.36*

In the final result in Fig. 3.35 we have weighted the new constraint terms with a constant K which we can choose depending on how strongly I want to enforce the constraint. Sure enough now if I do the simulation (see Fig. 3.36), by including the K, what we'll find is, well, when K was 0, we had these two extra peaks. But once we put in the K, we only get the two peaks that we want. And to what extent these unwanted peaks are suppressed will depend on what K I use. So here I use the K of 4, if I had used something less like one or half, then they wouldn't be completely suppressed. We would still see some of it.

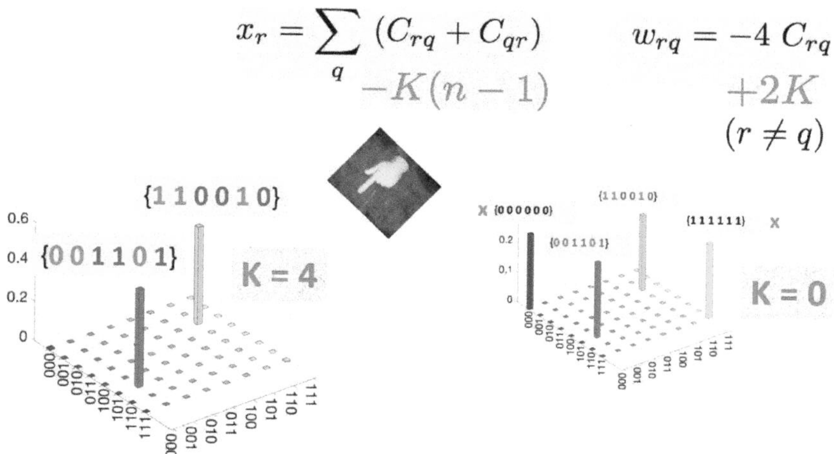

Fig. 3.36 State space response with ($K = 4$) and without ($K = 0$) constraint, MATLAB code included at end of book.

3.3.3.4 *Figs. 3.37-3.38: From min-cut to max-cut*

So this is what you might call the min-cut problem as we discussed (see Fig. 3.37). So this is where you're trying to minimize the energy of cutting the two groups apart, okay? Now, if you want to solve the max cut problem, then what you do is you just add a minus sign because an energy that minimizes something if you put a minus sign then it will maximize it. So let's say you have 1, so you prefer 1 relative to 10 but then if you put a minus sign, then of course you'll prefer -10 relative to -1.

3.3.3.5 *Fig. 3.37*

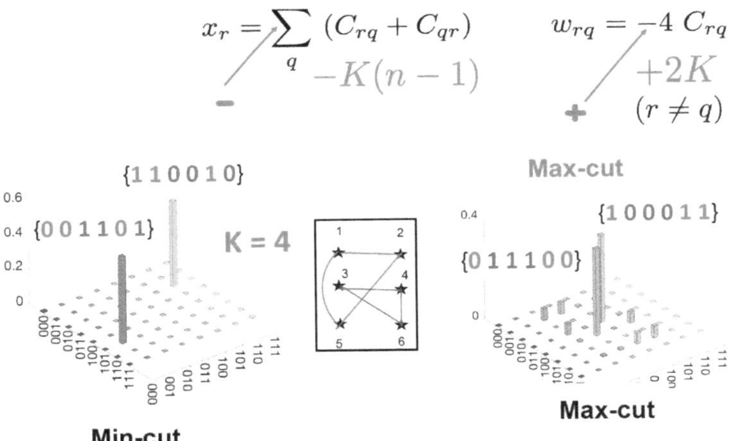

Fig. 3.37 From min-cut to max-cut, same MATLAB code as Fig. 3.36.

3.3.3.6 *Fig. 3.38*

So you just have to add the -1. You don't change anything about the term that has the K in it because that is intended to ensure that you have the same number of 0's and 1's in both groups. So now if you do that, sure enough, you solve the max-cut problem and we'll get a different set of peaks and now in this case the groups are 2 3 4 is one group and 1 5 6 is the other group, {011100} and {100011}. So in other words (see Fig. 3.38), you like to keep the 2 3 and 4 together and 1 5 and 6 together, and you can kind of see why, if you look at the connection matrix. You see, there's a 12 that

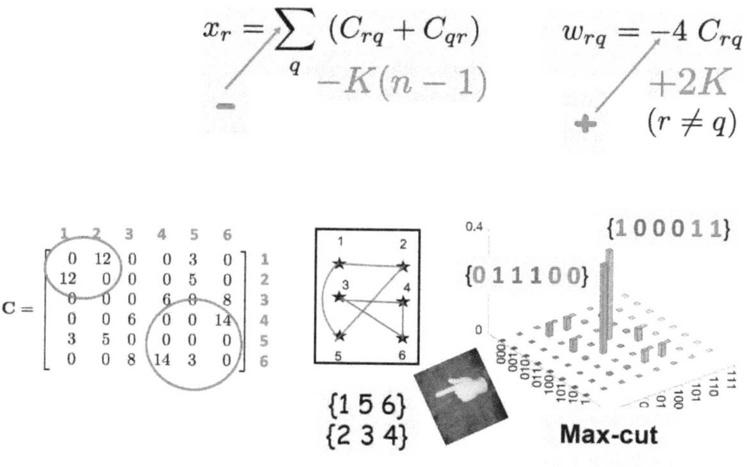

$$x_r = \sum_q (C_{rq} + C_{qr}) - K(n-1) \qquad w_{rq} = -4\, C_{rq} + 2K \quad (r \neq q)$$

$$\mathbf{C} = \begin{bmatrix} 0 & 12 & 0 & 0 & 3 & 0 \\ 12 & 0 & 0 & 0 & 5 & 0 \\ 0 & 0 & 0 & 6 & 0 & 8 \\ 0 & 0 & 6 & 0 & 0 & 14 \\ 3 & 5 & 0 & 0 & 0 & 0 \\ 0 & 0 & 8 & 14 & 3 & 0 \end{bmatrix}$$

Fig. 3.38 Max-cut.

connects 1 and 2. So you want to put 1 and 2 in separate groups so that when you cut it, you're cutting a 12. And remember, this is the max-cut problem, where you want to cut as much as possible.

Anyway, the bottom line is that (see Fig. 3.39), you could solve the min-cut problem or the max-cut problem just by changing the sign of the second term. The first term is just for imposing the constraint that you should have equal number of 0's and 1's.

3.3.4 *Figs. 3.39-3.40: Summary*

3.3.4.1 *Fig. 3.39*

Our final result for x and w can be written compactly in matrix form as shown in Fig. 3.39. For example, $w_{rq} = 2K \mp 4C_{rq}$ becomes $w = \mp 4[C]$ in matrix notation, and so on.

3.3.4.2 *Fig. 3.40*

So, summing up then what we're trying to show in this lecture is how you can use probabilistic circuits to solve constrained optimization problems (see Fig. 3.40). And I showed it using this example of min-cut and max-cut. You have a graph with a connection matrix, and the point is how to divide it into two groups so that when you cut, you cut as few connections

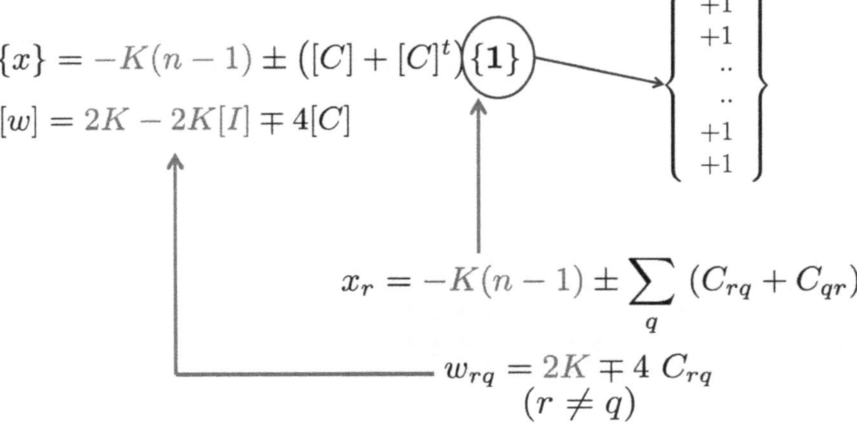

$\{x\} = -K(n-1) \pm ([C] + [C]^t)\{\mathbf{1}\}$
$[w] = 2K - 2K[I] \mp 4[C]$
+1
+1
..
..
+1
+1
$x_r = -K(n-1) \pm \sum_q (C_{rq} + C_{qr})$
$w_{rq} = 2K \mp 4\, C_{rq}$
$(r \neq q)$

Fig. 3.39 x, w in matrix notation.

as possible. Or as many connections as possible. And you could easily go from one problem to the other by changing the sign of the second term. And this constraint term weighted by the constant K tries to make the two groups be of equal size.

K: *constant*, [C]: *connection matrix for graph*

$$\{x\} = -K(n-1) \pm ([C] + [C]^t)\{\mathbf{1}\}$$

$$[w] = 2K - 2K[I] \mp 4[C]$$

Upper sign: *min-cut*
Lower sign: *max-cut*

$$\tilde{E} = \sum_r s_r x_r + \frac{1}{2} \sum_{r,q} s_r w_{rq} s_q$$

Cost function for constrained optimization

1 2 3 4 5 6

Fig. 3.40 Summary.

Finally I should note that in this lecture I chose the mincut / maxcut problem because it translates straightforwardly to a cost or energy function of the form $\widetilde{E}$ of the form $s^T x + 0.5 s^T w s$. Things may not be as straightforward if we consider otherwise optimization problems, like say the traveling salesman problem (TSP): A salesman has to visit say N cities in sequence.

Which route corresponds to the shortest overall path? This problem can be translated to $E = s^T x + 0.5 s^T w s$, but it requires N^2 *p-bits*. More efficient approaches are well-known and routinely used. It remains to be seen if the TSP problem can be translated to *p-bit* networks in a way that would provide an improvement over established methods.

3.3.5 *Quiz*

3.3.5.1 *Question 1*

The energy of a system of n classical spins (s is a binary variable with two values 0 and 1) is given by $\widetilde{E} = \left(s^T x + 0.5\ s^T w s\right) \times E_0$.
Suppose $x_r = -(n-1)$, $w_{rq} = 2$ if $r \neq q$ and $w_{rq} = 0$ if $r = q$.

Which states have the highest probability?[8]

3.3.5.2 *Question 2*

The energy of a system of 4 classical spins (s is a binary variable with two values 0 and 1) is given by $\widetilde{E} = \left(s^T x + 0.5\ s^T w s\right) \times E_0$.

Consider a graph with a connection matrix given by $C = \begin{bmatrix} 0 & 1 & 0 & 0 \\ 1 & 0 & 0 & 0 \\ 0 & 0 & 0 & 1 \\ 0 & 0 & 1 & 0 \end{bmatrix}$

Suppose we choose $w_{rq} = -4C_{rq}$ and $x_r = 2$.

What are the highest probability peaks?[9]

[8] Those having equal number of zeros and ones.
[9] {0000}, {1111}, {0011} and {1100}.

3.4 Inference

This is Lecture 3.4: Watch youtube video

In the last lecture I used the mincut / maxcut problem because it translates straightforwardly to a cost or energy function of the form $\widetilde{E}$ of the form $s^T x + 0.5 s^T ws$. However, as I mentioned at the end, not all problems are quite as straightforward. In general we may want an arbitrary set of peaks as shown in Fig. 3.41. Powerful learning algorithms have been developed to find the appropriate x and w and in the next lecture I will try to give you an example. In this lecture let me just try to give you an idea of how such arbitrary peaks in state space could help us address practical applications, assuming we have some way to learn the necessary x and w.

3.4.1 *Figs. 3.41-3.45: Logic gates*

3.4.1.1 *Fig. 3.41*

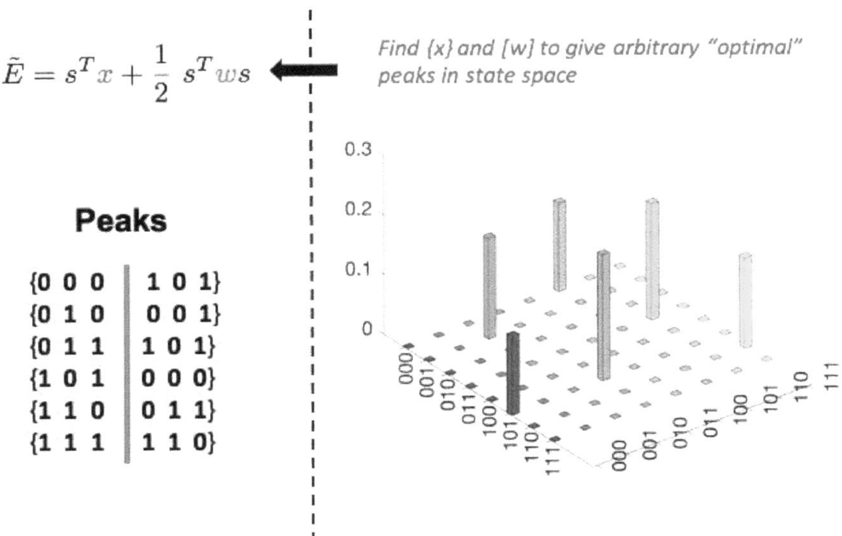

Fig. 3.41 Generating arbitrary peaks in state space.

Okay, so, these peaks are just randomly chosen actually with nothing in particular in mind (see Fig. 3.41). Each peak is labeled with a 6-digit binary number like say {000101}. Now this is something you could view as a truth table, that is if you are familiar with logic gates in electrical engineering or digital circuits. They usually have a truth table for inputs and outputs.

3.4.1.2 *Fig. 3.42*

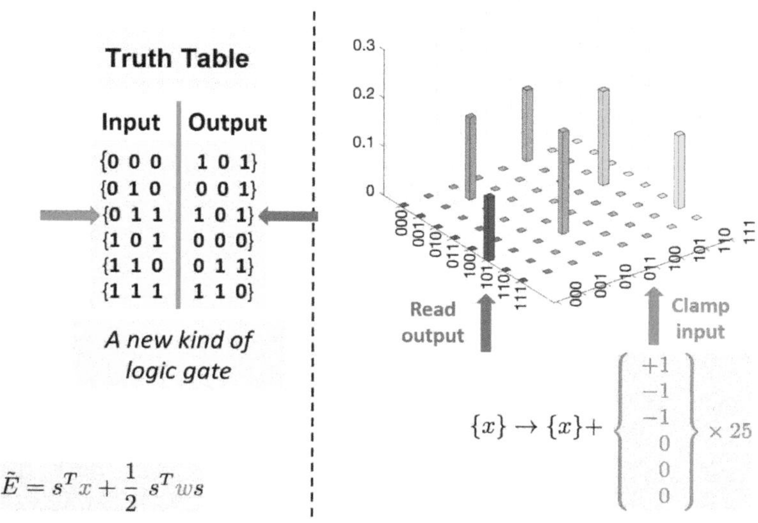

Fig. 3.42 Clamping inputs for the problem in Fig. 3.41.

Once x and w have been designed to give us these peaks, we could operate the *p-bit* network like a digital circuit in the sense that you could go in and apply an input and look at the output. So whenever I put an input say {011}, I'll get this output {101}.

Now how do you apply input? Well, you have to clamp these three bits to {011}. So how do you clamp it? Well, because left to itself of course they would be fluctuating all over the place, but you say well, no these three bits needs to be {011}. So how do you do that? Well, in your bias vector, x you add a big positive number to clamp it to 0 and a big negative number to clamp it to 1.

Once you clamp your input, you could then go and look at the output because you see originally, all of these six peaks were equally likely, they all had low energies they had high probability. But now that you have clamped it in the sense you have made it energetically favorable for this to be {011}, the output will just lock into one of them. And then you can read it and call that your output.

3.4.1.3 *Figs. 3.43 and 3.44*

So that looks just like a digital circuit. But it's really a very different kind of like digital circuit in the sense that it is much more versatile. It can work backwards and forwards in different ways.

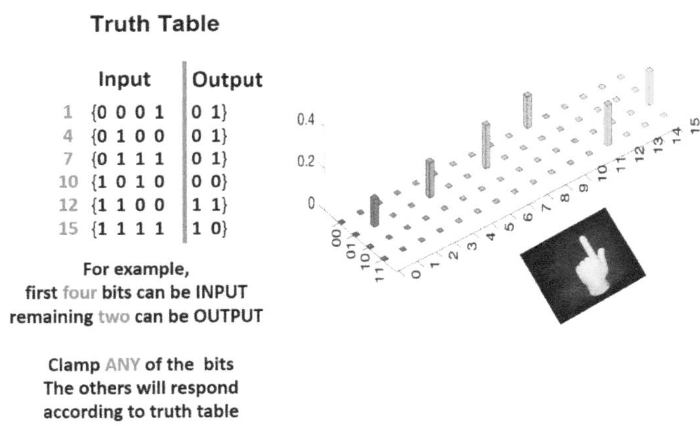

Truth Table
Input Output
1 {0 0 0 1 0 1}
4 {0 1 0 0 0 1}
7 {0 1 1 1 0 1}
10 {1 0 1 0 0 0}
12 {1 1 0 0 1 1}
15 {1 1 1 1 1 0}
For example,
first four bits can be INPUT
remaining two can be OUTPUT
Clamp ANY of the bits
The others will respond
according to truth table
0.4
0.2
0
00
01
10
11
0 1 2 3 4 5 6 7 8 9 10 11 12 13 14 15

Fig. 3.43 Redefining input and output as 4+2 instead of 3+3.

For example (see Fig. 3.43), what we could do is to define the first four *p-bits* as inputs and the last two as outputs. So these first four, that's what is on this axis. So four of them give you 16 numbers, which I have written in decimal, rather than write it out as {0001}, I've written it as 1. So the first line {0001} that's 1. Next is {0100} that's like a 4 and so on.

So now you can think of the first four bits as your input and the last two as your output. So, you could now go in and clamp the input (see Fig. 3.44), you could say, okay, the input is, let's say, seven which is like {0111}. Now, what will happen then is the output will go to the corresponding value on this side. So instead of having all these six peaks like I'd shown before, now you'll just have one peak and that peak you can now read output which is {01}.

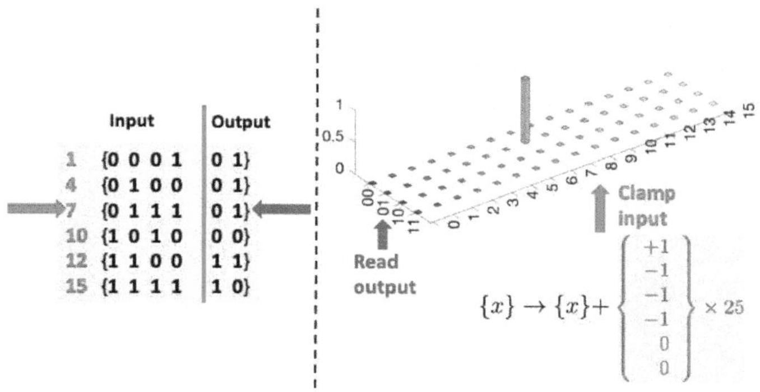

Fig. 3.44 Clamping example for the problem in Fig. 3.43.

3.4.1.4 *Fig. 3.45*

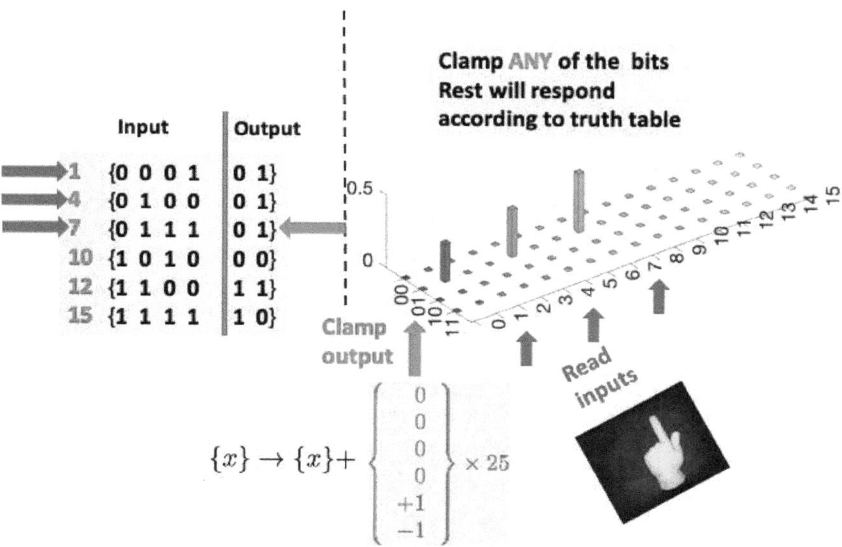

Fig. 3.45 Multiple inputs consistent with a clamped output.

An even more interesting thing is that our *p-circuit* can actually work backwards an tell us all possible inputs that could have produced a particular output. So what you could do is you could go in and say I'll clamp the output to {01} (see Fig. 3.45). How do I do that? Well, take the last two bits and put in a big bias there, positive if you want a 0, negative if you want a 1 as we have discussed. The original truth table, of course had all six possibilities. But after clamping, only the three that correspond to {01} on the output will show up. That gives us all three possible inputs 1, 4 and 7.

So I just clamped the output and the circuit gives me all three possible inputs that correspond to that particular output. This is something that a normal digital circuit would never do. They all work in one direction. You put inputs, you get outputs. But here you can run it the other way as well.

3.4.2 *Fig. 3.46: Image classification*

Another use for *p-circuits* could be for image classification (see Fig. 3.46). To see this note that what I called the input, {0001}, could represent a series of black and white pixels {black, black, black and white}. So in that sense, a binary input could define an image like say a handwritten digit as shown, and what the output could do is to classify them as 0, 1, 2 etc.

Now of course, real images have many bits because usually something like this will have 28 pixels on one side and 28 pixels on the other side. So it's a total of 784 pixels. And you'd have to indicate whether each pixel is a 1 or 0 whether it's bright or dark. The *p-circuit* could take a binary

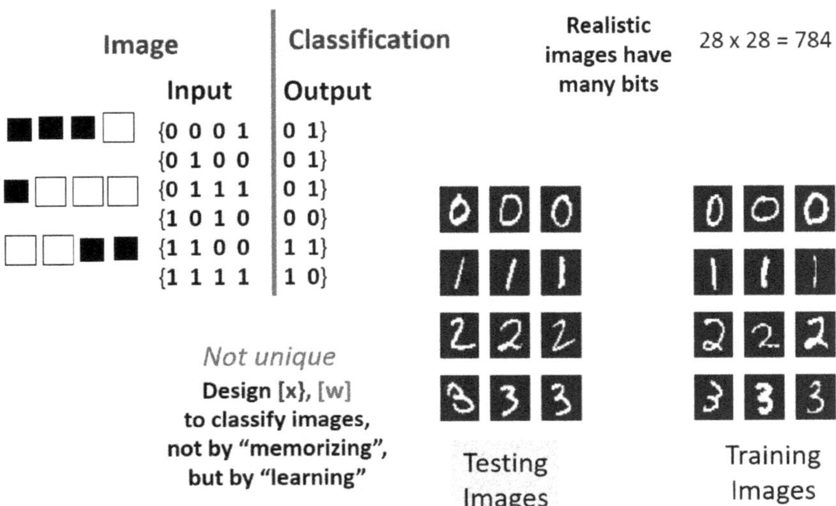

Fig. 3.46 Image classification.

string with 784 digits and classify it as one of ten decimal numbers. image classification.

The question is how do I design my x and w so that it will be able to recognize all the different ways people write say a 4 and classify them all as four. And you want to make sure that you have actually learned the images and haven't just memorized them meaning that you come out with x and w that recognizes the training images very well, but if you showed it something a little different, it may not recognize it at all. So usually, you'd have a set of training images, but then you test it with other images, which are not exactly the same but a little different and if the x and w have been properly chosen, then not only will it have memorized the training images, but also have learned how to recognize the testing images. So these are among the many issues you would discuss in a proper machine learning course, but we won't be going into it. Right now the main point I wanted to make is that for a lot of applications like invertible logic, image classification, etc. what you want is to design your x and w in such a way that you get these multiple peaks in your 2^n space that solve the problem at hand.

3.4.3 *Figs. 3.47-3.48:* ***A simple learning rule***

3.4.3.1 *Fig. 3.47*

In general then the problem amounts to you're given a set of peaks that you want (see Fig. 3.47), which we can call the truth table, $[t]$. The number of columns in $[t]$ is the number of *p-bits*, n and the number of rows is the number of peaks, $[n_t]$. Given $[t]$, how do I write x and w.

Next lecture we'll discuss learning in more detail. Let me just finish up this lecture by giving you a simple rule that you could use to write x and w in terms of t. This rule is of limited utility in the sense it works when you have just a few lines in your truth table, but you get in trouble if you have too many lines. But it's a nice simple place to start from.

It is easier to state the learning rule in the bipolar representation which is different from the binary representation we have been using. So let me first explain this new representation. In any case this representation is used a lot in the physics literature and so it is good to be able to relate to it.

So what is this bipolar representation? The idea is that, so far we've been doing binary where s is the variable and it's 0 or 1. Now, you could instead have used a bipolar representation where instead of 0 and 1, it's actually -1 and $+1$ and as I said that's widely used in this physics literature. Now, a truth table in binary $[t]$ can be transformed to bipolar using the

$[t]$ n
{0 0 0 1 0 1}
{0 1 0 0 0 1}
{0 1 1 1 0 1}
{1 0 1 0 0 0}
{1 1 0 0 1 1}
{1 1 1 1 1 0}
n_t

$$t_m = 2t - 1$$

$[t_m]$ n
{-1 -1 -1 +1 -1 +1}
{-1 +1 -1 -1 -1 +1}
{-1 +1 +1 +1 -1 +1}
{+1 -1 +1 -1 -1 -1}
{+1 +1 -1 -1 +1 1}
{+1 +1 +1 +1 +1 -1}
n_t

Widely used in physics literature

Given [t] **Write** [x}, [w]

Binary $s = 0$, $= 1$

Bipolar $m = -1$, $= +1$

Easiest to state in bipolar representation

$$\tilde{E} = s^T x + \frac{1}{2}\, s^T ws \qquad\qquad \tilde{E} = m^T h + \frac{1}{2}\, m^T Jm$$

Fig. 3.47 Bipolar representation.

rule $t_m = 2t - 1$, which means if an element in t is 1, you get $+1$ in $[t_m]$, if t is 0, you get -1.

Now, you could write the energy function, we had written it earlier in terms of s and x, $\widetilde{E} = s^{\mathrm{T}}x + (1/2)s^{\mathrm{T}}ws$, and this w, instead of s, you could have m which is the bipolar representation, and then the corresponding bias and weight matrices I'll write as h and J, $\widetilde{E} = m^{\mathrm{T}}h + (1/2)m^{\mathrm{T}}Jm$, following what is often done in the physics literature. So these are two expressions, $\widetilde{E} = s^{\mathrm{T}}x + (1/2)s^{\mathrm{T}}ws$ and $\widetilde{E} = m^{\mathrm{T}}h + (1/2)m^{\mathrm{T}}Jm$, which should give you the same energy because you're still trying to solve the same problem. As we will see, a little algebra gets us to a simple expression for interconverting back and forth between x, w and h, J.

3.4.3.2 *Fig. 3.48*

The simple learning rule I mentioned earlier is easy to state in the bipolar representation: $J = (-1/n^t)t_m^{\mathrm{T}}t_m$, whereas $h = (-1/n^t)t_m^{\mathrm{T}}\widetilde{\mathbf{1}}$, where $\widetilde{\mathbf{1}}$ is a $n_t \times 1$ column vector containing all 1's. I've put a tilde on $\widetilde{\mathbf{1}}$ because it has n_t number of rows, whereas the 1 vector appearing in $-J\mathbf{1} - J^{\mathrm{T}}\mathbf{1}$ without a tilde has n rows.

In the next lecture I will try to motivate where this rule comes from[10] and how some of the recent work on the so-called modern Hopfield networks seeks to go beyond it. For the moment let us just focus on how we use this simple rule.

Suppose we are given a truth table t in binary representation. To use the learning rule stated above in bipolar representation, We first convert to $t_m = 2t - 1$, then write h and J using the rule stated above, and then convert to x, w using these relations, $x = 2h - J\mathbf{1} - J^{\mathrm{T}}\mathbf{1}$ and $w = 4J$. How these relations are obtained is explained in the next few slides.

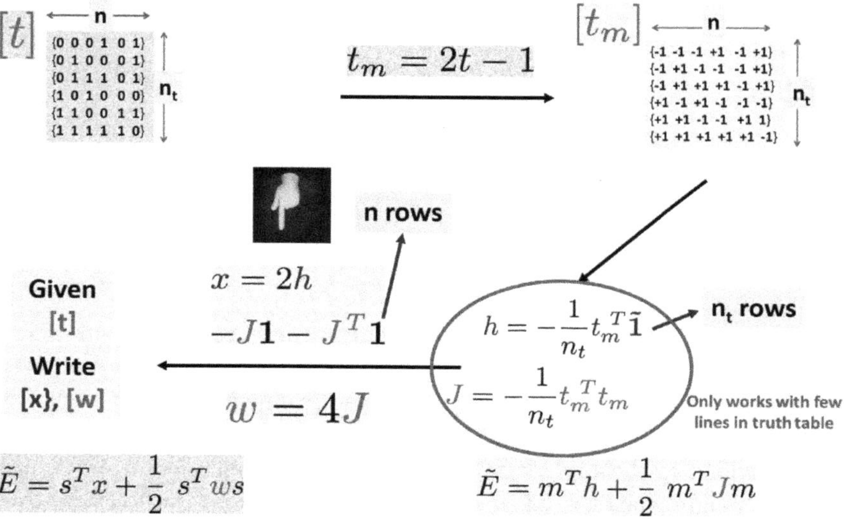

Fig. 3.48 Simple learning rule in bipolar representation.

3.4.4 *Figs. 3.49-3.50: Binary-bipolar interconversion*

Figs. 3.49 and 3.50 show the algebra needed to obtain the expressions connecting h, J to x,w. The basic approach is to start from the bipolar energy expression $\widetilde{E} = m^{\mathrm{T}}h + (1/2)m^{\mathrm{T}}Jm$, insert $m = 2s - 1$, and then compare with the binary energy expression $\widetilde{E} = s^{\mathrm{T}}x + (1/2)s^{\mathrm{T}}ws$.

Similarly you can also figure out the reverse transformation (see Fig. 3.50) that you could use if you are given w, x and you want to find J, h.

---

[10]Interested readers can look up *Hebbian learning*.

$$\tilde{E} = -1^T h + 2\,(1^T J 1) + 2s^T h - s^T J 1 - 1^T J s + 2s^T J s$$

$$\tilde{E} = 2s^T h - s^T J 1 - s^T J^T 1 + 2s^T J s$$

compare

$$\tilde{E} = s^T x + \frac{1}{2}\, s^T w s$$

$$\tilde{E} = (2s-1)^T h + \frac{1}{2}\,(2s-1)^T J (2s-1)$$

$$m = 2s - 1$$

$$\tilde{E} = m^T h + \frac{1}{2}\, m^T J m$$

Fig. 3.49 Converting h, J to x, w.

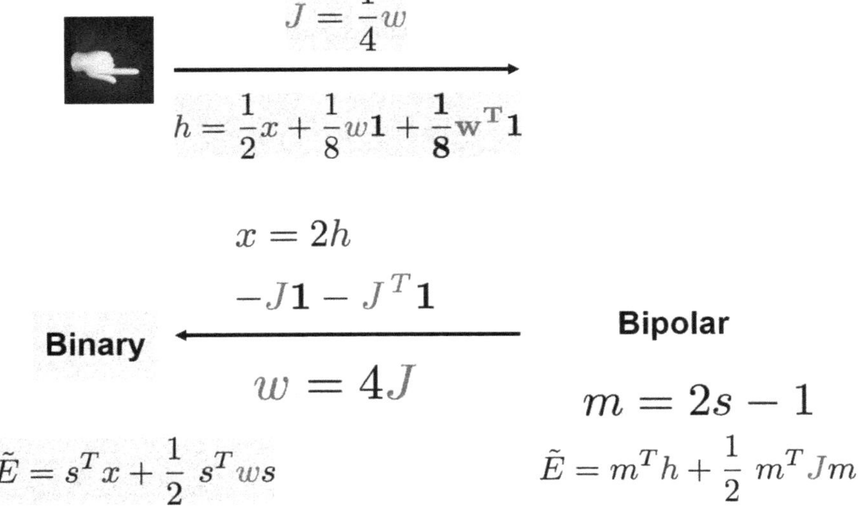

$J = \frac{1}{4} w$
$h = \frac{1}{2} x + \frac{1}{8} w\mathbf{1} + \frac{1}{8} \mathbf{w}^T \mathbf{1}$
$x = 2h - J\mathbf{1} - J^T \mathbf{1}$
Binary
Bipolar
$w = 4J$
$m = 2s - 1$
$\tilde{E} = s^T x + \frac{1}{2}\, s^T w s$
$\tilde{E} = m^T h + \frac{1}{2}\, m^T J m$

Fig. 3.50 Interconverting x, w and h, J.

3.4.5 *Quiz*

3.4.5.1 *Question 1*

The energy of a system of 2 classical spins in bipolar notation (m is a bipolar variable with two values -1 and $+1$) is given by

$$\widetilde{E} = m^T h + 0.5\ m^T J m$$

while in terms of a binary variable s with values 0 and 1,

$$\widetilde{E} = s^T x + 0.5\ s^T w s$$

Suppose $h = \begin{Bmatrix} 0 \\ 0 \end{Bmatrix}$ and $J = \begin{bmatrix} 0 & 1 \\ 1 & 0 \end{bmatrix}$

What is the choice of $\{x\}$ and $[w]$ that will give the same values of $\widetilde{E}$ for all configurations?[11]

3.4.5.2 *Question 2*

The energy of a system of 3 classical spins in bipolar notation (m is a bipolar variable with two values -1 and $+1$) is given by

$$\widetilde{E} = m^T h + 0.5\ m^T J m$$

What choice of h and $[J]$ will give us only two peaks at $\{+1 - 1 + 1\}$ and at $\{-1 + 1 - 1\}$?[12]

[11] $x = \begin{Bmatrix} -2 \\ -2 \end{Bmatrix}$ and $J = \begin{bmatrix} 0 & 4 \\ 4 & 0 \end{bmatrix}$.

[12] $h = \begin{Bmatrix} 0 \\ 0 \\ 0 \end{Bmatrix}$ and $J = \begin{bmatrix} 0 & +2 & -2 \\ +2 & 0 & +2 \\ -2 & +2 & 0 \end{bmatrix}$.

3.5 Learning

This is Lecture 3.5: Watch youtube video

3.5.1 *Fig. 3.51: Learning rule #1*

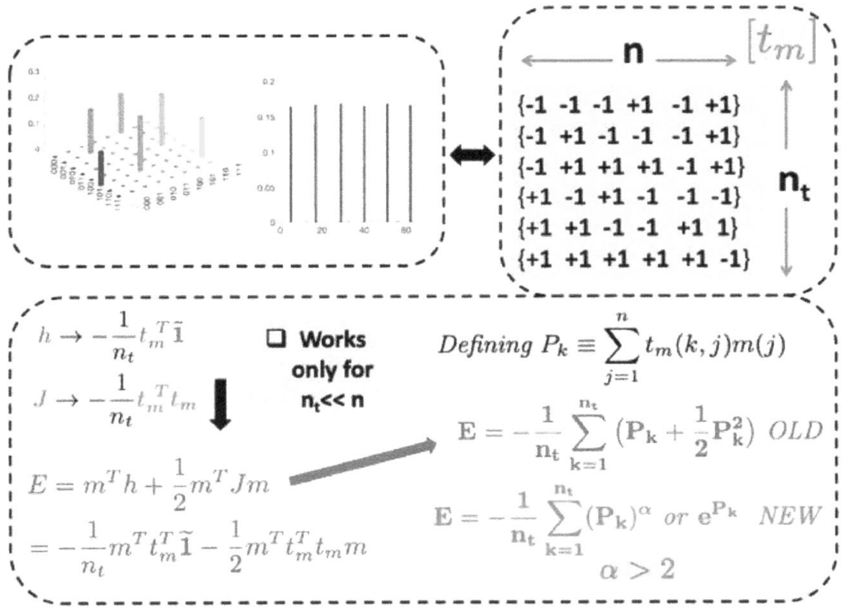

Fig. 3.51 Learning rule #1.

In the last lecture, we showed why it would be interesting to be able to create arbitrary peaks in your state space response, because you could use that for interesting applications like invertible logic and image classification. The state space response can be described by a truth table like the one in Fig. 3.51, each row describing a particular peak. The number of columns, that's the number of *p-bits* that you have, six in this case, and we have six peaks, as well. But those two don't have to be equal.

Using h, J from the learning rule stated in Fig. 3.48 we can write the energy function in terms of the quantity P_k which tells us how much overlap the current state m with each row k of the truth table. Any Boltzmann machine minimizes E which corresponds to maximizing $P_k + (1/2)P_k^2$. This seems reasonable since our purpose is to maximize the overlap with the truth table described by P_k. This rule often works well when you have many more bits than there are peaks.

A recent development is the *modern Hopfield network* that replaces $P_k + (1/2)P_k^2$ with higher powers of P_k, or even an exponential function e^{P_k}. These higher powers tend to favor solutions that maximize one of the P_k in comparison to those that give medium values for multiple P_k. This is desirable since we really want solutions that strongly match a particular line of the truth table, and not those that have a medium match with many lines. This seems like a promising approach but is still a work in progress. We will not discuss it further.

3.5.2 *Figs. 3.52-3.55: Average value and correlation matrix*

Let us talk about a different learning rule that has been widely used. The quantities h, J in the old rule play an important role in this new rule. First let's look at this quantity $h = -(1/n_T)t_m^{\mathrm{T}}\tilde{1}$ (see Fig. 3.52). A little reflection will tell you that it can be written as $\langle m_r \rangle = \sum_{k=1}^{n_t} (1/n_t)[t_m]_{k,r}$, which can be interpreted as the value of each *p-bit* averaged over all rows of the truth table.

n $[t_m]$

{+1 +1 +1 +1 +1 +1} × {-1 -1 -1 +1 -1 +1}
{-1 +1 -1 -1 -1 +1}
{-1 +1 +1 +1 -1 +1}
{+1 -1 +1 -1 -1 -1}
{+1 +1 -1 -1 +1 1}
{+1 +1 +1 +1 +1 -1}

n_t

$\{\,0\ \ +\frac{1}{3}\ \ 0\ \ 0\ \ -\frac{1}{3}\ \ +\frac{1}{3}\,\}$ {0 +2 0 0 -2 +2}/6

$\langle \{m\}^T \rangle$

$\frac{1}{n_t}\tilde{\mathbf{1}}^{\mathbf{T}}\mathbf{t_m}$

$h \rightarrow -\frac{1}{n_t} t_m^T \tilde{1}$

$J \rightarrow -\frac{1}{n_t} t_m^T t_m$

Fig. 3.52 Average value.

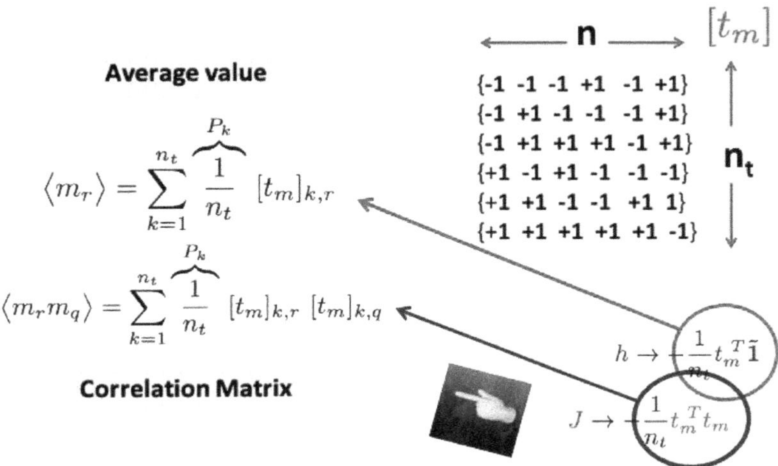

Fig. 3.53 Average value and correlation matrix.

3.5.2.1 *Fig. 3.53*

Now similarly, if you look at that second thing, the one that is the expression for the J matrix, $-(1/n_T)t_m^{\mathrm{T}}t_m$, that involves a product of t_m's, product of two of them. Again, mathematically, you could write it this way, $\langle m_r m_q \rangle = \sum_{k=1}^{n_t} (1/n_t)[t_m]_{k,r}[t_m]_{k,q}$. What it tells you is, the average value of the product of what you have for the r-th *p-bit* and what you have for the q-th *p-bit* so you could call that the correlation matrix, correlation between the r-th and q-th bits, m_r, m_q, averaged over all lines of the truth table.

3.5.2.2 *Fig. 3.54*

We defined the average value and correlation matrix in terms of the dream response, the one that has the six peaks exactly where you want them. Now, in general, if you just took any network, of course, it would have peaks all over the place. All the different configurations would have some probability and you could still define an average value which would look just like this $\langle m_r \rangle = \sum_{k=1}^{n_t} (1/n_t)[t_m]_{k,r}$ except that, now it's not that there's only six lines of your truth table which contribute, it's like every configuration contributes and so that you have to put in the probability of that configuration, the equilibrium probability, and then sum over all possible all 2^n configurations, $\langle m_r \rangle = \sum_{i=1}^{2^n} p_i[t_m]_{i,r}$. The same with the

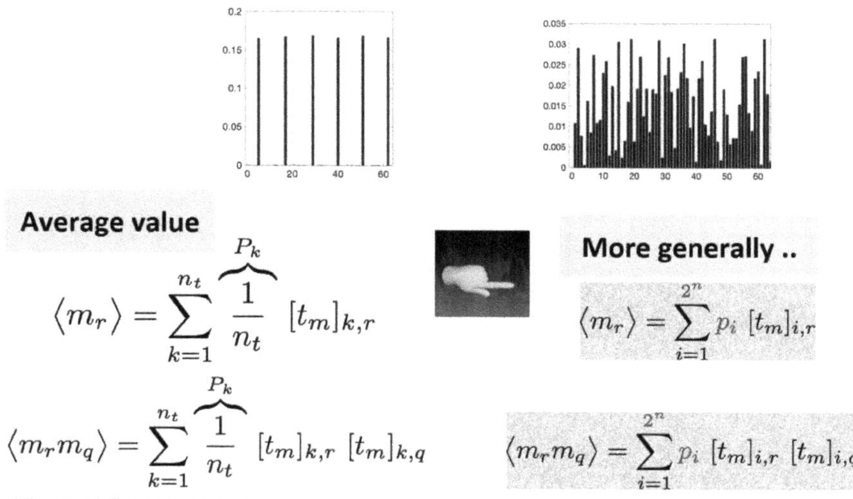

Fig. 3.54 Average value and correlation matrix.

correlation matrix, you'd have to sum over all 2^n configurations, $\langle m_r m_q \rangle = \sum_{i=1}^{2^n} p_i [t_m]_{i,r} [t_m]_{i,q}$ to get the correct correlation values.

3.5.2.3 *Fig. 3.55*

Now, so in general, in a particular problem (see Fig. 3.55), the situation is like this. There is a target that you have in mind, you want to get a certain $\langle m_r \rangle$, and a certain $\langle m_r m_q \rangle$, but you don't have it because you don't have the correct weight matrices, the h and J. Instead, what you have is giving you some junk and that junk has a corresponding average value and average correlations. So this is what you have, $\langle m_r \rangle = \sum_{i=1}^{2^n} p_i [t_m]_{i,r}$ and $\langle m_r m_q \rangle = \sum_{i=1}^{2^n} p_i [t_m]_{i,r} [t_m]_{i,q}$, and this, $\langle m_r \rangle = \sum_{k=1}^{n_t} (1/n_t) [t_m]_{k,r}$ and $\langle m_r m_q \rangle = \sum_{k=1}^{n_t} (1/n_t) [t_m]_{k,r} [t_m]_{k,q}$, is what you'd really like to do.

3.5.3 *Figs. 3.56-3.58: Learning rule #2*

How do you get from where you are to where you want to be? Well, that's where you have the learning rule. The learning rule tells you that if the target average is bigger than the actual, then you should decrease the h

Target

$$\langle m_r \rangle = \sum_{k=1}^{n_t} \overbrace{\frac{1}{n_t}}^{P_k} [t_m]_{k,r}$$

$$\langle m_r m_q \rangle = \sum_{k=1}^{n_t} \overbrace{\frac{1}{n_t}}^{P_k} [t_m]_{k,r} [t_m]_{k,q}$$

Actual

$$\langle m_r \rangle = \sum_{i=1}^{2^n} p_i [t_m]_{i,r}$$

$$\langle m_r m_q \rangle = \sum_{i=1}^{2^n} p_i [t_m]_{i,r} [t_m]_{i,q}$$

Fig. 3.55 Average and correlations: Target and actual.

value corresponding to that neuron. It's a decrease, so that means if this what's inside if it's positive, then the delta should be negative. That's why the minus sign, and this ε is what you call a learning parameter, $\Delta h_r = -\varepsilon(\langle m_r \rangle_{target} - \langle m_r \rangle_{actual})$. See, try to keep it small but not too small. I'll explain why this works in a minute.

The other rule is how do I adjust the weight matrix values? Well, there again, you look at the correlations and if the target is bigger than the actual, then you reduce the corresponding J. So that's the rule, you see. And what you do is to start from some arbitrary h and J, where you got this mess of a response and then if you keep iterating, you'll eventually get to your target where you really want to be.

$$\Delta h_r = -\varepsilon\big(\langle m_r \rangle_{target} - \langle m_r \rangle_{actual} \big)$$
$$\Delta J_{rq} = -\varepsilon\big(\langle m_r m_q \rangle_{target} - \langle m_r m_q \rangle_{actual} \big)$$

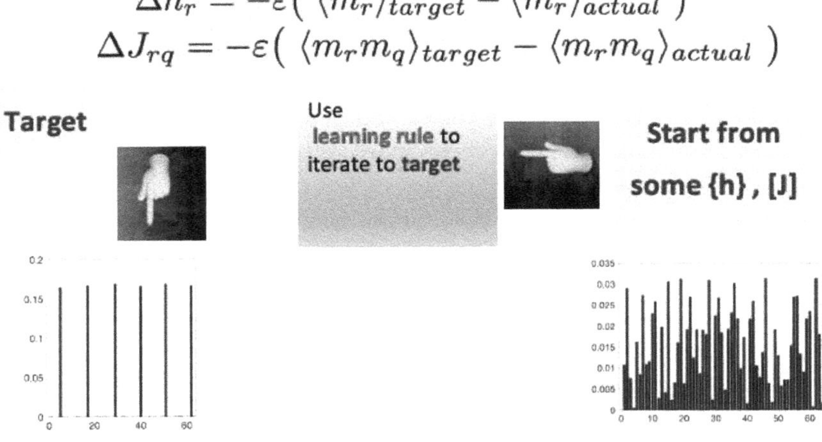
Target
Use
learning rule to
iterate to target
Start from
some {h}, [J]

Fig. 3.56 Learning rule #2.

$$\Delta h_r = -\varepsilon\big(\, \langle m_r \rangle_{target} - \langle m_r \rangle_{actual} \,\big)$$
$$\Delta J_{rq} = -\varepsilon\big(\, \langle m_r m_q \rangle_{target} - \langle m_r m_q \rangle_{actual} + \lambda J_{rq} \,\big)$$

Learning Rule

Regularization

Decreasing $\mathbf{h_r}$
lowers the energy//
raises the probability of
$\mathbf{m_r = +1}$ relative to $\mathbf{m_r = -1}$:

INCREASES $< m_r >$
taking **actual** towards **target**

Decreasing $\mathbf{J_{rq}}$
lowers the energy//
raises the probability of
$\mathbf{m_r\, m_q = +1}$ relative to $\mathbf{m_r\, m_q = -1}$:

INCREASES $< m_r m_q >$
taking **actual** towards **target**

$$\tilde{E} = \sum_r h_r m_r + \frac{1}{2} \sum_{r,q} J_{rq} m_r m_q$$

Fig. 3.57 Learning rule.

3.5.3.1 *Fig. 3.57*

Why does this work? Well think of it like this. Suppose the target value is bigger than the actual, then what you really want to do is do something, so that the actual increases. So how do you make the actual increase? Well, what I claim is decreasing h will do it. Why? Because you see h appears in this energy expression, $\widetilde{E} = \sum_r h_r m_r + (1/2) \sum_{r,q} J_{rq} m_r m_q$ and a positive h puts an energy penalty towards being $+1$. So, if I decrease h, $+1$ will become more probable relative to -1. So overall, the average value of m will want to increase because there's more $+1$'s then -1's. That's exactly what we want to see, because the actual is less than the target, And the same argument goes with the Js, you see again if you look at the energy expression, if you want to increase the correlation, what you should do is decrease this corresponding J.

I should mention here that we have written the energy as $\widetilde{E} = \sum_r h_r m_r + (1/2) \sum_{r,q} J_{rq} m_r m_q$. Often in the physics literature, they define energy with an extra minus sign here. If you do that, it would reverse the signs in the learning rule, but the basic logic is the same.

In the literature you'll see more rigorous derivations of the learning rules, but what I wanted to show you here is how you can intuitively understand why it works. There are other details like, sometimes people add a term that they called regularization. They don't want the weights J to increase too much. So they put an energy penalty, towards being too large $\Delta J_{rq} = -\varepsilon(\langle m_r m_q \rangle_{target} - \langle m_r m_q \rangle_{actual} + \lambda J_{rq})$.

3.5.3.2 *Fig. 3.58*

Now, how do you actually implement it? It means that at every step you have to evaluate the bias and correlation matrix for the target and the actual, and then use them to learn. Now for the target, it's relatively easy, Why? Because I just have to do these summations, $\langle m_r \rangle = \sum_{k=1}^{n_t} P_k[t_m]_{k,r}$ and $\langle m_r m_q \rangle = \sum_{k=1}^{n_t} P_k[t_m]_{k,r}[t_m]_{k,q}$, over my desired peaks, and there's only 6 of them or 10 of them, maybe 100 of them.

But it's much harder to evaluate the actual. It requires me to do a sum over 2^n terms, $\langle m_r \rangle = \sum_{i=1}^{2^n} p_i[t_m]_{i,r}$ and $\langle m_r m_q \rangle = \sum_{i=1}^{2^n} p_i[t_m]_{i,r}[t_m]_{i,q}$, and as I've mentioned many times, the 2^n can be a huge number. So, in this context, what you really want to do is not really evaluate this entire sum, but use the sampling method, the one that works in n space, but you have to take enough samples, so that you get a accurate idea of these average values. And that often can be time consuming. In the literature, often the target is called the data, actual is called the model, data is easy to evaluate, model needs to be approximated.

3.5.4 *Fig. 3.59: Learning a full adder*

So here's an example of learning a truth table (see Fig. 3.59), where the truth table I took is that corresponding to a full adder, which means it has three inputs, and it produces two outputs, a sum and a carry term. So this is a system with five *p-bits*. I'm writing it in binary notation. The details aren't important. Basically I've got five bits, so there are 32 possibilities, and I want to have eight peaks in my answer which I have labeled with their corresponding decimal values. So that's what I've shown: the red ones are the peaks I want.

At first, I start with $h = 0$, $J = 0$ so that all 32 values from 0 to 31 are equally probable. And then gradually as you learn, you adjust the h and the J and the reds pick up gradually, the blues go down as you can see in the video.

Watch Videoclip: .. 13:00 to 15:00
Learning a full adder: Courtesy of Jan Kaiser

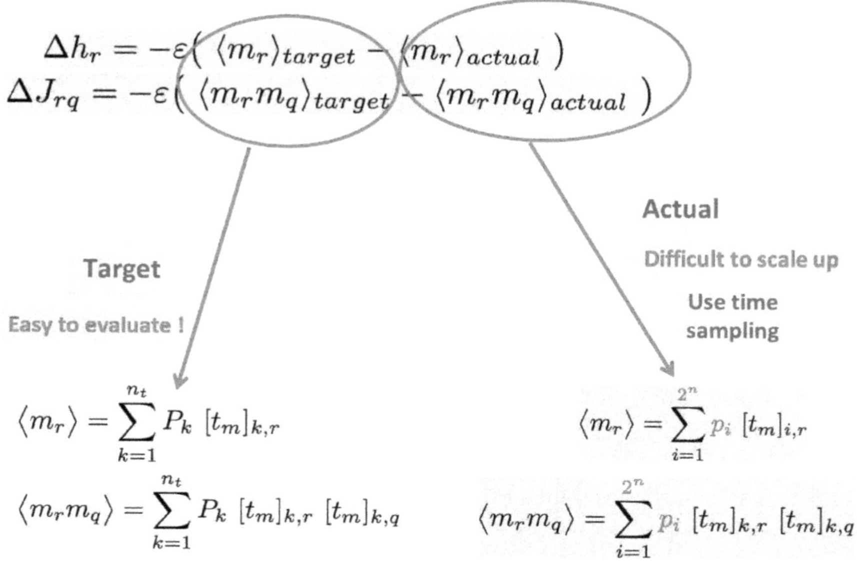

$\Delta h_r = -\varepsilon\left(\langle m_r \rangle_{target} - \langle m_r \rangle_{actual} \right)$
$\Delta J_{rq} = -\varepsilon\left(\langle m_r m_q \rangle_{target} - \langle m_r m_q \rangle_{actual} \right)$
Actual
Difficult to scale up
Use time sampling
Target
Easy to evaluate !
$\langle m_r \rangle = \sum_{k=1}^{n_t} P_k \, [t_m]_{k,r}$
$\langle m_r m_q \rangle = \sum_{k=1}^{n_t} P_k \, [t_m]_{k,r} \, [t_m]_{k,q}$
$\langle m_r \rangle = \sum_{i=1}^{2^n} p_i \, [t_m]_{i,r}$
$\langle m_r m_q \rangle = \sum_{i=1}^{2^n} p_i \, [t_m]_{k,r} \, [t_m]_{k,q}$

Fig. 3.58 Learning Rule

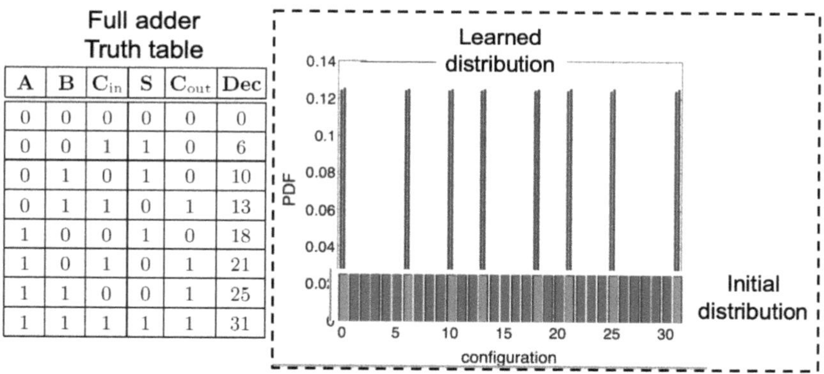

Full adder Truth table

A	B	C_{in}	S	C_{out}	Dec
0	0	0	0	0	0
0	0	1	1	0	6
0	1	0	1	0	10
0	1	1	0	1	13
1	0	0	1	0	18
1	0	1	0	1	21
1	1	0	0	1	25
1	1	1	1	1	31

Fig. 3.59 Full adder: Truth table and response with learned bias (x) and weight (w), MATLAB code included at end of book

3.5.5 *Figs. 3.60-3.62: Learning with hidden units*

3.5.5.1 *Fig. 3.60*

Before finishing up, let me mention a few ideas to indicate the richness of this subject. Suppose instead of 6 peaks with the 6 bits, we wanted 10 peaks. So then you'd find that if we just use the straight forward learning method, it may not work too well. Often what people do is, they introduce a set of hidden bits, ones I don't look at. So I want these 10 peaks, but these ten peaks correspond to the 6 visible units, and not these other four that are hidden that I don't even look at. But the h, J matrices involve all ten units. How do I train them?

The learning rule is still the same but remember to get the learning rule of course, I have to evaluate these average values. Now it's a little more harder to do this evaluation for the hidden bits because when I specify the peaks in terms of the visible units. As far as the hidden units are concerned, I don't really care what they are. So I'm not really specifying them at all and there is no target value. Even that has to be evaluated by sampling.

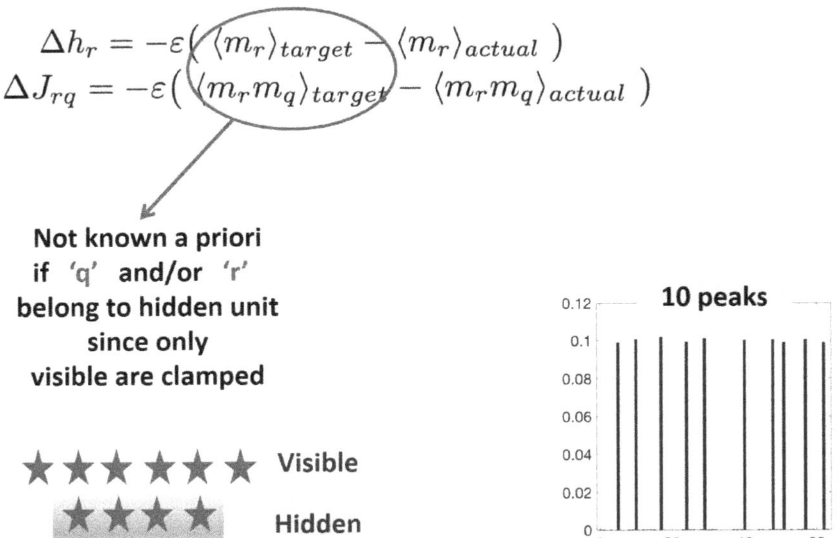

Fig. 3.60 Introducing hidden units, same code as Fig. 3.59.

3.5.5.2 *Fig. 3.61*

Here's an example that we ran with this where you had 10 peaks (see Fig. 3.61) with six visible units, and four hidden units. I have used a two-dimensional representation with the $2^6 = 64$ visible configurations on one axis, and $2^4 = 16$ hidden configurations on the other, giving a total of $2^10 - 1024$ configurations in all. Now if you look from the visible side I got 10 Peaks, but each one is located at a different point in the hidden axis. But of course, I hadn't specified anything for the hidden axes. It's not like I told it to have the peak there. It just figured that out on its own. So in a way as if the hidden layer, found some patterns in the data that you showed it, and classified them in some way, as if it labeled the data and this is generally what people refer to as unsupervised learning. Not like someone took the data and labeled it but it, discovered the patterns and labeled it for itself.

Another thing you often hear in this field is about generative models. The idea that well you show it a few images and train it, but then after that, if you let it run it will generate new images which will look like what you had and will have patterns in common with it, but these are not things that it had seen before. So I'm telling you all this just to give you a rough idea of the richness of this topic, but if you want to explore that you need to take a real course on machine learning.

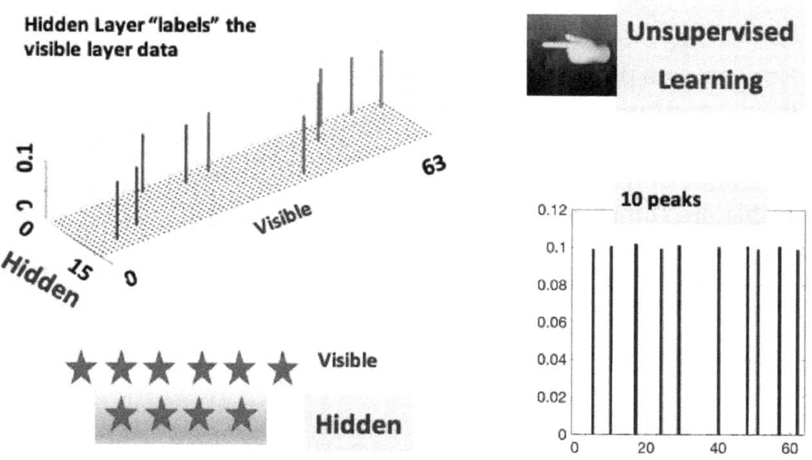

Fig. 3.61 Introducing hidden units, MATLAB code included at end of book.

3.5.5.3 *Fig. 3.62*

One final note. One of the problems you have with Boltzmann machines is that when you try to scale it up the training gets to be difficult. Boltzmann machines, are always undirected, that is $w_{ij} = w_{ji}$. It goes equally both ways.

Now the training process is actually easier if you have directed connections. So a lot of the action in the field of machine learning is based on directed networks, the ones where the interactions are one way if $w_{ij} \neq 0$ then $w_{ji} = 0$. And for directed networks, the energy function does not come naturally as it does for Boltzmann machines. But there is a lot of work on defining energy-based models for such directed networks. One of these will be evident after we discuss transition matrices and Feynman paths in the next chapter.

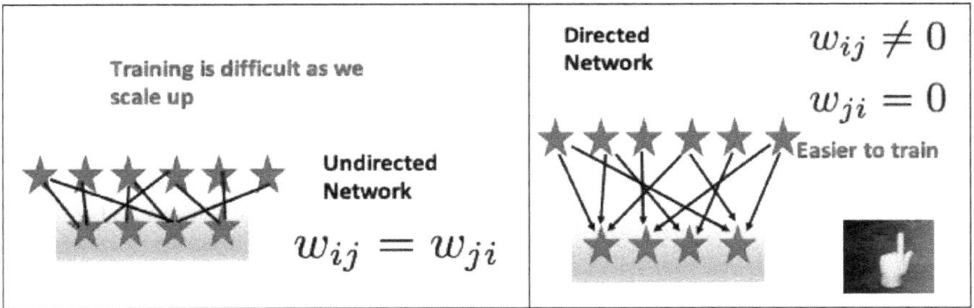

Fig. 3.62 Directed networks are easier to train.

3.5.6 *Quiz*

3.5.6.1 *Question 1*

A network of 3 spins shows two peaks, one at $\{+1-1+1\}$ and one at $\{-1+1-1\}$.

What is the matrix describing the average correlations $\langle m_r m_q \rangle$?[13]

3.5.6.2 *Question 2*

Suppose for a given network, $\langle m_r m_q \rangle = 0.5$ while our target value for $\langle m_r m_q \rangle$ is 0.4. How should we change the parameters in order to train the network?[14]

3.5.6.3 *Question 3*

Suppose for a given network, $\langle m_r m_q \rangle = 0.5$ while our target value for $\langle m_r m_q \rangle$ is 0.7. How should we change the parameters in order to train the network?[15]

---

13 $\begin{bmatrix} +1 & -1 & +1 \\ -1 & +1 & -1 \\ +1 & -1 & +1 \end{bmatrix}$.

14 Increase J_{rq}.

15 Decrease J_{rq}.

3.6 Fig. 3.63: 5-minute Summary

This is Chapter 3 summary: Watch youtube video, until 2:05

In Lecture 2.1, we started by introducing this sampling method. Is time sampling, which works in this n-space, but allows us to get accurate results for the response in the 2^n space. As you know, one of the basic points I've always stressed is, how 2^n can be huge when you scale up.

In Lecture 2.2, we discussed how you can control the response in this 2^n space, by adjusting the bias and weight x and w, which are in n space.

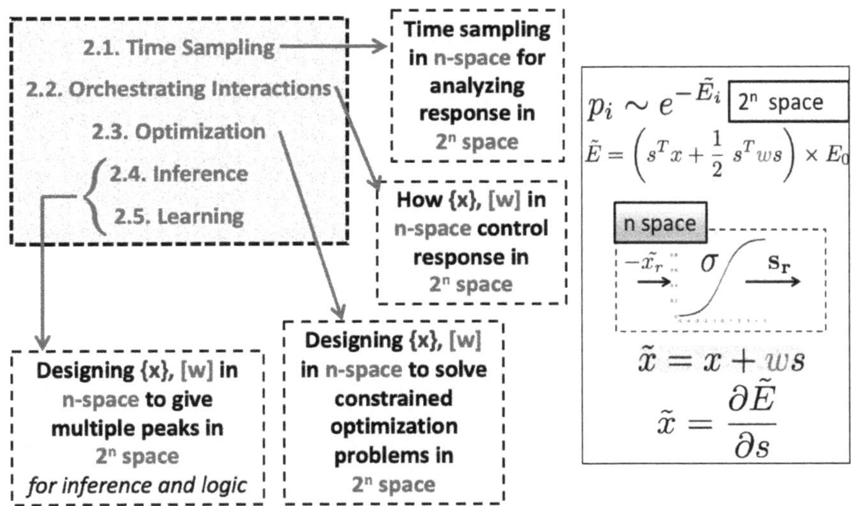

Fig. 3.63 Summary of Lectures 3.1-3.5.

In Lecture 3.3 we talked about how you could design x and w to solve useful problems that we generally refer to as constrained optimization. We took a very specific example, this max cut and min cut problem, where the translation to x, w is straightforward.

In Lectures 3.4 and 3.5 we talked about a general approach for designing x and w to give us arbitrary peaks in the 2^n space, which could be used for a new kind of logic and image classification for example.

Chapter 4

Transition Matrix

4.1 Markov Chain Monte Carlo

This is Lecture 4.1: Watch youtube video

We started in Chapter 2 with the general Boltzmann law opertaing in 2^n space and then in Chapter 3 introduced the sampling method which operates in n space. Now we'll introduce a third method, which operates in 2^n space, but as you'll see, it gives us a lot of insight into how the sampling method works and leads to this concept of Feynman paths, which is useful in connecting to the world of quantum computing.

4.1.1 *Figs. 4.1-4.4: Transition matrix*

4.1.1.1 *Fig. 4.1: Definition*

So what is this third method? Well, the idea is that if you have a system in some configuration $\{111001\}$ denoted by i. You want to know what will happen at the next time step. And the answer is that in a probabilistic circuit, it will go to different configurations j with different probabilities. (see Fig. 4.1). And those are the probabilities that should appear in the i-th column of the transition matrix $[W]$. So the i-th column, the column tells you what's the input, that is what the configuration was at time t. And j-th row then tells you the probability that the system will go from i on to j.

In general, you can take the probability distribution function at a time t. Multiply it by W, and it will give you the new probability distribution at time $t+1$, $[W]pdf(t) = pdf(t+1)$. So, this matrix kind of propagates your probability distribution function from one time point to the next (see Fig. 4.1).

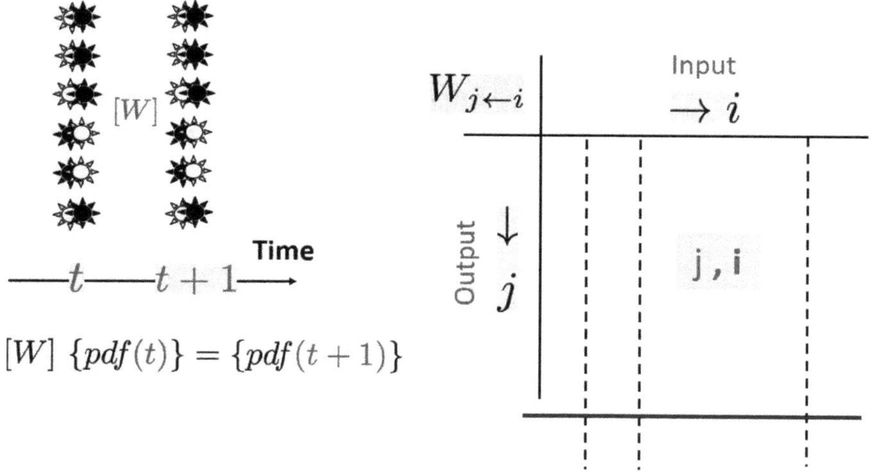

Fig. 4.1 Transition matrix.

4.1.1.2 *Fig. 4.2: Properties*

Matrices of this type appear in diverse fields and are generally called stochastic matrices which have some very useful properties.

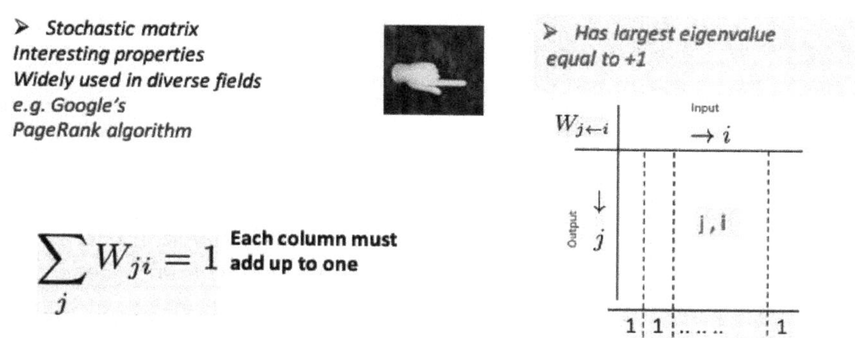

Fig. 4.2 Properties of stochastic matrix.

One such property is that every column must add up to 1. Why is that? Well, because each column represents the probability that the system will go to some state j, given that it is in i at this time. But of course it must go somewhere, which means if I add up all the j's, the answer should be 1, $\sum_j W_{ji} = 1$.

4.1.1.3 *Fig. 4.3*

Another important property is that it has an eigenvalue equal to one. This is a huge matrix 2^n by 2^n. So, it has 2^n eigenvalues. But one of these actually the largest one, is equal to 1. To show this takes a little discussion. First consider the transpose of the W matrix. For the W matrix, the columns add up to 1, so for the transpose, it is the row that adds up to 1: So, $\sum_j [W^{\mathrm{T}}]_{ij}$.

Now what that means is that a constant vector, all of whose components are equal to a particular number c, is actually an eigenvector of the transpose matrix W, $[W^{\mathrm{T}}]$ with an eigenvalue of 1.

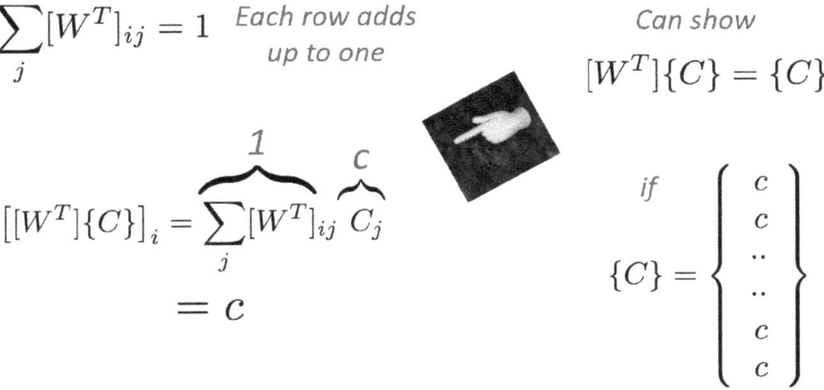

Fig. 4.3 W^T has one eigenvalue equal to 1.

4.1.1.4 *Fig. 4.4*

Now, I am of course, interested not in W transpose, W^{T}, but in W, and then there is this theorem that you may remember from somewhere in linear algebra. That W and W^{T} have the same eigenvalues though not necessarily the same eigenvectors. Eigenvectors could be same but don't have to be. But the point is they will always have the same eigenvalues.

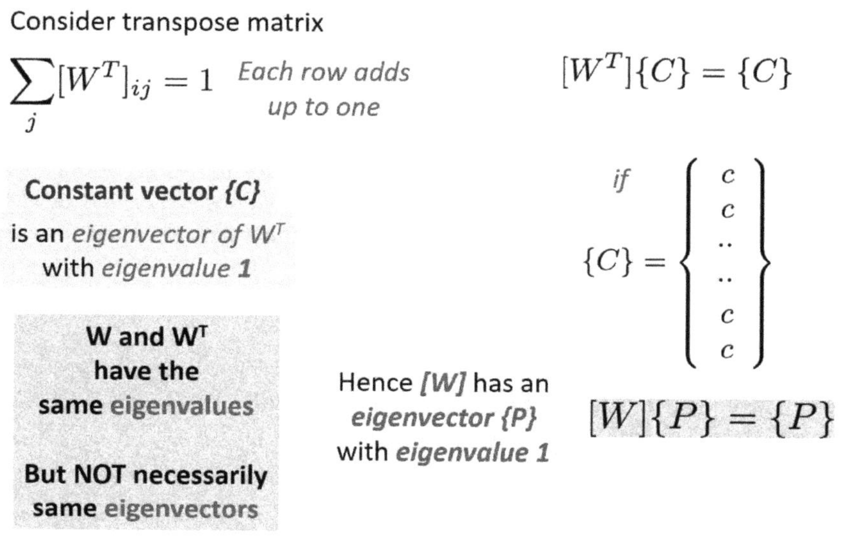

Consider transpose matrix

$$\sum_j [W^T]_{ij} = 1$$ *Each row adds up to one*

$$[W^T]\{C\} = \{C\}$$

if

$$\{C\} = \begin{Bmatrix} c \\ c \\ .. \\ .. \\ c \\ c \end{Bmatrix}$$

Constant vector *{C}* is an *eigenvector of* W^T with *eigenvalue* **1**

W and W^T have the same eigenvalues

But NOT necessarily same eigenvectors

Hence ***[W]*** has an ***eigenvector {P}*** with ***eigenvalue 1***

$$[W]\{P\} = \{P\}$$

Fig. 4.4 W^T and W have the same eigenvalues though not necessarily the same eigenvectors.

So, what we can deduce is that since W^{T} has eigenvalue 1 and eigenvector C, W must also have an eigenvector, but not necessarily C, we'll call it P, with an eigenvalue of 1 such that $[W]P = P$.

4.1.2 *Figs. 4.5-4.9: Stationary distribution*

4.1.2.1 *Fig. 4.5*

Now, this P is what you could call the stationary distribution. Why is that? Well, this W matrix as we discussed takes the probability distribution function from one point in time and propagates it to the next point. So if at a given time t you have a distribution P, then $[W]P = P$. So at $t+1$ also you'll have the same distribution. In other words, the distribution, once it reaches P, will stay that way forever and so you call it a stationary distribution.

4.1.2.2 *Fig. 4.6*

Now what if initially at time t, the distribution was something else. I'll call that Q. Well, the answer is that after a few time steps, and we'll talk about how many, the probability distribution function will converge to P.

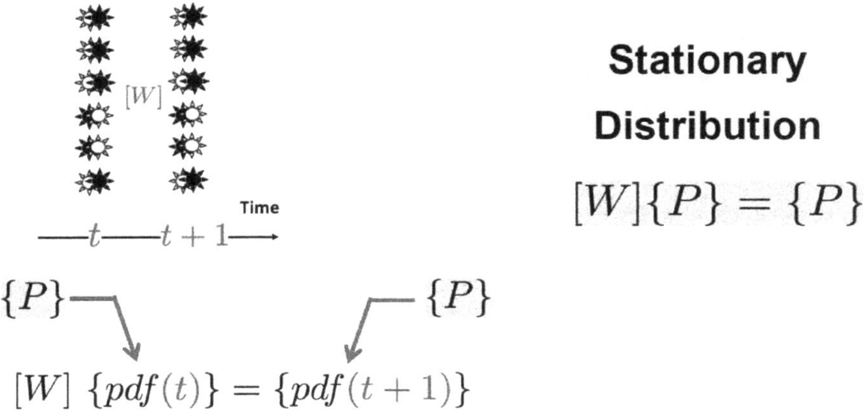

Fig. 4.5 Stationary distribution.

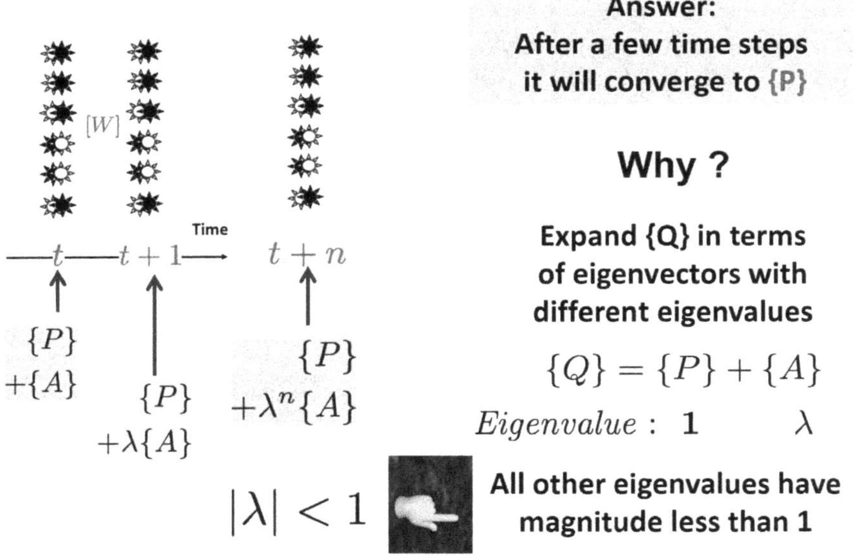

Fig. 4.6 Converging to a stationary distribution.

Why is that? Well, one way to think is, take the Q and write it in terms of the eigenvectors of the W matrix. So, as I said P is one of the eigenvectors with eigenvalue 1. Let's say there's another eigenvector A with eigenvalue λ and of course, there'll be many more eigenvectors and some eigenvalues will even be complex. But here, just for illustrative purposes, I'm considering one other. The argument we'll make will apply to all of these other eigenvectors.

Now, you see, if at time t we have $P+A$, then what will happen at time $t+1$? Well, it will get multiplied by W, and WP will give me P, but WA will give me λA. Why? Because A is also an eigenvector of W, but with an eigenvalue λ.

And so, every time I propagate one time step the P stays P, but the A, that part keeps picking up a factor of λ. So after n time steps, we have $P+\lambda^n A$. And the point is, I'd mentioned before that this eigenvalue of 1 is actually the one with the largest magnitude. Every other one, all other λ's, they may be complex, but the point is their magnitude will be less than 1. That's one of the properties of this stochastic matrix. So because it's less than 1, when you raise it to the power n, it gradually disappears. If you take 0.1 and raise the power 100, it becomes a very small number. And so eventually only the P remains, everything else disappears.

4.1.2.3 *Fig. 4.7*

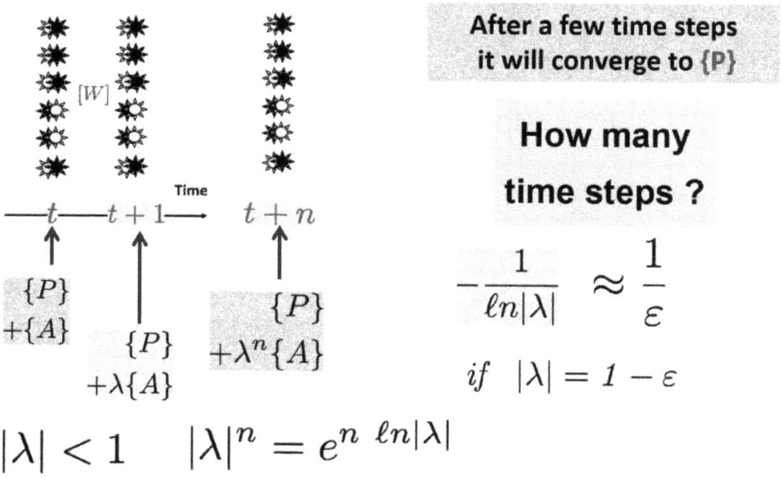

Fig. 4.7 Stationary distribution.

So how many time steps does it take for these other components to disappear? Well, you can estimate it this way, take $|\lambda|^n$, and write it in this form $|\lambda|^n = \exp(n \ln |\lambda|)$.

You can always write λ as $\exp(\ln |\lambda|)$, that's an identity (see Fig. 4.7). So, you could take this quantity and write it this way $|\lambda|^n = \exp(n \ln |\lambda|)$. What that means is, that if the number of time steps n is equal to $-1/(\ln |\lambda|)$, then you see this $|\lambda|^n$ would be $\exp(-1)$, which means after $-1/(\ln |\lambda|)$ time steps. This component will have decayed to $1/e$ of its original value.

So how much is that? Well, if λ we'll say a little less than 1, write it as $1 - \varepsilon$, then you can show that this number will be $1/\varepsilon$. This is an approximate result, but it works well if ε is small. So what that means is if say, this eigenvalue happened to be 0.99, that means, ε is 0.01. Then it would take like hundred time steps before this component becomes $1/e$ of its original value.

4.1.2.4 *Fig. 4.8*

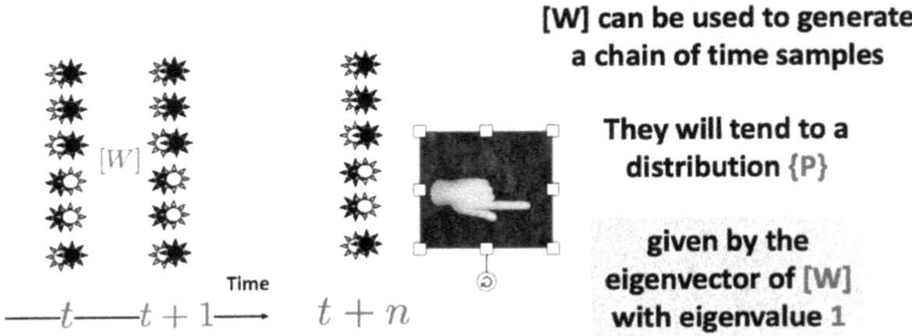

Fig. 4.8 Markov Chain Monte Carlo.

So, bottom line is, we have this $[W]$ matrix, the transition matrix, you can use it to generate a chain of time samples. And they will tend to this distribution P, the stationary distribution P. And what distribution is it? Well, it's given by the eigenvector of $[W]$ with this eigenvalue 1 (see Fig. 4.8).

4.1.2.5 *Fig. 4.9*

Now, what we want is a method of time sampling where the samples obey the Boltzmann law, $p_i = (1/Z)\exp(-\widetilde{E}_i)$ which is our target distribution.

How can you make the Boltzmann distribution p the stationary distribution for W. By making $[W]\{p\} = \{p\}$. One way to do this is to impose detailed balance. Which means that we require $W_{ji}p_i$ to be equal to $W_{ij}p_j$. If this is true then I can show that $[W]\{p\} = \{p\}$. The algebra is shown in Fig. 4.9.

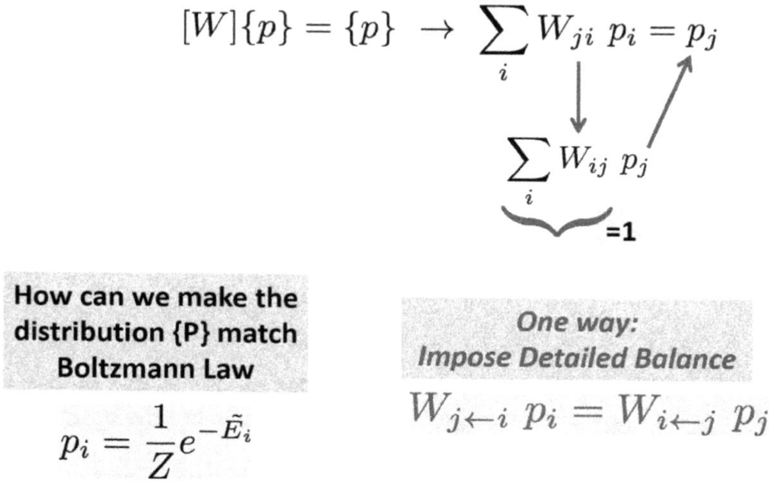

$$[W]\{p\} = \{p\} \;\rightarrow\; \sum_i W_{ji}\, p_i = p_j$$

$$\sum_i W_{ij}\, p_j \quad \left(\sum_i W_{ij} = 1\right)$$

How can we make the distribution {P} match Boltzmann Law

$$p_i = \frac{1}{Z}e^{-\tilde{E}_i}$$

One way: Impose Detailed Balance

$$W_{j\leftarrow i}\, p_i = W_{i\leftarrow j}\, p_j$$

Fig. 4.9 How to make the Boltzmann distribution p the stationary distribution for W?

4.1.3 *Fig. 4.10: Metropolis algorithm*

There's a very well known algorithm that is widely used in statistical physics. It's called the Metropolis algorithm. Consider any two states, i and j and let's say i has a bigger energy than j.

Say I am currently sitting at i and I am trying to figure out the probability of going to j. I choose the probability as 1 for going down in energy, which means for i to j, $W_{j\leftarrow i}$. If j has a lower energy than i take it for sure. But for the reverse process, $W_{i\leftarrow j}$, I choose the probability as proportional to $p_j/p_i = \exp(-(\widetilde{E}_i - \widetilde{E}_j))$.

This will ensure that I meet the condition of detailed balance. It should lead us to a stationary distribution that follows Boltzmann law, but it is not the only way. Any other choice that satisfies detailed balance should work too, though one choice might reach the stationary distribution faster than another. In the next lecture we will look at another popular choice, one that we have been using, often referred to as Gibbs sampling.

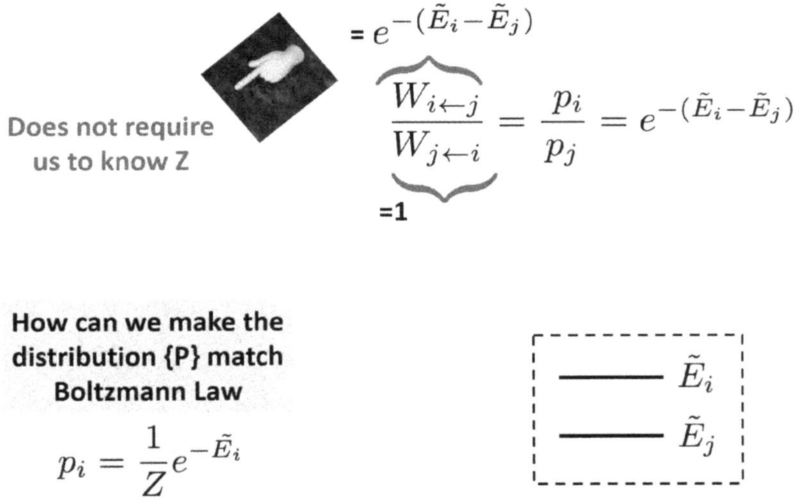

Does not require us to know Z

$$\overbrace{\frac{W_{i\leftarrow j}}{W_{j\leftarrow i}}}^{=e^{-(\tilde{E}_i-\tilde{E}_j)}}_{=1} = \frac{p_i}{p_j} = e^{-(\tilde{E}_i-\tilde{E}_j)}$$

How can we make the distribution {P} match Boltzmann Law

$$p_i = \frac{1}{Z}e^{-\tilde{E}_i}$$

$\tilde{E}_i$

$\tilde{E}_j$

Fig. 4.10 Metropolis algorithm.

4.1.4 *Quiz*

4.1.4.1 *Question 1*

For any transition matrix $[W]$, what is (a) the sum of each column, (b) the largest eigenvalue?[1]

4.1.4.2 *Question 2*

A single spin has a transition matrix given by $W = \begin{bmatrix} 0.2 & 0.4 \\ 0.8 & 0.6 \end{bmatrix}$

What is the stationary probability distribution?[2]

[1] 1,1.

[2] $\begin{Bmatrix} 1/3 \\ 2/3 \end{Bmatrix}$.

4.2 Gibbs' Sampling

This is Lecture 4.2: Watch youtube video

In the last lecture, we introduced the concept of a transition matrix whose eigenvector with eigenvalue 1 gives us the stationary probability distribution. We then showed that a transition matrix that obeys detailed balance $W_{i \leftarrow j}/W_{j \leftarrow i} = \exp(-(\widetilde{E}_i - \widetilde{E}_j))$, will lead to a stationary distribution that follows the Boltzmann law: $p_i = (1/Z)\exp(-\widetilde{E}_i)$.

Now, what we'll be talking about in this lecture is what's called Gibbs' sampling. Basically it is the sampling algorithm that we have been using the one that I introduced in the very first lecture of in Chapter 3. In this lecture and the next, we'll see how to write down the transition matrix for this kind of sampling, and why some approaches work and some don't work.

4.2.1 *Figs. 4.11-4.12: How it works*

4.2.1.1 *Fig. 4.11*

Now, so how does this Gibbs sampling work? Well, the idea is that you go to one of your *p-bits*, say the r-th, and either set it equal to 0 or equal to 1, according to a certain algorithm. When you are updating the r-th *p-bit* you don't mess with any other *p-bit* say the q-th if there are terms in the energy function $\widetilde{E}$ that involve both s_r and s_q. So when you're working on the r-th *p-bit*, you just have two choices, you can either set it to 0 or to 1 but you're not supposed to mess with the other ones. The other *p-bits* remain wherever they are, whatever configuration α they may be in.

So our choice is between $\alpha 0$, meaning, rest of the *p-bits* in α and the r-th one in 0, or rest in α and the r-th one in 1. And when we try to write down the $[W]$ matrix, that's the transition matrix, we are basically trying to write down this 2 by 2 section.

Note of course, that the matrix itself is much bigger. You see, even with 6 *p-bits*, the matrix would be 2^6 by 2^6, which would be 64×64 and in general could be even bigger, depending on the number of *p-bits*, it grows exponentially. But for this method of sampling, when you're dealing with the r-th neuron, the only nonzero elements are in this 2 by 2 block, labeled with $\alpha 0$ and $\alpha 1$.

And what are the elements of this block? Well, the procedure is you first find this quantity that we call $\widetilde{x}_r$, which you obtain from the difference in the energies between the two possibilities, 1 and 0, $\widetilde{x}_r = \widetilde{E}_{\alpha 1} - \widetilde{E}_{\alpha 0}$, and

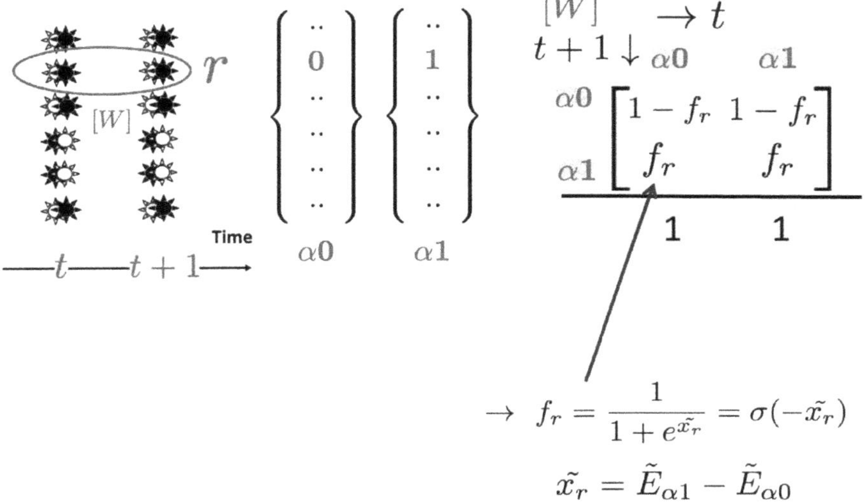

Fig. 4.11 Gibbs sampling.

that is what, as we discussed, you could write also as the derivative of the energy function, $\partial\widetilde{E}/\partial s_r$, and that's because s is a binary variable.

I should also mention that in general, you often calculate this $\widetilde{x}_r$ using the synapse equation, $\widetilde{x} = x + [w]s$ and what we are doing here is kind of equivalent. In fact, this is more general, because it would work, even if energy functions had higher order terms beyond quadratic, as we have discussed earlier.

Now, what do you do once you have the $\widetilde{x}_r$? Well, you find the Fermi function of $\widetilde{x}_r$, which is the mirror image of the sigmoidal function, $f_r = 1/(1 + \exp\widetilde{x}_r) = \sigma(-\widetilde{x}_r)$. The sigmoid function is something you see a lot in the neural network literature and the Fermi function is what you'd normally see in, I guess, solid state devices and solid state physics courses.

Okay, now once you have this Fermi function, the rule is that probability that this *p-bit* will be set to 1 is equal to the Fermi function. Note that this probability is independent of what the *p-bit* currently is, that doesn't matter. You just calculate $\widetilde{x}_r$ or find f_r, and then depending on f_r, you set it to 1 or 0.

So remember when we write the $[W]$ matrix, the columns correspond to the current state, the state at time t, whereas the rows tell you the state at time $t+1$. And so since the state at time $t+1$ really doesn't depend on the state at time t, we put f_r on both columns here. Similarly, if you want to write the probability of putting a 0 on that neuron, well that's $1 - f_r$, and again, it's the same for both columns.

Finally, one property of transition matrices I'd mentioned is that every column must add up to 1, and it does (see Fig. 4.11). That's trivially clear, but you might wonder that well, you told me $[W]$ was a huge matrix, and you're just writing this little 2×2 block, but it's that huge matrix where the columns should add up to 1. That's true, but the way we're doing it here, all other elements of that matrix are actually 0, because in a particular step, the only element that can change is the r-th *p-bit*. Okay, and so if these add up to 1, it means the columns of the entire big matrix also would add up to 1.

4.2.1.2 *Fig. 4.12*

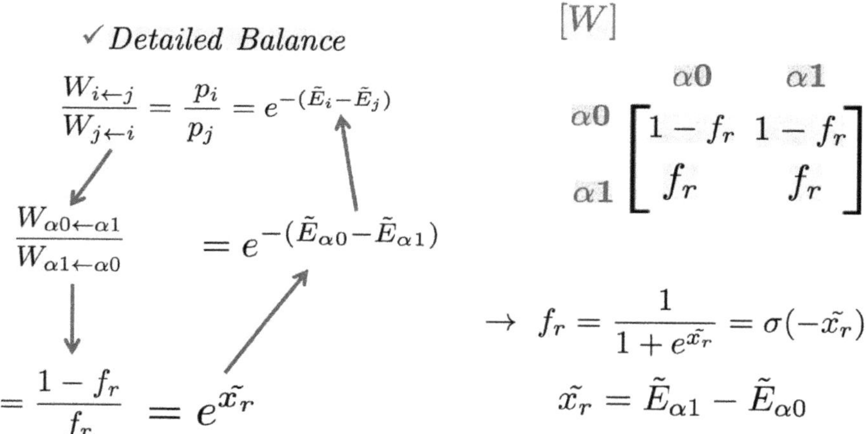

Fig. 4.12 Gibbs sampling.

Another question you could ask is about detailed balance, $W_{i\leftarrow j}/W_{j\leftarrow i} = p_i/p_j = \exp -(\widetilde{E}_i - \widetilde{E}_j)$, because if you remember, in the last lecture, we said that one way to ensure that the $[W]$ matrix will give a stationary distribution that matches the Boltzmann distribution is to ensure this detailed balance.

The question is what we wrote down here, does that satisfy this condition? Well, we can check. With a little algebra you can show that $(1 - f_r)/f_r = e^{\widetilde{x}_r}$ and use it to show that we are satisfying detailed balance.

4.2.2 *Figs. 4.13-4.20: Toy example with n = 2*

4.2.2.1 *Fig. 4.13*

Now let's look at a toy example with just two *p-bits*. How do we write down the $[W]$ matrices? We start, of course, with the energy expression, which in matrix form would be written like this, $\widetilde{E} = s^{\mathrm{T}}x + (1/2)s^{\mathrm{T}}ws$, but with just two *p-bits*, you could actually spell it out, and it wouldn't be too inconvenient. The matrix version is particularly useful when you have lots of *p-bits*, because it's hard to write out all the terms. But here you could easily write this out, the first term will give you $s_1x_1 + s_2x_2$ and the interaction term will give you this $w_{12}s_1s_2$. Note, of course, these are Boltzmann networks for which the w matrix is symmetric, that is, w_{12} is equal to w_{21}.

By the way, I should mention that the small w, which is the weight matrix, is very different from this big $[W]$, which is the transition matrix. The small w is n by n, the big $[W]$ is 2^n by 2^n, a different matrix. Even when w is symmetric W need not be.

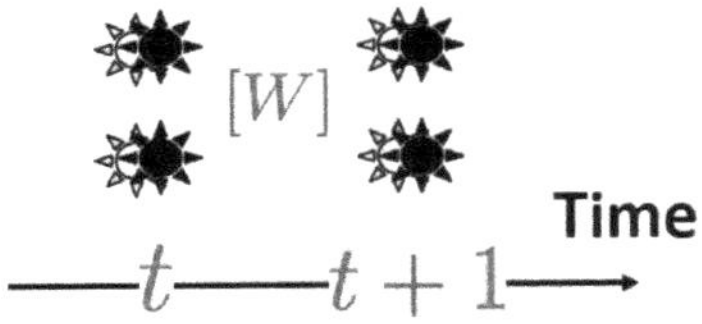

$$\tilde{E}_{00} = 0$$

$$\tilde{E}_{01} = x_2$$

$$\tilde{E}_{10} = x_1$$

$$\tilde{E}_{11} = x_1 + x_2 + w_{12}$$

$$\tilde{E} = s^T x + \frac{1}{2} s^T ws = s_1x_1 + s_2x_2 + \overbrace{w_{12}}^{= w_{21}}s_1s_2$$

Fig. 4.13 $[W]$ with $n = 2$.

Anyway, from the expression $\widetilde{E} = s_1x_1 + s_2x_2 + w_{12}s_1s_2$, we can write out the energies of all the configurations. How many configurations? Well 2 *p-bits*, so there are $2^2 = 4$ configurations: $\{00\}$, $\{01\}$, $\{10\}$ and $\{11\}$ where $\{00\}$ means $s_1 = 0$, $s_2 = 0$ etc.

4.2.2.2 *Fig. 4.14: Transition matrix for updating p-bit 1*

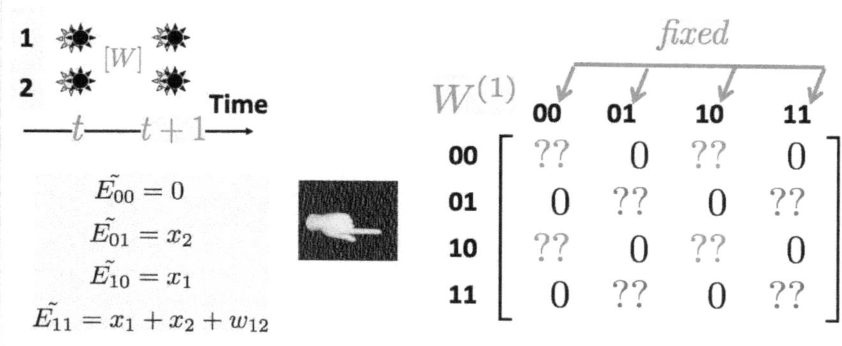

Fig. 4.14 Non-zero elements in $[W^{(1)}]$.

Let us write down the $[W]$ matrix for updating *p-bit* 1, and I've put a superscript, $W^{(1)}$ to indicate that. The point to note is that the second *p-bit* is fixed. So from $\{00\}$, you can go to $\{10\}$, but you cannot go to $\{01\}$ or to $\{11\}$, because you are not allowed to change the second one. So when you write this $W^{(1)}$ matrix, you have these red question marks and these blue question marks, those would be the nonzero elements, rest will be zeros. Because the rest will require changing both *p-bits* and that's not allowed. In this sampling scheme, you update one *p-bit* at a time.

4.2.2.3 *Figs. 4.15-4.16*

Okay, so let's just focus on the red ones, involving a transition between $\{00\}$ and $\{10\}$. So the corresponding $\widetilde{x_1}$, is $\widetilde{E}_{10} - \widetilde{E}_{00}$, and that's really x_1, as you can see.

Incidentally, you could have got the same answer starting from the synapse equation as well, $\widetilde{x} = x + [w]s$ setting $s_2 = 0$. Remember that this synapse equation is equivalent if the energy expression has only a linear and a quadratic term as in this case.

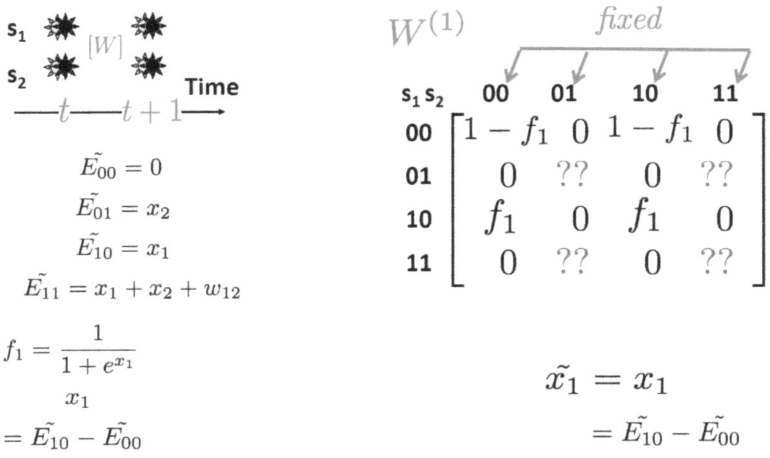

s_1 s_2 $[W]$ Time t $t+1$

$\tilde{E_{00}} = 0$

$\tilde{E_{01}} = x_2$

$\tilde{E_{10}} = x_1$

$\tilde{E_{11}} = x_1 + x_2 + w_{12}$

$f_1 = \frac{1}{1+e^{x_1}}$

x_1

$= \tilde{E_{10}} - \tilde{E_{00}}$

$W^{(1)}$ *fixed*

$$\begin{array}{c|cccc} s_1 s_2 & 00 & 01 & 10 & 11 \\ \hline 00 & 1-f_1 & 0 & 1-f_1 & 0 \\ 01 & 0 & ?? & 0 & ?? \\ 10 & f_1 & 0 & f_1 & 0 \\ 11 & 0 & ?? & 0 & ?? \end{array}$$

$\tilde{x_1} = x_1$

$= \tilde{E_{10}} - \tilde{E_{00}}$

Fig. 4.15 $[W^{(1)}]$.

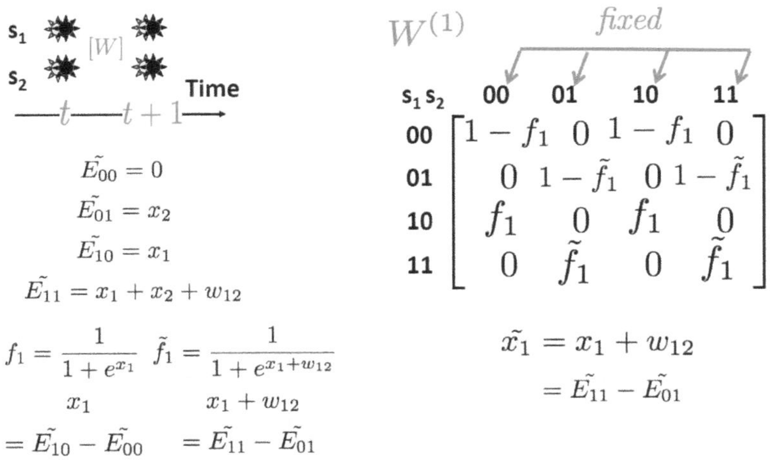

Fig. 4.16 $[W^{(1)}]$.

Now the probability of updating *p-bit* 1 to one is given by the Fermi function $f_1(\widetilde{x_1})$, and the probability of updating it to zero is given by $1 - f_1(\widetilde{x_1})$. And so we can fill up the red question marks in Fig. 4.14 as shown in Fig. 4.15.

Next you can go onto the blue question marks which involve a transition between 01 and 11 and the difference is that now we have to look at the energy difference between 11 and 01, so this $\widetilde{x_1} = \widetilde{E}_{01} - \widetilde{E}_{11}$ which is $x_1 + w_{12}$. The last time the energy difference was just x_1. So we'll define a new Fermi function with a tilde, $\widetilde{f_1} = 1/(1 + \exp(x_1 + w_{12}))$, and fill up the blue question marks accordingly.

4.2.2.4 *Figs. 4.17-4.18*

Is detailed balance satisfied? You can easily check it is, the way we did it earlier (see Fig. 4.12).

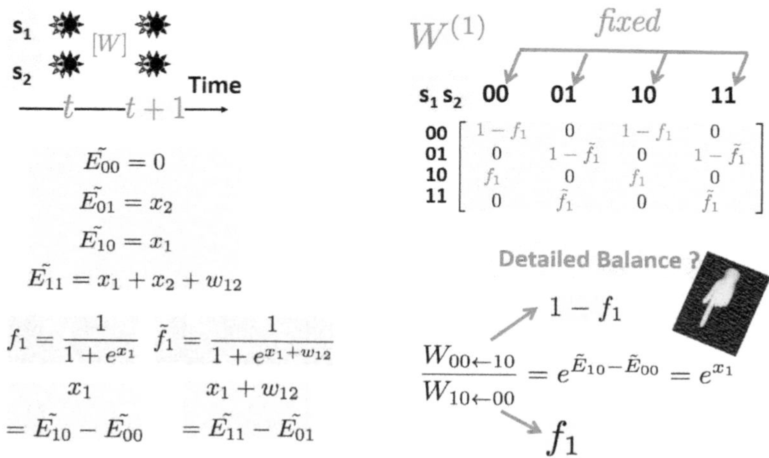

Fig. 4.17 Checking for detailed balance.

4.2.2.5 *Fig. 4.19: Transition matrix for updating p-bit 2*

Next we have to write down $W^{(2)}$, that is the W matrix for updating *p-bit* 2 keeping *p-bit* 1 fixed. Remember that previously we updated *p-bit* 1 keeping *p-bit* 2 fixed. Now you can see that we have a different set of elements that are non-zero. These are the blocks where the first *p-bit* does not change, it's either 0 or 1 and stays fixed.

And so you can go ahead and fill them up, again much the same principles, but now the energy differences involved would be between {01} and {00}, and between {10} and {11}. But it's the same pattern with f_2 and $\widetilde{f_2}$ defined as shown.

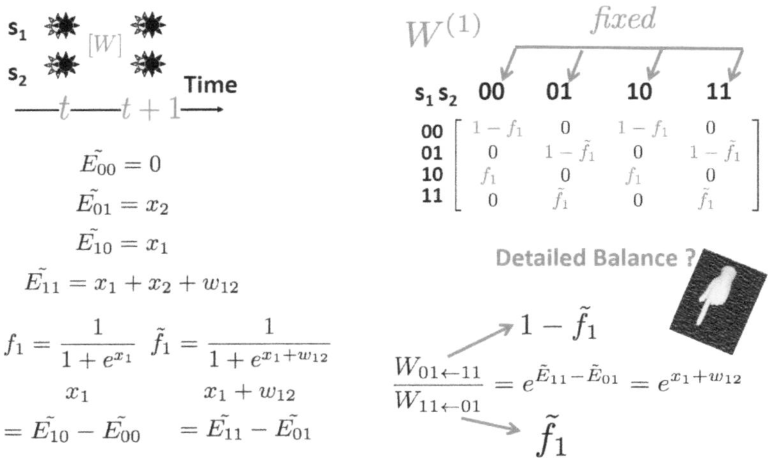

Fig. 4.18 Checking for detailed balance.

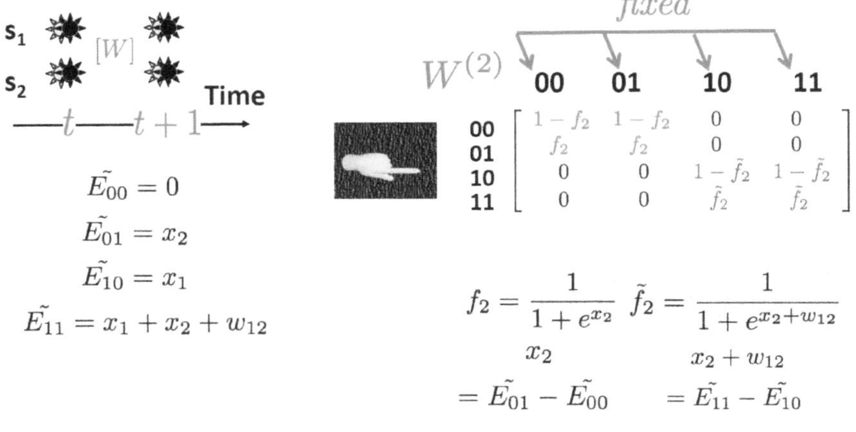

Fig. 4.19 $[W^{(2)}]$.

4.2.2.6 *Fig. 4.20*

So collecting all the results, We have these two $[W]$ matrices, one for updating 1, one for updating 2, and they depend on these various Fermi functions that appear, each one corresponding to a different energy difference.

Now, I'll stop here for this lecture. What we'll do is continue with this in the next lecture with a specific numeral example and see what we get

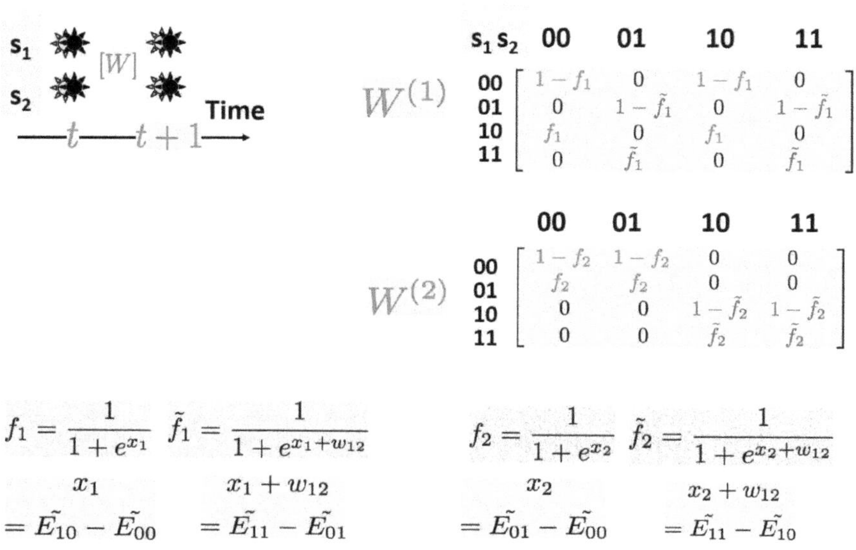

s1 s2 [W] Time — t — t + 1 →

$$W^{(1)} \quad \begin{array}{c|cccc} s_1 s_2 & 00 & 01 & 10 & 11 \\ \hline 00 & 1-f_1 & 0 & 1-f_1 & 0 \\ 01 & 0 & 1-\tilde{f}_1 & 0 & 1-\tilde{f}_1 \\ 10 & f_1 & 0 & f_1 & 0 \\ 11 & 0 & \tilde{f}_1 & 0 & \tilde{f}_1 \end{array}$$

$$W^{(2)} \quad \begin{array}{c|cccc} & 00 & 01 & 10 & 11 \\ \hline 00 & 1-f_2 & 1-f_2 & 0 & 0 \\ 01 & f_2 & f_2 & 0 & 0 \\ 10 & 0 & 0 & 1-\tilde{f}_2 & 1-\tilde{f}_2 \\ 11 & 0 & 0 & \tilde{f}_2 & \tilde{f}_2 \end{array}$$

$$f_1 = \frac{1}{1+e^{x_1}} \quad \tilde{f}_1 = \frac{1}{1+e^{x_1+w_{12}}} \qquad f_2 = \frac{1}{1+e^{x_2}} \quad \tilde{f}_2 = \frac{1}{1+e^{x_2+w_{12}}}$$

$$x_1 = \tilde{E}_{10} - \tilde{E}_{00} \quad x_1 + w_{12} = \tilde{E}_{11} - \tilde{E}_{01} \qquad x_2 = \tilde{E}_{01} - \tilde{E}_{00} \quad x_2 + w_{12} = \tilde{E}_{11} - \tilde{E}_{10}$$

Fig. 4.20 Collecting all results for $[W^{(1)}]$ and $[W^{(2)}]$.

for sequential updating the way we discussed. And then compare it with what you get when you try to update 1 and 2 simultaneously.

4.2.3 *Quiz*

The transition matrix for updating one spin in a network of 2 spins is

$$W = \begin{bmatrix} 1-f_1 & 0 & 1-f_1 & 0 \\ 0 & 1-\widetilde{f}_1 & 0 & 1-\widetilde{f}_1 \\ f_1 & 0 & f_1 & 0 \\ 0 & \widetilde{f}_1 & 0 & \widetilde{f}_1 \end{bmatrix}$$

4.2.3.1 *Question 1*

What is $(1-f_1)/f_1$ in terms of the energy function $\widetilde{E}$?[3]

4.2.3.2 *Question 2*

What is $(1-\widetilde{f}_1)/\widetilde{f}_1$ in terms of the energy function $\widetilde{E}$?[4]

---

[3] $exp(\widetilde{E}_{10} - \widetilde{E}_{00})$.

[4] $exp(\widetilde{E}_{11} - \widetilde{E}_{01})$.

4.3 Sequential Versus Simultaneous Updates

This is Lecture 4.3: Watch youtube video

4.3.1 *Figs. 4.21-4.23: Sequential update*

4.3.1.1 *Fig. 4.21: Toy example*

This lecture is kind of a continuation of the last one and what we'll try to do is define a specific two *p-bit* problem and compare what you get when you update *p-bits* sequentially and what happens when you update them simultaneously, and show that the W matrix gives you a nice analytical way of seeing those results.

Now, recall the toy example that we used in the last lecture, two *p-bits* with energy given by $\widetilde{E} = s^{\mathrm{T}}x + (1/2)s^{\mathrm{T}}ws$. The Figure shows the probabilities of the four different configurations, {00}, {01}, {10}, {11}, assuming the weight w shown along with two choices of the bias x.

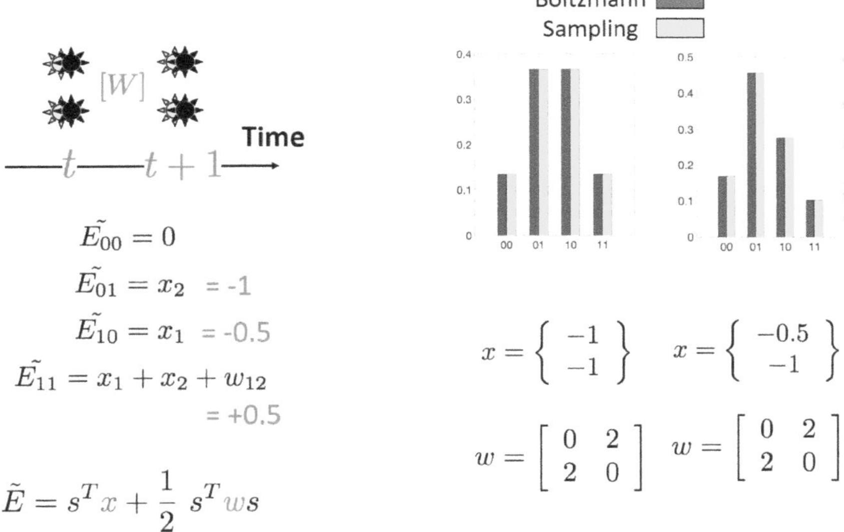

Fig. 4.21 Numerical example.

Now how can you understand the probabilities. Well, the easiest is by in terms of the Boltzmann distribution because as you know, the probability is exponential of $-E$. So what you need to find out is the energies of these different configurations. With a bias $x = \{-1 \ \ -1\}^T$, if you put in the numbers you will see that 11 has the same energy, equal to zero, as 00 and so they have exactly the same probability. The ratio of the probabilities of the first and second groups is e^0/e^{-1} which is what the plot shows. All probabilities add up to one.

Now, if you change the bias on *p-bit* #2 to say -0.5, then the energies come out a little different: 11 now has a slightly higher energy than 00 and so it's probability goes down. 01 and 10 are also not equal anymore, 01 has a lower energy and hence a higher probability. So that's the toy example we will use to compare the Boltzmann result to what we get directly from two different sampling approaches along with what we get from the eigenvectors of the corresponding W matrices that have an eigenvalue of 1.[5]

4.3.1.2 *Fig. 4.22: Transition matrix*

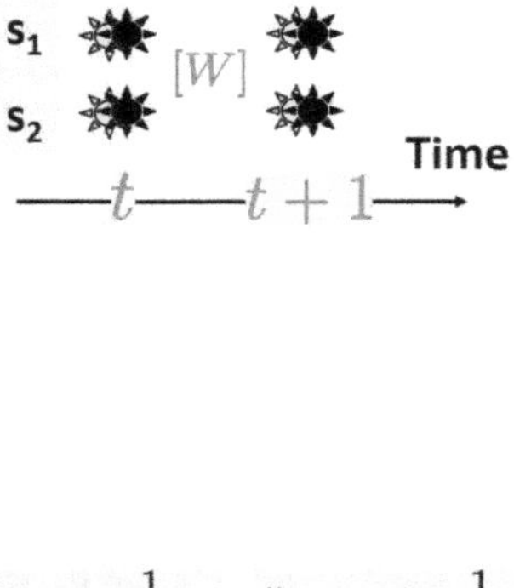

s_1, s_2 — $[W]$ — Time: t → $t+1$

$$W^{(1)} = \begin{array}{c|cccc} s_1 s_2 & 00 & 01 & 10 & 11 \\ \hline 00 & 1-f_1 & 0 & 1-f_1 & 0 \\ 01 & 0 & 1-\tilde{f}_1 & 0 & 1-\tilde{f}_1 \\ 10 & f_1 & 0 & f_1 & 0 \\ 11 & 0 & \tilde{f}_1 & 0 & \tilde{f}_1 \end{array}$$

$$W^{(2)} = \begin{array}{c|cccc} & 00 & 01 & 10 & 11 \\ \hline 00 & 1-f_2 & 1-f_2 & 0 & 0 \\ 01 & f_2 & f_2 & 0 & 0 \\ 10 & 0 & 0 & 1-\tilde{f}_2 & 1-\tilde{f}_2 \\ 11 & 0 & 0 & \tilde{f}_2 & \tilde{f}_2 \end{array}$$

$$f_1 = \frac{1}{1+e^{x_1}} \quad \tilde{f}_1 = \frac{1}{1+e^{x_1+w_{12}}} \qquad f_2 = \frac{1}{1+e^{x_2}} \quad \tilde{f}_2 = \frac{1}{1+e^{x_2+w_{12}}}$$

$$x_1 = \tilde{E}_{10} - \tilde{E}_{00} \qquad x_1 + w_{12} = \tilde{E}_{11} - \tilde{E}_{01} \qquad x_2 = \tilde{E}_{01} - \tilde{E}_{00} \qquad x_2 + w_{12} = \tilde{E}_{11} - \tilde{E}_{10}$$

Fig. 4.22 Recalling $W^{(1)}$ and $W^{(2)}$ from last lecture.

In the last lecture we spent some time writing the W matrices, $W^{(1)}$ and $W^{(2)}$, for updating *p-bit* 1 with *p-bit* 2 fixed and for updating *p-bit* 2

[5]Recall that the eigenvector of W with an eigenvalue of 1 represents the stationary distribution.

with *p-bit* 2 fixed. As you can see, the elements of these W matrices involve different Fermi functions corresponding to different energy differences.

4.3.1.3 *Fig. 4.23*

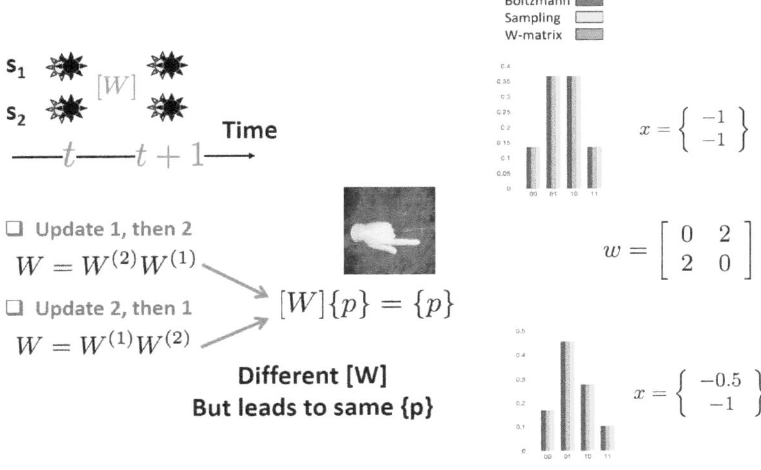

Fig. 4.23 $[W] = [W^{(1)}][W^{(2)}]$.

Now, how do you apply it to the problem to calculate the stationary distribution? Well first you have to write the composite W matrix, which depends on whether you first update 1 and then 2, or the other way. If you update *p-bit* 1 first then you put the $W^{(1)}$ first. First meaning to the right because that's the one that operates on your distribution first, and then $W^{(2)}$. But if you update 2 first, then $W^{(2)}$ is the one on the right and then $W^{(1)}$. The composite matrix W is then given either by the product $W = W^{(2)}W^{(1)}$ or $W = W^{(1)}W^{(2)}$.

You can then find the eigenvector of W with eigenvalue equal to 1. And if you do that, you will get results that will match the Boltzmann result very nicely, along with the sampling results. So, I have now added this third method, the W matrix method. You see the first two methods, Boltzmann and sampling, we had in Chapters 2 and 3. This W matrix method is what we are adding now.

All three methods agree nicely for the two numerical examples we are discussing.

4.3.2 *Fig. 4.24: Simultaneous update*

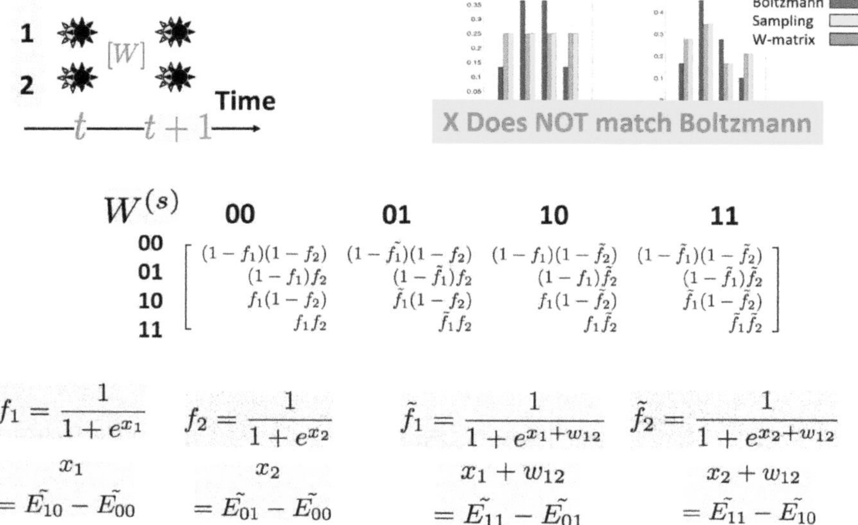

$$W^{(s)} = \begin{bmatrix} (1-f_1)(1-f_2) & (1-\tilde{f}_1)(1-f_2) & (1-f_1)(1-\tilde{f}_2) & (1-\tilde{f}_1)(1-\tilde{f}_2) \\ (1-f_1)f_2 & (1-\tilde{f}_1)f_2 & (1-f_1)\tilde{f}_2 & (1-\tilde{f}_1)\tilde{f}_2 \\ f_1(1-f_2) & \tilde{f}_1(1-f_2) & f_1(1-\tilde{f}_2) & \tilde{f}_1(1-\tilde{f}_2) \\ f_1 f_2 & \tilde{f}_1 f_2 & f_1\tilde{f}_2 & \tilde{f}_1\tilde{f}_2 \end{bmatrix}$$

$$f_1 = \frac{1}{1+e^{x_1}} \quad f_2 = \frac{1}{1+e^{x_2}} \quad \tilde{f}_1 = \frac{1}{1+e^{x_1+w_{12}}} \quad \tilde{f}_2 = \frac{1}{1+e^{x_2+w_{12}}}$$

$$x_1 = \tilde{E}_{10} - \tilde{E}_{00} \quad x_2 = \tilde{E}_{01} - \tilde{E}_{00} \quad x_1 + w_{12} = \tilde{E}_{11} - \tilde{E}_{01} \quad x_2 + w_{12} = \tilde{E}_{11} - \tilde{E}_{10}$$

Fig. 4.24 Simultaneous update.

Now what I want to talk about is, what it would look like if instead of updating them one by one, I am a little impatient and I say no, let's do it quickly, update them both, why not? With a little thought, we can write down the elements of the corresponding transition matrix $W^{(s)}$ as shown. Now, let us again compare the three methods, the Boltzmann method, the sampling method and the W matrix method. The sampling now is not Gibbs sampling, but it's this simultaneous update method.

You'll notice the sampling and the W matrix they match exactly. So the yellow and the green, they are matched very nicely. So that tells you that this W matrix method actually describes this sampling procedure very well. But you'll notice they don't match the Boltzmann answer which is this blue peak. So when you do simultaneous update, whatever stationary distribution you get by sampling will not look like the Boltzmann distribution, which is generally what you want. That's why the simultaneous updating is not used at all.

4.3.3 Figs. 4.25-4.26: Sequential versus simultaneous

4.3.3.1 Fig. 4.25

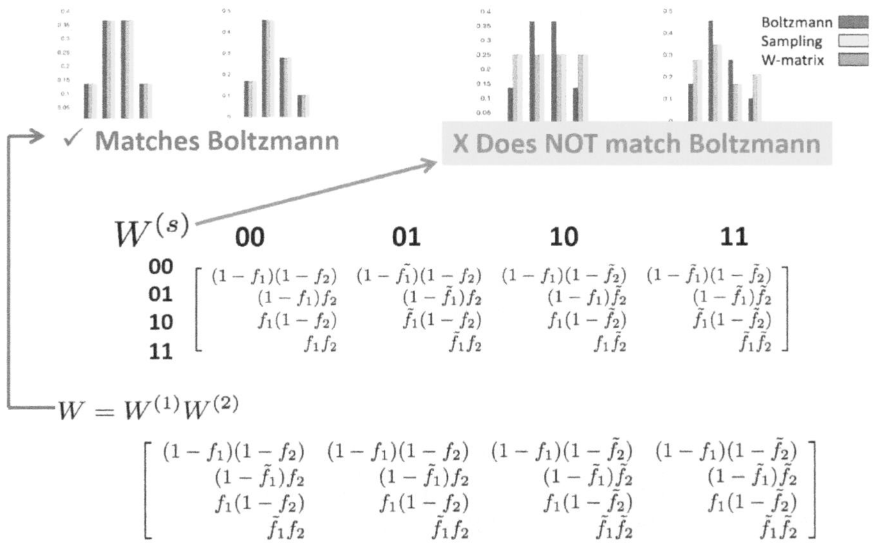

Fig. 4.25 Sequential update.

We saw earlier that sequential updating works very well irrespective of the order, you could do $W^{(1)}$, $W^{(2)}$ or $W^{(2)}W^{(1)}$, in either case it matches Boltzmann very nicely. But simultaneous updating does not. So you might wonder, well, how do the W matrices compare for these two updating schemes? Why is it that one's working beautifully and the other is not working? And you'll notice the differences are pretty subtle.

You see if you actually took our $W^{(1)}$ and $W^{(2)}$ and multiplied them out you'd get something looking a little different from $W^{(s)}$. The basic structure is very similar, but it is just that the tildes are in different places. These are subtle differences and yet they lead to a major difference in the stationary distributions.

4.3.3.2 Fig. 4.26

Now you might have noticed that the difference between the sequential $W^{(1)}W^{(2)}$ and the simultaneous $W^{(s)}$ comes from the difference between

f_1 and $\widetilde{f_1}$ which comes from the interaction term w_{12}. What would happen if the interaction was 0?

The answer is, if we set w, this interaction matrix, to 0, sure enough, even the simultaneous update will match the Boltzmann nicely because then you see this is kind of the trivial situation, where you have a whole bunch of *p-bits* that don't know about each other. In that case, it really doesn't matter whether you updated them sequentially or all simultaneously, they're all independent anyway.

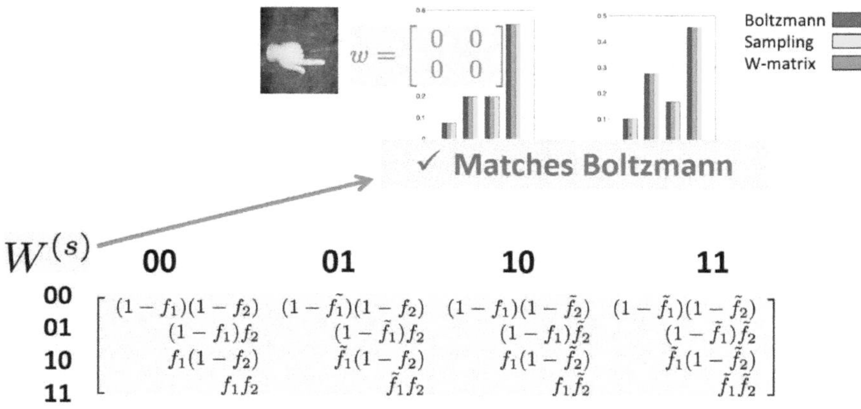

Fig. 4.26 Simultaneous update works for unconnected *p-bits*.

4.3.4 *Fig. 4.27: Restricted Boltzmann machine*

Now, one can make use of this fact that unconnected *p-bits* can be updated simultaneously, to architect Boltzmann networks in a way that allows updates to be performed much faster than one could otherwise. The idea is to bunch all the *p-bits* in two groups, the A group and the B group. And there is no connection internally among the A group and no connection internally among the B group, but there's lots of connection between the two groups. So when I look at the weight matrix, it has zero connections between A and A or B and B. But, it has all the connections going B to A and A to B.

What's the advantage? Well what this means is now I can update all *p-bits* in Group A simultaneously because they have no connections amongst

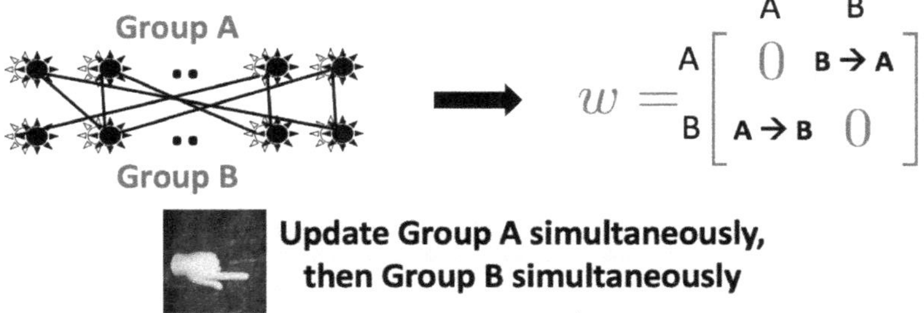

Fig. 4.27 Restricted Boltzmann machine (RBM).

them and so whether it's simultaneous or sequential doesn't really matter. Similarly I can update all of Group B simultaneously.

This is a big advantage because if you had 1 million *p-bits* half in Group A, half in Group B it means you could update half a million at a time. And then go on to the other half a million and back and forth. This can speed up the update process enormously and so practical Boltzmann machines often use this restricted architecture.

4.3.5 *Quiz*

The transition matrix for updating one spin in a network of 2 spins is

$$W = \begin{bmatrix} 1-f_1 & 0 & 1-f_1 & 0 \\ 0 & 1-\widetilde{f_1} & 0 & 1-\widetilde{f_1} \\ f_1 & 0 & f_1 & 0 \\ 0 & \widetilde{f_1} & 0 & \widetilde{f_1} \end{bmatrix}$$

4.3.5.1 *Question 1*

How should we time sample a system of spins all connected to each other (all $w_{ij} = w_{ji} \neq 0$), such that the samples follow the Boltzmann distribution?[6]

4.3.5.2 *Question 2*

For simultaneous updating of a system of 2 spins, the transition matrix is given by $W =$

$$\begin{bmatrix} (1-f_1)(1-f_2) & (1-\widetilde{f_1})(1-f_2) & (1-f_1)(1-\widetilde{f_2}) & (1-\widetilde{f_1})(1-\widetilde{f_2}) \\ (1-f_1)f_2 & (1-\widetilde{f_1})f_2 & (1-f_1)\widetilde{f_2} & (1-\widetilde{f_1})\widetilde{f_2} \\ f_1(1-f_2) & \widetilde{f_1}(1-f_2) & f_1(1-\widetilde{f_2}) & \widetilde{f_1}(1-\widetilde{f_2}) \\ f_1 f_2 & \widetilde{f_1} f_2 & f_1\widetilde{f_2} & \widetilde{f_1}\widetilde{f_2} \end{bmatrix}$$

Suppose the energies of the 00, 01, 10 and 11 states are such that $f_1 = f_2 \approx 1$ and $\widetilde{f_1}\widetilde{f_2} \approx 0$. If the system starts out in the 00 state, how will it behave thereafter?[7]

---

[6]Sample one at a time in any order.

[7]It will go to 11, then come back to 00, then oscillate back and forth.

4.4 Bayesian Networks

This is Lecture 4.4: Watch youtube video

In this Chapter we started by defining this transition matrix $[W]p = p$ and showing how you could get the stationary probability distribution from that matrix. Then we spend the next two lectures talking about this sampling technique and writing down the transition matrix and discussing why certain updating sequences work whereas the simultaneous updating doesn't work, if the nodes are connected.

4.4.1 *Figs. 4.28-4.35: Bayesian versus reciprocal networks*

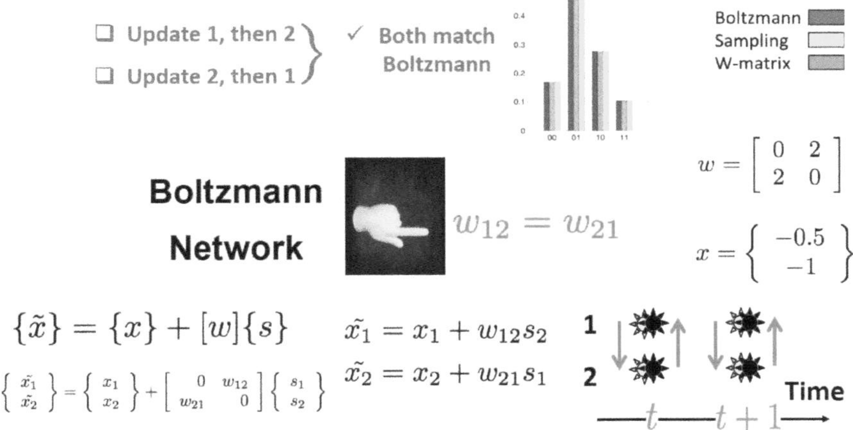

Fig. 4.28 Boltzmann network.

What we'll do in this lecture is we'll talk about a different kind of network, see, which is different from the Boltzmann networks that we have been talking about. In this network, the connections are one way. By contrast, Boltzmann networks are always reciprocal, if there's a w_{12}, there's a w_{21} and they are equal.

4.4.1.1 *Figs. 4.29-4.30: Bayesian networks*

Bayesian networks are directed. So, w_{12} is 0, but w_{21} is nonzero (see Fig. 4.29) and such networks are quite widely used particularly because

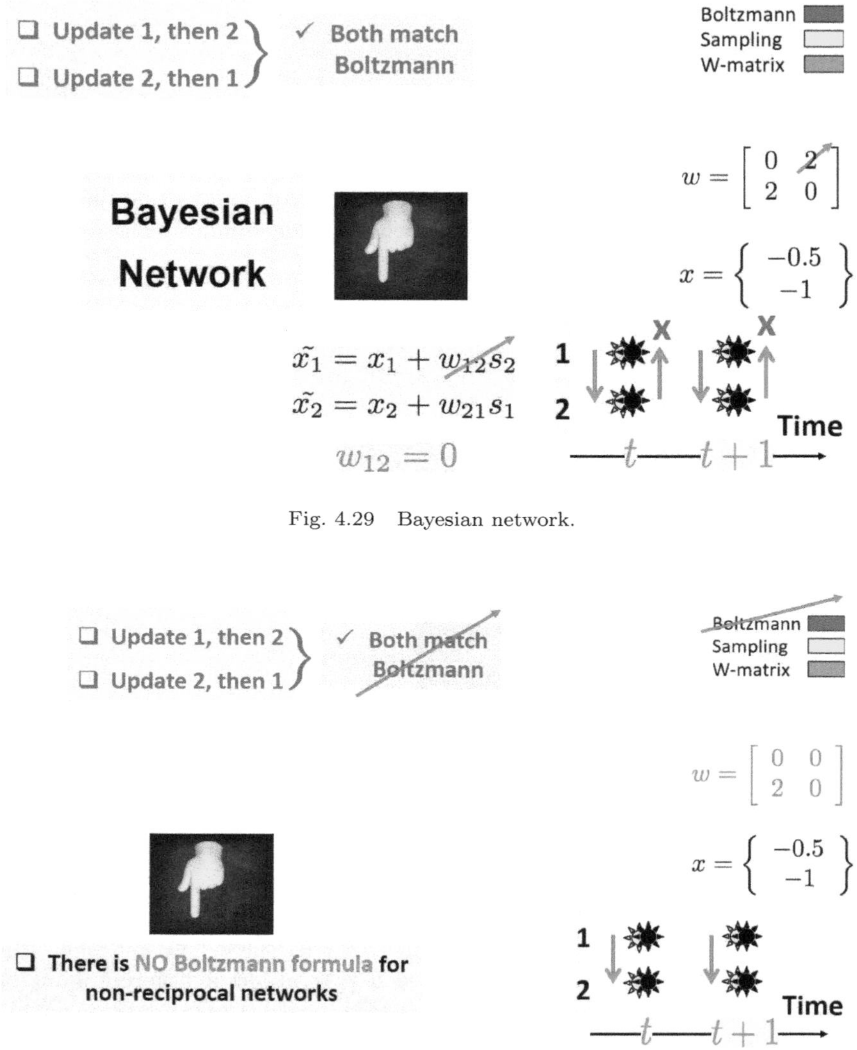

Fig. 4.29 Bayesian network.

Fig. 4.30 Bayesian network.

they are much easier to train than the Boltzmann networks we have focused on. In this lecture I'd like to say a few words about this type of network.

So first point about these networks is that there is no obvious Boltzmann formula. You see this whole Boltzmann approach, is based on the concept of an energy function. If the connection is not reciprocal, then there is no simple way to write an energy function.

We have talked about three methods the Boltzmann method, the sampling method, and the transition matrix method. As we'll see, the sampling method and the W matrix method they still agree very well. That is, the transition matrix method does give a very good description of how the sampling method works, that's fine, although there is no Boltzmann to compare to.

4.4.1.2 *Fig. 4.31*

So if you use the sampling method or the transition matrix method they both give the same answer. But the answer is different depending on the sequence of updating. You see with Boltzmann networks it doesn't matter which way you update. It could be 1 and then 2 or it could be 2 and then 1. But now the answers will be different.

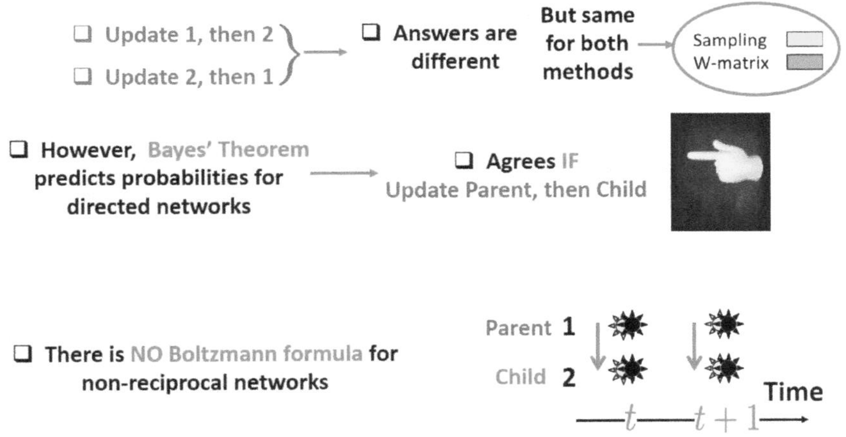

Fig. 4.31 Bayesian network.

What do we compare these answers to? We don't have Boltzmann but there is a Bayes' theorem that allows you to predict the probabilities for directed networks and the answer that you get will match Bayes' theorem if you update it in the order of parent to child. You see in Bayesian networks, you can identify parent nodes and child nodes who are influenced by their parents. The correct way of sampling is one that gives results that agree with Bayes' theorem, which generally describes phenomena in the real world very well. And to agree with Bayes' theorem, the updating order should be first parent, then child.

Let's talk about these points one by one.

4.4.1.3 *Fig. 4.32: Why no energy function*

So first point is, why is there no energy function for non reciprocal networks? Well, if you write down the energy function like let's say with two *p-bits*, you'll get a set of terms looking like this, $\widetilde{E} = s_1x_1 + s_2x_2 + (1/2)w_{12}s_1s_2 + (1/2)w_{21}s_1s_2$, and we'll notice how w_{12} and w_{21} are kind of part of the same term.

Now let's calculate this synaptic functions you know the $\widetilde{x}_1$ that determines the updating of *p-bit* 1, or $\widetilde{x}_2$ which determines the updating of *p-bit* 2. The way you're supposed to do it is by taking the derivative of the energy function with respect to s_1 or s_2: $\partial\widetilde{E}/\partial s_1$ or $\partial\widetilde{E}/\partial s_2$. And if you just go from an energy function, you get the same factor in both places, $\widetilde{x}_1 = x_1 + ((w_{12} + w_{21})/2)s_2$ and $\widetilde{x}_2 = x_2 + ((w_{12} + w_{21})/2)s_1$.

This is not really an accident. It's kind of inevitable if you're starting from an energy function. because $\partial\widetilde{x}_1/\partial s_2 = \partial\widetilde{x}_2/\partial s_2 = \partial^2\widetilde{E}/\partial s_1\partial s_2$. So usually, you cannot start from an energy function and get a directed network out of it, and if you don't have an energy function, you don't have a Boltzmann formula either.

$$\tilde{E} = s^T x + \frac{1}{2}\, s^T w s$$
$$= s_1x_1 + s_2x_2 + \frac{1}{2}w_{12}s_1s_2 + \frac{1}{2}w_{21}s_1s_2$$

$$\frac{\partial\tilde{x}_1}{\partial s_2} = \frac{w_{12}+w_{21}}{2} = \frac{\partial^2\tilde{E}}{\partial s_2\partial s_1}$$
$$\frac{\partial\tilde{x}_2}{\partial s_1} = \frac{w_{12}+w_{21}}{2} = \frac{\partial^2\tilde{E}}{\partial s_1\partial s_2}$$

$$\tilde{x}_1 = \tilde{E}(s_1=1) - \tilde{E}(s_1=0) = \frac{\partial\tilde{E}}{\partial s_1} = x_1 + \frac{w_{12}+w_{21}}{2}s_2$$
$$\tilde{x}_2 = \tilde{E}(s_2=1) - \tilde{E}(s_2=0) = \frac{\partial\tilde{E}}{\partial s_2} = x_2 + \frac{w_{12}+w_{21}}{2}s_1$$

❑ **There is NO Boltzmann formula for non-reciprocal networks**

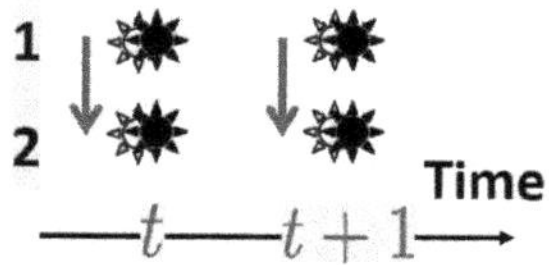

Fig. 4.32 Why no energy function.

4.4.1.4 *Fig. 4.33*

One thing we could do is forget about energy, and just start from the synaptic equations getting rid of the term $w_{12}s_2$ while keeping $w_{21}s_1$ since the weight term acts only one way.

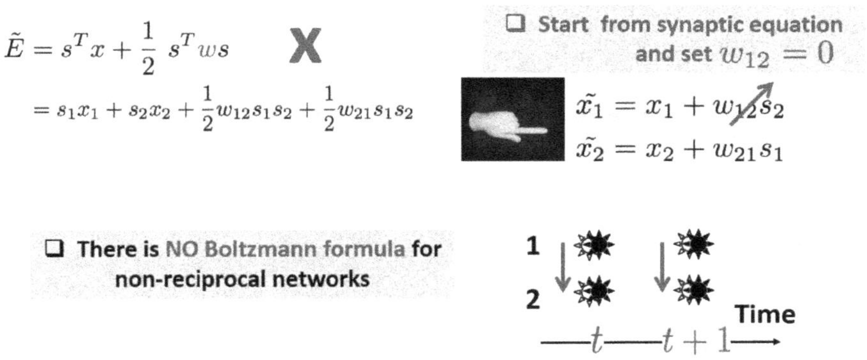

$$\tilde{E} = s^T x + \frac{1}{2} s^T w s$$

$$= s_1 x_1 + s_2 x_2 + \frac{1}{2} w_{12} s_1 s_2 + \frac{1}{2} w_{21} s_1 s_2$$

❑ Start from synaptic equation and set $w_{12} = 0$

$$\tilde{x_1} = x_1 + w_{12} s_2$$

$$\tilde{x_2} = x_2 + w_{21} s_1$$

❑ There is NO Boltzmann formula for non-reciprocal networks

1

2

Time

t — $t+1$

Fig. 4.33 Synaptic functions without an energy function.

4.4.1.5 *Fig. 4.34*

You could use the $[W]$ matrix method, to emulate both update orders for the sampling process. It could be 1 and then 2 or 2 and then 1, and in either case we can write down a composite W matrix just as we did in the last lecture (Fig. 4.22). It's just that we drop the w_{12} but keep the w_{21} as shown.

4.4.1.6 *Fig. 4.35*

Here we show two problems, one reciprocal with $w_{12} = 2, w_{21} = 2$, and one non-reciprocal $w_{12} = 0, w_{21} = 2$ and compare the results from direct sampling and from the eigenvectors of the W matrix. In either case, the sampling method and the $[W]$ matrix method they agree, showing that the $[W]$ matrix method describes the sampling process for different networks quite well.

But the point to note is that the update order makes no difference to the reciprocal network, but does make a difference to the Bayesian one. But which one is more correct? With Boltzmann networks, we could have

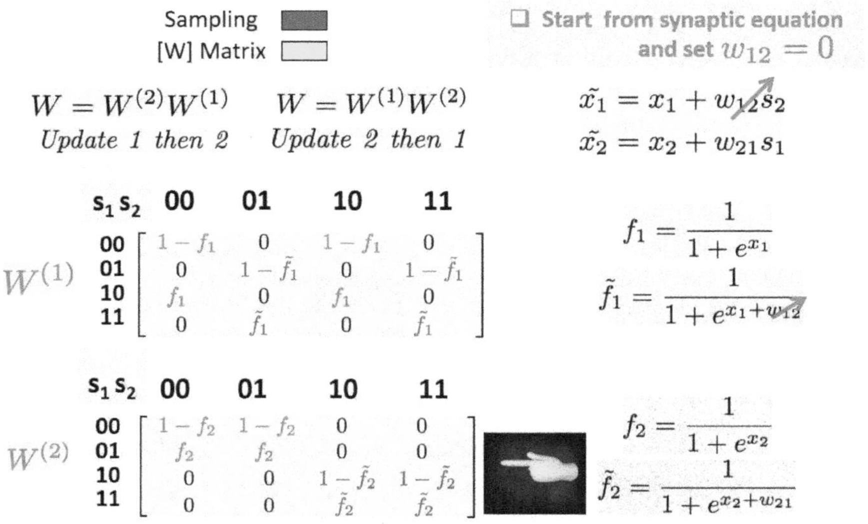

Sampling
[W] Matrix

❑ Start from synaptic equation and set $w_{12} = 0$

$W = W^{(2)}W^{(1)}$ *Update 1 then 2*

$W = W^{(1)}W^{(2)}$ *Update 2 then 1*

$$\tilde{x}_1 = x_1 + w_{12}s_2$$
$$\tilde{x}_2 = x_2 + w_{21}s_1$$

$$W^{(1)} = \begin{array}{c|cccc} s_1s_2 & 00 & 01 & 10 & 11 \\ \hline 00 & 1-f_1 & 0 & 1-f_1 & 0 \\ 01 & 0 & 1-\tilde{f}_1 & 0 & 1-\tilde{f}_1 \\ 10 & f_1 & 0 & f_1 & 0 \\ 11 & 0 & \tilde{f}_1 & 0 & \tilde{f}_1 \end{array}$$

$$f_1 = \frac{1}{1+e^{x_1}} \qquad \tilde{f}_1 = \frac{1}{1+e^{x_1+w_{12}}}$$

$$W^{(2)} = \begin{array}{c|cccc} s_1s_2 & 00 & 01 & 10 & 11 \\ \hline 00 & 1-f_2 & 1-f_2 & 0 & 0 \\ 01 & f_2 & f_2 & 0 & 0 \\ 10 & 0 & 0 & 1-\tilde{f}_2 & 1-\tilde{f}_2 \\ 11 & 0 & 0 & \tilde{f}_2 & \tilde{f}_2 \end{array}$$

$$f_2 = \frac{1}{1+e^{x_2}} \qquad \tilde{f}_2 = \frac{1}{1+e^{x_2+w_{21}}}$$

Fig. 4.34 [W] matrix.

compared to the Boltzmann result, but for Bayesian networks, what do we compare to? Answer: Bayes' theorem which we will talk about next.

4.4.2 *Figs. 4.36-4.37: Bayes theorem*

In a Bayesian network you have a parent node that influences the child node and the way you should do it is, you should first write down the parent distribution because that doesn't depend on anybody else and then use Bayes' theorem to write the overall probabilities. This should get clearer once we look at our simple example.

In our problem, we first note that the state of the parent (*p-bit* 1) is determined solely by its bias x_1 irrespective of the state of the child. So $P(s_1 = 0) = 1 - f_1$ and $P(s_1 = f_1)$, where $f_1 = 1/(1 + exp(x_1))$.

Next, suppose I want to know probability of 00. We first take the probability that the parent is 0 and then multiply it by the probability that the *child is 0 given that the parent is 0*: $P(00) = P(s_2 = 0)|_{s_1=0}P(s_1 = 0)$. This is basically the Bayes' theorem that we are talking about.

So what is the probability that this child is 0 given that the parent is 0? Given that the parent is 0 means s_1 equal to 0. So then the $\tilde{x}_2$ is just x_2 and so the state of the child is determined by $f_2 = 1/(1 + \exp x_2)$.

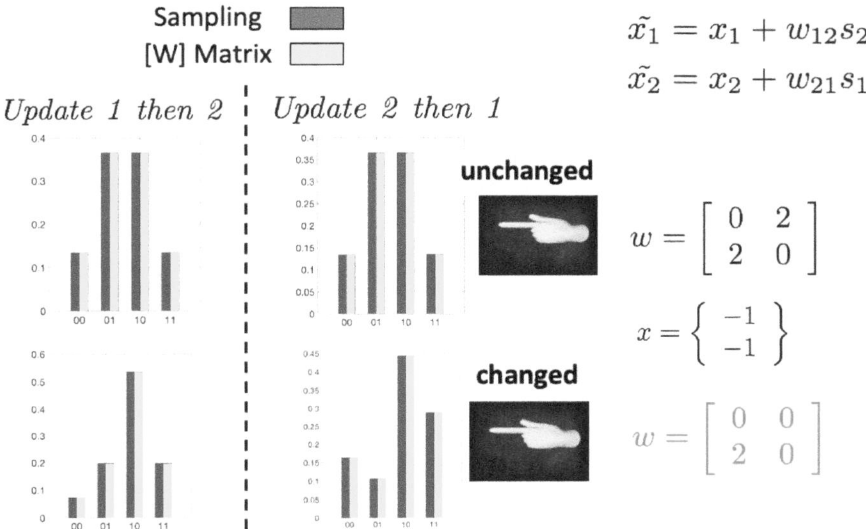

Fig. 4.35 Bayesian versus reciprocal networks.

$$f_1 = \frac{1}{1+e^{x_1}} \quad f_2 = \frac{1}{1+e^{x_2}} \quad \tilde{f}_2 = \frac{1}{1+e^{x_2+w_{21}}}$$

PARENT CHILD

$$P(00) + P(01) = 1 - f_1$$
$$P(10) + P(11) = f_1$$

PARENT pdf
is independent
of CHILD

Use Bayes Theorem
to write composite pdf

$$\tilde{x}_1 = x_1 + w_{12}s_2$$
$$\tilde{x}_2 = x_2 + w_{21}s_1$$

$$P(00) = \overbrace{P(s_2=0)\big|_{s_1=0}}^{1-f_2} \times \underbrace{P(s_1=0)}$$
$$P(01) = \overbrace{P(s_2=1)\big|_{s_1=0}}^{f_2} \times \overbrace{P(s_1=0)}^{1-f_1}$$
$$P(10) = \overbrace{P(s_2=0)\big|_{s_1=1}}^{1-\tilde{f}_2} \times \underbrace{P(s_1=1)}$$
$$P(11) = \overbrace{P(s_2=1)\big|_{s_1=1}}^{\tilde{f}_2} \times \overbrace{P(s_1=1)}^{f_1}$$

Fig. 4.36 Bayes theorem.

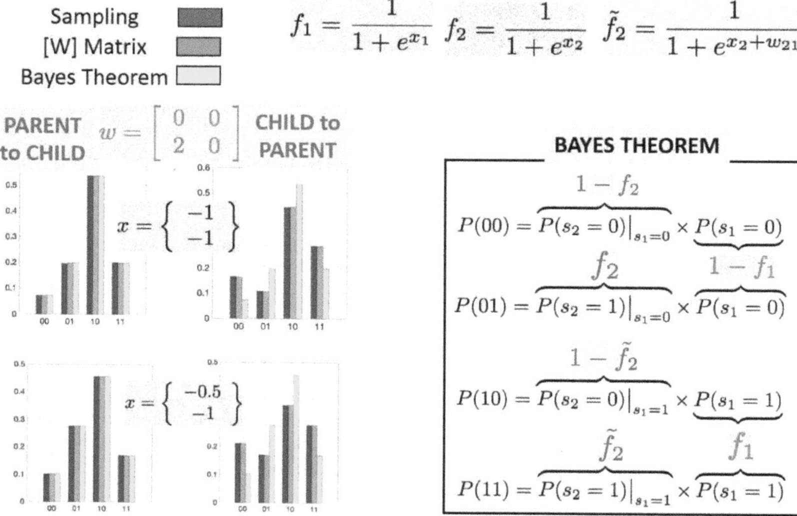

Fig. 4.37 Bayes theorem.

The probability the child is 0 is $1 - f_2$. And so overall $P(00)$ is $P(00) = (1 - f_2)(1 - f_1)$.

Similary you can fill up $P(01)$, $P(10)$ and $P(11)$ as shown. So the basic procedure, remember, parent you can write right away, and then you have to find the child using these conditional probabilities. Okay, so that's the Bayes theorem.

Now if you compare what you get from sampling and from $[W]$ matrix method with Bayes theorem, we see in this problem very clearly that when you update from parent to child, they match beautifully. When you update from child to parent, the sampling and the $[W]$ matrix agree as we had discussed, but not with Bayes' theorem (see Fig. 4.37)

So, this is the basic point we want to get across here that when it comes to directed networks, the order of update indeed matters and when you do things parent to child, they work very well. When you do child to parent, it doesn't agree with Bayes' theorem.

4.4.3 *Quiz*

4.4.3.1 *Question 1*

How should we time sample a system of spins all with directed connections (all $w_{ij} \neq 0, w_{ji} = 0$), such that the samples follow the Bayes rule?[8]

4.4.3.2 *Question 2*

Suppose we have a network of 2 spins labeled 00, 01, 10, 11 in the order $\{Parent \;\; Child\}$. The Parent node is equally likely to be 0 or 1, while the child node is exactly the opposite of the parent node. According to Bayes theorem, what are the probabilities of {00 01 10 11}?[9]

[8] The spins are updated one at a time in parent-child order.

[9] {0 0.5 0.5 0}.

4.5 Feynman Paths

This is Lecture 4.5: Watch youtube video

4.5.1 *Figs. 4.38-4.42: Multiplying W-matrices*

4.5.1.1 *Fig. 4.38: Why W-matrix?*

One of the reasons I'm spending so much time on this $[W]$ matrix method is because it gives you a deeper understanding of how this whole sampling technique works. But from a practical sense though, you could say that, well, the Boltzmann law needed a 2^n space to work on, which was unwieldy. But the $[W]$ matrix, it is a 2^n by 2^n matrix. Now, such a huge unwieldy matrix, is it really useful? Well, one use is just understanding how sampling works, but the other use is, it gives you a nice physical picture, which also provides this conceptual bridge to quantum computing and that's what this lecture is about. It's based on this concept of Feynman paths.

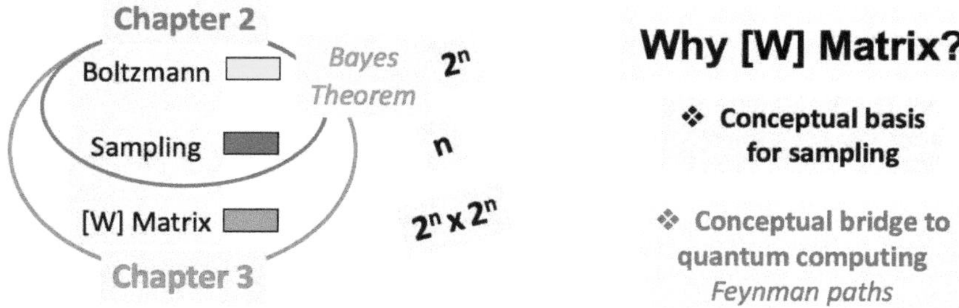

Fig. 4.38 Why $[W]$ matrix?

4.5.1.2 *Fig. 4.39*

Now, as you remember, the way I introduced this $[W]$ matrix, is that it is the matrix which propagates a probability distribution function, from one time point to the next. Now, for this lecture I'd like to generalize this a little bit. And that is to note that firstly, you see the components of $[W]$ as we have seen depends on this bias matrix and the weight matrix, x and w, and these could in principle be changing with time.

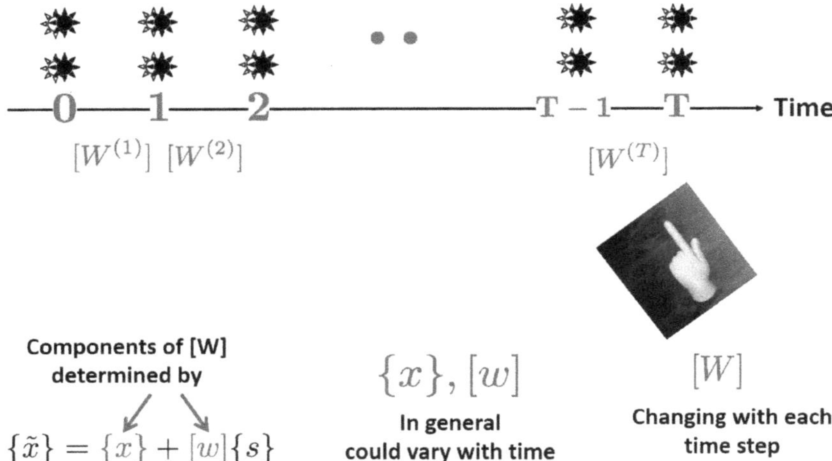

Fig. 4.39 [W] matrix.

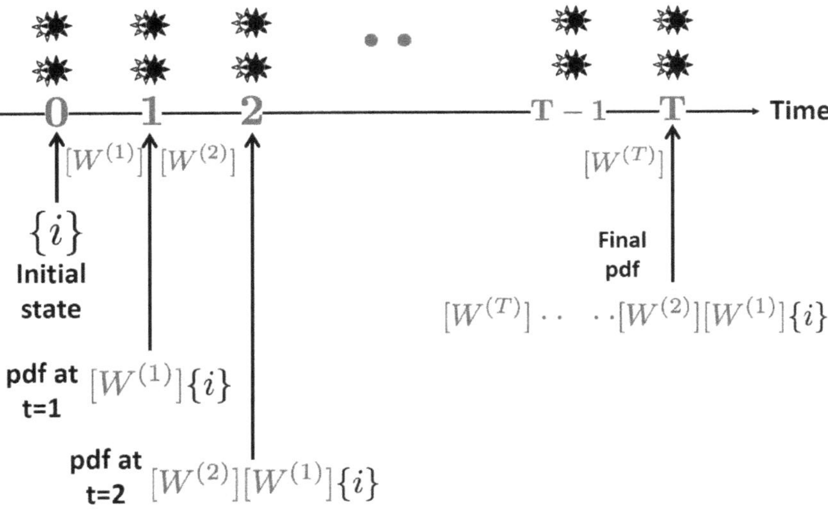

Fig. 4.40 [W] matrix.

So all these capital [W]'s don't have to be the same, they could be different, it could be evolving with a different bias, or a different weight matrix. So going forward, what I'll do is I'll put a superscript on top, 1,

2, up to T. Where this $[W^{(1)}]$ is the transition matrix for step one, this $[W^{(2)}]$ is the transition matrix for step two, and so on until step T, $[W^{(\mathrm{T})}]$.

4.5.1.3 *Fig. 4.40*

Now, If I start with some initial state, what happens is the probability distribution function at time 1 is equal to this $[W^{(1)}]$, times the initial distribution i. Again, you go on to time 2, and you will have a product of $[W^{(1)}]$ and $[W^{(2)}]$. And then in the end, after a long time T, you'd have multiplied it out by all these matrices one by one, $[W^{(1)}]$, $[W^{(2)}]$, all the way up to $[W^{(\mathrm{T})}]$, and so this i is the initial distribution. Then you have multiplied it out, and that's how you get final probability distribution function.

4.5.1.4 *Figs. 4.41-4.42*

Now, just look at a numerical example, a two *p-bit* system which has four configurations, 00, 01, 10, and 11. Suppose you're starting it out in the 00 state, which means the initial distribution looks like $\{1000\}$.

Now, after we apply the $[W]$, and here I just took some numerical values corresponding to certain parameters that I used. It's from one of the examples we had discussed earlier, and you see that the distribution which was originally 100% (00) has now spread out, it is now 7% (00), 20% (01), 53% (10), and 20% (11).

You apply again, the distribution has again changed, 12%, 33%, 40%, 15%, and of course when you add them up, it's 100%, since it's a probability distribution.

4.5.1.5 *Fig. 4.42*

Now, after some time, after you've applied the same $[W]$ a few times, it gets to a stationary state, which is actually the Boltzmann distribution, 13% for (00) and (11), and a higher percentage like 37% for (01) and (10) each. So that's how you would gradually evolve to this final state.

So if you wanted to now know that well, I started in (00), but what is the probability that I'll end up in (01)? The answer is 37%. What is the probability I'll end up in (11)? Well, it's 13%. So basically then if you want to know the probability that you'll be in state f, if you have started from i, then what you should do is look at the f component in the final distribution: $P_{f\leftarrow i} = \left[[W^{(\mathrm{T})}]\cdots[W^{(2)}][W^{(1)}]\{i\}\right]_f$.

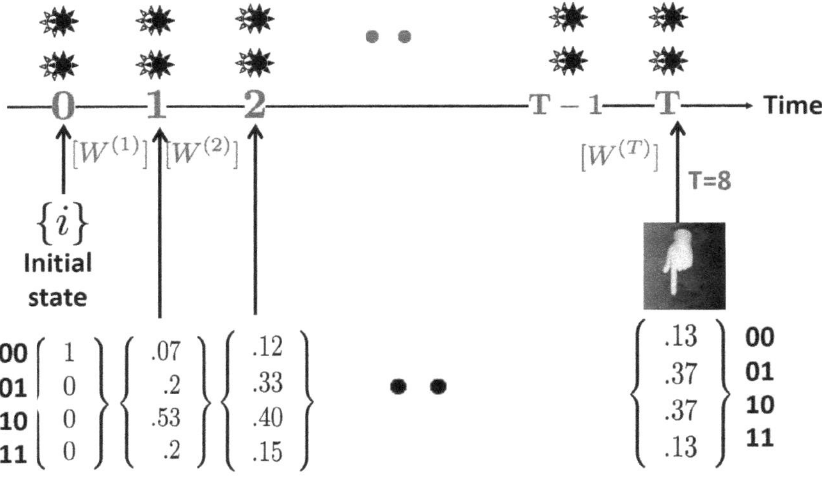

Fig. 4.41 [W] matrix.

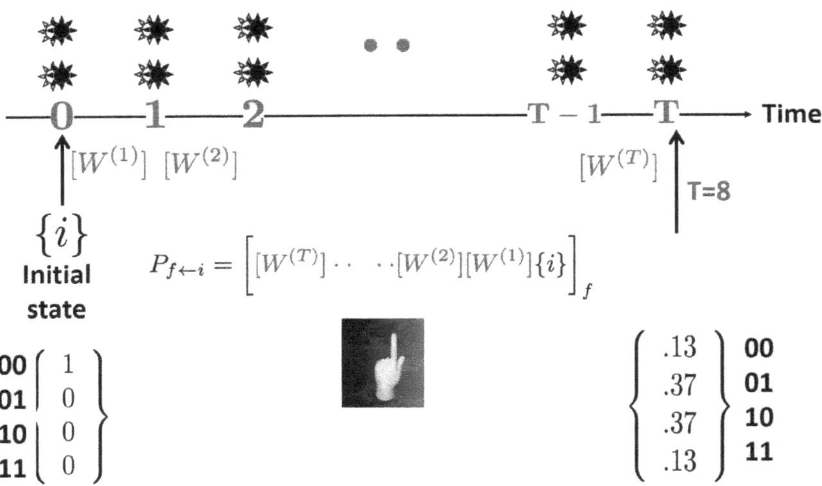

Fig. 4.42 [W] matrix.

4.5.2 *Figs. 4.43-4.45: Matrix multiplication as sum over paths*

Now, we are going to make use of the *rule of matrix multiplication.* So what we have here is a string of matrices that are getting multiplied. The rule for matrix multiplication says that when you say take $[AB]$, and you want to know the ij element of the product, it is like $A_{ia}B_{aj}$, and you have to sum over all a: $[AB]_{ij} = \sum_a A_{ia}B_{aj}$. This is the basic rule of matrix multiplication. So every time you multiply two matrices, you pick up a summation.

In our problem you see I want the final probability of i to f. And what I would have done is, a string of these summations, one for each multiplication essentially. So you'd have a_1, and then a_2, and then a_3, one after the other, up to a_{T-1}, and all these multiplied, and the first index here will be i, that's the state you start it from, initial state, and the last index will be f, that's the state you end up in. So this is a purely mathematical expansion of this matrix multiplication, but the reason I'm doing it is, it gives you a very interesting way of viewing this whole sampling procedure, and how we think about these things.

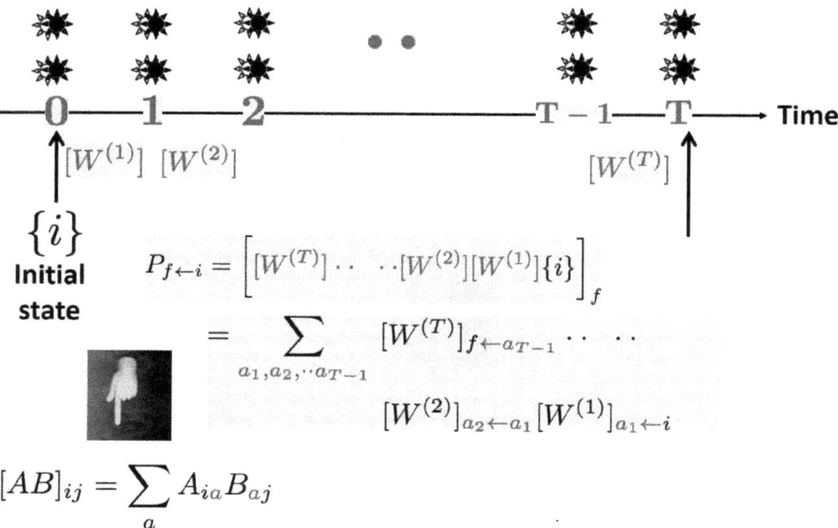

Fig. 4.43 [W] matrix multiplication involves summing over intermediate states.

4.5.2.1 *Fig. 4.44*

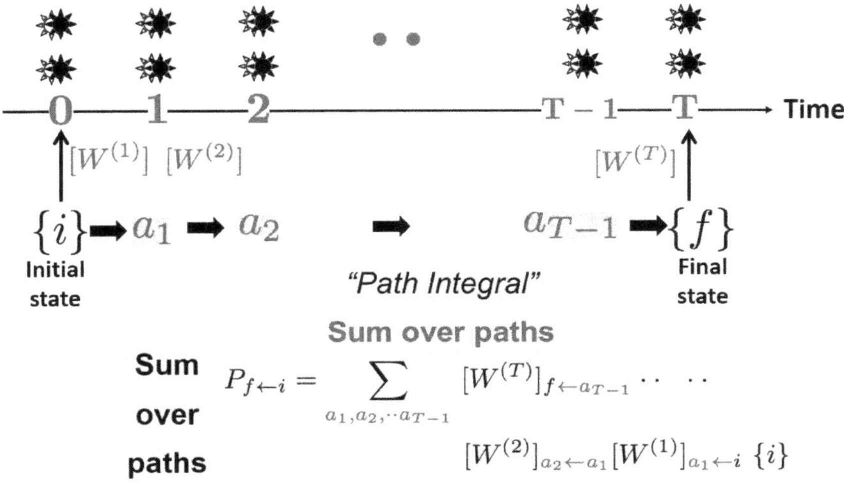

Fig. 4.44 [W] matrix.

So this is what you could call a relatively simple special case of the Feynman path integral. We can write the overall probability, as a sum over paths, that is, this summation $P_{f\leftarrow i} = \sum_{a_1,a_2,\ldots,a_{T-1}}[W^{(T)}]_{f\leftarrow a_{T-1}}\cdots [W^{(2)}]_{a_2\leftarrow a_1}[W^{(1)}]_{a_1\leftarrow i}\{i\}$.

Why sum over paths?

Well, you see, you could view this a_1, a_2, etc, as intermediate states. In the sense you could think of it this way, that I started from $\{i\}$, and I have a probability of going to different states in the middle, a_1 is one such state, this could be 00, 01, 10, and 11, a_2 again could be 00, 01, 10, 11, etc. So if I put down a specific one, then I have a specific path. So this is one possible path from i to f, and that path has a certain probability, which is obtained by multiplying out the corresponding elements of your [W] matrix. But then there is, of course many, many paths, why? Because at each stage I've got four possibilities. So as you go down the list, you have so many possibilities, so many paths, a very large number of paths, and each one has a certain probability and the overall probability that we observe is a sum of the probabilities over all those paths.

4.5.2.2 *Fig. 4.45*

Now, how do you actually calculate them? Well, it's probably much more convenient to multiply out the matrices if you could have written them down, but then they are huge matrices. So what we are really doing in our sampling methods is we're saying look, doing this entire summation by multiplying matrices, that's impossible, that's too hard.

So instead what we'll do is, we'll try to find which ones are the paths with the highest probabilities, and we'll add them up and hopefully, that will get us close enough to the correct answer. So these different algorithms for sampling, like the Metropolis algorithm or Gibbs sampling, all of these in the end I think are saying that, I can't do this summation exactly, but I'll try to have an algorithm, so that I pick out the ones with the highest probabilities and then I'll sum them up, and try to get to the right answer.

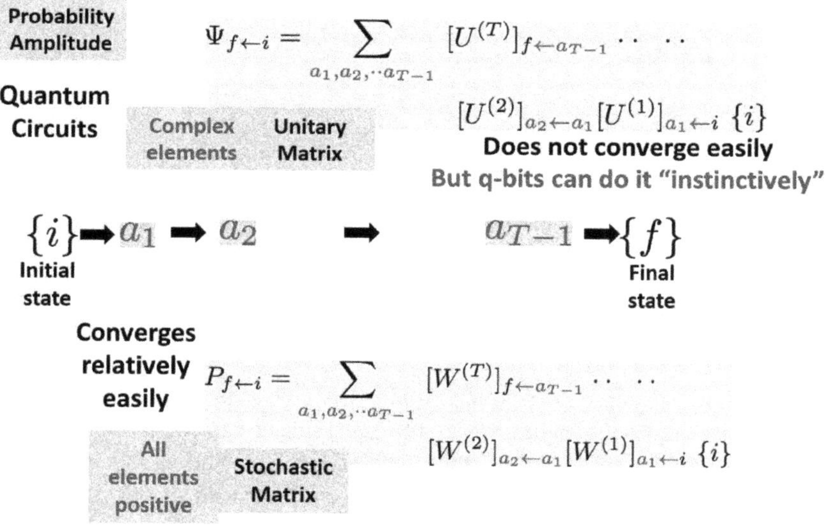

Fig. 4.45 Sum over paths.

But one important conceptual value of this view is in connecting to the quantum world. As we will see in Chapter 6, quantum problems are described by a quantum transition matrix U which is of size $2^n \times 2^n$ just like the classical counterpart W we have been discussing. However, unlike W, it's elements are not positive numbers but are complex numbers and instead of the probability distribution P we have a complex probability amplitude or wavefunction ψ whose squared magnitude gives the probability.

But the mathematics is very similar and we can express the final wavefunction as a sum over Feynman paths. Indeed you will see this concept of Feynman paths more often in the context of quantum problems. But there's a very big difference, between adding probabilities and adding probability amplitudes. Probabilities are always positive and so when you add them up, they tend to converge relatively easily, because it's all positive numbers that you're adding up. But if you're adding complex numbers or even numbers that are both positive and negative, you can get a small number by adding and subtracting huge numbers, like if you had $+100$ and -99 and they give you 1, that's a harder number to get it right, because you miss one sample, and you get a totally wrong answer.

So these things don't converge easily, and that is where the strength of quantum computing lies. Quantum bits or q-bits can actually do these summations "instinctively". It is as if they kind of sense all these paths and add up their complex amplitudes, and behave accordingly. A classical sampling algorithm in order to figure out all these cancellations, would actually have to sum many, many samples to get it right. The challenge of quantum computing, however, is that in order to sum complex amplitudes accurately it needs stringent control of the phase of different paths, and there is a worldwide effort to achieve that with different physical representations of q-bits. By contrast, *p-bits* can be built with existing technology operating at room temperature.

4.5.3 *Quiz*

4.5.3.1 *Question 1*

A system with just one spin has a transition matrix given by $W = \begin{bmatrix} 0.1 & 0.3 \\ 0.9 & 0.7 \end{bmatrix}$

It evolves from an initial state 0 at t, to a final state at $t+2$ after 2 time steps. What is the probability that it took the path $0 \to 1 \to 1$?[10]

4.5.3.2 *Question 2*

A system of three spins evolves from an intial state 000 at t to a final state 111 at $t+10$ after ten steps. How many Feynman paths leading from an initial 0 to a final 1.[11]

4.5.3.3 *Question 3*

A system of four spins evolves from an intial state 0000 at t to a final state 1111 at $t+10$ after ten steps. How many Feynman paths leading from an initial 0 to a final 1.[12]

---

[10] $0.9 \times 0.7 = 0.63$.
[11] 8^9.
[12] 16^9.

4.6 Fig. 4.46: 5-minute Summary

This is Chapter 4 summary: Watch youtube video, after 2:05

In week 3, we introduced this transition matrix method. In Chapter 3 we had these two methods, namely the direct Boltzmann probabilities, and the sampling method. Now, in Chapter 4 we have introduced a third method based on the transition matrix from which also you could calculate the stationary probability distribution. We first use it to discuss the sampling method, why it works, why it is important to update *p-bits* sequentially and not simultaneously. Then in the fourth lecture, we talked about the Bayesian networks which are widely used and behave very differently from the Boltzmann networks that we largely focus on.

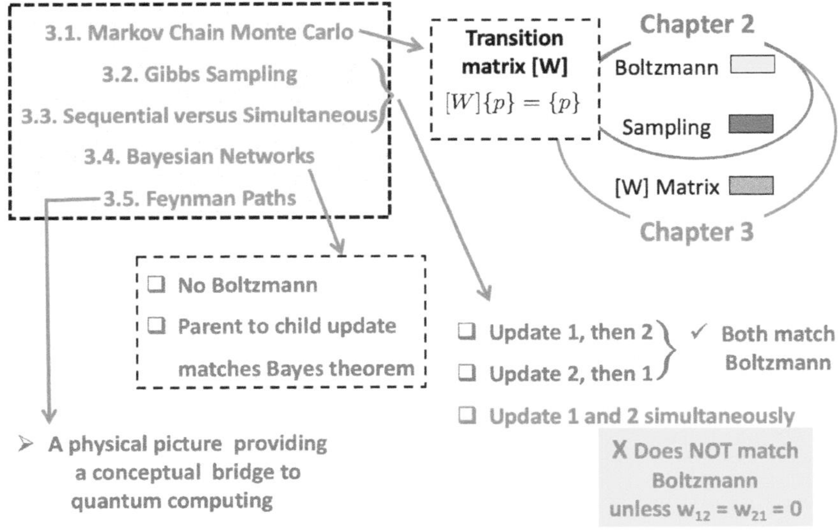

Fig. 4.46 Week 2.

Finally, we talked about Feynman paths which gives you a nice conceptual picture, of how to think about these probabilistic circuits using W matrices and it provides you a conceptual bridge to our next topic, which is about quantum computing where instead of probabilities evolving through stochastic W matrices, we have complex probability amplitudes or wavefunctions evolving through unitary U matrices.

Chapter 5

Quantum Boltzmann Law

5.1 Quantum Spins

This is Lecture 5.1: Watch youtube video

Now, Chapters 5 and 6, that's the quantum part of this course. Loosely speaking, they are the quantum counterparts of Chapters 3 and 4. Mathematically, as you'll see in this chapter we'll introduce this equation, which looks like a lot like the classical Boltzmann Law. It's just that instead of a probability distribution function, we have this density matrix. And instead of energy you have the energy matrix or the Hamiltonian.

And in chapter 6, we'll introduce this quantum transition matrix which loosely corresponds to the classical transition matrix, where you had a probability distribution function that evolved with time. Here you have a wave function that evolves with time. Anyway, so let's get started with the quantum Boltzmann law.

5.1.1 *Figs. 5.1-5.3: Classical spin*

5.1.1.1 *Fig. 5.1*

So how do you go from this Classical Boltzmann Law to what I call this Quantum Boltzmann Law? Now, in order to make this transition, it is convenient to start from the bipolar representation. If you remember in Lecture 3.4, we introduced this bipolar representation, which is equivalent to the binary representation which we commonly used in Chapters 3 and 4. In binary representation the spin has the values 1 and 0, whereas in the bipolar representation it has the values +1 and −1. Now, for the purposes of making this transformation to the Quantum Boltzmann law, the bipolar

Bipolar m = {+1,-1}

$$\tilde{E} = m^T h + \frac{1}{2} m^T J m$$

Lecture 2.4

Binary s = {1,0}

$$\tilde{E} = s^T x + \frac{1}{2} s^T w s$$

Fig. 5.1 Classical binary and bipolar representations.

one is more convenient, it corresponds more directly, okay? So this is where we'll start.

5.1.1.2 *Fig. 5.2*

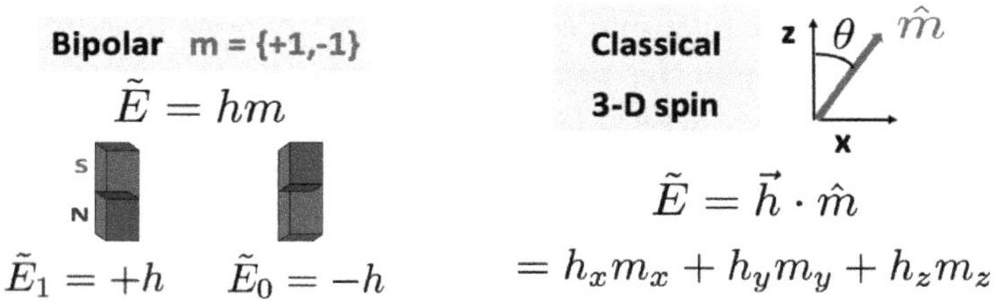

Bipolar m = {+1,-1}

$$\tilde{E} = hm$$

S N

$$\tilde{E}_1 = +h \qquad \tilde{E}_0 = -h$$

Classical 3-D spin

z θ $\hat{m}$ x

$$\tilde{E} = \vec{h} \cdot \hat{m}$$
$$= h_x m_x + h_y m_y + h_z m_z$$

Fig. 5.2 Classical bipolar spin versus 3-D spin.

Now, for starters, let's ignore this interaction term and just think of one spin, right? In Lectures 4 and 5 of this chapter we'll pick up the interactions. For the moment, let's just focus on one spin. But what we want to describe now is quantum spins. And the best example of that is a single electron because every electron is actually like a little magnet but it's a quantum magnet, as we mentioned in the Prologue, see Fig. 1.2. And what I'll try to describe in this lecture is what that means and how you describe it.

So this elementary magnet you might think, okay, I've got this electron it has no particular preferred direction. Unlike a magnet where you could say okay, this is the long axis. Well, the electron has no particular axis, it could point in any direction. And so you might say, well, what I really need to do is take my basic description that I had before and turn it into a 3D spin, something where the magnetization of the magnetic moment can have a three components m_x, m_y, and m_z, and instead of this one parameter h, allow her h_x and h_y and h_z. I could write the energy as say $\vec{h} \cdot \widehat{m}$.

But a quantum magnet is neither a classical bipolar magnet or a classical 3-D magnet, you could say it is something in-between.

5.1.1.3 *Fig. 5.3*

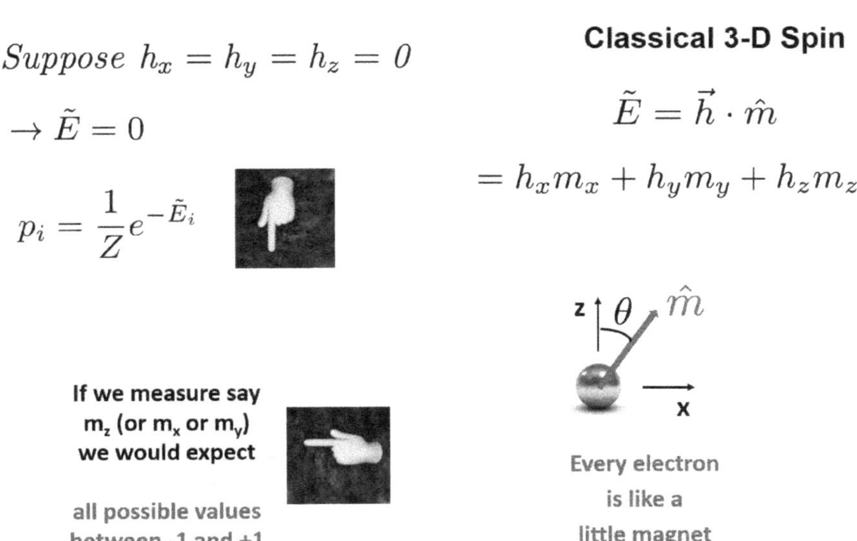

Fig. 5.3 What we expect to see for classical 3-D spin.

What would we expect to see if the electron were a 3-D classical spin? Suppose we put all h's equal to 0, then the energy is equal to 0, which means regardless of which direction this elementary magnet points, the energy is the same. And so you can apply Boltzmann Law and say, all directions have equal energy and hence equal probability. Well, so if I went in and measured a particular component of the spin or the magnetic moment, say the z-component or the x-component or the y-component, you'd think that you'd get all values between -1 and $+1$. Because after all the magnet could be pointing in any direction, and so z-component could have any value, between the extremes.

Fig. 5.4 Experiment shows that a quantum spin can point in any 3D direction, but any measurement will yield a bipolar result!

5.1.2 *Figs. 5.4-5.5: Quantum spins*

5.1.2.1 *Fig. 5.4*

Well, what 100 years ago, Stern and Gerlach reported this experiment, which essentially revolutionized our conception of electron (see Fig. 5.4), and what they showed was that when they measured m_x or m_z or m_y, there's only two values -1 and $+1$, not this continuous spectrum of values. In short, a quantum spin can point in any 3D direction, but any measurement will yield a bipolar result!

Of course, in science, facts come first, and so if the facts don't fit the math, then you have to change the math. So what is the new math that will fit the new facts?

5.1.2.2 *Fig. 5.5*

So that's how the quantum theory started. And in the quantum theory then, the m, this magnetic moment gets replaced by a operator $\vec{\sigma}$, which as you'll see is a 2×2 matrix. So instead of $\vec{h} \cdot \widehat{m}$, you write this energy matrix or what's called the Hamiltonian matrix H, which is $\vec{h} \cdot \vec{\sigma}$ (see Fig. 5.5).

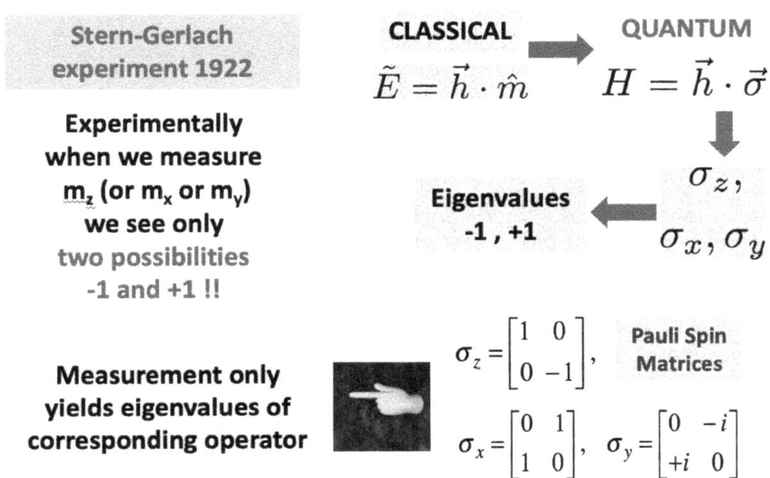

Fig. 5.5 Quantum spin.

Now, what is this $\vec{\sigma}$? Well, we have these three Pauli spin matrices, one corresponding to each direction, σ_z, σ_x and σ_y, and these are the three matrices and so $\vec{h} \cdot \vec{\sigma}$ means $h_x\sigma_x + h_y\sigma_y + h_z\sigma_z$ and when you measure any quantity, let's say you want to know, I measured m_z, what values will I get? And the answer is the measurement will only yield eigenvalues of the corresponding operator. So what are the eigenvalues?

Well, for σ_z since its diagonal, it's easy to see the eigenvalues it's $+1$ and -1, whatever is on the diagonal. But what about σ_x? Well, it's not as easy to see, but you can check for the eigenvalues and the answer is still $+1$ and -1 (see Fig. 5.5). And if you look at σ_y, it looks different, but here too the eigenvalues are $+1$ and -1. So whether you measure m_z or m_x or m_y, what you'll measure will be the eigenvalues of the corresponding operator and those are -1 and $+1$. And that obviously fits the fact here.

5.1.3 *Fig. 5.6: Density matrix*

Now, quantitatively how do we predict probabilities of measuring -1 and $+1$? So that is where this density matrix comes in (see Fig. 5.6). So classically the probability was as you know, related to the energy. Now we

$p_i = \frac{1}{Z} e^{-\tilde{E}_i}$
Classical Probability
CLASSICAL
$\tilde{E} = \vec{h} \cdot \hat{m}$
$\rho = \frac{1}{Z} e^{-H}$
Quantum Probability
Density Matrix
$H = \vec{h} \cdot \vec{\sigma}$
QUANTUM
ρ, H are both Hermitian
$H_{ij} = H_{ji}^*$
$\begin{bmatrix} a & c \\ c^* & b \end{bmatrix}$
real
$\sigma_z = \begin{bmatrix} 1 & 0 \\ 0 & -1 \end{bmatrix}$,
Pauli Spin Matrices
$\sigma_x = \begin{bmatrix} 0 & 1 \\ 1 & 0 \end{bmatrix}$, $\sigma_y = \begin{bmatrix} 0 & -i \\ +i & 0 \end{bmatrix}$

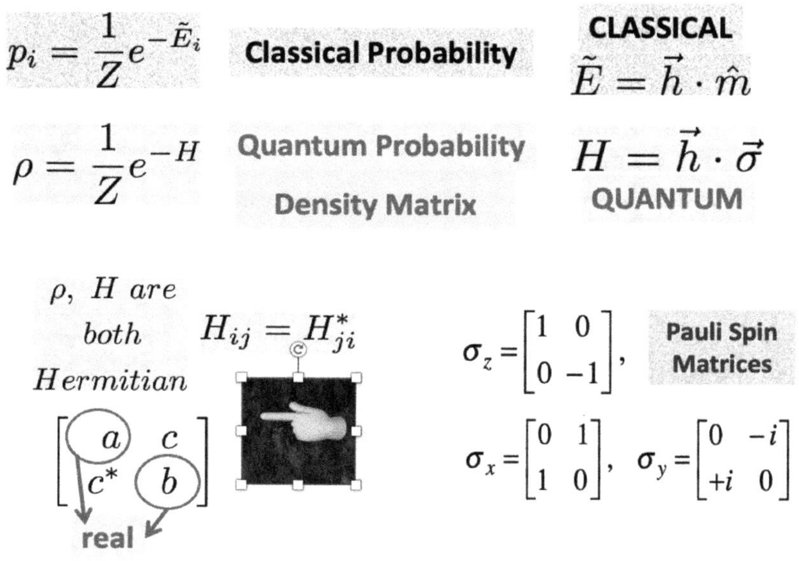

Fig. 5.6 Density matrix.

have a density matrix, which is $\exp(-H)$, H being this energy matrix or Hamiltonian matrix.

A little side note. This H matrix is Hermitian. And Hermitian means that the matrix is equal to it's conjugate transpose. So if you look at the (i, j) component, it is equal to the complex conjugate of the (j, i) component. So all these three spin matrices you will notice are Hermitian. σ_z is Hermitian because there isn't any off-diagonal element and h_{ii} and the diagonal elements h_{11} or h_{22}, those are all real. So they are of course, equal to their complex conjugate. And σ_x again you'll notice 1 is equal to its complex conjugate and here also in σ_y, $-i$ is equal to the complex conjugate of $+i$. So H is Hermitian, and so is ρ which is obtained by exponentiating this H, and I should note that this exponentiation is in a matrix sense, not an element by element sense. And these will become clear when we look at the actual examples.

Now, if you write out this matrix, then this Hermitian matrix, it will always have the form shown: there will be real quantities a, b on the diagonal. The off-diagonal elements can be complex, but then they'll be complex conjugates, c and c^*.

5.1.4 *Figs. 5.7-5.10: Predicting measurements*

5.1.4.1 *Figs. 5.7*

Now, these diagonal elements basically give you the probability of measuring m_z equals $+1$ or -1 (see Fig. 5.7). Now, what about m_x and m_y? Well, you might be tempted to say that I should look at the off diagonal terms. Well, no, that won't quite work because after all, these off-diagonal elements are complex and they cannot be interpreted as probability.

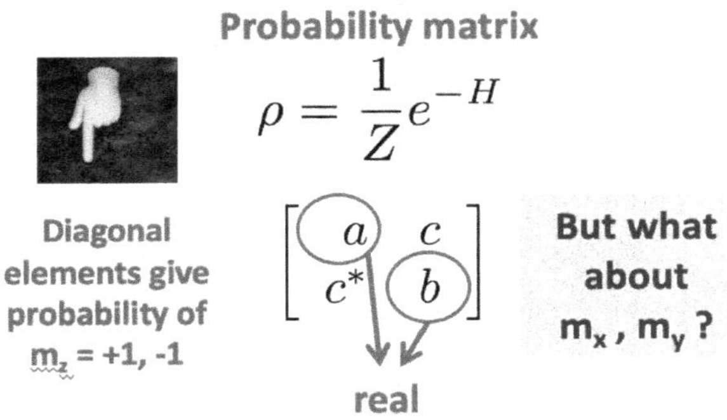

Fig. 5.7 Predicting measurements.

5.1.4.2 *Fig. 5.8*

The general rule for predicting measured values is the following. Given any quantity S, there is a corresponding operator S_{op}. And the way you find the average value of that quantity is by taking the *trace* of this operator times the density matrix and when you take *trace*, it doesn't matter in what order you multiply the matrices. So you could multiply the density matrix times the operator, answer would be the same. So if you wanted m_x, well, you take whatever density matrix you have and multiply it by the operator representing m_x, which is σ_x, and then take the *trace* and you'd have the average value. Same procedure if you want m_y, except that you use the operator representing m_y, which is σ_y.

Now, what if I wanted to predict the value of the correlation between m_x and m_y? So I go and measure both m_x and m_y, and I want to know

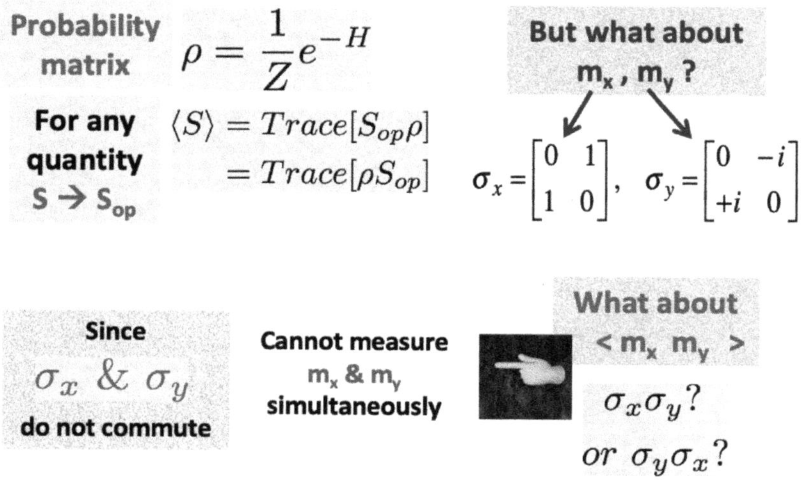

Probability matrix $\rho = \frac{1}{Z}e^{-H}$

For any quantity S → S_{op} $\langle S \rangle = Trace[S_{op}\rho] = Trace[\rho S_{op}]$

But what about m_x, m_y?

$\sigma_x = \begin{bmatrix} 0 & 1 \\ 1 & 0 \end{bmatrix}, \quad \sigma_y = \begin{bmatrix} 0 & -i \\ +i & 0 \end{bmatrix}$

Since σ_x & σ_y do not commute

Cannot measure m_x & m_y simultaneously

What about $< m_x \, m_y >$

$\sigma_x \sigma_y$? or $\sigma_y \sigma_x$?

Fig. 5.8 Predicting measurements (contd.).

the average value of the product. And you might say, well, that's simple, I could define the operator for $m_x m_y$ as $\sigma_x \sigma_y$. Well, not quite, because what's not clear is whether I should use $\sigma_x \sigma_y$ or $\sigma_y \sigma_x$? And now when you are talking of numbers like m_x and m_y, of course, the order doesn't matter, but here we have matrices. With matrices, A times B is not necessarily equal to B times A. And in this case, actually it isn't, you can check it out. If you take σ_x times σ_y, you'll get $+i\sigma_z$. And if you take σ_y times σ_x, you'll get $-i\sigma_z$, and neither of these is actually Hermitian, anyway. So the bottom line is if you really wanted to know the expectation value of $m_x m_y$, the quantum theory I just described to you wouldn't give you an answer? Well, then how do we use quantum theory?

And the answer is that well, experimentally there is no way to measure m_x and m_y simultaneously. If you could, then you see quantum theory would essentially fail. But it stands on the general experimental fact that for these elemental magnets, there is no way to measure two components simultaneously. You can either measure x or y or z, but not any two of them. In general, whenever you have two operators, if they do not commute, meaning if AB is not equal to BA, then you cannot measure them simultaneously.

5.1.4.3 *Fig. 5.9*

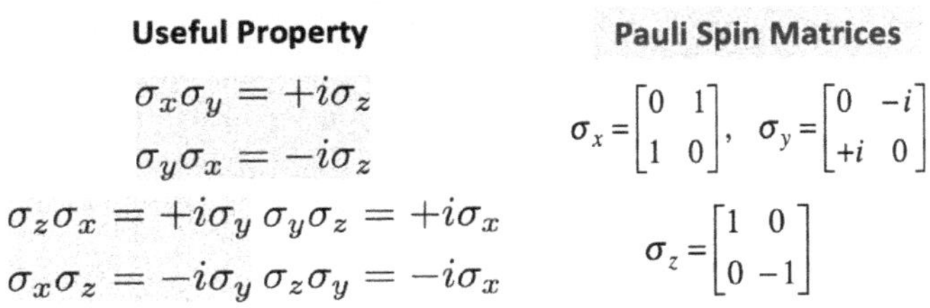

Useful Property

$$\sigma_x\sigma_y = +i\sigma_z$$
$$\sigma_y\sigma_x = -i\sigma_z$$
$$\sigma_z\sigma_x = +i\sigma_y \quad \sigma_y\sigma_z = +i\sigma_x$$
$$\sigma_x\sigma_z = -i\sigma_y \quad \sigma_z\sigma_y = -i\sigma_x$$

Pauli Spin Matrices

$$\sigma_x = \begin{bmatrix} 0 & 1 \\ 1 & 0 \end{bmatrix}, \quad \sigma_y = \begin{bmatrix} 0 & -i \\ +i & 0 \end{bmatrix}$$
$$\sigma_z = \begin{bmatrix} 1 & 0 \\ 0 & -1 \end{bmatrix}$$

Fig. 5.9 Useful property.

Note that the Pauli spin matrices have this cyclic property shown in the figure. This is a very useful property that often comes in handy.

5.1.4.4 *Fig. 5.10*

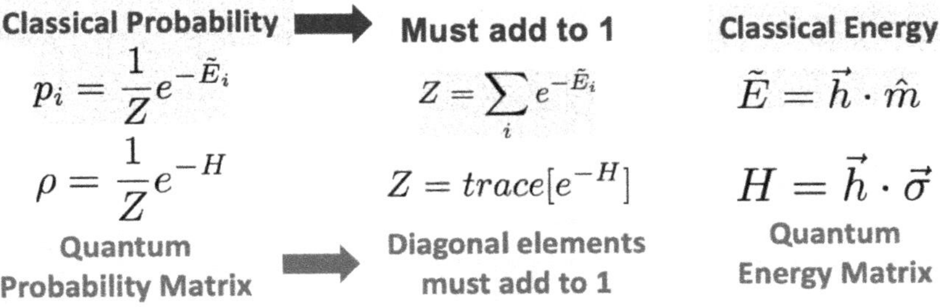
Classical Probability
Must add to 1
Classical Energy
$p_i = \frac{1}{Z}e^{-\tilde{E}_i}$
$Z = \sum_i e^{-\tilde{E}_i}$
$\tilde{E} = \vec{h} \cdot \hat{m}$
$\rho = \frac{1}{Z}e^{-H}$
$Z = trace[e^{-H}]$
$H = \vec{h} \cdot \vec{\sigma}$
Quantum Probability Matrix
Diagonal elements must add to 1
Quantum Energy Matrix

Fig. 5.10 Finding Z.

Now, one last thing, and that is to calculate the probability, as you know, you also need to figure out the constant in front. And in the classical case, the idea is that all probabilities must add up to 1. And so this constant Z is actually the sum of all the exponentials. The corresponding thing for the quantum law is, that you see that diagonal elements of the density matrix they represent a probability, and they must add up to 1, which means the trace of ρ must be equal to 1. And that leads to the condition that Z should be equal to Trace $(\exp(-H))$.

So to sum up then what we did in this lecture was introduced this quantum version of the energy, which gives us this Hamiltonian matrix H. And you can use this matrix to find the density matrix which is like the quantum version of probability. And once you have the density matrix, you can predict the expected measured value of any quantity: For whatever quantity you're interested in, you have to figure out the corresponding operator and then find the trace of the opertaor times the density matrix. In the next lecture we'll look at an example of a one q-bit system and apply the rules we just laid down.

5.1.5 *Quiz*

5.1.5.1 *Question 1*

Suppose the density matrix is given by $\rho = \frac{1}{2}\begin{bmatrix} 1 & 1 \\ 1 & 1 \end{bmatrix}$

What is the expected value $\langle m_x \rangle$ of the spin in the x-direction?[1]

5.1.5.2 *Question 2*

Suppose the density matrix is given by $\rho = \frac{1}{2}\begin{bmatrix} +1 & -1 \\ -1 & +1 \end{bmatrix}$

What is the expected value $\langle m_x \rangle$ of the spin in the x-direction?[2]

5.1.5.3 *Question 3*

Consider the Pauli spin matrices

$$\sigma_x = \begin{bmatrix} +1 & 0 \\ 0 & -1 \end{bmatrix}, \sigma_y = \begin{bmatrix} 0 & -i \\ +i & 0 \end{bmatrix}, \sigma_z = \begin{bmatrix} 0 & 1 \\ 1 & 0 \end{bmatrix}$$

What is the matrix $\sigma_x\sigma_y - \sigma_y\sigma_x$?[3]

---

[1] +1.

[2] −1.

[3] −2i $\sigma_z = \begin{bmatrix} -2i & 0 \\ 0 & +2i \end{bmatrix}$.

5.2 One q-bit System

This is Lecture 5.2: Watch youtube video

In the last lecture, we introduced this quantum energy matrix or the Hamiltonian matrix where you replace the classical spin variable with a spin operator, σ, with three components σ_z, σ_x, and σ_y, each one of which is a two by two matrix. You can calculate the quantum probability matrix or what's called the density matrix, $\rho = (1/Z)\exp(-H)$ from H, and knowing the operator S for a particular observable S, you can calculate its expectation value from $trace[\rho S]$.

Now, what we'll do in this lecture is work out a specific example which should give you a more concrete feeling for how this whole thing works.

5.2.1 *Fig. 5.11: Hamiltonian*

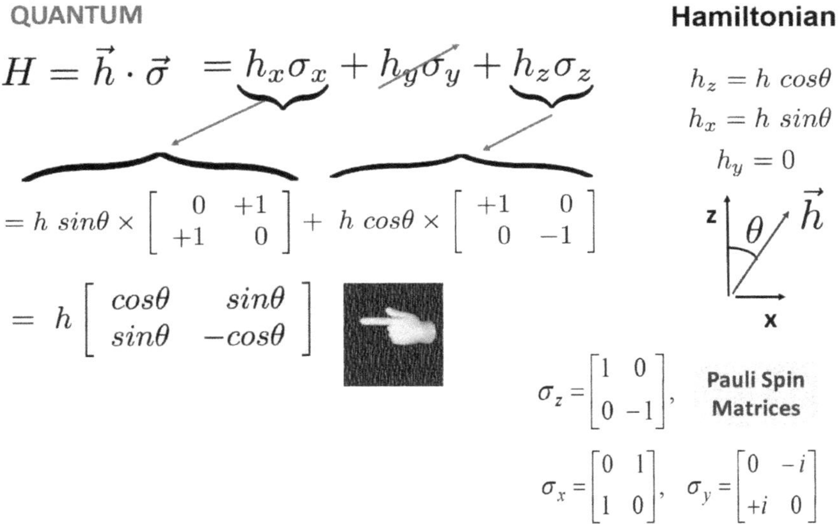
QUANTUM
Hamiltonian
$H = \vec{h} \cdot \vec{\sigma} = h_x\sigma_x + h_y\sigma_y + h_z\sigma_z$
$h_z = h\ cos\theta$
$h_x = h\ sin\theta$
$h_y = 0$
$= h\ sin\theta \times \begin{bmatrix} 0 & +1 \\ +1 & 0 \end{bmatrix} + h\ cos\theta \times \begin{bmatrix} +1 & 0 \\ 0 & -1 \end{bmatrix}$
$= h \begin{bmatrix} cos\theta & sin\theta \\ sin\theta & -cos\theta \end{bmatrix}$
z
θ
$\vec{h}$
x
$\sigma_z = \begin{bmatrix} 1 & 0 \\ 0 & -1 \end{bmatrix}$,
Pauli Spin Matrices
$\sigma_x = \begin{bmatrix} 0 & 1 \\ 1 & 0 \end{bmatrix}$, $\sigma_y = \begin{bmatrix} 0 & -i \\ +i & 0 \end{bmatrix}$

Fig. 5.11 Hamiltonian.

Now, for a single q-bit, the energy matrix is given by, $H = \vec{h}\cdot\vec{\sigma}$, which you can write as, $H = h_x\sigma_x + h_y\sigma_y + h_z\sigma_z$. Now for this example, we'll assume that h_y is 0. You could put in a nonzero h_y as well, it's just that algebra looks more messy, so we'll put that to 0 for this discussion, and assume that $\vec{h}$ lies in the z-x plane, pointing in some direction θ from the z-axis.

So what does the energy matrix look like then? A little algebra leads us to the result shown with $h\cos\theta$ on the diagonal and $h\sin\theta$ off diagonal.

5.2.2 *Figs. 5.12-5.14: Density matrix*

5.2.2.1 *Fig. 5.12*

General approach to finding f(M) function of a matrix M

Diagonalize M

$$D = VMV^{+}$$

$$f(D) = \begin{bmatrix} f(D_{11}) & 0 \\ 0 & f(D_{22}) \end{bmatrix}$$

Note

$$V^{+} = \left[V^{T}\right]^{*}$$

Hermitian conjugate

Reverse transform

$$f(M) = V^{+}f(D)V$$

$$e^{-\vec{h}\cdot\vec{\sigma}} = ??$$

With "some algebra"

$$\rho = \frac{1}{Z}e^{-\mathbf{H}}$$

$$H = \vec{h}\cdot\vec{\sigma}$$

$$= h\begin{bmatrix} cos\theta & sin\theta \\ sin\theta & -cos\theta \end{bmatrix}$$

$$f(-\vec{h}\cdot\vec{\sigma}) = [I]\,\frac{f(h)+f(-h)}{2} - [\vec{h}\cdot\vec{\sigma}]\,\frac{f(h)-f(-h)}{2h}$$

Fig. 5.12 Density matrix.

Now, so we have written down the energy matrix, now to find the density matrix, that's this probability matrix, we need to evaluate this quantity, $(1/Z)\exp(-H)$ (see Fig. 5.12). So how would we do that? We need the $\exp(-H)$. Now, this question is how do we evaluate $\exp(-\vec{h}\cdot\vec{\sigma})$? Remember, this exponentiation is not in an element by element sense, it is in the matrix sense.

Now, the general approach to finding any function of a matrix works like this, given a matrix M, you first diagonalize it. You find the transformation, $VMV^{\dagger}$ that will turn it into a diagonal matrix. These transformations work also in reverse that is from diagonal matrix you can go back to the original by applying $V^{\dagger}$ and then V, in that order, $M = V^{\dagger}DV$. Remember we are writing this $V^{\dagger}$ to denote Hermitian conjugate, which is the conjugate transpose.

Now, the way you proceed to find any function is the following, that given a diagonal matrix, the function is simply the functions of the diagonal elements and the off diagonal stays 0 (see Fig. 5.12). So after you have transformed it, So you find the function in the transformed bases and then transform it back. So this is a general procedure for finding any function.

Of course, if you're calculating things numerically, you do not have to worry about this. There's a command in MATLAB® or in Python that will do just that. It's EXPM, that if you leave out the M, just say EXP, then it will get you the element by element exponentiation, which is not what we want, we want the EXPM.

Anyway, we are trying to do this analytically without invoking numerical computations. Then what you can show with some algebra is that any function of this quantity $-\vec{h}\cdot\vec{\sigma}$ can be written as, $f(-\vec{h}\cdot\vec{\sigma}) = [I]((f(h)+f(-h))/2) - [\vec{h}\cdot\vec{\sigma}]((f(h)-f(-h))/2h)$.

5.2.2.2 *Fig. 5.13*

$$e^{-\vec{h}\cdot\vec{\sigma}} =$$

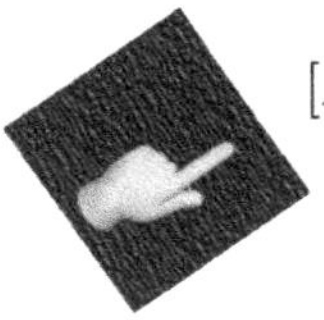

$$[I]\ cosh(h) - \frac{[\vec{h}\cdot\vec{\sigma}]}{h}\ sinh(h)$$

$$e^{-\vec{h}\cdot\vec{\sigma}} = [I]\ \frac{e^{+h}+e^{-h}}{2} - [\vec{h}\cdot\vec{\sigma}]\ \frac{e^{+h}-e^{-h}}{2h}$$

$$\rho = \frac{1}{Z}e^{-\mathbf{H}}$$

$$H = \vec{h}\cdot\vec{\sigma}$$

$$= h\begin{bmatrix} cos\theta & sin\theta \\ sin\theta & -cos\theta \end{bmatrix}$$

$$f(-\vec{h}\cdot\vec{\sigma}) = [I]\ \frac{f(h)+f(-h)}{2} - [\vec{h}\cdot\vec{\sigma}]\ \frac{f(h)-f(-h)}{2h}$$

Fig. 5.13 Density matrix.

So if we use this relation along with the result we obtained earlier for $\vec{h}\cdot\vec{\sigma}$ we get the result shown: $\exp(-\vec{h}\cdot\vec{\sigma}) = [I]\cosh(h) - ([-\vec{h}\cdot\vec{\sigma}]/h)\sinh(h)$.

5.2.2.3 *Fig. 5.14*

$$\rho = \frac{1}{2}\left([I] - \frac{[\vec{h}\cdot\vec{\sigma}]}{h}\, tanh(h) \right) = \frac{1}{2}\begin{bmatrix} 1 - tanh(h)\, cos\theta & tanh(h)\, sin\theta \\ tanh(h)\, sin\theta & 1 + tanh(h)\, cos\theta \end{bmatrix}$$

$$I = \begin{bmatrix} 1 & 0 \\ 0 & 1 \end{bmatrix}$$

$$\rho = \frac{1}{Z} e^{-\mathbf{H}}$$

$$Z = trace[e^{-H}] = 2\, cosh(h)$$

$$H = \vec{h}\cdot\vec{\sigma} = h\begin{bmatrix} cos\theta & sin\theta \\ sin\theta & -cos\theta \end{bmatrix}$$

$$e^{-\vec{h}\cdot\vec{\sigma}} = [I]\, cosh(h) - \frac{[\vec{h}\cdot\vec{\sigma}]}{h}\, sinh(h)$$

Fig. 5.14 Finding Z.

Finally to get the density matrix, I also need to know this number in front Z, and what is Z? Well, I need to take the trace of $\exp(-\vec{h}\cdot\vec{\sigma})$. Now, what is the trace? Well, for the identity matrix, the trace is 2, it's 1 plus 1. For all these σ matrices, the trace is 0. So the trace of $\exp(-\vec{h}\cdot\vec{\sigma})$ is $2\cosh(h)$, and that's the Z. So now, we can write down the density matrix ρ as shown.

5.2.3 *Figs. 5.15-5.17: Predicting m_z*

5.2.3.1 *Fig. 5.15*

Now, we can file that away, because this density matrix is what we need to calculate any quantity of interest. We'll look at different operators and how to find the expected value, and how to predict the results of measurements of different quantities.

Let us say you want to know the average value of m_z. Okay, then I am supposed to take the trace of σ_z times the density matrix and when I multiply those two quantities take the trace I get $\rho_{11} - \rho_{22}$. From our result for the density matrix we know that $\rho_{11} = 0.5(1 - \tanh(h)\cos\theta)$ and $\rho_{22} = 0.5(1 + \tanh(h)\cos\theta)$ and the difference is $\langle m_z\rangle = -\tanh(h)\cos(\theta)$.

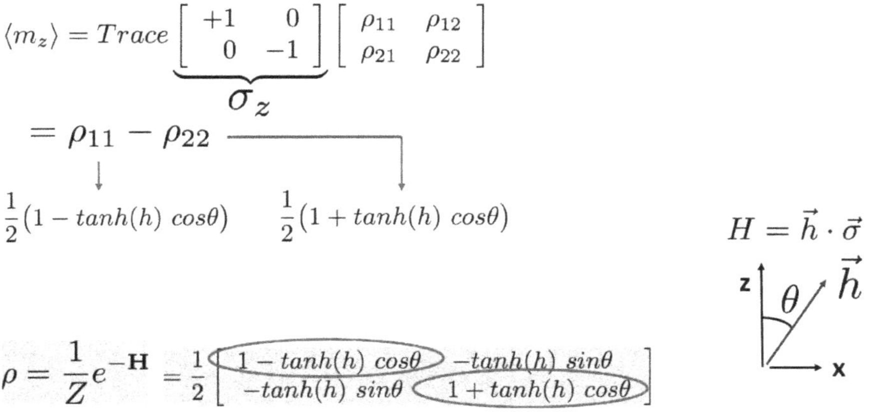

$$\langle m_z \rangle = Trace \underbrace{\begin{bmatrix} +1 & 0 \\ 0 & -1 \end{bmatrix}}_{\sigma_z} \begin{bmatrix} \rho_{11} & \rho_{12} \\ \rho_{21} & \rho_{22} \end{bmatrix}$$

$$= \rho_{11} - \rho_{22}$$

$$\frac{1}{2}(1 - tanh(h)\ cos\theta) \qquad \frac{1}{2}(1 + tanh(h)\ cos\theta)$$

$$H = \vec{h} \cdot \vec{\sigma}$$

z θ $\vec{h}$ x

$$\rho = \frac{1}{Z} e^{-\mathbf{H}} = \frac{1}{2} \begin{bmatrix} 1 - tanh(h)\ cos\theta & -tanh(h)\ sin\theta \\ -tanh(h)\ sin\theta & 1 + tanh(h)\ cos\theta \end{bmatrix}$$

Fig. 5.15 Predicting m_z.

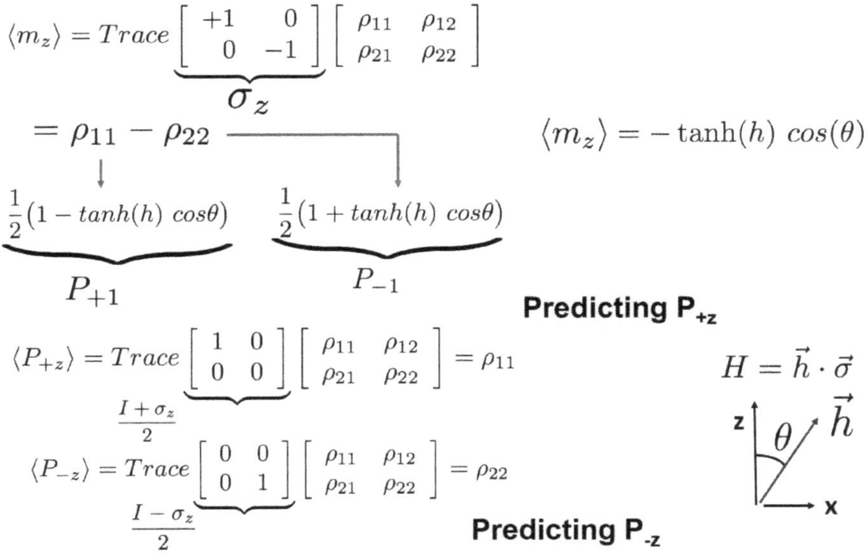

$$\langle m_z \rangle = Trace \underbrace{\begin{bmatrix} +1 & 0 \\ 0 & -1 \end{bmatrix}}_{\sigma_z} \begin{bmatrix} \rho_{11} & \rho_{12} \\ \rho_{21} & \rho_{22} \end{bmatrix}$$

$$= \rho_{11} - \rho_{22}$$

$$\langle m_z \rangle = -\tanh(h)\ cos(\theta)$$

$$\underbrace{\frac{1}{2}(1 - tanh(h)\ cos\theta)}_{P_{+1}} \qquad \underbrace{\frac{1}{2}(1 + tanh(h)\ cos\theta)}_{P_{-1}}$$

Predicting P_{+z}

$$\langle P_{+z} \rangle = Trace \underbrace{\begin{bmatrix} 1 & 0 \\ 0 & 0 \end{bmatrix}}_{\frac{I+\sigma_z}{2}} \begin{bmatrix} \rho_{11} & \rho_{12} \\ \rho_{21} & \rho_{22} \end{bmatrix} = \rho_{11}$$

$$H = \vec{h} \cdot \vec{\sigma}$$

z θ $\vec{h}$ x

$$\langle P_{-z} \rangle = Trace \underbrace{\begin{bmatrix} 0 & 0 \\ 0 & 1 \end{bmatrix}}_{\frac{I-\sigma_z}{2}} \begin{bmatrix} \rho_{11} & \rho_{12} \\ \rho_{21} & \rho_{22} \end{bmatrix} = \rho_{22}$$

Predicting P_{-z}

Fig. 5.16 Predicting P_{+z} and P_{-z}.

5.2.3.2 *Fig. 5.16*

So we have seen that $m_z = \rho_{11} - \rho_{22}$. Now, one thing I should point out is that you could interpret ρ_{11} and ρ_{22} as the probability that the spin will have a value +1 and −1 respectively. How do you see that? By writing down the operators representing the probability of the spin being +1 or −1 as shown. We then get $P_{+z} = \rho_{11}$ and $P_{-z} = \rho_{22}$ and the difference is what gives you the average value $\langle m_z \rangle$.

5.2.3.3 *Fig. 5.17*

$$\langle m_z \rangle = Trace \underbrace{\begin{bmatrix} +1 & 0 \\ 0 & -1 \end{bmatrix}}_{\sigma_z} \begin{bmatrix} \rho_{11} & \rho_{12} \\ \rho_{21} & \rho_{22} \end{bmatrix}$$

$$= \rho_{11} - \rho_{22} \qquad \langle m_z \rangle = -\tanh(h)\ cos(\theta)$$

$$\langle m_x \rangle = Trace \underbrace{\begin{bmatrix} 0 & 1 \\ 1 & 0 \end{bmatrix}}_{\sigma_x} \begin{bmatrix} \rho_{11} & \rho_{12} \\ \rho_{21} & \rho_{22} \end{bmatrix} = \rho_{12} + \rho_{21} = -tanh(h)\ sin(\theta)$$

Predicting m_x

$$H = \vec{h} \cdot \vec{\sigma}$$

z, θ, $\vec{h}$, x

$$\rho = \frac{1}{Z} e^{-\mathbf{H}} = \frac{1}{2} \begin{bmatrix} 1 - tanh(h)\ cos\theta & -tanh(h)\ sin\theta \\ -tanh(h)\ sin\theta & 1 + tanh(h)\ cos\theta \end{bmatrix}$$

Fig. 5.17 Predicting $\langle m_x \rangle$.

One more example. Suppose you want the average value of m_x, then you take the operator for m_x namely σ_x, multiply it by the density matrix and take the trace as shown. In this case, you can show that what you'll get is $\rho_{12} + \rho_{21}$, now, those it will depend on the off diagonal terms, and we'll add it up, add those two, and you'll get this answer, $-\tanh(h)\sin\theta$, that would be $\langle m_x \rangle$.

So the point I am trying to make is that any question you want to ask in this quantum framework, what you have to do is figure out the corresponding operator. And then you can multiply it with the density matrix and take the trace, and you'd have your answer, that's the message.

5.2.4 *Quiz*

5.2.4.1 *Question 1*

A single quantum spin has a Hamiltonian matrix $H = \overrightarrow{h} \cdot \overrightarrow{\sigma}$. If $h_z = h_x = 0$, $h_y \neq 0$, what is [H]?[4]

5.2.4.2 *Question 2*

A single quantum spin has a Hamiltonian matrix $H = \overrightarrow{h} \cdot \overrightarrow{\sigma}$. If $h_z = 0$, $h_x \neq 0$, $h_y \neq 0$, what is [H]?[5]

5.2.4.3 *Question 3*

The density matrix is given by

$$\rho = \frac{1}{2}\begin{bmatrix} 1 - tanh(h)cos(\theta) & -tanh(h)sin(\theta) \\ -tanh(h)sin(\theta) & 1 + tanh(h)cos(\theta) \end{bmatrix}$$

What is the expectation value $\langle m_z \rangle$?[6]

---

[4] $\begin{bmatrix} 0 & -ih_y \\ +ih_y & 0 \end{bmatrix}$.

[5] $\begin{bmatrix} 0 & h_x - ih_y \\ h_x + ih_y & 0 \end{bmatrix}$.

[6] $-tanh(h)cos\theta$.

5.3 Spin-Spin Interactions

This is Lecture 5.3: Watch youtube video

In the first two lectures we have seen how we can write down the energy or Hamiltonian matrix for one quantum spin, and use it to obtain the density matrix, from which we can calculate the expectation value of any quantity S if we can write down the operator S_{op} corresponding to it. In this lecture we will see how we write down the energy matrix for multiple spins with interactions, which can then be used to calculate the density matrix and make predictions.

5.3.1 *Figs. 5.18-5.19: Interaction Hamiltonian*

5.3.1.1 *Fig. 5.18*

In the last two lectures, we wrote the energy for just one spin. If there are two non-interacting spins, then it's easy, you just add the second one. The classical picture would be $\widetilde{E} = \overrightarrow{h_1} \cdot \hat{m}_1 + \overrightarrow{h_2} \cdot \hat{m}_2$, and the corresponding quantum picture would be $H = \overrightarrow{h_1} \cdot \overrightarrow{\sigma_1} + \overrightarrow{h_2} \cdot \overrightarrow{\sigma_2}$.

QUANTUM
$H = \vec{h_1} \cdot \vec{\sigma_1} + \vec{h_2} \cdot \vec{\sigma_2}$
$+J\ \vec{\sigma_1} \cdot \vec{\sigma_2}$
Two spins
Interactions
CLASSICAL
$\tilde{E} = \vec{h_1} \cdot \hat{m}_1 + \vec{h_2} \cdot \hat{m}_2$
$+J\hat{m}_1 \cdot \hat{m}_2$

Fig. 5.18 Interactions.

If you want to include interactions, then classically you would add J times this interaction term times $\hat{m}_1 \cdot \hat{m}_2$. Correspondingly in the quantum picture you'd have $\overrightarrow{\sigma_1} \cdot \overrightarrow{\sigma_2}$.

5.3.1.2 *Fig. 5.19*

Now if you write it out, you will see all the components, $h_{1x}\sigma_{1x}$, etc. and here, $\vec{\sigma_1} \cdot \vec{\sigma_2}$ means $\sigma_{1x}\sigma_{2x}$, $\sigma_{1y}\sigma_{2y}$, $\sigma_{1z}\sigma_{2z}$. By the way I've written J_x, J_y, J_z because in general, those three could be different, although in Fig. 5.19 I had assumed the same J for all three components.

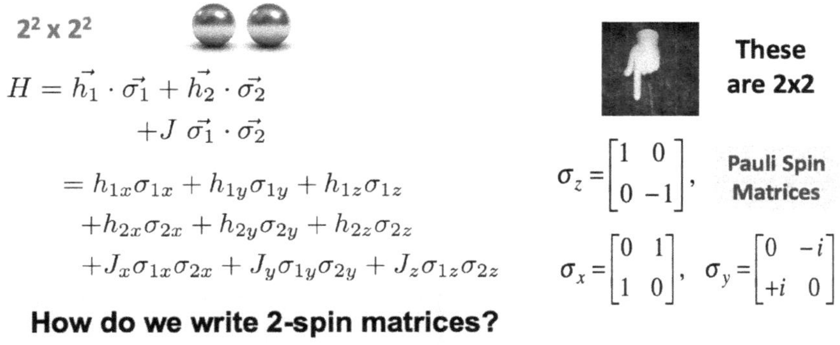

$2^2 \times 2^2$

$$H = \vec{h_1} \cdot \vec{\sigma_1} + \vec{h_2} \cdot \vec{\sigma_2} + J\, \vec{\sigma_1} \cdot \vec{\sigma_2}$$
$$= h_{1x}\sigma_{1x} + h_{1y}\sigma_{1y} + h_{1z}\sigma_{1z} + h_{2x}\sigma_{2x} + h_{2y}\sigma_{2y} + h_{2z}\sigma_{2z} + J_x\sigma_{1x}\sigma_{2x} + J_y\sigma_{1y}\sigma_{2y} + J_z\sigma_{1z}\sigma_{2z}$$

How do we write 2-spin matrices?

These are 2x2

$$\sigma_z = \begin{bmatrix} 1 & 0 \\ 0 & -1 \end{bmatrix},$$

Pauli Spin Matrices

$$\sigma_x = \begin{bmatrix} 0 & 1 \\ 1 & 0 \end{bmatrix}, \quad \sigma_y = \begin{bmatrix} 0 & -i \\ +i & 0 \end{bmatrix}$$

Fig. 5.19 Interactions.

Okay, now, the tricky part is that actually when you have two spins, this energy matrix is $2^2 \times 2^2$. If it were n spins, it will be 2^n by 2^n. So it's a matrix in this 2^2 space, whereas the matrices we had written down earlier, those were 2×2 matrices, the Pauli spin matrices. So question is, how do we write down these 2-spin matrices, which are 4×4? If we knew how to do that, then after that, it's straightforward again. You have the energy matrix, you can calculate density matrix, and then calculate any operator.

5.3.2 *Figs. 5.20-5.21: 2-spin matrices*

5.3.2.1 *Fig. 5.20*

So supposing we want to write σ_{1x}, which means the x-directed spin of spin 1. So for 1, I have σ_x but for 2, I do nothing which is represented by the identity matrix. So the corresponding operators are σ_x and I, but you have to take the Kronecker product of the two: kron(σ_x, I).

Now, how does this Kronecker product work? It's not a matrix product. With matrix products, if you took a 2×2 matrix and multiply by another 2×2 matrix, you would have got another 2×2 matrix, but when you take this Kronecker product or tensor product, you actually get a 4×4 matrix, using the procedure shown.

5.3.2.2 *Fig. 5.21*

Now, if you want σ_{2x}, which means I want the x component of the spin two, then you see it's a little different, we want kron(I, σ_x), since I have

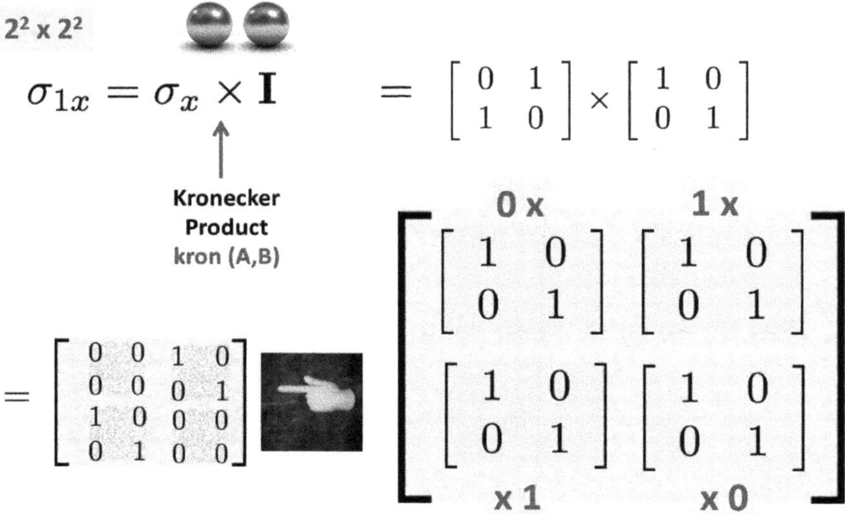
2² x 2²
$\sigma_{1x} = \sigma_x \times \mathbf{I} = \begin{bmatrix} 0 & 1 \\ 1 & 0 \end{bmatrix} \times \begin{bmatrix} 1 & 0 \\ 0 & 1 \end{bmatrix}$
Kronecker
Product
kron (A,B)
$= \begin{bmatrix} 0 & 0 & 1 & 0 \\ 0 & 0 & 0 & 1 \\ 1 & 0 & 0 & 0 \\ 0 & 1 & 0 & 0 \end{bmatrix}$
0 x
1 x
x 1
x 0

Fig. 5.20 2-spin matrices.

labeled the order of the spins in my mind as 1 and then 2. And the point to note is that for the Kronecker product, the order matters: $kron(I, \sigma_x) \neq kron(\sigma_x, I)$. Of course, if you're using MATLAB or Python, that's what the computer would do for you and give you the 4×4 matrices, which are different for σ_{1x} and σ_{2x} as shown.

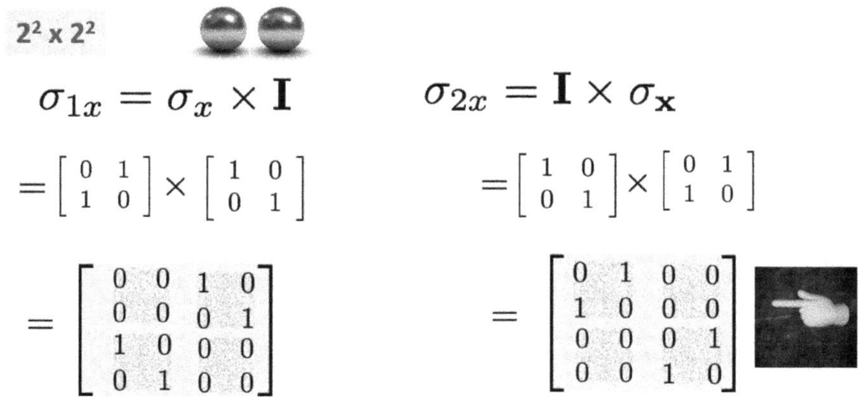

2² x 2²

$$\sigma_{1x} = \sigma_x \times \mathbf{I} \qquad \sigma_{2x} = \mathbf{I} \times \sigma_{\mathbf{x}}$$

$$= \begin{bmatrix} 0 & 1 \\ 1 & 0 \end{bmatrix} \times \begin{bmatrix} 1 & 0 \\ 0 & 1 \end{bmatrix} \qquad = \begin{bmatrix} 1 & 0 \\ 0 & 1 \end{bmatrix} \times \begin{bmatrix} 0 & 1 \\ 1 & 0 \end{bmatrix}$$

$$= \begin{bmatrix} 0 & 0 & 1 & 0 \\ 0 & 0 & 0 & 1 \\ 1 & 0 & 0 & 0 \\ 0 & 1 & 0 & 0 \end{bmatrix} \qquad = \begin{bmatrix} 0 & 1 & 0 & 0 \\ 1 & 0 & 0 & 0 \\ 0 & 0 & 0 & 1 \\ 0 & 0 & 1 & 0 \end{bmatrix}$$

Fig. 5.21 2-spin matrices.

5.3.3 *Figs. 5.22-5.26: Product matrices*

5.3.3.1 *Fig. 5.22*

Once we have the 4×4 matrices representing σ_{1x} and σ_{2x}, finding their product $\sigma_{1x}\sigma_{2x}$ is straightforward matrix multiplication. What if I multiply them in reverse order, $\sigma_{2x}\sigma_{1x}$? Interestingly, you end up with the same matrix at the end, indicating that the matrices σ_{1x} and σ_{2x} *commute.* Indeed you would have got the same answer if you had taken the Kronecker product $kron(\sigma_x, \sigma_x)$.

The fact that we get the same matrix for both $\sigma_{1x}\sigma_{2x}$ and $\sigma_{2x}\sigma_{1x}$ means that we can identify it as the operator for $m_{1x}m_{2x}$ without any ambiguity. Experimentally the question we are asking is, what is the expectation or average value of the product of the measurement of x spin on spin 1 and x spin on spin 2? When I measure the x spin of spin 1, I get $+1$ or -1, and the same for the x spin of spin 2, and I want to know what is the average value of the product. Well, to answer this question I should be using the operator $\sigma_{1x}\sigma_{2x} = \sigma_{2x}\sigma_{1x}$.

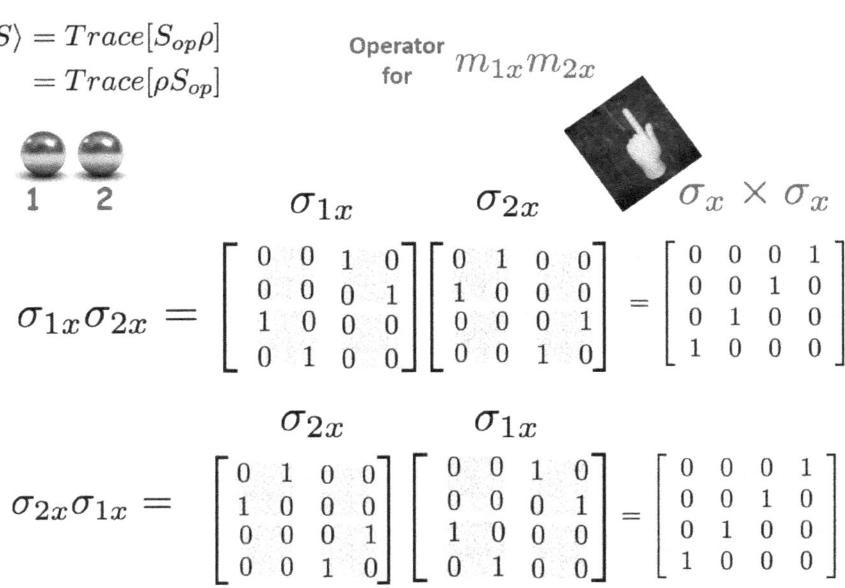
$\langle S \rangle = Trace[S_{op}\rho] = Trace[\rho S_{op}]$
Operator for $m_{1x}m_{2x}$
1 2
σ_{1x} σ_{2x} $\sigma_x \times \sigma_x$
$\sigma_{1x}\sigma_{2x} = \begin{bmatrix} 0 & 0 & 1 & 0 \\ 0 & 0 & 0 & 1 \\ 1 & 0 & 0 & 0 \\ 0 & 1 & 0 & 0 \end{bmatrix} \begin{bmatrix} 0 & 1 & 0 & 0 \\ 1 & 0 & 0 & 0 \\ 0 & 0 & 0 & 1 \\ 0 & 0 & 1 & 0 \end{bmatrix} = \begin{bmatrix} 0 & 0 & 0 & 1 \\ 0 & 0 & 1 & 0 \\ 0 & 1 & 0 & 0 \\ 1 & 0 & 0 & 0 \end{bmatrix}$
σ_{2x} σ_{1x}
$\sigma_{2x}\sigma_{1x} = \begin{bmatrix} 0 & 1 & 0 & 0 \\ 1 & 0 & 0 & 0 \\ 0 & 0 & 0 & 1 \\ 0 & 0 & 1 & 0 \end{bmatrix} \begin{bmatrix} 0 & 0 & 1 & 0 \\ 0 & 0 & 0 & 1 \\ 1 & 0 & 0 & 0 \\ 0 & 1 & 0 & 0 \end{bmatrix} = \begin{bmatrix} 0 & 0 & 0 & 1 \\ 0 & 0 & 1 & 0 \\ 0 & 1 & 0 & 0 \\ 1 & 0 & 0 & 0 \end{bmatrix}$

Fig. 5.22 $\sigma_{1x}\sigma_{2x}$ and $\sigma_{2x}\sigma_{1x}$.

5.3.3.2 *Fig. 5.23*

Now, what if I wanted to know the x spin on 1 and the y spin on 2? Well, then the operator would be like $\sigma_x \times \sigma_y$, or you could write $\sigma_{1x}\sigma_{2y}$ or $\sigma_{2y}\sigma_{1x}$. You can multiply them in either order and again you get the same answer. And it is exactly the matrix you would have got if you just Kroneckered σ_x and σ_y. So this is how you would write the operator for answering questions about measurements of x spin on 1 and y spin on 2: $\langle m_{1x}m_{2y}\rangle$.

$$\langle S\rangle = Trace[S_{op}\rho] = Trace[\rho S_{op}]$$

Operator for $m_{1x}m_{2y}$

1 2

$$\sigma_{1x} = \sigma_x \times \mathbf{I} \qquad \sigma_{2y} = \mathbf{I} \times \sigma_{\mathbf{y}} \qquad = \sigma_x \times \sigma_y$$

$$\sigma_{1x}\sigma_{2y} = \begin{bmatrix} 0 & 0 & 1 & 0 \\ 0 & 0 & 0 & 1 \\ 1 & 0 & 0 & 0 \\ 0 & 1 & 0 & 0 \end{bmatrix} \begin{bmatrix} 0 & -i & 0 & 0 \\ +i & 0 & 0 & 0 \\ 0 & 0 & 0 & -i \\ 0 & 0 & +i & 0 \end{bmatrix} = \begin{bmatrix} 0 & 0 & 0 & -i \\ 0 & 0 & +i & 0 \\ 0 & -i & 0 & 0 \\ +i & 0 & 0 & 0 \end{bmatrix}$$

$$\sigma_{2y} = \mathbf{I} \times \sigma_{\mathbf{y}} \qquad \sigma_{1x} = \sigma_x \times \mathbf{I}$$

$$\sigma_{2y}\sigma_{1x} = \begin{bmatrix} 0 & -i & 0 & 0 \\ +i & 0 & 0 & 0 \\ 0 & 0 & 0 & -i \\ 0 & 0 & +i & 0 \end{bmatrix} \begin{bmatrix} 0 & 0 & 1 & 0 \\ 0 & 0 & 0 & 1 \\ 1 & 0 & 0 & 0 \\ 0 & 1 & 0 & 0 \end{bmatrix} = \begin{bmatrix} 0 & 0 & 0 & -i \\ 0 & 0 & +i & 0 \\ 0 & -i & 0 & 0 \\ +i & 0 & 0 & 0 \end{bmatrix}$$

Fig. 5.23 $\sigma_{1x}\sigma_{2y} = \sigma_{2y}\sigma_{1x}$.

5.3.3.3 *Fig. 5.24*

Now, you might say, well, what if I want to know the x spin and y spin, but on spin 2, both on spin 2? Now, if you remember from our first lecture, this is something quantum mechanics says you cannot do because you can never measure the two components on the same spin and indeed, if you try to write the operator for this, you'd get in trouble. We end up with different matrices for $\sigma_{2x}\sigma_{2y}$ and for $\sigma_{2y}\sigma_{2x}$.

Actually one is the negative of the other. You could show is that one is $+i\sigma_{2z}$, and the other is $-i\sigma_{2z}$, and this is related to the identity I had mentioned in Lecture 5.1, that $\sigma_x\sigma_y = +i\sigma_z$ and $\sigma_y\sigma_x = -i\sigma_z$. Although we are writing 4×4 matrices, it's basically what you would have expected just for one spin. Here as you may have noticed, all our measurements are on spin 2 and spin 1 is just going along for the ride.

Anyway the bottom line is that there's no unambiguous way of defining a proper operator to answer questions about $\langle m_{2x} m_{2y} \rangle$ since the corresponding operators do not commute. And so we cannot answer such questions. That is fine because it turns out that experimentally too you cannot measure both x and y components of the same spin.

$$\langle S \rangle = Trace[S_{op}\rho] = Trace[\rho S_{op}]$$

$m_{2x}m_{2y}$ NOT allowed to ask $\qquad \sigma_{2x}\sigma_{2y} \neq \sigma_{2y}\sigma_{2x}$

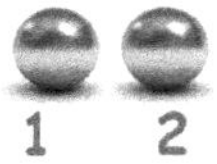

1 2

$$\sigma_{2x}\sigma_{2y} = \underbrace{\begin{bmatrix} 0 & 1 & 0 & 0 \\ 1 & 0 & 0 & 0 \\ 0 & 0 & 0 & 1 \\ 0 & 0 & 1 & 0 \end{bmatrix}}_{\sigma_{2x} = \mathbf{I} \times \sigma_{\mathbf{x}}} \underbrace{\begin{bmatrix} 0 & -i & 0 & 0 \\ +i & 0 & 0 & 0 \\ 0 & 0 & 0 & -i \\ 0 & 0 & +i & 0 \end{bmatrix}}_{\sigma_{2y} = \mathbf{I} \times \sigma_{\mathbf{y}}} = \underbrace{\begin{bmatrix} +i & 0 & 0 & 0 \\ 0 & -i & 0 & 0 \\ 0 & 0 & +i & 0 \\ 0 & 0 & 0 & -i \end{bmatrix}}_{+i\sigma_{2z}}$$

$$\sigma_{2y}\sigma_{2x} = \underbrace{\begin{bmatrix} 0 & -i & 0 & 0 \\ +i & 0 & 0 & 0 \\ 0 & 0 & 0 & -i \\ 0 & 0 & +i & 0 \end{bmatrix}}_{\sigma_{2y} = \mathbf{I} \times \sigma_{\mathbf{y}}} \underbrace{\begin{bmatrix} 0 & 1 & 0 & 0 \\ 1 & 0 & 0 & 0 \\ 0 & 0 & 0 & 1 \\ 0 & 0 & 1 & 0 \end{bmatrix}}_{\sigma_{2x} = \mathbf{I} \times \sigma_{\mathbf{x}}} = \underbrace{\begin{bmatrix} -i & 0 & 0 & 0 \\ 0 & +i & 0 & 0 \\ 0 & 0 & -i & 0 \\ 0 & 0 & 0 & +i \end{bmatrix}}_{-i\sigma_{2z}}$$

Not the same !!

Fig. 5.24 $\sigma_{2x}\sigma_{2y} \neq \sigma_{2y}\sigma_{2x}$.

5.3.3.4 *Fig. 5.25*

To sum up, when operators do not commute, like σ_{2x} and σ_{2y}, we cannot measure the corresponding quantities m_{2x} and m_{2y} simultaneously and we cannot define an operator for the product $m_{2x}m_{2y}$.

But when operators do commute, like σ_{1x} and σ_{2y}, the corresponding quantities m_{1x} and m_{2y} can be measured simultaneously and we can define an operator for the product $m_{1x}m_{2y}$ and use it to answer questions regarding it.

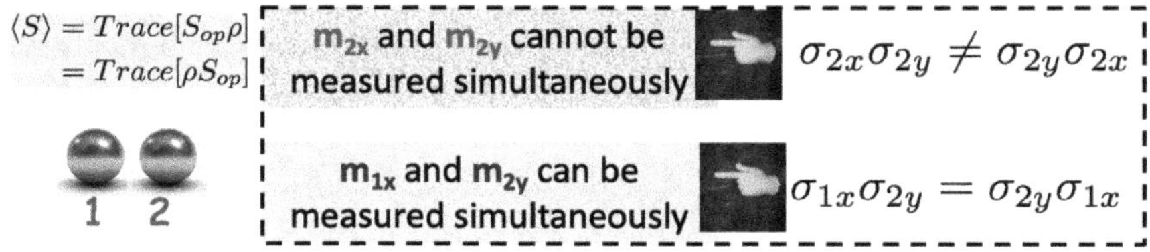

$\langle S\rangle = Trace[S_{op}\rho]$
$= Trace[\rho S_{op}]$

m_{2x} and m_{2y} cannot be measured simultaneously $\sigma_{2x}\sigma_{2y} \neq \sigma_{2y}\sigma_{2x}$

1 2

m_{1x} and m_{2y} can be measured simultaneously $\sigma_{1x}\sigma_{2y} = \sigma_{2y}\sigma_{1x}$

Fig. 5.25 $m_{1x}m_{2y}$ versus $m_{2x}m_{2y}$.

5.3.3.5 *Fig. 5.26*

Getting back to the original 2-spin problem with interactions, we now have everything we need. We have seen is how to write σ_{1x}, σ_{2x}, σ_{1y}, σ_{2y}, σ_{1z}, σ_{2z}. Each of these are 4×4 matrices and we can combine them as needed using straightforward matrix algebra to obtain the composite H matrix. Once you have H, you could find the probability or density matrix which we could use to find the expectation value for any measured quantity S as long as we can wirte down the corresponding operator S_{op}.

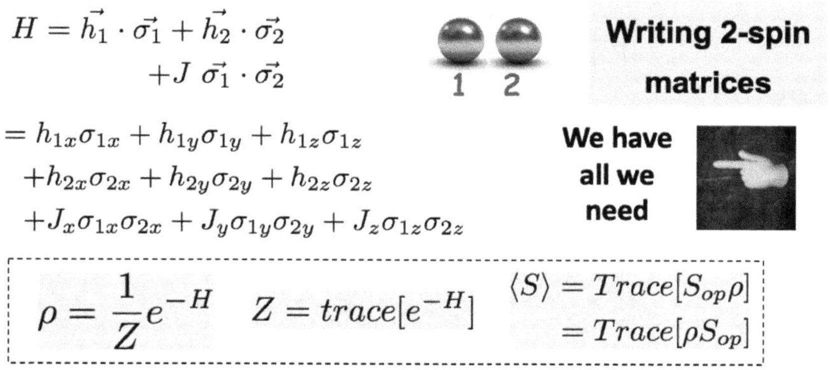

$$H = \vec{h_1}\cdot\vec{\sigma_1} + \vec{h_2}\cdot\vec{\sigma_2} + J\,\vec{\sigma_1}\cdot\vec{\sigma_2}$$

$$= h_{1x}\sigma_{1x} + h_{1y}\sigma_{1y} + h_{1z}\sigma_{1z} + h_{2x}\sigma_{2x} + h_{2y}\sigma_{2y} + h_{2z}\sigma_{2z} + J_x\sigma_{1x}\sigma_{2x} + J_y\sigma_{1y}\sigma_{2y} + J_z\sigma_{1z}\sigma_{2z}$$

1 2

Writing 2-spin matrices

We have all we need

$$\rho = \frac{1}{Z}e^{-H} \quad Z = trace[e^{-H}] \quad \langle S\rangle = Trace[S_{op}\rho] = Trace[\rho S_{op}]$$

Fig. 5.26 We have everything we need for the two interacting spin problem.

5.3.4 *Fig. 5.27: n-spin matrices*

In principle, this is how you could talk about an n-spin system also. If you had n spins with pairwise or two-body interactions then the general expression would be something like this, $H = \sum_{r=1}^{n} \vec{h_r} \cdot \vec{\sigma_r} + (1/2) \sum_{r \neq q}^{n} \sum_{q=1}^{n} J_{rq} \vec{\sigma_r} \cdot \vec{\sigma_q}$ and each one of these sigmas would actually be a $2^n \times 2^n$ matrix.

For example, suppose you had a 4-spin system and you want to know what is σ_{2x}. Well, then, the σ_{2x} matrix would be like a Kronecker product of $I \times \sigma_x \times I \times I$ giving a 16×16 matrix at the end.

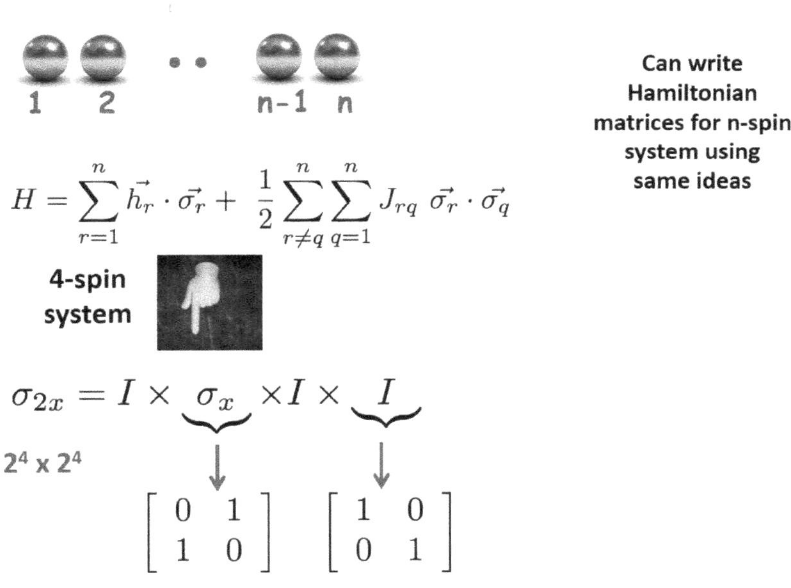

Fig. 5.27 Writing n-spin matrices.

5.3.5 *Figs. 5.28-5.29: Why quantum computers?*

5.3.5.1 *Fig. 5.28*

So in principle, that's all there is to it. In practice, of course, the problem gets huge as n gets bigger because of this exponential problem that I had mentioned before that as n grows, 2^n power grows exponentially and that is what makes it practically difficult to deal with large quantum spin problems in general (see Fig. 5.28). That is, in a way, the basic rationale for building a quantum computer.

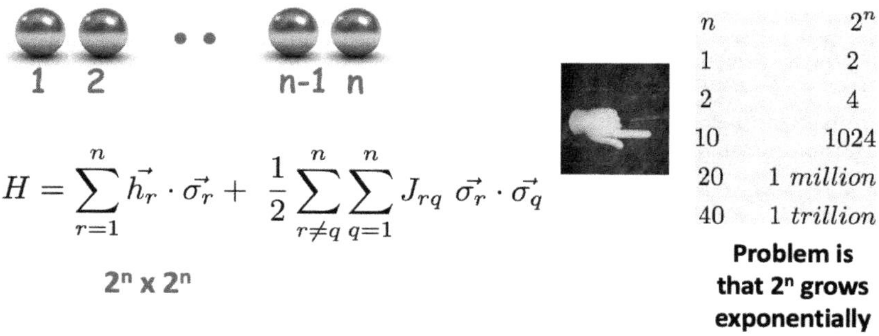

1 2 .. n-1 n

$$H = \sum_{r=1}^{n} \vec{h_r} \cdot \vec{\sigma_r} + \frac{1}{2} \sum_{r \neq q}^{n} \sum_{q=1}^{n} J_{rq}\ \vec{\sigma_r} \cdot \vec{\sigma_q}$$

2^n x 2^n

n	2^n
1	2
2	4
10	1024
20	1 *million*
40	1 *trillion*

Problem is that 2^n grows exponentially

Fig. 5.28 Exponential growth in matrix size.

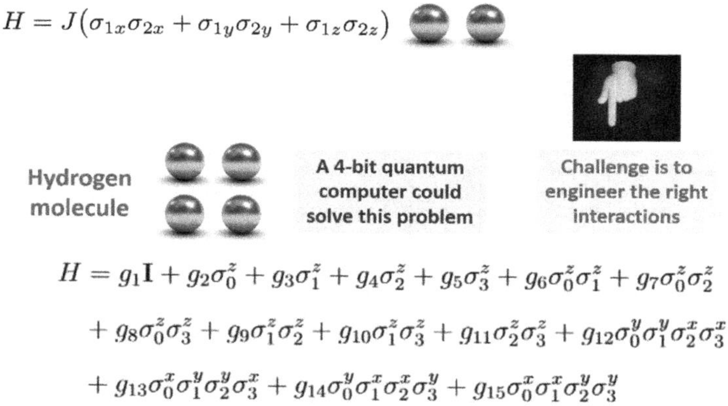

$$H = J\big(\sigma_{1x}\sigma_{2x} + \sigma_{1y}\sigma_{2y} + \sigma_{1z}\sigma_{2z}\big)$$

Hydrogen molecule

A 4-bit quantum computer could solve this problem

Challenge is to engineer the right interactions

$$\begin{aligned} H = {} & g_1\mathbf{I} + g_2\sigma_0^z + g_3\sigma_1^z + g_4\sigma_2^z + g_5\sigma_3^z + g_6\sigma_0^z\sigma_1^z + g_7\sigma_0^z\sigma_2^z \\ & + g_8\sigma_0^z\sigma_3^z + g_9\sigma_1^z\sigma_2^z + g_{10}\sigma_1^z\sigma_3^z + g_{11}\sigma_2^z\sigma_3^z + g_{12}\sigma_0^y\sigma_1^y\sigma_2^x\sigma_3^x \\ & + g_{13}\sigma_0^x\sigma_1^y\sigma_2^y\sigma_3^x + g_{14}\sigma_0^y\sigma_1^x\sigma_2^x\sigma_3^y + g_{15}\sigma_0^x\sigma_1^x\sigma_2^y\sigma_3^y \end{aligned}$$

Fig. 5.29 H_2 molecule.

5.3.5.2 *Fig. 5.29*

As an example, for a hydrogen molecule one of the simpler models would lead to a Hamiltonian with four spins, σ_0, σ_1, σ_2, and σ_3, as shown. So it's a four spin system, and each one of the matrices appearing here would be $2^4 \times 2^4$. We could write out the 16×16 Hamiltonian matrix, find the density matrix and calculate the properties you're interested in.

On the other hand, you could build a 4-bit quantum computer to solve this problem. Of course, in this case, the direct calculation isn't too hard, because the matrices are 16 × 16, but this goes up exponentially. When you have bigger molecules and you want to calculate the structure, the direct calculation would involve huge matrices of size 2^n, but if you build a relatively small quantum computer with just n qubits, and in principle it could solve the problem for you.

Of course the challenge is how to engineer all these interactions. That how do you make sure that the interaction between say the z component of the second spin, and the z component of the third spin is indeed g_{11}, etc. That is the part that is hard to engineer, that is the challenge that people face when actually trying to build quantum computer. But the driving vision is that a 40 q-bit quantum computer could solve a 40 spin problem, something that would ordinarily involve $10^{12} \times 10^{12}$ matrices!

5.3.6 *Quiz*

5.3.6.1 *Question 1*

An operator for a 2-spin system is given by $\begin{bmatrix} 0 & 0 & 1 & 0 \\ 0 & 0 & 0 & 1 \\ 1 & 0 & 0 & 0 \\ 0 & 1 & 0 & 0 \end{bmatrix}$

Can you write it as the Kronecker product of the identity matrix and/or the Pauli spin matrices $\sigma_x, \sigma_y, \sigma_z$?[7]

5.3.6.2 *Question 2*

An operator for a 2-spin system is given by $\begin{bmatrix} +1 & 0 & 0 & 0 \\ 0 & -1 & 0 & 0 \\ 0 & 0 & -1 & 0 \\ 0 & 0 & 0 & +1 \end{bmatrix}$

Can you write it as the Kronecker product of the identity matrix and/or the Pauli spin matrices $\sigma_x, \sigma_y, \sigma_z$?[8]

---

[7] $\sigma_x \times I$.

[8] $\sigma_z \times \sigma_z$.

5.3.6.3 *Question 3*

An operator for a 2-spin system is given by $\begin{bmatrix} 0 & 0 & 0 & -i \\ 0 & 0 & +i & 0 \\ 0 & -i & 0 & 0 \\ +i & 0 & 0 & 0 \end{bmatrix}$

Can you write it as the Kronecker product of the identity matrix and/or the Pauli spin matrices $\sigma_x, \sigma_y, \sigma_z$?[9]

[9] $\sigma_x \times \sigma_y$.

5.4 Two q-bit System

This is Lecture 5.4: Watch youtube video

Now that we have established the basic framework for the quantum description, let us consider a two q-bit system described by an energy operator of this form, $H = \overrightarrow{h_1} \cdot \overrightarrow{\sigma_1} + \overrightarrow{h_2} \cdot \overrightarrow{\sigma_2} + J\overrightarrow{\sigma_1} \cdot \overrightarrow{\sigma_2}$. and work out some of the consequences. Hopefully this will give you a better feeling of how these things work.

5.4.1 *Figs. 5.30-5.31: Hamiltonian*

5.4.1.1 *Figs. 5.30*

Let us assume that all the one spin terms $\overrightarrow{h_1}, \overrightarrow{h_2}, \overrightarrow{h_3}$ are zero and consider just the interaction term $J\overrightarrow{\sigma_1} \cdot \overrightarrow{\sigma_2}$ which is the sum of three terms $J(\sigma_{1x}\sigma_{2x} + \sigma_{1y}\sigma_{2y} + \sigma_{1z}\sigma_{2z})$. Following the procedure discussed in the last lecture we write out the 4×4 matrices for each of the terms.

1 2

$$H = J\big(\sigma_{1x}\sigma_{2x} + \sigma_{1y}\sigma_{2y} + \sigma_{1z}\sigma_{2z}\big)$$

$$\sigma_{1x} = \sigma_x \times \mathbf{I} \quad \sigma_{2x} = \mathbf{I} \times \sigma_{\mathbf{x}}$$

$$\begin{bmatrix} 0 & 0 & 1 & 0 \\ 0 & 0 & 0 & 1 \\ 1 & 0 & 0 & 0 \\ 0 & 1 & 0 & 0 \end{bmatrix} \begin{bmatrix} 0 & 1 & 0 & 0 \\ 1 & 0 & 0 & 0 \\ 0 & 0 & 0 & 1 \\ 0 & 0 & 1 & 0 \end{bmatrix} = \begin{bmatrix} 0 & 0 & 0 & 1 \\ 0 & 0 & 1 & 0 \\ 0 & 1 & 0 & 0 \\ 1 & 0 & 0 & 0 \end{bmatrix} \sigma_{1x}\sigma_{2x}$$

$$\sigma_{1y} = \sigma_y \times \mathbf{I} \quad \sigma_{2y} = \mathbf{I} \times \sigma_{\mathbf{y}}$$

$$\begin{bmatrix} 0 & 0 & -i & 0 \\ 0 & 0 & 0 & -i \\ +i & 0 & 0 & 0 \\ 0 & +i & 0 & 0 \end{bmatrix} \begin{bmatrix} 0 & -i & 0 & 0 \\ +i & 0 & 0 & 0 \\ 0 & 0 & 0 & -i \\ 0 & 0 & +i & 0 \end{bmatrix} = \begin{bmatrix} 0 & 0 & 0 & -1 \\ 0 & 0 & +1 & 0 \\ 0 & +1 & 0 & 0 \\ -1 & 0 & 0 & 0 \end{bmatrix} \sigma_{1y}\sigma_{2y}$$

$$\sigma_{1z} = \sigma_z \times \mathbf{I} \quad \sigma_{2z} = \mathbf{I} \times \sigma_{\mathbf{z}}$$

$$\begin{bmatrix} +1 & 0 & 0 & 0 \\ 0 & +1 & 0 & 0 \\ 0 & 0 & -1 & 0 \\ 0 & 0 & 0 & -1 \end{bmatrix} \begin{bmatrix} +1 & 0 & 0 & 0 \\ 0 & -1 & 0 & 0 \\ 0 & 0 & +1 & 0 \\ 0 & 0 & 0 & -1 \end{bmatrix} = \begin{bmatrix} +1 & 0 & 0 & 0 \\ 0 & -1 & 0 & 0 \\ 0 & 0 & -1 & 0 \\ 0 & 0 & 0 & +1 \end{bmatrix} \sigma_{1z}\sigma_{2z}$$

Fig. 5.30 Writing $J\overrightarrow{\sigma_1} \cdot \overrightarrow{\sigma_2}$ in matrix form.

5.4.1.2 *Fig. 5.31*

So now, if we want to write out the total matrix, we have to add up these three matrices. The items on the diagonal come from $\sigma_{1z}\sigma_{2z}$, because the other two have all 0's on the diagonal, while the off-diagonal terms come from the other two $\sigma_{1x}\sigma_{2x}$ and $\sigma_{1y}\sigma_{2y}$.

$$H = J\big(\sigma_{1x}\sigma_{2x} + \sigma_{1y}\sigma_{2y} + \sigma_{1z}\sigma_{2z}\big)$$

Two q-bit system

$$= J \begin{bmatrix} +1 & 0 & 0 & 0 \\ 0 & -1 & 2 & 0 \\ 0 & 2 & -1 & 0 \\ 0 & 0 & 0 & +1 \end{bmatrix} \quad (\text{columns/rows: } 00,\ 01,\ 10,\ 11)$$

$$= \begin{bmatrix} 0 & 0 & 0 & 1 \\ 0 & 0 & 1 & 0 \\ 0 & 1 & 0 & 0 \\ 1 & 0 & 0 & 0 \end{bmatrix} \ \sigma_{1x}\sigma_{2x}$$

$$= \begin{bmatrix} 0 & 0 & 0 & -1 \\ 0 & 0 & +1 & 0 \\ 0 & +1 & 0 & 0 \\ -1 & 0 & 0 & 0 \end{bmatrix} \ \sigma_{1y}\sigma_{2y}$$

$$= \begin{bmatrix} +1 & 0 & 0 & 0 \\ 0 & -1 & 0 & 0 \\ 0 & 0 & -1 & 0 \\ 0 & 0 & 0 & +1 \end{bmatrix} \ \sigma_{1z}\sigma_{2z}$$

Fig. 5.31 Writing $J\,\vec{\sigma_1}\cdot\vec{\sigma_2}$ in matrix form (contd.).

5.4.2 *Figs. 5.32-5.33: Ising spins*

5.4.2.1 *Fig. 5.32*

Now what we need to do is, find the density matrix which is $\exp(-H)$. If we ignore the off diagonal terms, which came from σ_x and σ_y, then this would be equivalent to doing just classical spins, sometimes referred to as Ising spins. You'd then have a purely diagonal matrix. It is easy then to write down the exponential as shown, with $\exp(-J)$, $\exp(+J)$, $\exp(+J)$, and $\exp(-J)$ on the diagonal, all the rest being zero.

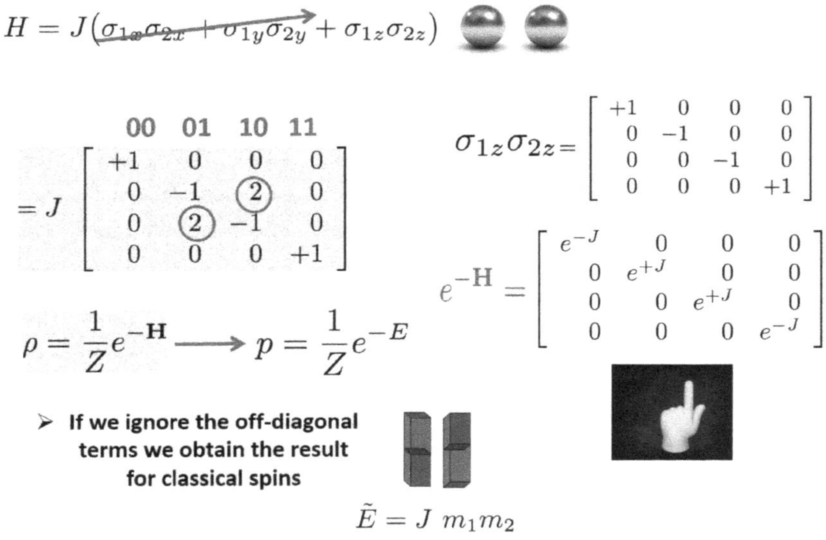

$$H = J(\sigma_{1x}\sigma_{2x} + \sigma_{1y}\sigma_{2y} + \sigma_{1z}\sigma_{2z})$$

00 01 10 11

$$= J\begin{bmatrix} +1 & 0 & 0 & 0 \\ 0 & -1 & 2 & 0 \\ 0 & 2 & -1 & 0 \\ 0 & 0 & 0 & +1 \end{bmatrix}$$

$$\sigma_{1z}\sigma_{2z} = \begin{bmatrix} +1 & 0 & 0 & 0 \\ 0 & -1 & 0 & 0 \\ 0 & 0 & -1 & 0 \\ 0 & 0 & 0 & +1 \end{bmatrix}$$

$$e^{-\mathbf{H}} = \begin{bmatrix} e^{-J} & 0 & 0 & 0 \\ 0 & e^{+J} & 0 & 0 \\ 0 & 0 & e^{+J} & 0 \\ 0 & 0 & 0 & e^{-J} \end{bmatrix}$$

$$\rho = \frac{1}{Z}e^{-\mathbf{H}} \longrightarrow p = \frac{1}{Z}e^{-E}$$

➢ **If we ignore the off-diagonal terms we obtain the result for classical spins**

$$\tilde{E} = J\ m_1 m_2$$

Fig. 5.32 Classical or Ising spins.

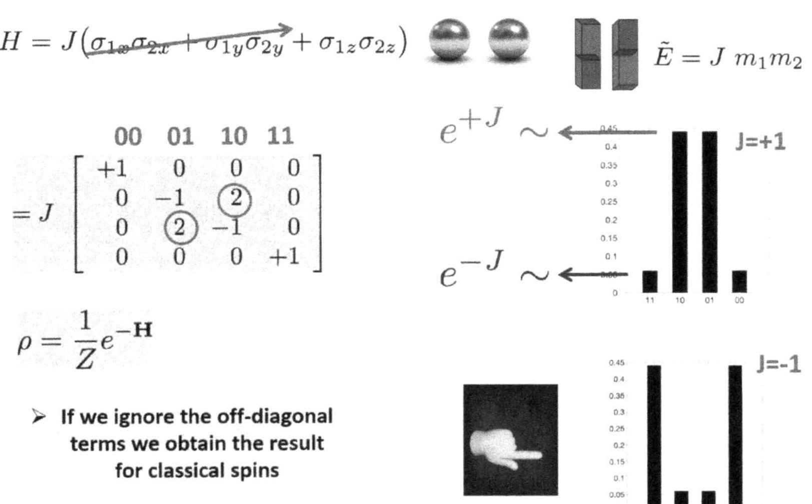
$H = J(\sigma_{1x}\sigma_{2x} + \sigma_{1y}\sigma_{2y} + \sigma_{1z}\sigma_{2z})$
$\tilde{E} = J\ m_1 m_2$
00 01 10 11
$= J\begin{bmatrix} +1 & 0 & 0 & 0 \\ 0 & -1 & 2 & 0 \\ 0 & 2 & -1 & 0 \\ 0 & 0 & 0 & +1 \end{bmatrix}$
$e^{+J} \sim$
$e^{-J} \sim$
J=+1
J=-1
$\rho = \frac{1}{Z}e^{-\mathbf{H}}$
➢ If we ignore the off-diagonal terms we obtain the result for classical spins
11
10
01
00

Fig. 5.33 Classical or Ising spins.

5.4.2.2 *Fig. 5.33*

So in this limit when you have ignored the σ_x and σ_y terms, we just get what we'd have got in the classical case that we looked at in Chapter 3. The heights for the states $\{01\}$ and $\{10\}$ are $\sim \exp(+J)$, which means if J is a positive quantity, these would be the tall peaks. The heights for $\{00\}$ and $\{11\}$ are $\sim \exp(-J)$, and of course, if J were negative, these would be the peaks. Easy to understand this, positive J makes it energetically favorable for the two spins to be antiparallel ($m_1 m_2 < 0$), while a negative J makes it favorable to be parallel ($m_1 m_2 > 0$). These are often referred to as antiferromagnetic and ferromagnetic interaction respectively.

5.4.3 *Figs. 5.34-5.35: Quantum spins*

5.4.3.1 *Fig. 5.34*

Now, if you keep the x and y terms, then you will get something that looks a little different (see Fig. 5.34). Qualitatively it's still similar in that positive J accentuates (01) and (10) while a negative J accentuates (00) and (11).

But in the quantum case, firstly, you will notice that for positive J, the (01) and (10) seem taller with respect to (00) (11) than in the classical case. But the result for negative J is more striking, it doesn't matter how big you make J, (01) and (10) never get suppressed beyond a factor of two. It is always half of this (see Fig. 5.34). By contrast, in the classical case, with negative J, (01) and (10) get suppressed exponentially as J gets more negative.

5.4.3.2 *Fig. 5.35*

It is straightforward to see the mathematical origin of this difference by performing the matrix exponentiation of the full H matrix, e^{-H}. Earlier we ignored the off-diagonal terms in H and got a diagonal matrix with $\exp(-J)$, $\exp(+J)$, $\exp(+J)$ and $\exp(-J)$ along the diagonal. When we include the off-diagonal terms in H the extremes still remain $\exp(-J)$, but in the middle we have a matrix as shown. The probabilities of (01) and (10) are given by $a = (e^{-J} + e^{+3J})/2$.

So based on this, you can understand what I had mentioned before, namely that for $J << 0$, the (01) and (10) peaks tend to half the (00) and (11) peaks, since $a \rightarrow e^{-J}/2$.

This quantum problem appears in many contexts and are often discussed in terms of what are called singlet and triplet states, but we will not discuss the physics any further. Our purpose is simply to illustrate the overall quantum methodology, which is straightforward to implement on MATLAB or Python even after including more details like the single spin terms, $\vec{h_1}, \vec{h_2}, \vec{h_3}$ that we ignored at the outset.

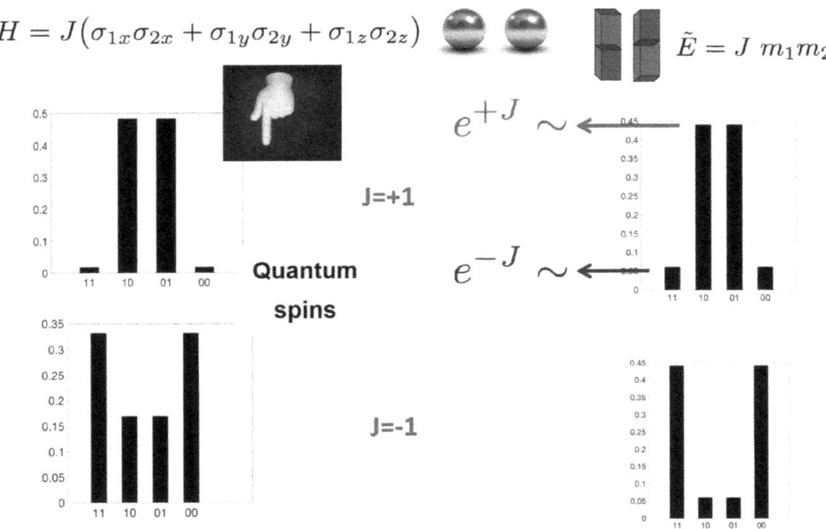

Fig. 5.34 Comparing Ising to quantum spins.

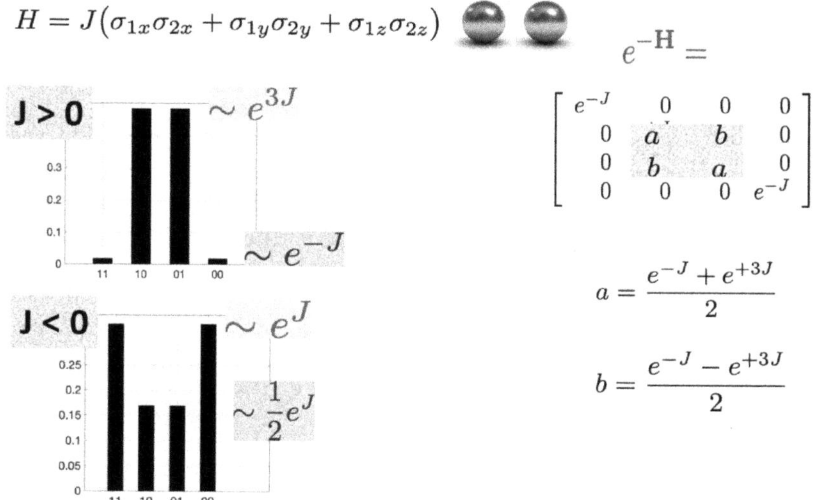

$H = J(\sigma_{1x}\sigma_{2x} + \sigma_{1y}\sigma_{2y} + \sigma_{1z}\sigma_{2z})$
J > 0
$\sim e^{3J}$
$\sim e^{-J}$
11 10 01 00
J < 0
$\sim e^{J}$
$\sim \frac{1}{2}e^{J}$
11 10 01 00
$e^{-H} = \begin{bmatrix} e^{-J} & 0 & 0 & 0 \\ 0 & a & b & 0 \\ 0 & b & a & 0 \\ 0 & 0 & 0 & e^{-J} \end{bmatrix}$
$a = \frac{e^{-J} + e^{+3J}}{2}$
$b = \frac{e^{-J} - e^{+3J}}{2}$

Fig. 5.35 Two quantum spins.

5.4.4 *Quiz*

5.4.4.1 *Question 1*

An operator for a 2-spin system is given by $\begin{bmatrix} +1 & 0 & 0 & 0 \\ 0 & -1 & 2 & 0 \\ 0 & 2 & -1 & 0 \\ 0 & 0 & 0 & +1 \end{bmatrix}$

Can you write it in terms of the 4×4 matrices like σ_{1x}, σ_{2y} etc?[10]

5.4.4.2 *Question 2*

Suppose for a 2-spin system we have $e^{-H} = \begin{bmatrix} 10 & 0 & 0 & 0 \\ 0 & 5 & 5 & 0 \\ 0 & 5 & 5 & 0 \\ 0 & 0 & 0 & 10 \end{bmatrix}$

What is the expectation value $\langle m_{1x} \rangle$?[11]

---

[10] $\sigma_{1x}\sigma_{2x} + \sigma_{1y}\sigma_{2y} + \sigma_{1z}\sigma_{2z}$.
[11] 0.

5.4.4.3 *Question 3*

An operator for a 2-spin system is given by $\begin{bmatrix} 0 & 0 & 0 & 1 \\ 0 & 0 & 1 & 0 \\ 0 & 1 & 0 & 0 \\ 1 & 0 & 0 & 0 \end{bmatrix}$

Can you write it in terms of the 4×4 matrices like σ_{1x}, σ_{2y} etc?[12]

[12] $\sigma_{1x}\sigma_{2x}$.

5.5 Quantum Annealing

This is Lecture 5.5: Watch youtube video

In Lecture 6.3 I had mentioned that one use for a system of quantum spins, this what you might call generally adiabatic quantum computer, would be chemical structure calculations, which can be cast in the form of H matrix describing the interactions of many spins. But as we noted, the challenge there is how to implement the complex interactions in the actual hardware. Now, in this lecture, what we'll talk about a possible application known as *quantum annelaing* on which there has been a lot of work because this requires relatively simple interactions. Even without a quantum computer the principle itself could be useful when implemented on a conventional computer, something that is referred to as *simulated quantum annealing.*

5.5.1 *Figs. 5.36-5.38: Why anneal?*

5.5.1.1 *Fig. 5.36*

Now, let me start from a problem that we discussed in Chapter 3 where we talked about this problem of optimization using classical spins. The idea was how to design the interactions so that the lowest energy state indicates the solution to some problem we're interested in and we used the min cut or max cut problem as an illustration. So the idea was, if you have say a bunch of nodes, I show six nodes, of which some are connected strongly and some are not connected and there's a connection matrix describing these connections. The problem is to find a way of separating them into two separate groups of three nodes each, such that the connections that you are cutting when you break them apart is a minimum or is a maximum. We showed that there is a simple way to choose the bias terms x and the interaction terms w, given the connection matrix, such that the lowest energy solutions will solve the problem you're interested in.

5.5.1.2 *Fig. 5.37*

Now going forwards, what we'll be trying to do is translating this into a quantum system seeing what that can add to this story. But before we go on, let me just re-plot this graph, not as a two dimensional thing, but in one dimension. What I mean is, here the way we did it is we had eight states on each axis. Instead we plot it with all 64 items on a single axis,

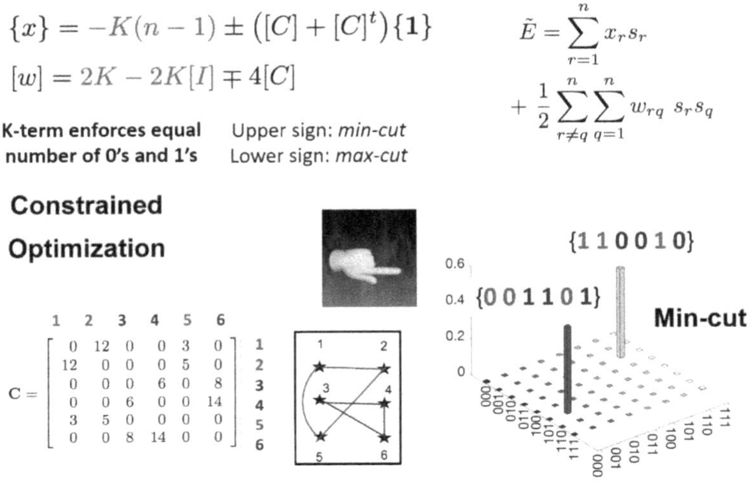

$$\{x\} = -K(n-1) \pm \big([C] + [C]^t\big)\{\mathbf{1}\}$$

$$[w] = 2K - 2K[I] \mp 4[C]$$

$$\tilde{E} = \sum_{r=1}^{n} x_r s_r + \frac{1}{2}\sum_{r \neq q}^{n}\sum_{q=1}^{n} w_{rq}\ s_r s_q$$

K-term enforces equal number of 0's and 1's

Upper sign: *min-cut*
Lower sign: *max-cut*

Constrained Optimization

$$C = \begin{bmatrix} 0 & 12 & 0 & 0 & 3 & 0 \\ 12 & 0 & 0 & 0 & 5 & 0 \\ 0 & 0 & 0 & 6 & 0 & 8 \\ 0 & 0 & 6 & 0 & 0 & 14 \\ 3 & 5 & 0 & 0 & 0 & 0 \\ 0 & 0 & 8 & 14 & 0 & 0 \end{bmatrix}$$

{1 1 0 0 1 0}
{0 0 1 1 0 1}
Min-cut

Fig. 5.36 Constrained optimization.

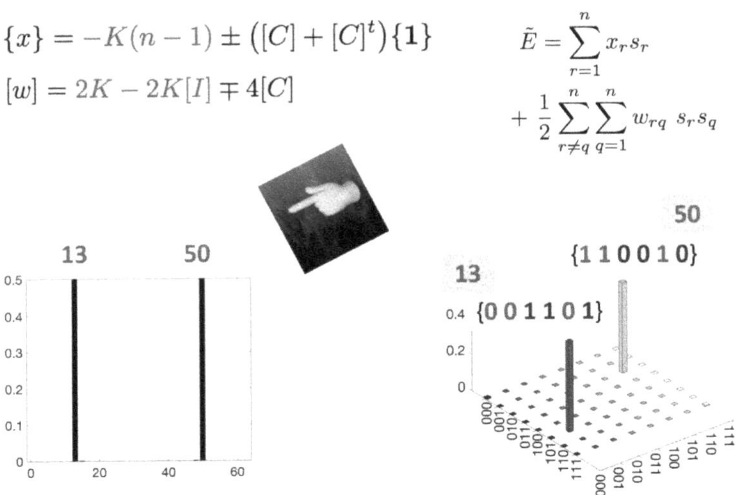

Fig. 5.37 Re-plotting in 1D.

The two solutions then look like a 13 and a 50, obtained by converting the binary number to a decimal one.

5.5.1.3 *Fig. 5.38*

Now in solving problems of this type, there is a common difficulty that I didn't talk about earlier. This is is not a problem you'd encounter with six *p-bits* usually, but with many *p-bits* what could often happen is that as you try to find the lowest energy states when you're sampling, you could get stuck in other states which are not really the lowest energy. If you take many, many samples, wait a long time, theoretically it should always get there, but with a reasonable number of samples, it often may be difficult to lock in on the right answers.

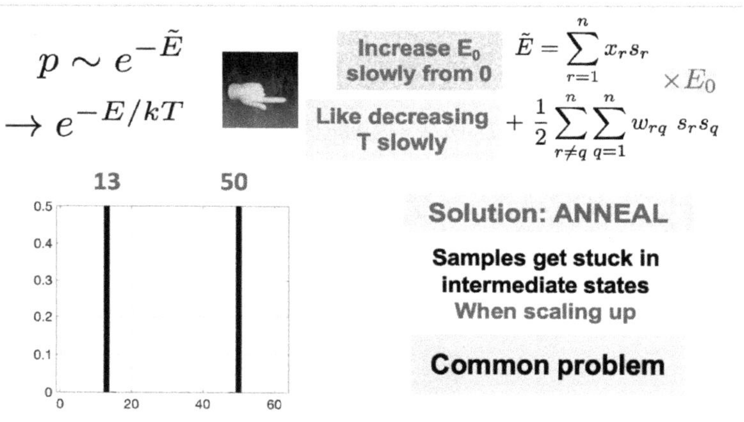

Fig. 5.38 Annealing.

So one solution that people use is what's called annealing (see Fig. 5.38). They multiply the energy by a number E_0, which is slowly turned up from zero. When E_0 is 0, all states are equally probable and then as you increase E_0, gradually the correct peaks rise up. In Chapter 1 we saw that for physical systems, $\widetilde{E} = E/kT$ and by analogy one could view our E_0 as $1/kT$ so that we are kind of starting at a high temperature and gradually lowering it. That is the origin of this word annealing. In physical systems, when people are trying to grow a crystal, a solid often gets stuck in higher energy states with many defects in it, and one way to get rid of defects is to anneal by lowering the temperature slowly. In this case, of course, we are not changing the physical temperature, we are just changing the energy function $\widetilde{E}$ through the constant E_0.

5.5.2 *Figs. 5.39-5.40: Translating to quantum spins*

5.5.2.1 *Fig. 5.39*

Now, what we want to talk about is the quantum version of this, and as I had noted earlier, when translating to quantum spins, it's more convenient to work from the bipolar formulation. So we do this in two steps as shown, first from binary to bipolar (Fig. 5.39), and then from bipolar to the quantum model with z-spins only (Fig. 5.40).

Note that m_r, m_q becomes σ_{zr}, σ_{zq}, and the point is that the coefficients h and J remain unchanged from what they were in Chapter 3.

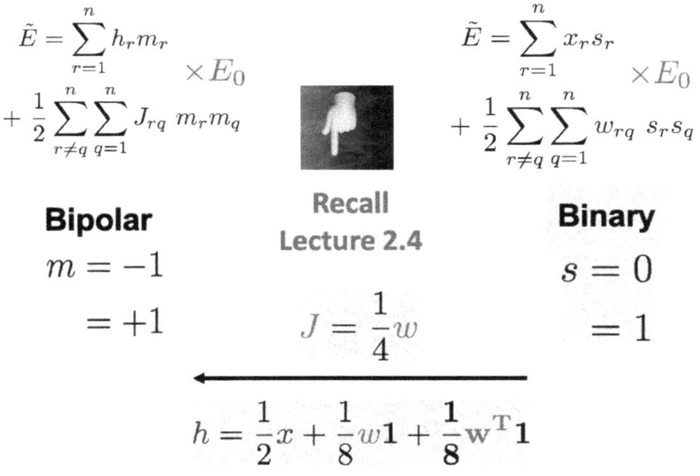

$$\tilde{E} = \sum_{r=1}^{n} h_r m_r + \frac{1}{2}\sum_{r\neq q}^{n}\sum_{q=1}^{n} J_{rq}\; m_r m_q \quad \times E_0$$

$$\tilde{E} = \sum_{r=1}^{n} x_r s_r + \frac{1}{2}\sum_{r\neq q}^{n}\sum_{q=1}^{n} w_{rq}\; s_r s_q \quad \times E_0$$

Bipolar $m = -1$, $= +1$

Recall Lecture 2.4

Binary $s = 0$, $= 1$

$$J = \frac{1}{4}w$$

$$h = \frac{1}{2}x + \frac{1}{8}w\mathbf{1} + \frac{1}{8}\mathbf{w}^{\mathrm{T}}\mathbf{1}$$

Fig. 5.39 Translating binary to bipolar.

5.5.3 *Fig. 5.41: Add transverse term*

Of course, if that was all, then you'd say, well, why do I even want to do it? The classical one is much simpler, we can go from there. But what the quantum one lets you also do is add other terms to it that are not in the z direction. So you could for example add a term like this, $\sum_{r=1}^{n} h_{xr}\sigma_{xr}$, which correspond to an energy term that involves the m_x component.

$$\tilde{E} = \sum_{r=1}^{n} h_r m_r + \frac{1}{2} \sum_{r \neq q}^{n} \sum_{q=1}^{n} J_{rq}\, m_r m_q \times E_0 \qquad H = \left(\sum_{r=1}^{n} h_{zr} \sigma_{zr} + \frac{1}{2} \sum_{r \neq q}^{n} \sum_{q=1}^{n} J_{rq}\, \sigma_{zr} \sigma_{zq} \right) \times E_0$$

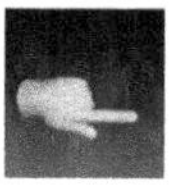

Fig. 5.40 Translating bipolar to quantum with z-spins only.

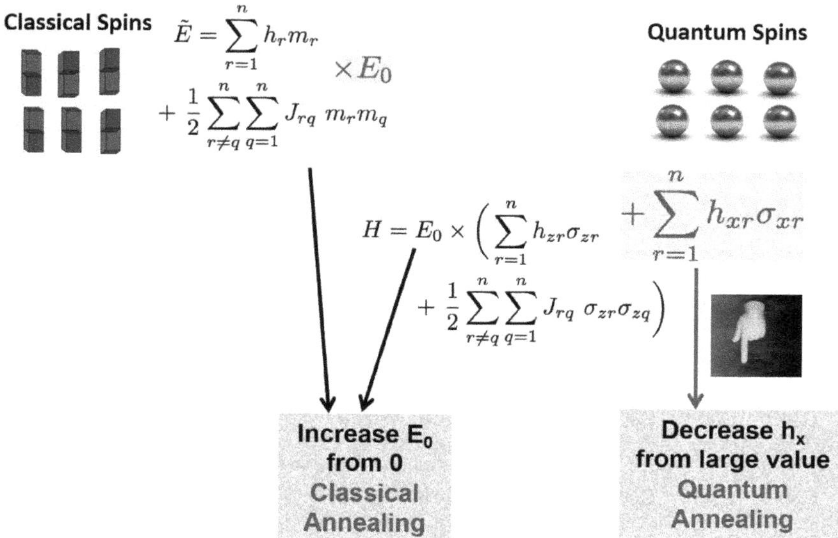

Fig. 5.41 Add x-spin term.

Now, the way classical annealing works is that you start with $E_0 = 0$, so all configurations have the same energy and then gradually you increase E_0, and the peaks gradually rise up. With quantum annealing what you could do is to could keep E_0 fixed, whatever your normal value is, but you gradually decrease this transverse h_x from a large value. This is something you couldn't have done with your classical spins.

5.5.4 *Fig. 5.42: Classical versus quantum annealing*

Now, just to give you an example, with $E_0 = 1$ and $h_{xr} = 0$ we have this solution I've shown before, two peaks at 13 and 50. In classical annealing you could approach the final result by starting with $E_0 = 0.04$ and increasing to $E_0 = 1$, while in quantum annealing you could start with $h_{xr} = 15$ and work your way down to $h_{xr} = 0$. As you can see both have qualitatively the same effect, start with lots of peaks and gradually lock down to the desired ones.

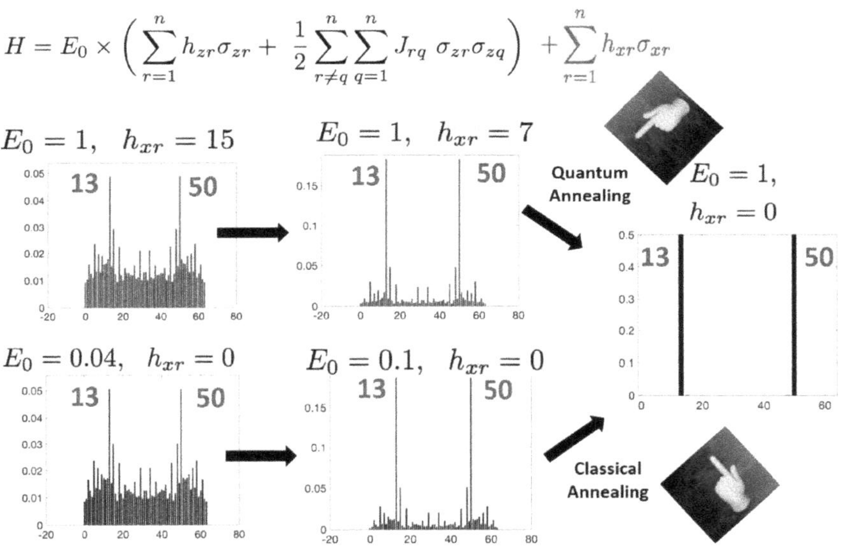

Fig. 5.42 Classical versus quantum annealing, MATLAB code included at end of book.

But why would you think that quantum annealing might be better than classical annealing? Well, there is a theorem that says that when you gradually change a parameter in your Hamiltonian, if you do it slowly enough, that if initially it was in some ground state, then it will stay there and eventually you will actually get to the ground state. But in the classical case, there is really no theorem that guarantees that you will get to the ground state.

Now in practice how well this will work, how slowly you have to go to actually take advantage of these? These are all still debated and pretty much up in the air. So there have been demonstrations of various kinds, there's a lot of work that has gone into this, but the motivation is that quantum annealing might allow you to get to the ground state faster and more reliably than the classical one.

5.5.5 *Figs. 5.43-5.44: How the transverse term works*

5.5.5.1 *Figs. 5.43*

Now, why does the x term have the same effect as lowering E_0, namely making all states equally likely? Well, one way to think about it is to recall from Lecture 5.1 that the expectation value of m_z is given by $-\tanh(h)\cos(\theta)$. So if you put an h in the x direction corresponding to θ being 90 degrees, then $\cos(\theta)$ being 0, it says that the expectation value of m_z is 0 (see Fig. 5.43).

What that means is that with large h_{xr}, for each spin r, both $+1$ and -1 states are equally likely, which makes all states kind of equally probable.

$$H = E_0 \times \left(\sum_{r=1}^{n} h_{zr}\sigma_{zr} + \frac{1}{2}\sum_{r \neq q}^{n}\sum_{q=1}^{n} J_{rq}\ \sigma_{zr}\sigma_{zq} \right) + \sum_{r=1}^{n} h_{xr}\sigma_{xr}$$

Why x-term works

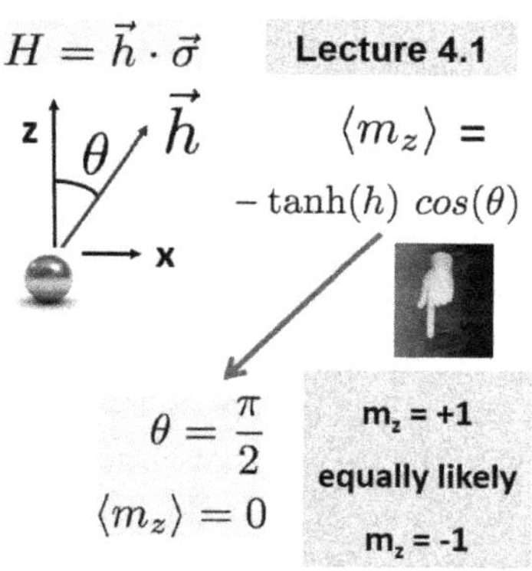

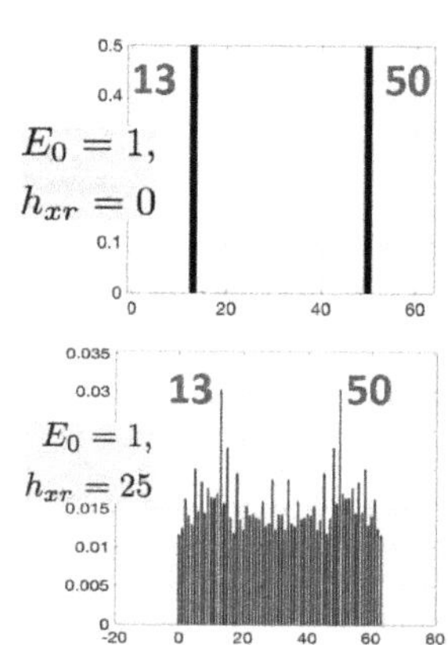

Fig. 5.43 How the x-term works.

5.5.5.2 *Fig. 5.44: Density matrix to wavefunction*

You can get a little more insight if you actually go from density matrices to wave functions, which is not always possible, and in the next week we'll

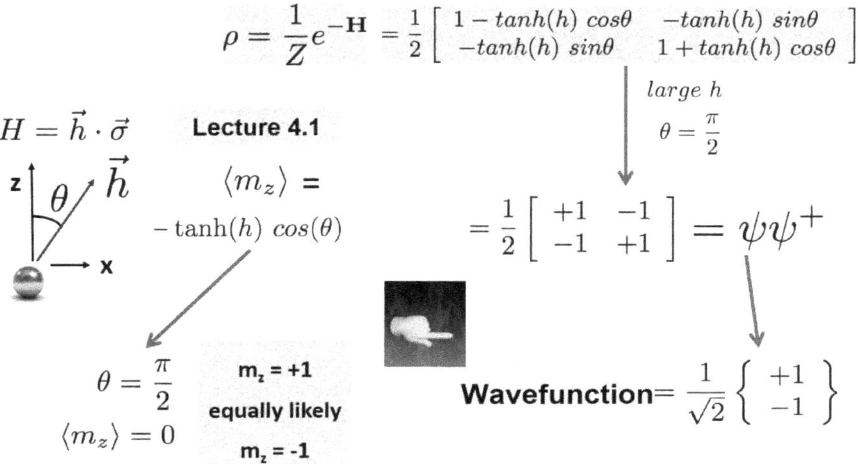

Fig. 5.44 Density matrix to wavefunction.

discuss this much more. For the moment we note that if you put a large h at 90 degrees, the density matrix takes a simple form that can be factorized to give us a wavefunction ψ such that $\rho = \psi\psi^+$.

As we'll discuss next week, there are systems where you can take the density matrix and factorize it, and in that case, you can think in terms of a wave function, which is a little easier because it's just got two components as opposed to the density matrix, which is a matrix.

With wavefunctions, the squared magnitude of the first component tells you the probability of up ($m_z = +1$) and the second one tells you the probability of down ($m_z = -1$). In this case the two components of the wavefunction are equal indicating that up and down states are equally likely.

Next chapter we'll see more of wavefunctions.

5.5.6 *Quiz*

5.5.6.1 *Question 1*

A classical spin system has an energy function given by

$$\widetilde{E} = \sum_{r=1}^{n} b_r s_r + \frac{1}{2} \sum_{r \neq q}^{n} \sum_{q=1}^{n} w_{rq} s_r s_q$$

in binary representation 0, 1 (using b_r instead of our usual x_r to avoid confusion with the coordinate x).

In bipolar representation it is given by

$$\widetilde{E} = \sum_{r=1}^{n} h_r m_r + \frac{1}{2} \sum_{r \neq q}^{n} \sum_{q=1}^{n} J_{rq} m_r m_q$$

What is the Hamiltonian matrix for the corresponding quantum spin system?[13]

5.5.6.2 *Question 2*

A quantum spin system has a Hamiltonian matrix given by

$$H = E_0 \times \sum_{r=1}^{n} h_{zr} \sigma_{zr} + \frac{1}{2} \sum_{r \neq q}^{n} \sum_{q=1}^{n} J_{rq} \sigma_{zr} \sigma_{zq} + \sum_{r=1}^{n} h_{xr} \sigma_{xr}$$

How would you implement classical annealing on this system?[14]

5.5.6.3 *Question 3*

A quantum spin system has a Hamiltonian matrix given by

$$H = E_0 \times \sum_{r=1}^{n} h_{zr} \sigma_{zr} + \frac{1}{2} \sum_{r \neq q}^{n} \sum_{q=1}^{n} J_{rq} \sigma_{zr} \sigma_{zq} + \sum_{r=1}^{n} h_{xr} \sigma_{xr}$$

How would you implement quantum annealing on this system?[15]

[13] $H = \sum_{r=1}^{n} h_r \sigma_{zr} + \frac{1}{2} \sum_{r \neq q}^{n} \sum_{q=1}^{n} J_{rq} \sigma_{zr} \sigma_{zq}$.
[14] Slowly changing E_0 from a low value to a large value.
[15] Slowly changing h_{xr} from a large value to a small value.

5.6 EPR Experiment

In this chapter we have introduced the quantum methodology: To every observable S, there is a corresponding operator S_{op} and knowing the density matrix ρ we can find the average value of measurements from the relation $trace[\rho S_{op}]$. Let us end this chapter with an example that shows that the methodology is straightforward to apply, but understanding the results can take much longer!

5.6.1 *Fig. 5.45: Problem statement*

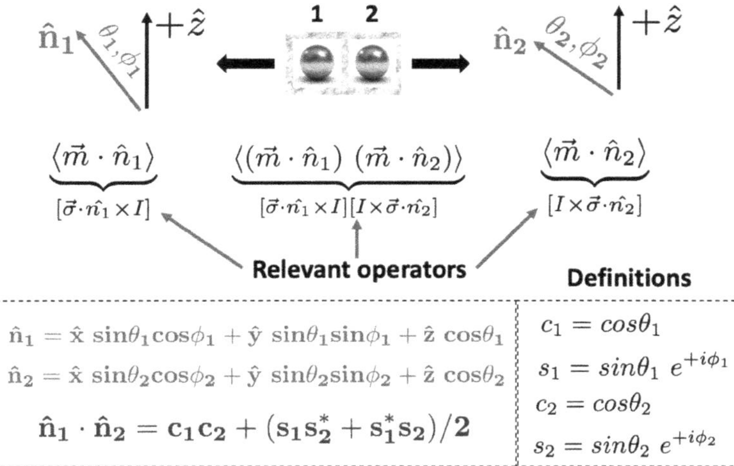

Fig. 5.45 A pair of electrons is initially prepared in some state: their spins are then measured respectively along two arbitrary directions $\hat{n}_1$ and $\hat{n}_2$. Problem is to predict the averages of each measurement and the average of their product. The operators corresponding to these observables are indicated.

The problem we consider is the following. A pair of electrons is initially prepared in some state and their spins are then measured respectively along two arbitrary directions $\hat{n}_1$ and $\hat{n}_2$. Problem is to predict the averages of the measurements of $\vec{m} \cdot \hat{n}_1$, $\vec{m} \cdot \hat{n}_2$ and their product $(\vec{m} \cdot \hat{n}_1)(\vec{m} \cdot \hat{n}_2)$. The operators corresponding to these three observables are obtained from the 2×2 matrices obtained by replacing $\vec{m}$ with $\vec{\sigma}$. But before we write down the observables let us talk about the initial states we consider and their density matrices.

5.6.2 *Fig. 5.46: Density matrix*

We consider four separate initial states: First is the state (01) with spin 1 pointing along $+\hat{z}$ and spin 2 pointing along $-\hat{z}$. The corresponding density matrix has only one non-zero element for [01, 01]. Second is the state (10) with the spins reversed. The density matrix now has its non-zero element for [10, 10]. Third is a state that is a 50 − 50 mixture of the two, and the corresponding density matrix is a 50 − 50 combination of the last two. We will refer to it as the *classical mixture state.*

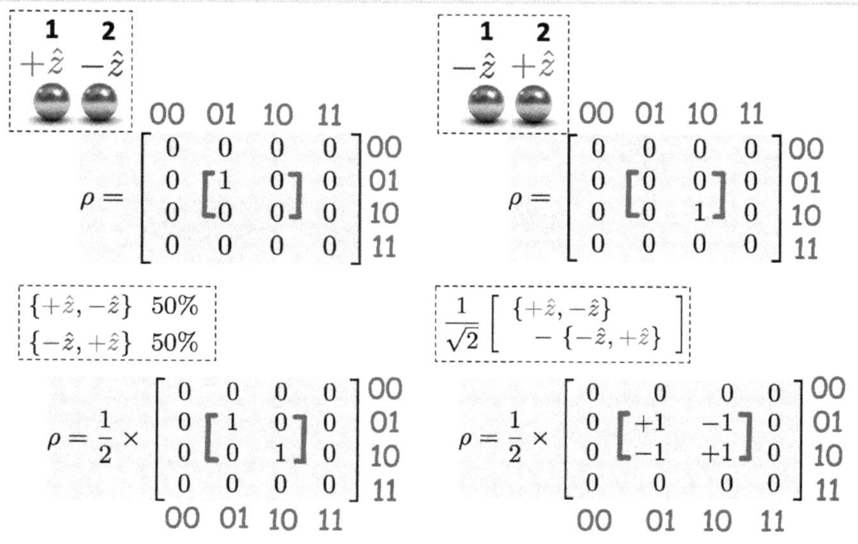

Fig. 5.46 Four different initial states that we consider and the corresponding density matrices.

These three initial states are all classical states that we have included to provide a contrast to the fourth state which is the *quantum entangled state* that the EPR experiment is actually about. Earlier in this chapter we saw that a pair of electrons when subject to a large antiferromagnetic interaction ($J >> 0$) go to a ground state with a density matrix as shown having two additional *off-diagonal* terms compared to the third initial state. In this case the density matrix can actually be factorized ($\rho = \psi\psi^T$) to give a wavefunction $\psi = \{0 \ +1 \ -1 \ 0\}^T/\sqrt{2}$ indicating that it is a superposition of (01) and (10) with a negative sign.

5.6.3 *Fig. 5.47: Operators for observables*

Next we write down the operators corresponding to the three observables in the problem. The 4×4 matrix corresponding to $\vec{m} \cdot \hat{n}_1$ is obtained by replacing $\vec{m}$ with the 2×2 spin matrix $\vec{\sigma}$, and then taking the Kronecker product with the identity matrix representing spin 2. Similarly the matrix corresponding to $\vec{m} \cdot \hat{n}_2$ is obtained from the Kronecker product of I with $\vec{\sigma} \cdot \hat{n}_2$. Finally the matrix corresponding to the product $(\vec{m} \cdot \hat{n}_1)(\vec{m} \cdot \hat{n}_2)$ is obtained from the matrix product of the two 4×4 matrices we just wrote down. Alternatively we could take the Kronecker product of the 2×2 matrices $\vec{\sigma} \cdot \hat{n}_1$ and $\vec{\sigma} \cdot \hat{n}_2$.

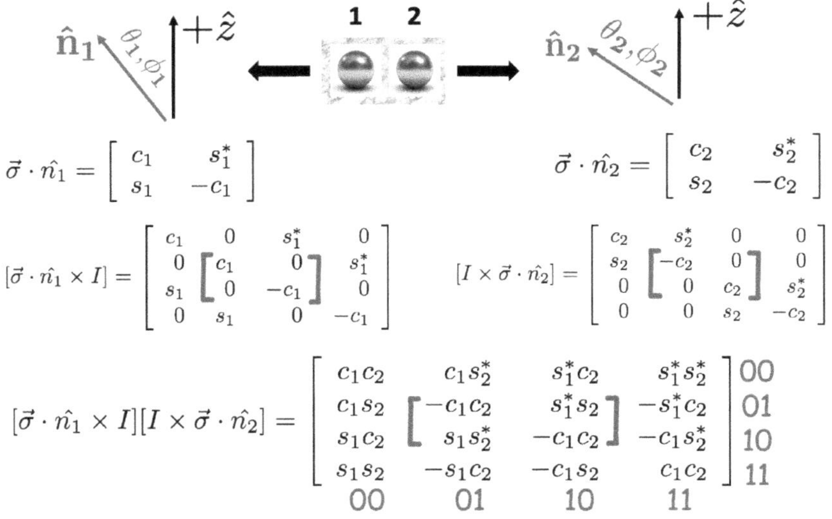

Fig. 5.47 Operators corresponding to the three observables we consider.

5.6.4 *Fig. 5.48: Predicting the averages*

Now that we have both the density matrices ρ and the operators S_{op} for each observables S, we are ready to compute the predictions for the average value from the relation $trace[\rho S_{op}]$. Note that all the density matrices have non-zero elements only in the middle 2×2 block indicated in red in Figs. 5.46 and 5.47. Although the matrices are 4×4, we only need to consider the 2×2 sections indicated, making the algebra fairly simple.

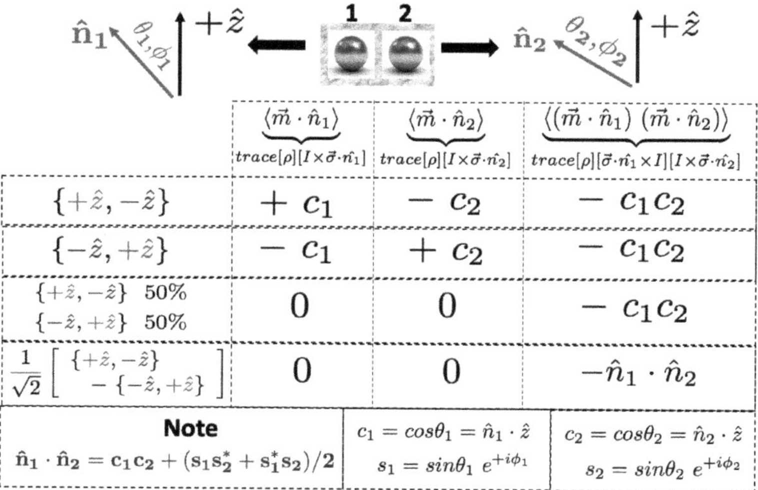

	$\underbrace{\langle \vec{m} \cdot \hat{n}_1 \rangle}_{trace[\rho][I \times \vec{\sigma} \cdot \hat{n}_1]}$	$\underbrace{\langle \vec{m} \cdot \hat{n}_2 \rangle}_{trace[\rho][I \times \vec{\sigma} \cdot \hat{n}_2]}$	$\underbrace{\langle (\vec{m} \cdot \hat{n}_1)\ (\vec{m} \cdot \hat{n}_2) \rangle}_{trace[\rho][\vec{\sigma} \cdot \hat{n}_1 \times I][I \times \vec{\sigma} \cdot \hat{n}_2]}$
$\{+\hat{z}, -\hat{z}\}$	$+\ c_1$	$-\ c_2$	$-\ c_1 c_2$
$\{-\hat{z}, +\hat{z}\}$	$-\ c_1$	$+\ c_2$	$-\ c_1 c_2$
$\{+\hat{z}, -\hat{z}\}$ 50% $\{-\hat{z}, +\hat{z}\}$ 50%	0	0	$-\ c_1 c_2$
$\frac{1}{\sqrt{2}} \left[\begin{array}{l} \{+\hat{z}, -\hat{z}\} \\ \quad - \{-\hat{z}, +\hat{z}\} \end{array} \right]$	0	0	$-\hat{n}_1 \cdot \hat{n}_2$

Note $\hat{\mathbf{n}}_1 \cdot \hat{\mathbf{n}}_2 = \mathbf{c}_1 \mathbf{c}_2 + (\mathbf{s}_1 \mathbf{s}_2^* + \mathbf{s}_1^* \mathbf{s}_2)/2$	$c_1 = cos\theta_1 = \hat{n}_1 \cdot \hat{z}$ $s_1 = sin\theta_1\ e^{+i\phi_1}$	$c_2 = cos\theta_2 = \hat{n}_2 \cdot \hat{z}$ $s_2 = sin\theta_2\ e^{+i\phi_2}$

Fig. 5.48 Predicted results for the average value of the three observables for each of the initial states.

5.6.5 *Fig. 5.49: Interpreting the results*

To interpret the results it is useful to consider the actual histogram of results that is experimentally observed from which the average values in Fig. 5.48 are to be calculated. For example, the average value of $\vec{m} \cdot \hat{n}_1$ is given as $c_1 = cos\theta_1$. Experimentally one measures some spins that are up (u) along $\hat{n}_1$ and contribute +1 and some spins that are down (d) and contribute −1. The fraction of spins contributing +1 is $p_1 \equiv cos^2(\theta_1/2)$, while the fraction contributing −1 is $q_1 \equiv sin^2(\theta_1/2)$, so that the average value is $p_1 - q_1 = c_1$ as shown in Fig. 5.49.

You might say well it's nice that p_1 and q_1 give us the right average c_1 we calculated directly from the operator $\vec{\sigma} \cdot \hat{n}_1$. But isn't there a operator that would let me calculate p_1, the number of up's directly. Indeed we could do that using the operator $(I + \vec{\sigma} \cdot \hat{n}_1)/2$ as I had mentioned earlier (see Fig. 5.16). We would then have obtained $(1 + c_1)/2 = p_1$.[16]

[16]Incidentally you might have noticed that we are getting $p_1 = cos^2(\theta_1/2)$ for the probability of detecting an upsin along $\hat{n}_1$ which is at an angle θ_1 to the direction of the spin $\hat{z}$. With photons the answer would have been $p_1 = cos^2\theta_1$, obtained from the square of the dot product $\hat{n}_1 \cdot \hat{z}$. Photon polarization is represented by vectors and the dot product gives $cos\theta_1$. But electron spin is represented by spinors and the "dot product" gives $cos(\theta_1/2)$.

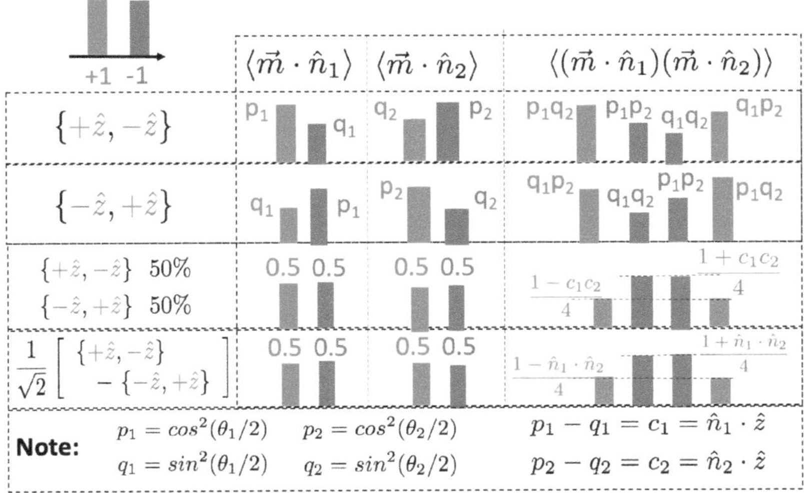

Fig. 5.49 Predicted histogram for the three observables for each of the initial states whose averages are shown in Fig. 5.48. On the right there are four bars, the red ones (uu and dd) contributing +1, and the blue ones (ud and du) contributing −1. On the left there are two bars, the red (u) contributing +1 and the blue (d) contributing −1.

Anyway, from this picture we can understand the results for the first two initial conditions and see how we get the average values of $\pm c_1$ and $\mp c_2$, and their product gives the average of the product or the correlation $-c_1c_2$. If we take the average of the first two we get the third, which makes good sense since the third case, the classical mixture state, is a $50-50$ mixture of the first two. This is all quite understandable.

What is intriguing is the correlation histogram for the fourth case, the quantum entangled state, where the fraction of {ud} & {du} measurements contributing −1 is $(1+\hat{n}_1\cdot\hat{n}_2)/2$ and the fraction of {uu} & {dd} measurements contributing +1 is $(1-\hat{n}_1\cdot\hat{n}_2)/2$, giving an average of $-\hat{n}_1\cdot\hat{n}_2$.

Consider first the case when both measurements are in the same direction, that is, $\hat{n}_1 = \hat{n}_2$. Each measurement will produce a sequence of random *up* and *down* results, but the two results will then be exactly anti-correlated. Something like this

Electron 1: $\{u\ u\ d\ u\ d\ d\ u\ u\ u\ d\ d\ u\ d\ u\ u\ d\cdots\}$
Electron 2: $\{d\ d\ u\ d\ u\ u\ d\ d\ d\ u\ u\ d\ u\ d\ d\ u\cdots\}$

And as long as $\hat{n}_1 = \hat{n}_2 \equiv \hat{n}$, this will be true no matter what direction $\hat{n}$ we choose! This means that one observer could make a measurement on one spin and immediately predict the result of the other person's measurement which could be happening far away at another location. Does that mean information is getting transmitted instantaneously? Not really. Each person's measurement looks like a random sequence of *up* and *down* that the other person has no control over. The magical correlation between them is evident only if they get together and compare notes, but that does not let them transmit any information.

5.6.6 *Figs. 5.50: Why is it surprising?*

Nevertheless one still wonders how correlations like this can be enforced between two remote measurements. With $\hat{n}_1 \neq \hat{n}_2$ the result is even more intriguing: the correlations are determined by $\hat{n}_1 \cdot \hat{n}_2$ even though both $\hat{n}_1$ and $\hat{n}_2$ can be chosen arbitrarily.

But you might say that a correlation is also observed for the classical $50-50$ mixture, the one that shows a correlation of $-c_1 c_2$. Why isn't that surprising? *Answer:* $c_1 c_2$ is equal to $(\hat{n}_1 \cdot \hat{z})$ times $(\hat{n}_2 \cdot \hat{z})$ which has a simple common sense interpretation. One electron is polarized along $+\hat{z}$, another along $-\hat{z}$, the two observers measure the components along $\hat{n}_1$ and $\hat{n}_2$ respectively and it does not matter which observer sees which electron, the product is always negative $-(\hat{n}_1 \cdot \hat{z}) \times (\hat{n}_2 \cdot \hat{z})$.

It is as if you took two marbles, one white and one black, chose one randomly and gave it to A, and gave the other to B. A and B traveled elsewhere and looked at their marbles, and sure enough their colors are anti-correlated. Nothing surprising here!

The quantum case is different. The electrons were not pointing $+\hat{z}$ or $-\hat{z}$ when they left the source. They were neither black nor white. Two independent observers chose two arbitrary directions $\hat{n}_1$ and $\hat{n}_2$ to measure their blackness or whiteness and their correlation is determined by $\hat{n}_1 \cdot \hat{n}_2$, no role is played by any property that the each electron may have carried with it from the source.

There is a rich literature on Bell's inequalities and related topics exploring different ways to pin down the surprising nature of quantum entanglement. For example the CHSH[17] inequality is based on the quantity S calculated from an experiment where one observer measures the spin randomly along one of two directions $\hat{n}_1$ or $\hat{n}'_1$ and the other observers does

[17]Clauser-Horne-Shimony-Holt.

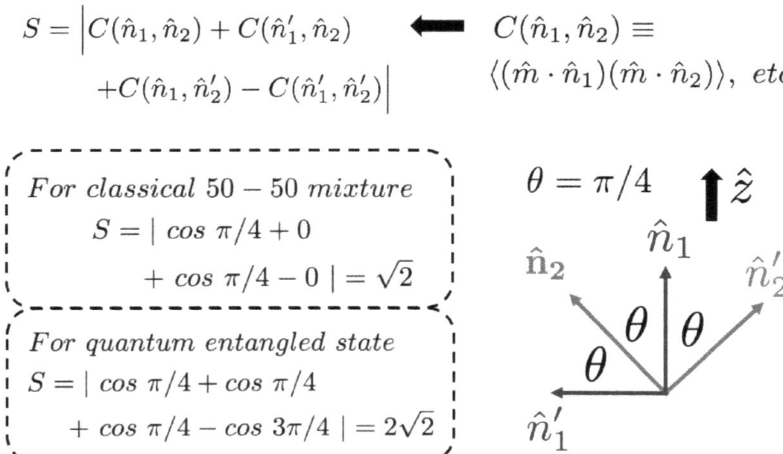

$S = \Big| C(\hat{n}_1, \hat{n}_2) + C(\hat{n}'_1, \hat{n}_2)$
$+ C(\hat{n}_1, \hat{n}'_2) - C(\hat{n}'_1, \hat{n}'_2) \Big|$
$C(\hat{n}_1, \hat{n}_2) \equiv$
$\langle (\hat{m} \cdot \hat{n}_1)(\hat{m} \cdot \hat{n}_2) \rangle$, *etc*
For classical 50 − 50 *mixture*
$S = |\ cos\ \pi/4 + 0$
$+\ cos\ \pi/4 - 0\ | = \sqrt{2}$
For quantum entangled state
$S = |\ cos\ \pi/4 + cos\ \pi/4$
$+\ cos\ \pi/4 - cos\ 3\pi/4\ | = 2\sqrt{2}$
$\theta = \pi/4$
$\hat{z}$
$\hat{n}_1$
$\hat{n}_2$
$\hat{n}'_2$
θ
θ
θ
$\hat{n}'_1$

Fig. 5.50 Comparing S for the classical 50-50 mixture and the quantum entangled states.

the same with two other directions $\hat{n}_2$ or $\hat{n}'_2$ as shown in the figure. For simplicity let us just consider the case with the directions equally spaced by an angle $\theta = \pi/4$ from each other. The quantum entangled state we discussed then leads to an S of $2\sqrt{2}$. Our classical $50 - 50$ mixture on the other hand gives an S that is only half as big.

Your first reaction may be to say that we have arbitrarily chosen the $\hat{z}$ direction to coincide with $\hat{n}_1$. Maybe a different choice would have given a larger S? Interestingly with $\theta = \pi/4$ we get the same answer irrespective of our choice of $\hat{z}$ though it takes a little more algebra to see it.

Perhaps one could replace $\hat{z}$ with an elaborate set of hidden variables that none of us know about and which control the correlations in a way that leads to the large S expected for the quantum entangled state? It has been shown that a certain class of hidden variable models will always obey the CHSH inequality $S \leq 2$ and cannot explain the values exceeding 2 that have been demonstrated experimentally, work that was recognized in 2022 with the physics Nobel prize.

5.7 Fig. 5.51: 5-minute Summary

This is Chapter 5 summary: Watch youtube video, upto 2:20

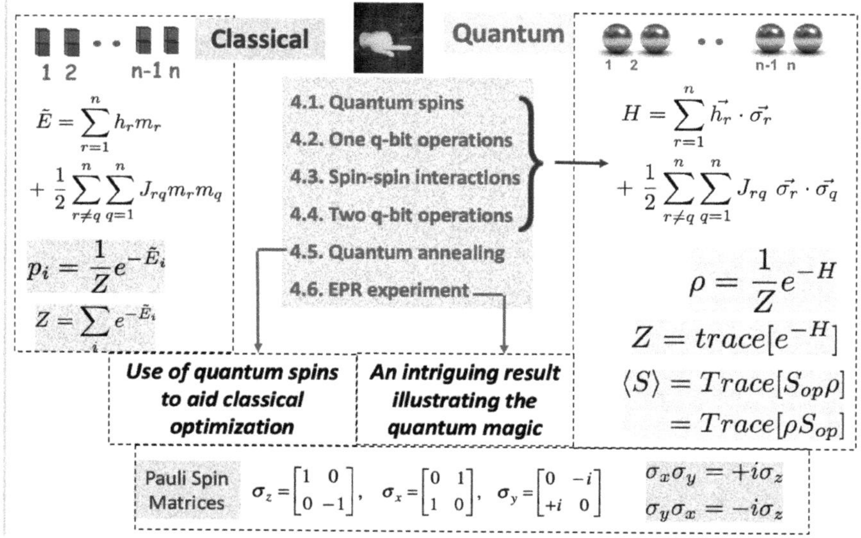

Fig. 5.51 Chapter 5 summary.

In this chapter, we started by making this transition from classical spins to quantum spins starting from the bipolar representation, and replacing m's with σ's which are 2×2 matrices, known as the Pauli spin matrices. So what used to be an energy function now becomes an energy matrix which you call the Hamiltonian matrix and that's what you use when you want to describe quantum spins.

Just as with classical spins, you find the probability from the energy, but now we find the probability matrix or the density matrix from the energy matrix. Then if you want to predict what the result of a particular measurement will be, that's when you need the operator corresponding to what you are trying to observe and then take the *trace* of its product with the density matrix.

The first two lectures illustrated the approach with one spin, while the next two lectures illustrated it with two-spin systems. The principles can be extended straightforwardly to n-spin systems for arbitrary n, the real difficulty being that the matrices are of size $2^n \times 2^n$, which increases exponentially with n. Hence the interest in building quantum computers whose natural physics can perform the computation for us. However, implementing arbitrary interactions presents a formidable challenge. Finally, in the last lecture we talked about quantum annealing, which is one approach that people have been working on to use quantum systems to improve classical optimization circuits.

In Section 5.6 we used the methods introduced in this chapter to discuss the celebrated EPR (Einstein-Podolsky-Rosen) experiment that has intrigued generations of scientists. Our aim is to convey that although the quantum approach is straightforward and can be implemented readily, "understanding" the results can be much more challenging, even for a simple two q-bit system.

Chapter 6

Quantum Transition Matrix

6.1 Adiabatic to Gated Computing

This is Lecture 6.1: Watch youtube video

What we discussed in Chapter 5 you could call adiabatic quantum computing, which assumes that the quantum system is in equilibrium with some reservoir. And in that case it is convenient to describe things in terms of the density matrix. In this chapter we will make the transition to what is called gated computing, where we'll talk more in terms of wave functions.

6.1.1 *Figs. 6.1-6.8: Density matrix and wavefunction*

6.1.1.1 *Fig. 6.1*

In the last chapter we set up the general framework for discussing quantum spins, of how you write the energy matrix, the density matrix, and deduce the expectation values of observables. We did this by extending the concepts from classical spins, which we had introduced in Chapters 2-4. When translating to quantum, we didn't have to bring up all those deep thoughts about reservoirs and the Boltzmann law, we just went from the energy function to this energy matrix.

But of course, the physical picture is still the same, the system interacts continually with the reservoir, which keeps it in equilibrium. Now, if we were to start from the full system plus reservoir, then we'd have a density matrix, that would also involve the reservoir states as shown in Fig. 6.1. The reservoir could be in state 1, state 2 etc, an enormous number of states, because reservoirs are usually huge things with many degrees of freedom. The density matrix that we've been calculating is like the sum of all these diagonal elements corresponding to individual states of the reservoir, and it all comes out naturally in our equilibrium calculations, because we're using this framework that we inherited from classical statistical mechanics.

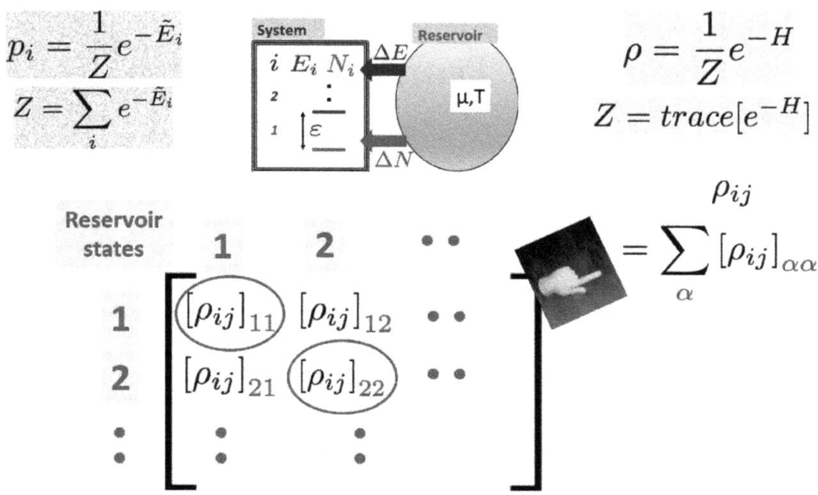

Fig. 6.1 Density matrix.

6.1.1.2 *Fig. 6.2*

Suppose instead we were dealing with an isolated system, then you see we'd be looking at only one of the density matrices along the diagonal in Fig. 6.1. In that case, you can write the density matrix as a product of what's called a wave function, so $\rho_{ij} = \psi_i \psi_j{}^*$. This is much simpler, of course, because ρ_{ij} is a matrix, whereas ψ is a column vector (see Fig. 6.2). But when you're trying to discuss an open system, you see, we have a sum over all the reservoir states and in that case, the ρ_{ij} cannot be simply factorized this way, which is why you really need the density matrix and that's what we'd been doing in the last chapter.

6.1.1.3 *Fig. 6.3*

But for an isolated system, the density matrix can be written as the product of a column vector ψ and its conjugate transpose, $\psi^\dagger$, a row vector. In this chapter we'll be talking more about an isolated system, and how it evolves

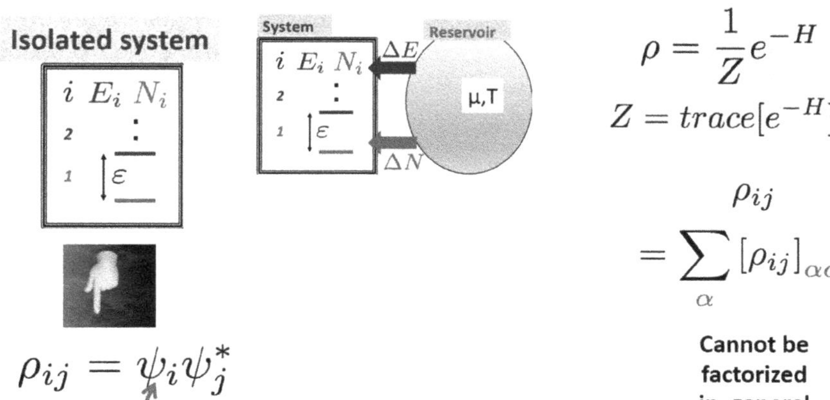

Fig. 6.2 Density matrix and wavefunction.

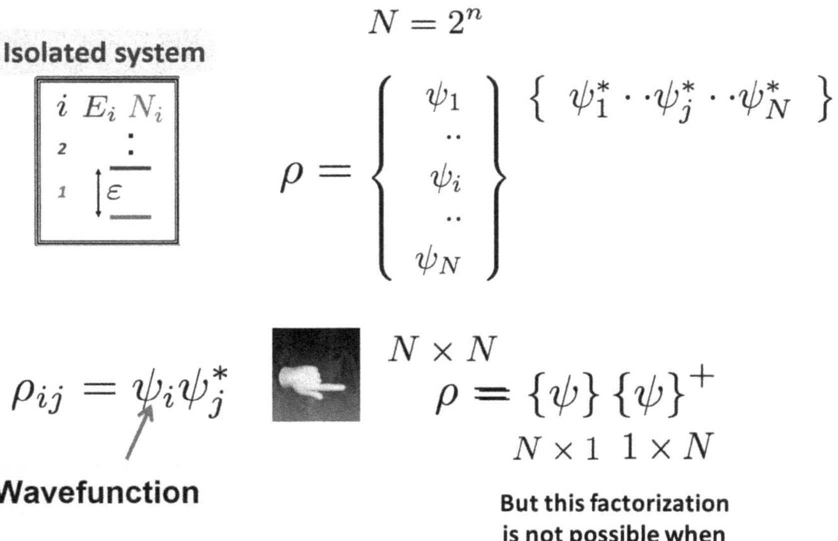

Fig. 6.3 Density matrix and wavefunction.

in time. In that case, you can talk in terms of the wave function, which is simpler, because it's got just N components, whereas, the density matrix has N^2 components. But when reservoirs are involved, you cannot have this factorization, which is why we hadn't talked about wave functions in the last chapter.

6.1.1.4 *Fig. 6.4*

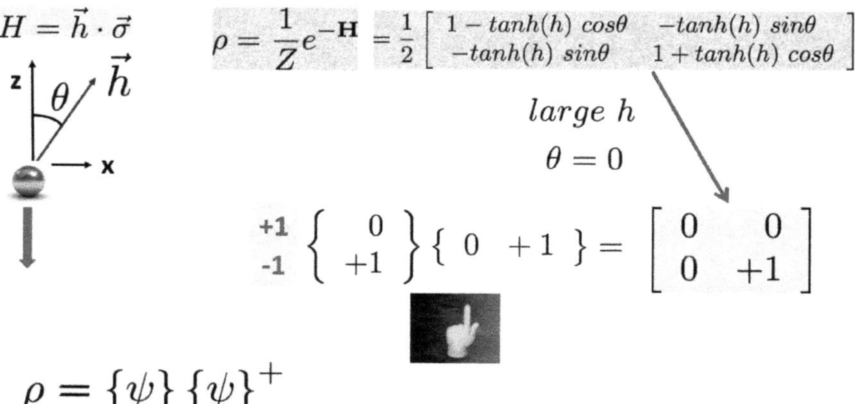

Fig. 6.4 Single q-bit: Density matrix and wavefunctions ($\theta = 0$).

Now, just to understand this distinction between density matrices and wavefunctions a little better, let's go back to the equilibrium density matrix for one q-bit that we discussed in Lecture 5.2 (Fig. 5.15), in the presence of a $\vec{h}$ pointing along θ.

Now, suppose $\theta = 0$, that means that this bias term is all in the z direction, and you put a large h, so that $tanh(h) \approx 1$. Now you can simplify the density matrix ρ and factorize it into $\{0 \quad +1\}^T$ times $\{0 \quad +1\}$ as shown. You can check this out when you multiply it, you'll will get this matrix. So now you have the wave function. $\{0 \quad +1\}$, and you could interpret it by saying, that this quantum spin is all in the -1 state, it's pointing downwards and that makes sense, because you're putting a large bias term in the z direction, which means, that if this were to point upwards, it would have a very big energy, and so, it wants to point downwards.

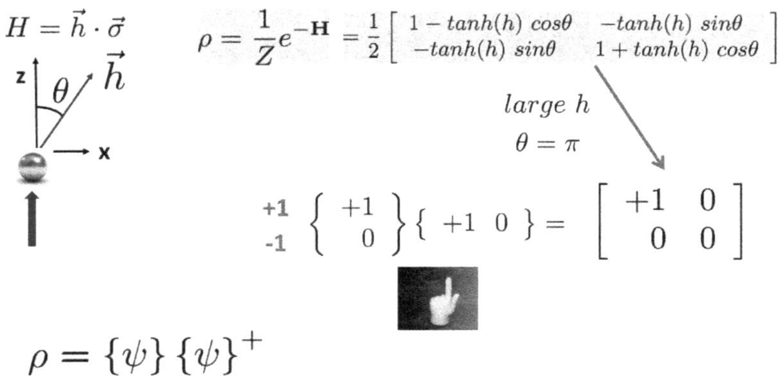

$$H = \vec{h} \cdot \vec{\sigma} \qquad \rho = \frac{1}{Z} e^{-\mathbf{H}} = \frac{1}{2} \begin{bmatrix} 1 - tanh(h)\ cos\theta & -tanh(h)\ sin\theta \\ -tanh(h)\ sin\theta & 1 + tanh(h)\ cos\theta \end{bmatrix}$$

large h

$\theta = \pi$

$$\begin{matrix} +1 \\ -1 \end{matrix} \left\{ \begin{matrix} +1 \\ 0 \end{matrix} \right\} \{ +1 \ \ 0 \} = \begin{bmatrix} +1 & 0 \\ 0 & 0 \end{bmatrix}$$

$$\rho = \{\psi\} \{\psi\}^{+}$$

Fig. 6.5 Single q-bit: Density matrix and wavefunctions ($\theta = \pi$).

6.1.1.5 *Fig. 6.5*

What if you put a large H in the opposite direction, that's $\theta = \pi$. Well in that case, $\cos\theta$ is -1, $\tanh(h)$ is still ≈ 1. Proceeding as before we can factorize the density matrix to obtain the wavefunction as $\{+1 \quad 0\}$, which shows you that the spin is all in the $+1$ state, pointing up. So if you put H pointing downwards, the spin will point upwards. Incidentally, I should mention that in a lot of the literature, people define the H with an additional minus sign here, and so their conclusions may be the opposite of ours. we are coming to, could be the exact opposite of what you might see in some of the literature. This is just to warn you, if you're trying to correlate this with what you might see elsewhere.

Anyway, but the main point here is, that when you get into one of these pure states, you can easily factorize.

6.1.1.6 *Fig. 6.6*

What if I put a large h in the x direction? Now, you see $cos\theta = 0$ leading to a more complicated density matrix, but it can still be factorized giving a wavefunction $\{+1 \quad -1\}$. So what this wave function tells you is that the probability of being up or down is equal, you see, it's $+1$. Remember, there's a half in the density matrix, so I should have a $1/\sqrt{2}$ multiplying each one of the wavefunctions, which I have left out for clarity.

But the important point I wanted to make is, that this actually represents a spin in the $-x$ direction (see Fig. 6.6), as you might expect, since

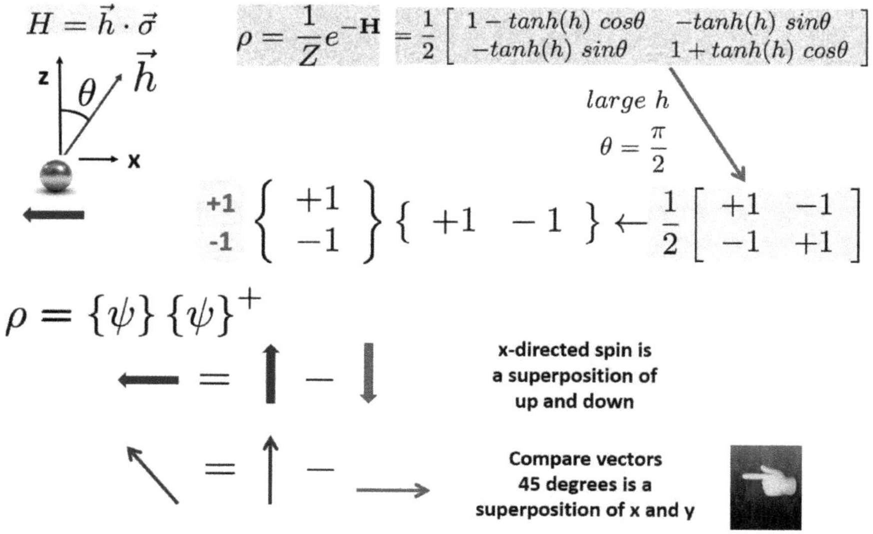

$$H = \vec{h} \cdot \vec{\sigma}$$

$$\rho = \frac{1}{Z} e^{-\mathbf{H}} = \frac{1}{2} \begin{bmatrix} 1 - tanh(h)\ cos\theta & -tanh(h)\ sin\theta \\ -tanh(h)\ sin\theta & 1 + tanh(h)\ cos\theta \end{bmatrix}$$

large h

$\theta = \frac{\pi}{2}$

$$\begin{Bmatrix} +1 \\ -1 \end{Bmatrix} \{ +1 \quad -1 \} \leftarrow \frac{1}{2} \begin{bmatrix} +1 & -1 \\ -1 & +1 \end{bmatrix}$$

$$\rho = \{\psi\}\{\psi\}^{+}$$

x-directed spin is a superposition of up and down

Compare vectors 45 degrees is a superposition of x and y

Fig. 6.6 Single q-bit: Density matrix and wavefunctions ($\theta = \pi/2$).

you're putting a big h along positive x, making the spin point to negative x. But a negative x is actually a superposition of up and down.

This is a little bit like vectors, it is just that the angles are twice as big. We know that for a vector pointing at 45 degrees, you can think of it as a superposition of a vertical vector and a horizontal vector. But what used to be 45 degrees for vectors becomes 90 degrees for spinors. So it's a superposition of up and down which are each at 90 degrees to the original.

6.1.1.7 *Fig. 6.7*

Now, let us look at a case where the density matrix cannot be factorized. Suppose h equals 0. and the spin can be up or down, because they both have the same energy. The density matrix looks like an identity matrix multiplied by 1/2. And the thing is, you can try this out. You **cannot** write it as $\{\psi\}\{\psi\}^{\dagger}$.

What you can do, however, is to write it as the sum of two factorizable terms as shown, one represents a pure *up* state, and the other a pure *down* state. So there is no unique wave function in this case, it is 50% of one, and 50% of the other. You might say, well, couldn't I have just added these two wave functions? No, then I would get $\{1 \quad 1\}$ which we know represents an

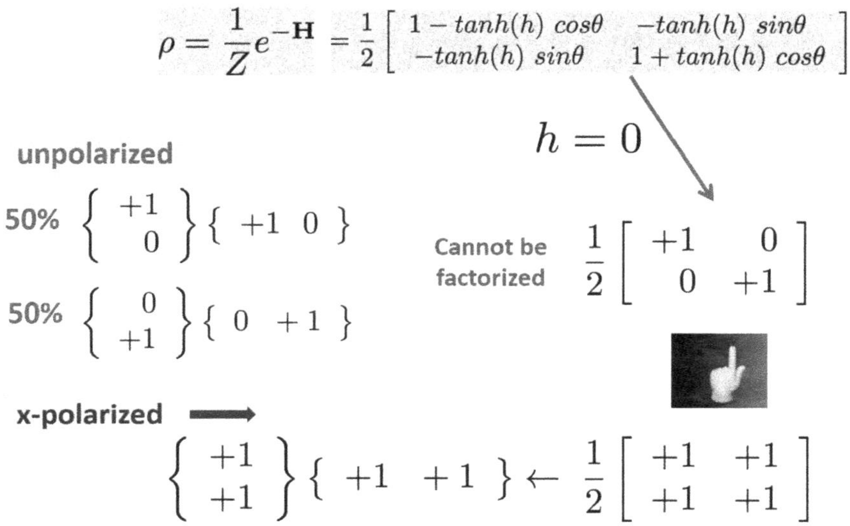

$$\rho = \frac{1}{Z} e^{-\mathbf{H}} = \frac{1}{2} \begin{bmatrix} 1 - tanh(h)\ cos\theta & -tanh(h)\ sin\theta \\ -tanh(h)\ sin\theta & 1 + tanh(h)\ cos\theta \end{bmatrix}$$

$$h = 0$$

unpolarized

50% $\begin{Bmatrix} +1 \\ 0 \end{Bmatrix} \{ +1 \ \ 0 \}$

50% $\begin{Bmatrix} 0 \\ +1 \end{Bmatrix} \{ 0 \ \ +1 \}$

Cannot be factorized $\frac{1}{2} \begin{bmatrix} +1 & 0 \\ 0 & +1 \end{bmatrix}$

x-polarized

$$\begin{Bmatrix} +1 \\ +1 \end{Bmatrix} \{ +1 \ \ +1 \} \leftarrow \frac{1}{2} \begin{bmatrix} +1 & +1 \\ +1 & +1 \end{bmatrix}$$

Fig. 6.7 Single q-bit: Density matrix and wavefunctions ($h = 0$).

x-polarized spin. What we actually have here is what you might call an unpolarized collection of electrons. Those are not the same thing, just as unpolarized light is not the same as 45 degree polarized light, it's the same with electrons.

6.1.1.8 *Fig. 6.8*

One more thing as we move from density matrices to wavefunctions assuming it is factorizable. Earlier we wrote the rule for calculating expectation values by taking the trace of the corresponding operator with the density matrix. Assuming that the density matrix can be factorized, we can rewrite this rule in terms of wavefunctions as shown. Note that we have made use of the property that when you take a trace of product of a, b, and c, you can permute these in cyclic order, and it stays the same.

6.1.2 *Figs. 6.9-6.10: Quantum transition matrix*

6.1.2.1 *Fig. 6.9*

In gated quantum computing, we will be talking about the time evolution of isolated quantum systems using the same Hamiltonian H that we used in Chapter 5. But is Chapter 5, we wanted the density matix e^{-H}, but

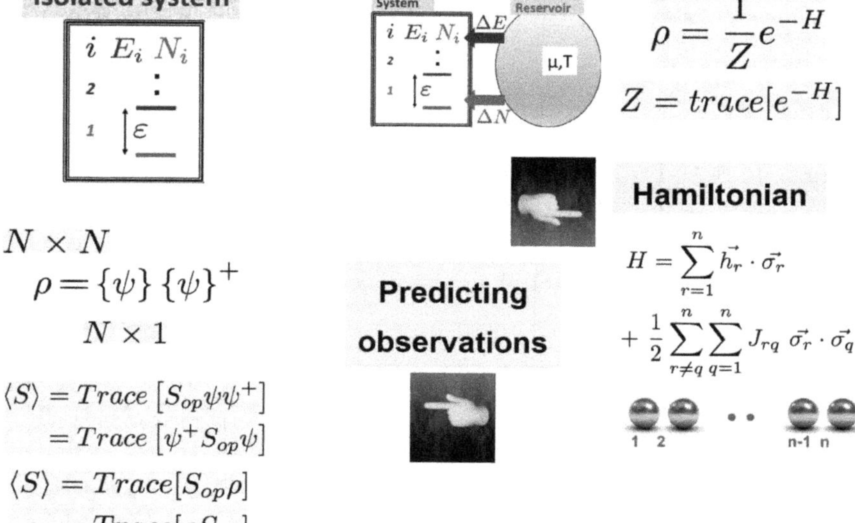

Fig. 6.8 Density matrix to wavefunctions.

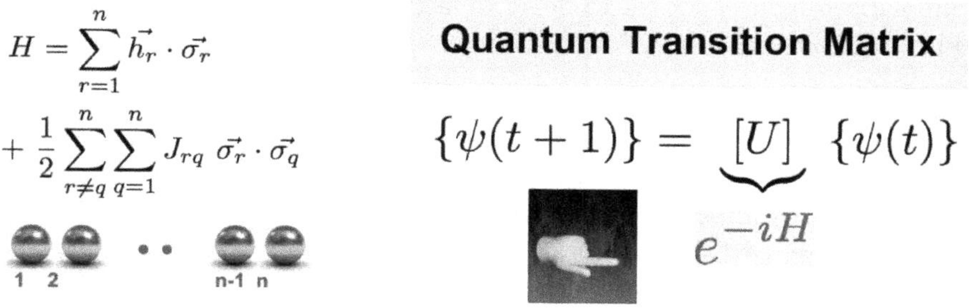

$$H = \sum_{r=1}^{n} \vec{h_r} \cdot \vec{\sigma_r} + \frac{1}{2}\sum_{r \neq q}^{n}\sum_{q=1}^{n} J_{rq}\, \vec{\sigma_r} \cdot \vec{\sigma_q}$$

1 2 .. n-1 n

Quantum Transition Matrix

$$\{\psi(t+1)\} = \underbrace{[U]}_{e^{-iH}} \{\psi(t)\}$$

Fig. 6.9 Quantum transition matrix.

now we want the the quantum transition matrix $U = e^{-iH}$, which evolves the wavefunctions from time t to $t+1$.

6.1.2.2 *Fig. 6.10*

You could compare the quantum transition matrix U with its classical counterpart W from Chapter 4. W describes the evolution of probabilities, whereas, the U describes the evolution of wave functions. Probabilities

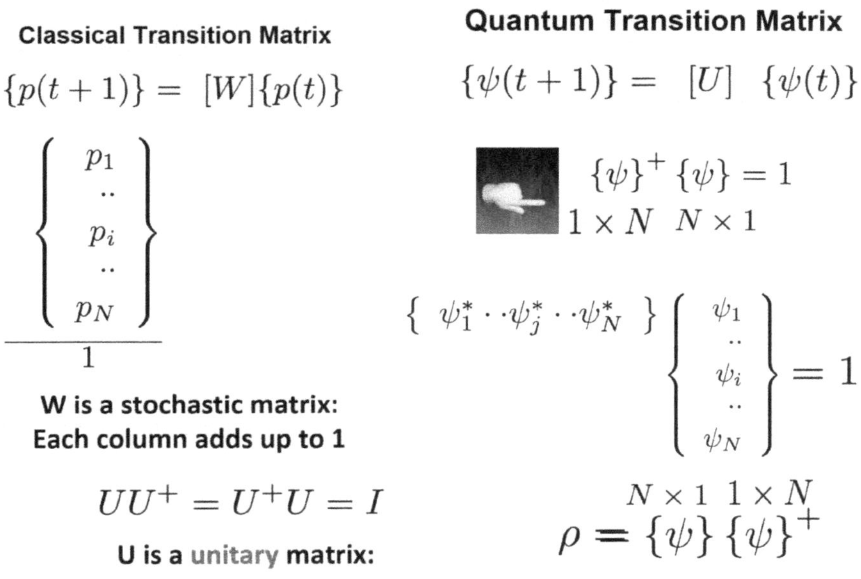

Classical Transition Matrix

$$\{p(t+1)\} = [W]\{p(t)\}$$

$$\begin{Bmatrix} p_1 \\ .. \\ p_i \\ .. \\ p_N \end{Bmatrix}$$

$$\overline{\qquad 1 \qquad}$$

W is a stochastic matrix:
Each column adds up to 1

$$UU^{+} = U^{+}U = I$$

U is a unitary matrix:

Quantum Transition Matrix

$$\{\psi(t+1)\} = [U] \; \{\psi(t)\}$$

$$\underset{1 \times N}{\{\psi\}^{+}} \; \underset{N \times 1}{\{\psi\}} = 1$$

$$\{\, \psi_1^* \cdot\cdot \psi_j^* \cdot\cdot \psi_N^* \,\} \begin{Bmatrix} \psi_1 \\ .. \\ \psi_i \\ .. \\ \psi_N \end{Bmatrix} = 1$$

$$\rho = \underset{N \times 1}{\{\psi\}} \; \underset{1 \times N}{\{\psi\}^{+}}$$

Fig. 6.10 Quantum transition matrix.

have the property that when you add up all the components, it must be 1, and so, to ensure that the probability stays normalized, W has the property that every column must add up to 1. So that's called a stochastic matrix.

For the quantum case, the ψ's don't add up to 1. What adds up to 1 is the sum of the squares, which can be written as, which means that $\{\psi\}^{\dagger}\{\psi\} = 1$. What you can show is, that in order to ensure this, the matrix U, must be unitary. Just as W must be a stochastic matrix with columns adding up to one, U must be a unitary matrix, with $UU^{\dagger} = U^{\dagger}U = 1$.

By the way note the subtle difference between $\{\psi\}^{\dagger}\psi$ and what we wrote for the density matrix after factorizing, namely $\{\psi\}\{\psi\}^{\dagger}$. If $\{\psi\}$ is an $N \times 1$ column vector, then the former is a number, while the latter is an $N \times N$ matrix. The former should equal one, while it's the *trace* of the latter that should equal one.

6.1.3 *Fig. 6.11: Quantum gates*

What we'll be doing this week then, is talk about quantum gates, which work on isolated systems where the wave functions are gradually transformed in time. By the way, it's convenient to draw the time axis

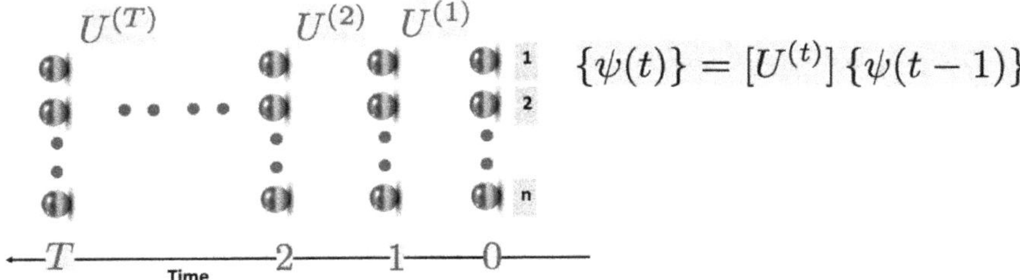

Fig. 6.11 Quantum gates.

from right to left, instead of left to right, because then the order of multiplication of matrices comes naturally.

Quantum gates will let you transform the wave function from an initial state as you go along and its classical equivalent might be the Bayesian networks we talked about briefly in Lecture 4.4 which transformed the probability density function. But these are very different from adiabatic quantum computing whose classical equivalent would be our Boltzmann networks.

The transformation of wavefunctions is described by the quantum transition matrix U and the challenge is to design them so that they do something useful. That is what we will talk about in the next three lectures.

6.1.4 *Quiz*

6.1.4.1 *Question 1*

Suppose the density matrix is given by $\frac{1}{2}\begin{bmatrix} 1 & 1 \\ 1 & 1 \end{bmatrix}$.
What is the corresponding wavefunction ψ?[1]

6.1.4.2 *Question 2*

Suppose the density matrix is given by $\frac{1}{2}\begin{bmatrix} 1 & -i \\ +i & 1 \end{bmatrix}$.
What is the corresponding wavefunction ψ?[2]

6.1.4.3 *Question 3*

What is the property that a properly normalized wavefunction ψ must have?[3]

---

[1] $\frac{1}{\sqrt{2}}\begin{bmatrix} 1 \\ 1 \end{bmatrix}$.

[2] $\frac{1}{\sqrt{2}}\begin{bmatrix} 1 \\ i \end{bmatrix}$.

[3] $\psi^\dagger\psi = 1$.

6.2 Hadamard Gates

This is Lecture 6.2: Watch youtube video

In the last lecture, we outlined this transition from density matrices to wavefunctions as we go from adiabatic to gated quantum computing. The next three lectures will be about how we use quantum gates to do useful interesting things. They all have this structure where you apply one gate after another sequentially: we draw the time axis going to the left so that you start with a wave function at the right and multiply by the U from these different gates to obtain a final wave function.

6.2.1 *Figs. 6.12-6.13: Transition matrix for H-gate*

6.2.1.1 *Fig. 6.12*

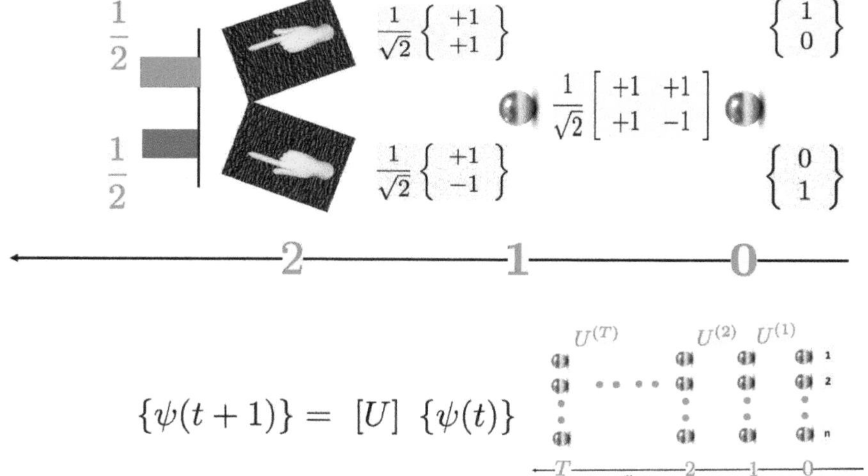

Fig. 6.12 Transition matrix for Hadamard gate.

Now, one gate that's very interesting and important that's widely used is this Hadamard gate whose U matrix is shown. Just a 2×2 matrix, but note that one element is -1, something you never see with classical W matrices.

Now if the initial state is say up, then if you multiply it with this U you get a superposition of up and down. If the initial state is down and you multiply it with this U again you will get a superposition but now the down component will have a negative sign. Now if you ask for the probabilities the negative sign doesn't matter because we square the wavefunction to get the probability, which in either case is 50% up and 50% down.

6.2.1.2 *Fig. 6.13*

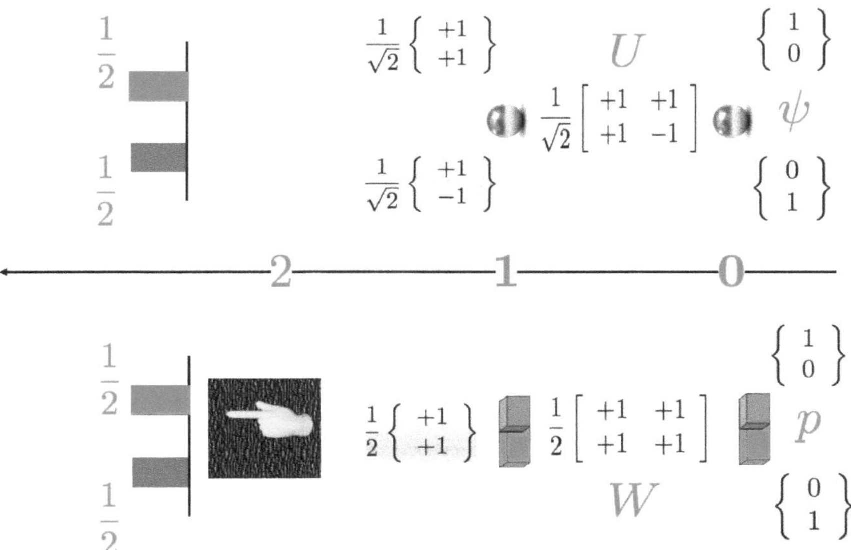

Fig. 6.13 Classical analog of H-gate.

It is interesting to compare with a classical probabilistic gate with a W that would give essentailly the same result as one Hadamard gate. This W will transform an initial probability distribution function that is all up or all down into half up and half down. So you might say why are we talking about the Hadamard gate? In effect it's doing much the same thing as the classical version. Well, they look the same because we are looking at the effect after one gate. The difference is striking when you apply the gate twice.

6.2.2 *Figs. 6.14: Two Hadamards in series*

So if you apply the same gate again, the effect is to multiply again with the same matrix. So it's the same U again and the interesting thing about the

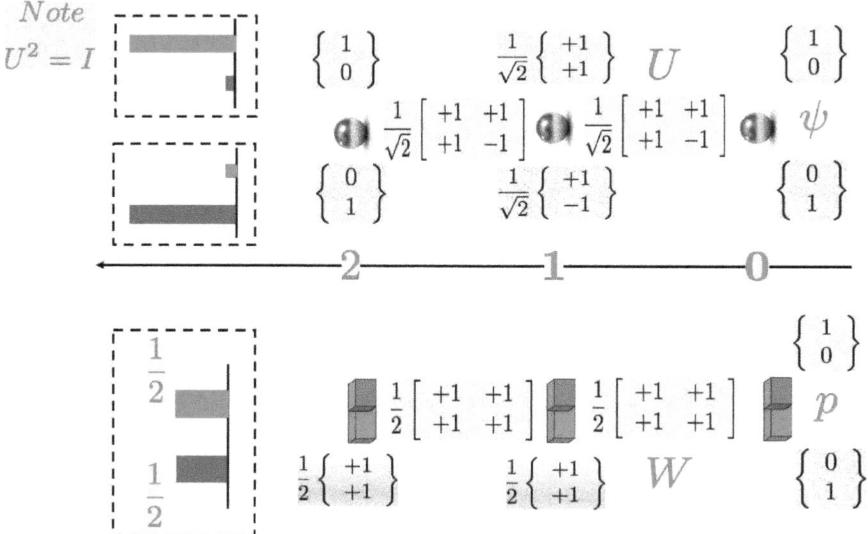

Fig. 6.14 Two Hadamards operating sequentially.

Hadamard gate is that U^2 is actually the identity gate, you can multiply it out and check. What that means is when you apply it twice you get back what you started with because it's basically like an identity matrix multiplying the original wavefunction. So if started all up, you end up being all up and if you started all down you end up being all down.

By contrast in the classical case if we apply that same gate again you will again get 50-50. No change in the classical case, but a big change in the quantum case. This is the very remarkable thing that this negative term in U is able to accomplish. When you apply the gate once it spreads out, but apply it twice and it comes back.

6.2.3 *Figs. 6.15-6.17: Example with two q-bits*

6.2.3.1 *Fig. 6.15*

Now, let's consider what happens when you have, 2-bits and you apply this Hadamard gate individually to each bit. We could think of it as a composite system which has four states, and these two individual Hadamard gates can be described by a single transformation matrix which is a 4×4 matrix obtained from the Kronecker product of the two individual 2×2 matrices.

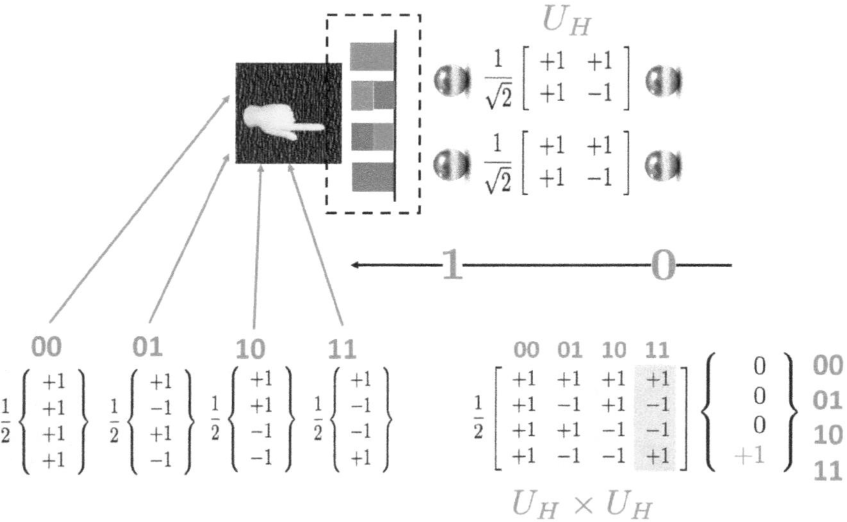

Fig. 6.15 2-bit Hadamards.

6.2.3.2 *Fig. 6.16*

So if you start out all in the (00) state then what would you get? We get what is in the first column of the $U_H \times U_H$ matrix, that's the way matrix multiplication works. If we start in the (01) state, we get the second column and so on. Since the different columns are all the same except for the signs, the histogram in any case would have all four states equally probable. But as we noted earlier with one q-bit, the magic of the Hadamard gate shows up when you apply it twice. You get back what you started with, since $(U_H \times U_H)^2$ is the identity matrix as you can check. So that's the amazing thing about this Hadamard gate, applied once it spreads out looks like all the information is lost. But apply it twice and it comes right back where you started.

6.2.3.3 *Fig. 6.17*

Now, it's convenient to express this property concisely because Hadamard gates are widely used in many of these quantum circuits. We label these columns as 0, 1, 2, 3 which is like the decimal equivalent of the binary representation. So we could name the columns of $(U_H \times U_H)$ as h_0, h_1, h_2, h_3.

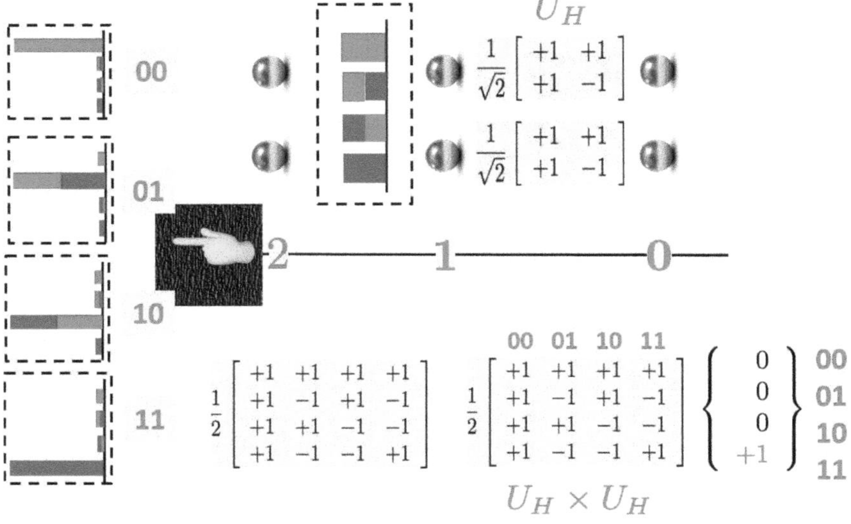

Fig. 6.16 2-bit Hadamards.

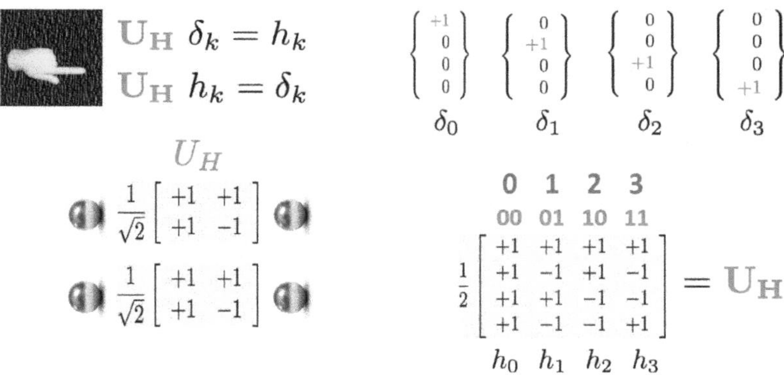

Fig. 6.17 Hadamard gate, compact expression.

What's h_0? It is this $(+1\ +1\ +1\ +1)^T$ multiplied by a half. What's h_1, well, it's $(+1\ -1\ +1\ -1)^T$ again multiplied by a half and so on.

We also define something like a delta function, δ_0 means you only have $+1$ in the (00) position, δ_1 means you will only have $+1$ in the (01) position, and so on. When you apply the Hadamard gate to a wave function that looks like δ_k, meaning a $+1$ in the k position you get the h_k which represents the column k of $(U_H \times U_H)$. Apply the Hadamard gate again to h_k and you get back δ_k.

6.2.4 *Fig. 6.18: Example with three q-bits*

$$\mathbf{U_H}\ \delta_k = h_k$$

$$\mathbf{U_H}\ h_k = \delta_k$$

$$\mathbf{U_H} = U_H \times U_H \times U_H$$

3-bit

Hadamard

$$\begin{array}{cccccccc} \mathbf{0} & \mathbf{1} & \mathbf{2} & \mathbf{3} & \mathbf{4} & \mathbf{5} & \mathbf{6} & \mathbf{7} \end{array}$$

$$\frac{1}{\sqrt{8}}\begin{bmatrix} +1 & +1 & +1 & +1 & +1 & +1 & +1 & +1 \\ +1 & -1 & +1 & -1 & +1 & -1 & +1 & -1 \\ +1 & +1 & -1 & -1 & +1 & +1 & -1 & -1 \\ +1 & -1 & -1 & +1 & +1 & -1 & -1 & +1 \\ +1 & +1 & +1 & +1 & -1 & -1 & -1 & -1 \\ +1 & -1 & +1 & -1 & -1 & +1 & -1 & +1 \\ +1 & +1 & -1 & -1 & -1 & -1 & +1 & +1 \\ +1 & -1 & -1 & +1 & -1 & +1 & +1 & -1 \end{bmatrix}$$

$$\begin{array}{cccccccc} h_0 & h_1 & h_2 & h_3 & h_4 & h_5 & h_6 & h_7 \end{array}$$

Fig. 6.18 Hadamard, 3-bit example.

These relations summarize the property of Hadamard gates and interestingly it can be extended beyond just two q-bits. If you had say 3 q-bits, then the overall matrix obtained from the Kronecker product of three elementary Hadamard matrices, $\mathbf{U_H} = \mathbf{U_H} \times \mathbf{U_H} \times \mathbf{U_H}$, is an 8×8 matrix. Once again we can define $\{h_k\}$, $\{\delta_k\}$ with k running from 0 to 7. With ten q-bits, the composite matrix would be of size 1024×1024, and we would have k running from 0 to 1023. But in the end we still have $\mathbf{U_H}\delta_k = h_k$ and $\mathbf{U_H}h_k = \delta_k$.

In the next two lectures we will talk about two classic quantum algorithms both of which make use of Hadamard gates to take a 0 state and spread it out and then later bring it back.

6.2.5 *Quiz*

6.2.5.1 *Question 1*

A Hadamard gate $\frac{1}{\sqrt{2}}\begin{bmatrix} 1 & 1 \\ 1 & -1 \end{bmatrix}$ acts on a wavefunction $\left\{\begin{matrix} 1 \\ 0 \end{matrix}\right\}$.
What is the final wavefunction ψ?[4]

6.2.5.2 *Question 2*

A Hadamard gate $\frac{1}{\sqrt{2}}\begin{bmatrix} 1 & 1 \\ 1 & -1 \end{bmatrix}$ acts on a wavefunction $\left\{\begin{matrix} 0 \\ 1 \end{matrix}\right\}$.
What is the final wavefunction ψ?[5]

6.2.5.3 *Question 3*

Two Hadamard gates $\frac{1}{\sqrt{2}}\begin{bmatrix} 1 & 1 \\ 1 & -1 \end{bmatrix}$ act separately on two spins with a composite wavefunction $\left\{\begin{matrix} 0 \\ 1 \\ 0 \\ 0 \end{matrix}\right\}$.
What is the final wavefunction ψ?[6]

---

[4] $\frac{1}{\sqrt{2}}\left\{\begin{matrix} 1 \\ 1 \end{matrix}\right\}$.

[5] $\frac{1}{\sqrt{2}}\left\{\begin{matrix} +1 \\ -1 \end{matrix}\right\}$.

[6] $\frac{1}{2}\left\{\begin{matrix} +1 \\ -1 \\ +1 \\ -1 \end{matrix}\right\}$.

6.3 Grover Search

This is Lecture 6.3: Watch youtube video

6.3.1 *Figs. 6.19-6.22: Grover cycle*

6.3.1.1 *Fig. 6.19: Classical versus Grover search*

In the last lecture, we introduced this Hadamard gate, and this magical property that when you apply it once to a delta function, you spread it out over all the components. But you apply it a second time, you again get back the δ. This is the property that is widely used in many quantum circuits and in this lecture, we'll see how it is used in Grover's algorithm along with other gates.

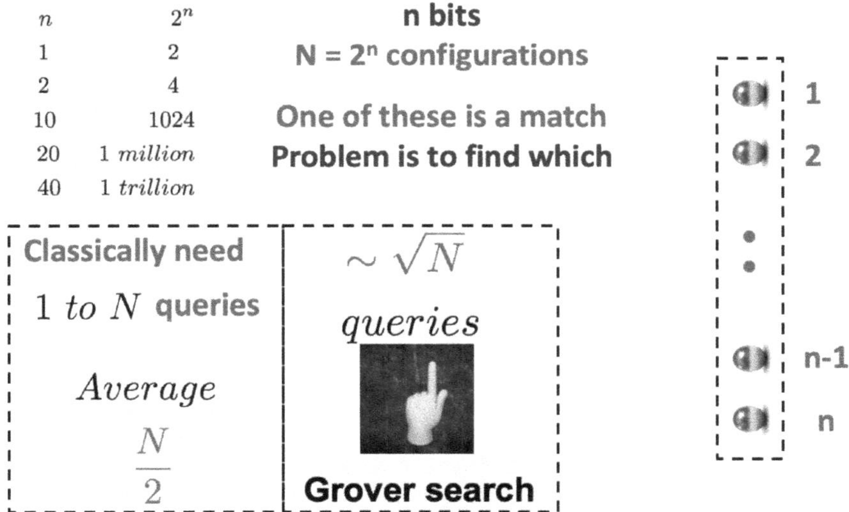

Fig. 6.19 An unstructured classical search needs $\sim N$ queries, Grover search needs $\sim \sqrt{(N)}$ queries.

The problem is something like this. We have a database with small n bits, which can host capital $N = 2^n$ configurations, and of these 2^n configurations, there is one which is the correct answer. That's the target that we want to find out of a total of 2^n configurations and N increases exponentially with n, so that with say 40 bits, you have like a trillion configurations, a lot to search from.

Now, classically, how many tries would you need? Well, the idea is that you'd go at it sequentially. You could say, okay, is this the right one? No. Is this the right one? No. Till you get a yes. If you're lucky, your first query would be the right one, so you'd have your answer in one query. If you're unlucky, it would take you N queries. On the average, it would be half of N, the point is it is of the order of N. But Grover's algorithm gives us a way to get an answer in $\sqrt{N}$ queries (see Fig. 6.19). That can be a huge improvement when N is large.

6.3.1.2 *Fig. 6.20: Grover cycle, Step 1, Hadamard*

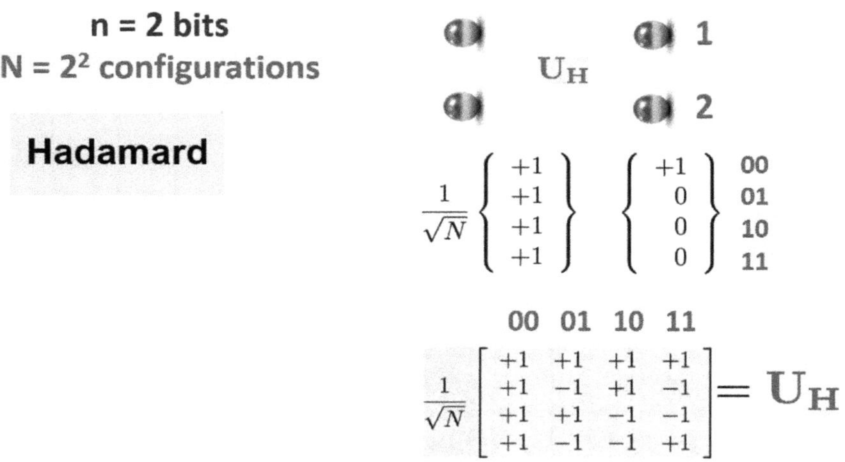

Fig. 6.20 Step 1 of Grover cycle: Hadamard.

So how does this work? For this discussion, we will assume $n = 2$ with $N = 4$ but you will see that it applies to any arbitrary number n. So the composite Hadamard matrix working on this two q-bit system will be written by the Kronecker product $\mathbf{U_H} = U_H \times U_H$. Now, if you come in with a $\{00\}$, so the initial wave function looks like $\delta_0 = \{+1\ 0\ 0\ 0\}^T$ and on applying the Hadamard gate, we get this first column, $h_0 = 1/\sqrt{N}\{1\ 1\ 1\ 1\}^T$. To keep it general I'm writing $1/\sqrt{N}$ instead of setting $N = 4$.

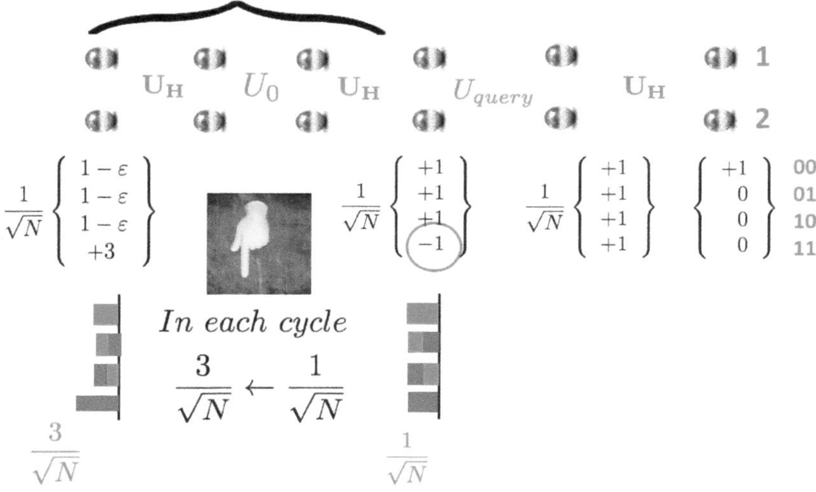

Fig. 6.21 Step 2 of Grover cycle: Query.

6.3.1.3 *Fig. 6.21: Grover cycle: Step 2, query*

Now comes the query. What it does is, that when you ask for the answer about the target, it will flip the sign of the target component as shown. Now if this were a course on quantum computing, the next question we'd be discussing is, how do you build the circuit that does this query? Can you do it with just a few circuits of the order of small n, or would you need $\sim 2^n$ circuits to do it? Actually, it's a fairly straightforward circuit using what are called controlled gates that you could use to implement this, but we won't go into that.

Okay, but the point is, supposing we had this circuit which flips the sign of the target every time we query it. How could we then identify the target? Because just flipping the sign doesn't help me. Because you see, in the end, when I'm making a measurement, I measure probabilities, I don't measure amplitudes. So the fact that this amplitude is -1 doesn't mean a thing, because as far as probabilities are concerned, all four look equally probable. So I can't really tell what happened.

So what happens next is there's a sequence of gates that are applied, which turn this simple flipping into a measurable thing, which means what happens after I apply these three gates, which I'll explain, the target becomes enhanced relative to the background, and the background is suppressed a little bit (see Fig. 6.21). Of course, if any one is enhanced, the rest must be suppressed in order to keep the normalization right, because overall, the sum of squares must be 1. So the point is every time you run this, the amplitude of the target, that is the correct answer, goes from $1/\sqrt{N}$ to $3/\sqrt{N}$. I'll show that in a minute, it's not obvious.

6.3.1.4 *Fig. 6.22: Grover cycle: Step 3*

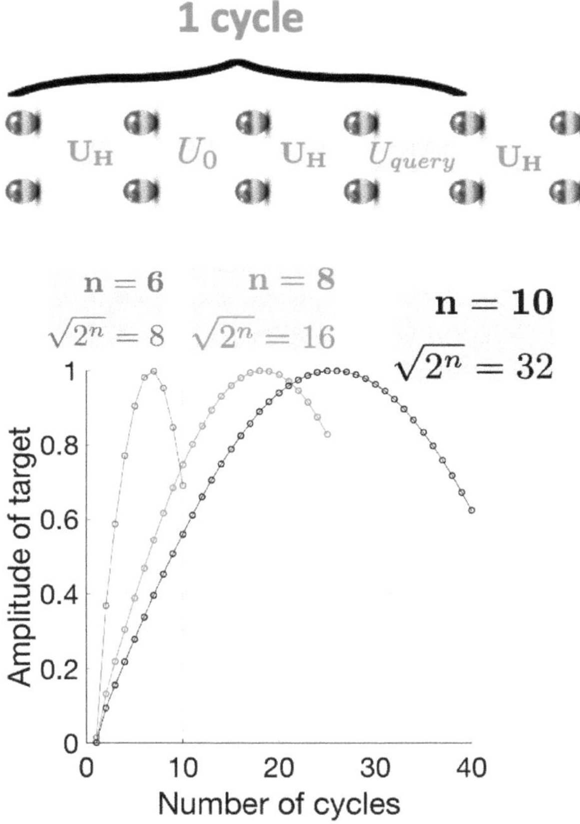

Fig. 6.22 The target amplitude increases in every cycle, reaches a maximum and continues to oscillate which we have not shown. MATLAB code included at end of book.

So in every cycle this enhancement occurs and if you apply the enhancement a number of times, then finally the target amplitude will become big enough that you will be easily able to detect it. How many would you need? Well, since it goes up by $2/\sqrt{N}$ every time, roughly speaking you need $\sim \sqrt{N}$ application cycles to build it up to ~ 1, at which point you can measure it and get your answer.

I have plotted the amplitude of the target as a function of the number of cycles and if you have say 6 bits, then you can see the number of cycles goes up to 1 rather quickly in less than 10 cycles and then actually comes down again. If you had 8 bits, it takes about 20 cycles. If you have 10 bits, it takes a little less than 30 cycles, and roughly you can see that the peak value occurs when the number of cycles is $\sqrt{N}$. So that's the point, for the Grover iteration the number of cycles which means the number of queries is of the order of $\sqrt{N}$, which is a big improvement over classical searches which require N queries. We will now work out a quantitative description that describes the results in Fig. 6.22 accurately. It will also show why the target amplitude increases at first, but eventually starts to decrease. Indeed we will see that with more cycles it continues to oscillate, which is not shown.

6.3.2 *Figs. 6.23-6.28: Quantitative analysis*

6.3.2.1 *Fig. 6.23: Role of query*

So how does this work? We are starting with something that's in the 0 state, and that's what we have named δ_0. When you apply a Hadamard, the δ_0 becomes h_0 as we discussed in the last lecture.

Now, what does the query do? It takes the target element and flips it. You could write that as h_0, where all elements are positive and subtract -2 from the target component, giving us $h_0 - (2\delta_t/\sqrt{N})$. That's what we get after applying the query.

6.3.2.2 *Fig. 6.24: The full cycle*

Next in the Grover cycle, we have this sequence $\mathbf{U_H} U_0\, \mathbf{U_H}$. What does the first Hadamard do? That's easy, as we have discussed, Hadamard takes δ and turns it into h, takes h and turns it into a δ. So after the first $\mathbf{U_H}$ we have $\delta_0 - 2h_t/\sqrt{N}$.

Next, we have this U_0 gate and its job is to flip the sign of all the elements except for the first one. So the first one stays what it is, but all the elements are flipped. Again, if this was a course about quantum computing, we'd talk about the kind of circuits you could use to actu-

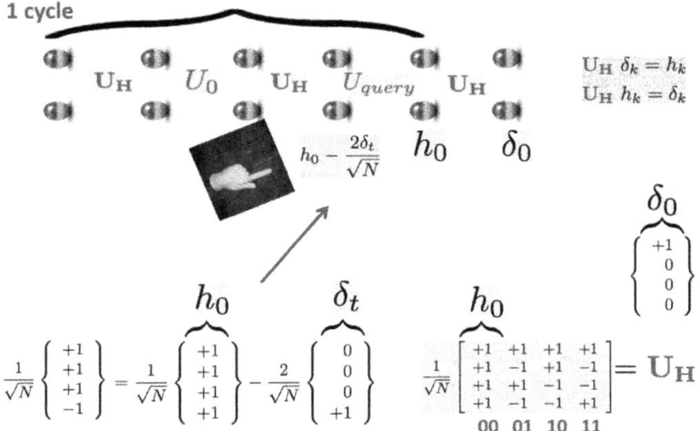

Fig. 6.23 Grover output after query.
Note that h_0 is defined to include the factor $1/\sqrt{N}$.

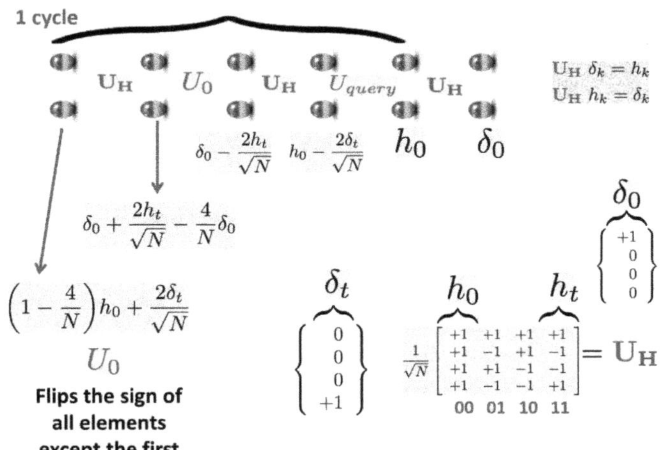

Fig. 6.24 Grover output after full cycle.
Note that h_0 and h_t are defined to include the factor $1/\sqrt{N}$.

ally do that. You'd need one of these controlled gates, but we won't go into it.

The question is, what does U_0 do to what we had, namely to $\delta_0 - (2h_t/\sqrt{N})$? Well, if you think about it, the δ_0 is unaffected. Why? Because in δ_0 the only non-zero element is the first one and we are doing nothing to the first one anyway.

Now, what about the h_t? Well, if you just flipped the sign of all its elements, $-2h_t/\sqrt{N}$ would become $+2h_t/\sqrt{N}$. But then you flipped all the signs except for the first one, so you need another term to account for that. You can show that this actually amounts to subtracting this δ_0, and the $4/N$ comes from $(2/\sqrt{N})^2$. So after applying U_0 we have $(1-4/N)\delta_0+(2h_t/\sqrt{N})$.

Next, we have another Hadamard and that's again easy because Hadamards just turn δ's into h and h's into δ. So at the end of the cycle, we have turned an initial h_0 into $(1-4/N)h_0 + (2\delta_t/\sqrt{N})$.

So we have two terms. The h_0 is $+1$ everywhere. That's the background and in the course of a cycle, it has been reduced by a factor $1-4/N$. And then there is δ_t, that's the target, which got enhanced by $2/\sqrt{N}$. So that's what we had said a Grover cycle does. It enhances the amplitude of the target from $1/\sqrt{N}$ to $3/\sqrt{N}$ and suppresses the background to compensate.

6.3.2.3 *Fig. 6.25: Transformation of a_k, b_k in each cycle*

Note, however, that in this case the cycle started with an initial state that contained just h_0. That is true of the first cycle but subsequent cycles will start with a combination of h_0 and δ_t and so we also need to know what the Grover cycle does to an initial δ_t. We will not go through the detailed arguments but the final result is shown in the Figure. We start with $a_0 = 1$, $b_0 = 0$ and the $(k+1)^{th}$ Grover cycle transforms a_k, b_k into a_{k+1}, b_{k+1} as shown.

6.3.2.4 *Fig. 6.26: Transformation from a_k, b_k to A_k, B_k*

We have described the wavefunction at each stage in terms of two components h_0 and δ_t but you can check that they are NOT orthogonal. The transformation properties of each Grover cycle can be made to look much cleaner if we subtract out the overlap with δ_t from h_0 to construct $\widetilde{h_0}$.

We now have a different set of coefficients A_k, B_k which are related to the old ones a_k, b_k at any value of k by the relations shown.

6.3.2.5 *Fig. 6.27: Transformation of A_k, B_k in each cycle*

We can now combine the transformation rules for a_k, b_k and A_k, B_k with the rule for the evolution of a_k, b_k in each cycle, to obtain the rule for the evolution of A_k, B_k in each cycle. Note that the resulting transformation

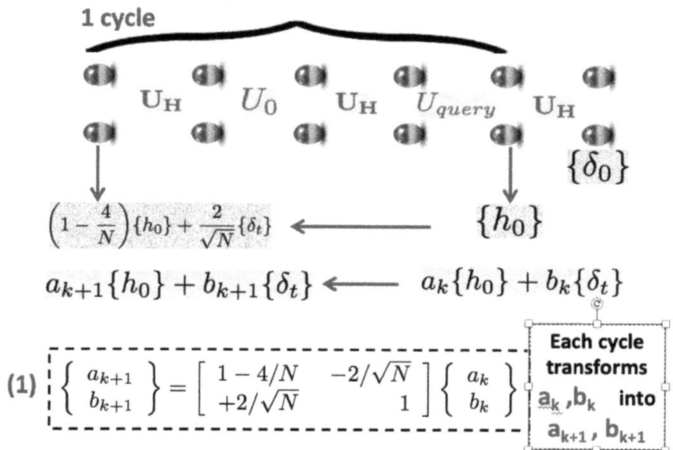

Fig. 6.25 Transformation of a_k, b_k in each cycle.

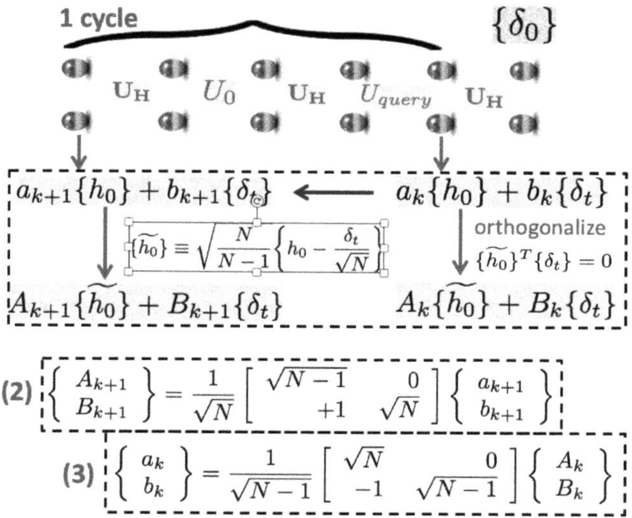

Fig. 6.26 We construct $\widetilde{h_0}$ from h_0 such that it is orthogonal to δ_t. This changes the coefficients a_k, b_k to A_k, B_k as shown.

matrix is a unitary one that can be written in the form of rotation matrix, as if A_k, B_k from an orthogonal $x - y$ coordinate system and each Grover cycle rotates the coordinates by θ. This simple transformation law is what we were seeking, the reason why we went to the trouble of constructing $\widetilde{h_0}$ from h_0 such that it was orthogonal to the other component δ_t.

Combine (1), (2) & (3)

$$\begin{Bmatrix} A_{k+1} \\ B_{k+1} \end{Bmatrix} = \frac{1}{\sqrt{N(N-1)}} \begin{bmatrix} \sqrt{N-1} & 0 \\ +1 & \sqrt{N} \end{bmatrix} \times \begin{bmatrix} 1-4/N & -2/\sqrt{N} \\ +2/\sqrt{N} & 1 \end{bmatrix} \begin{bmatrix} \sqrt{N} & 0 \\ -1 & \sqrt{N-1} \end{bmatrix} \begin{Bmatrix} A_k \\ B_k \end{Bmatrix}$$

$$\begin{Bmatrix} A_{k+1} \\ B_{k+1} \end{Bmatrix} = \begin{bmatrix} \overbrace{1-(2/N)}^{cos\theta} & -\overbrace{(2/N)\sqrt{N-1}}^{sin\theta} \\ +\underbrace{(2/N)\sqrt{N-1}}_{sin\theta} & \underbrace{1-(2/N)}_{cos\theta} \end{bmatrix} \begin{Bmatrix} A_k \\ B_k \end{Bmatrix}$$

Fig. 6.27 Transformation of A_k, B_k in each cycle.

6.3.2.6 *Fig. 6.28: Final solution after k cycles*

$$\begin{Bmatrix} A_k \\ B_k \end{Bmatrix} = \begin{bmatrix} cos\theta & -sin\theta \\ +sin\theta & cos\theta \end{bmatrix}^k \begin{Bmatrix} A_0 \\ B_0 \end{Bmatrix} = \begin{bmatrix} cos\ k\theta & -sin\ k\theta \\ +sin\ k\theta & cos\ k\theta \end{bmatrix} \begin{Bmatrix} A_0 \\ B_0 \end{Bmatrix} \rightarrow$$

$$sin\ K\theta = 1 \rightarrow K = \frac{\pi}{2\theta}$$

$$where\ \ sin\ \theta \equiv \frac{2}{N}\sqrt{N-1}$$

$$Large\ N \rightarrow\ K \approx \frac{\pi}{4}\sqrt{N}$$

Fig. 6.28 Number of cycles K needed for peak target amplitude.

Now that transformation property of each cycle has been reduced to a rotation, it is easy to see what k cycles will do: it will rotate the amplitudes by $k\theta$. When do we get a peak in the target amplitude? When $sin\ K\theta = 1$

which leads to a simple expression for K if we assume large N, so that $N-1 \approx N$ and $sin\ \theta \approx \theta$. This describes the numerical results in Fig. 6.22 accurately and shows why the target amplitude $sin\ k\theta$ is oscillatory as a function of the nunber of cycles k.

6.3.3 *Fig. 6.29: Summary*

Now, you may want to look at all the gates that were required to implement one Grover cycle. The Hadamard is used repeatedly to turn $\delta's$ into $h's$ and vice versa. In addition, we have a query gate that flips the sign of the target component and the U_0 gate which flips all signs except the first component. We have only shown two q-bits, but the real power of quantum circuits comes when we scale up the number n of q-bits, because the size of each matrix is $2^n \times 2^n$. So if this were a course on quantum computing we'd now talk about how to implement these transformations with controlled gates so that their complexity increases $\sim n$ and not $\sim 2^n$.

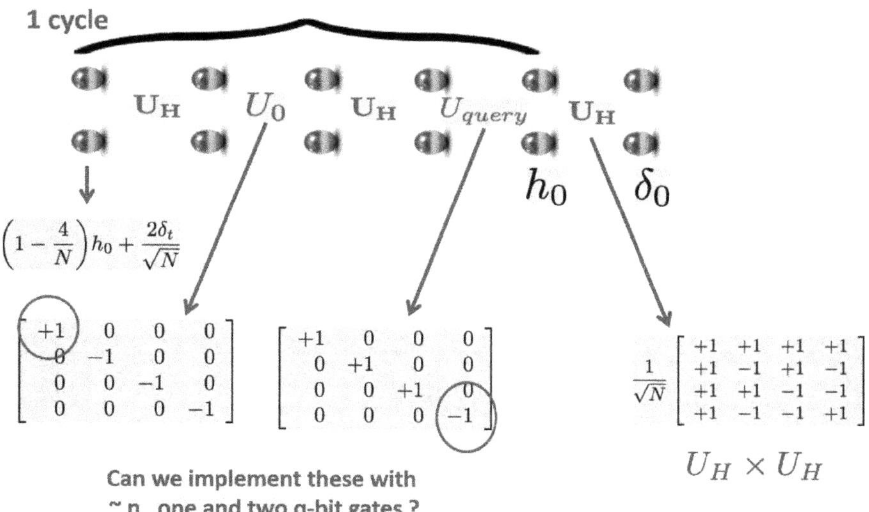

Fig. 6.29 All gates involved in Grover iteration.

Next we'll talk about another seminal algorithm in the quantum literature, known as Shor's algorithm.

6.3.4 *Quiz*

6.3.4.1 *Question 1*

If a system of 20 quantum spins is used to implement the Grover search algorithm, how many queries will be needed?[7]

6.3.4.2 *Question 2*

If a system of 4 quantum spins is used to implement the Grover search algorithm, then after one query cycle what will be the amplitude of the target relative to the background?[8]

[7] $\sim 2^{10}$.

[8] 11:3.

6.4 Shor's Algorithm

This is Lecture 6.4: Watch youtube video

In the last lecture, we talked about this Grover search algorithm, which makes use of quantum transformations to implement an efficient search algorithm. In this lecture, we'll talk about another celebrated quantum algorithm, one that allows you to factorize large numbers efficiently.

6.4.1 *Figs. 6.30-6.32: How the algorithm works*

6.4.1.1 *Fig. 6.30*

The way this works is, supposing I want to factorize a number F, then the first step is to find the period r of the function $a^x \text{mod}(F)$, where a is a number you can choose arbitrarily, any number you want, and what you have to find is the period of this function (see Fig. 6.30). When F is a big number, the difficult part is to find the period of this function and that's what the actual algorithm does, it uses quantum circuits to find the period.

Shor's algorithm

uses quantum circuits to find the period

To factorize a number F
Find the period r of the function

$$f(x) = a^x \ mod(F)$$

such that

$$f(x+r) = f(x)$$

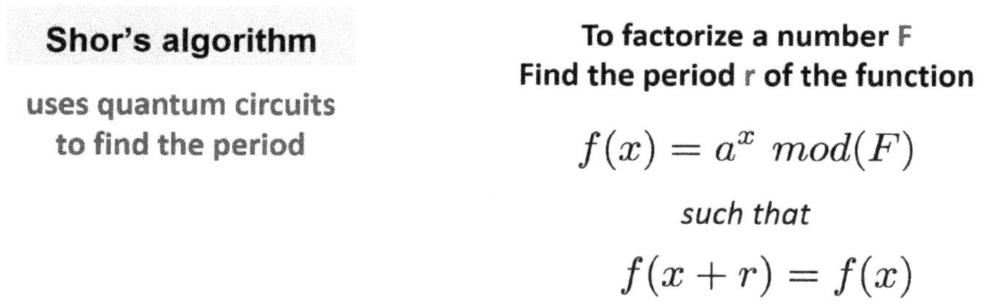

Fig. 6.30 Shor's algorithm.

6.4.1.2 *Figs. 6.31-6.32*

Supposing I'm trying to factorize 15 and I choose a equal to 11 (see Fig. 6.31). So 11^0mod(15) is 1, 11^1mod(15), is 11, 11^2mod(15), that's 121mod(15), which is 1 again, and so it keeps oscillating between 1 and 11. It's a periodic function whose period is 2. Now as I said, a is not unique, you can choose any a. So if you chose a equal 7, then you'd get a different period, 4. In either case you can find the gcd's as shown and obtain the factors 3 and 5. So that's how the overall thing works. Now the point is to find this period.

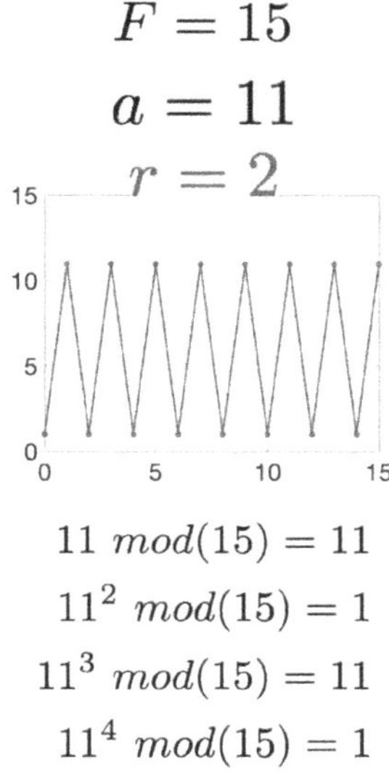

$F = 15$
$a = 11$
$r = 2$
15
10
5
0
0
5
10
15
$11\ mod(15) = 11$
$11^2\ mod(15) = 1$
$11^3\ mod(15) = 11$
$11^4\ mod(15) = 1$

To factorize a number F
Find the period r of the function

$$f(x) = a^x\ mod(F)$$

$a = 7$

$r = 4$

15

10

5

0

0 5 10 15

Fig. 6.31 Finding period of $a^x mod(F)$, MATLAB code included at end of book.

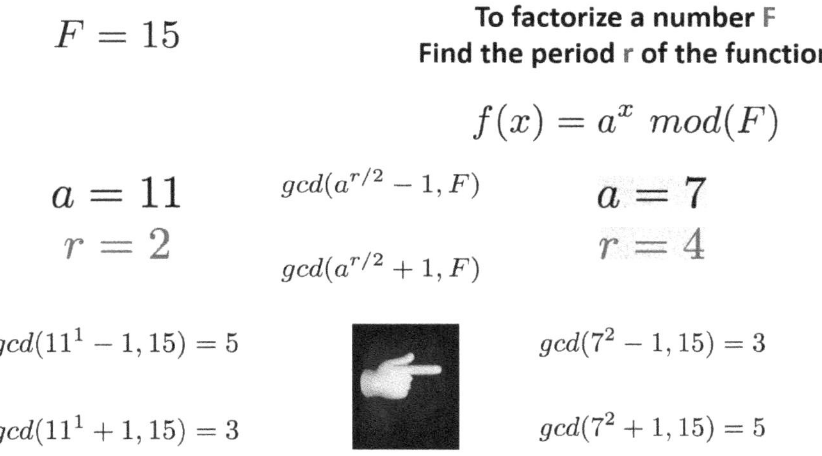

$F = 15$
To factorize a number F
Find the period r of the function
$f(x) = a^x\ mod(F)$
$a = 11$
$r = 2$
$gcd(a^{r/2} - 1, F)$
$gcd(a^{r/2} + 1, F)$
$a = 7$
$r = 4$
$gcd(11^1 - 1, 15) = 5$
$gcd(11^1 + 1, 15) = 3$
$gcd(7^2 - 1, 15) = 3$
$gcd(7^2 + 1, 15) = 5$

Fig. 6.32 Finding factors of F from period r of $a^x mod(F)$, same MATLAB code as in Fig. 6.31.

6.4.2 *Figs. 6.33-6.35: Period-finding with a quantum circuit*

6.4.2.1 *Fig. 6.33*

So how does a quantum circuit find the period? As shown, you have a main register and an auxiliary register each with a certain number of q-bits, and I've chosen 4 for illustration. Actually you'd need more than that even to factorize 15. But just to keep it from getting too messy, let me stick to 4. As you can see, I've already got $2^4 = 16$ components per register and it is kind of hard to see the thing clearly. Just so you can easily recognize which component we are talking about, I've put a red marker after every four of them. So the 4th one is red, 8th one is red, and the 12th one is red, and the 16th one is red indicating 0, 1, 2, 3 up to 15.

You start off with both registers in the zero state which means that the first item has an amplitude of 1, rest are all 0's. The first step is do the Hadamard transformation and we have discussed it often enough that you know immediately what to expect. You get our old friend h_0 from the last lecture, having +1 everywhere with the $1/\sqrt{2^4}$ in front. That's the main register and then, of course, we have the auxiliary register, which is still in the 0 state, what we had named δ_0 earlier. So the overall state of all eight q-bits is the Kronecker product of the two registers: $h_0 \times \delta_0$.

We now apply the gate U_f which performs a transformation so that for the x component of the main register it puts 1 for the $f(x)$ component of the auxiliary register. For our example $f(x)$ is either 1 or 11, for alternating components of the main register. So the composite wavefunction splits into two components $\psi_1 \times \delta_1 + \psi_2 \times \delta_{11}$ where ψ_1 contains all the components for which $f(x) = 1$ and ψ_2 contains the other components for which $f(x) = 11$.

Note that the elements are numbered from 0, so 11 appears at the 12th position which is one of the red-marked elements. As you probably realize, we get two components, $\psi_1 \times \delta_1$ and $\psi_2 \times \delta_{11}$ because the period is 2. If the period had been 4, then I'd have four terms to write. I chose this example so that I have only two parts and I can write it out cleanly.

6.4.2.2 *Fig. 6.34: Quantum Fourier Transform*

Next you apply is what's called the Quantum Fourier Transform, which takes what we have, namely $\psi_1 \times \delta_1 + \psi_2 \times \delta_{11}$ and operates only on the *main register* to produce a set of coefficients which are the

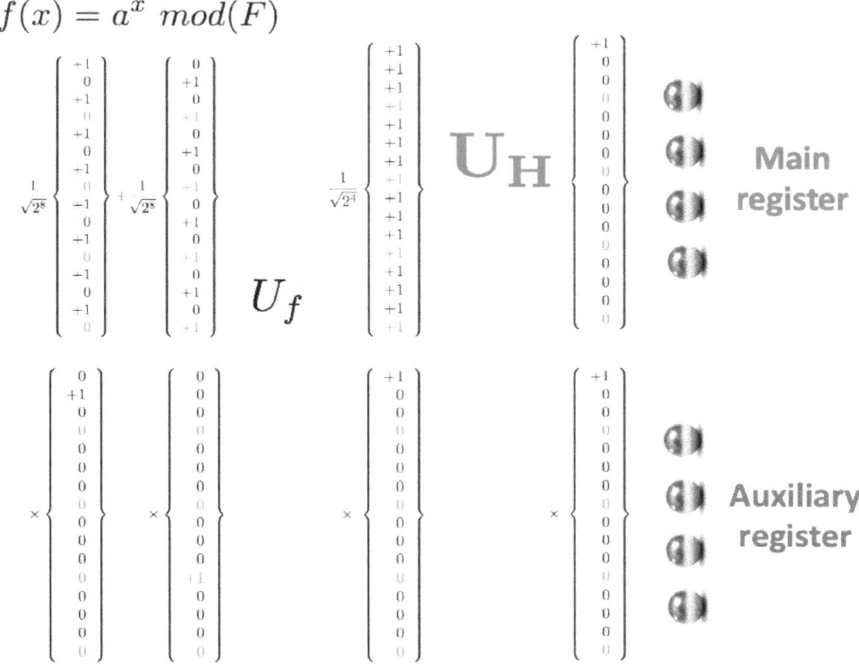

Fig. 6.33 Quantum circuits.

Fourier Transform of the original coefficients giving $\phi_1 \times \delta_1 + \phi_2 \times \delta_{11}$, where ϕ_1 and ϕ_2 are the Fourier transforms of ψ_1 and ψ_2 respectively.

Now both parts of our main register ψ_1 and ψ_2 are periodic functions with the same period, namely 2. So their Fourier transforms are essentially the same function except for an overall phase factor coming from the fact that ψ_1 and ψ_2 are shifted with respect to each other. So we could replace ϕ_1 and ϕ_2 with a common function ϕ having two peaks and write the composite wavefunction as $\sim \phi \times (\delta_1 + \delta_{11})$.

Now if you come in and measure the main register, you will see two peaks and when you see two peaks, you conclude that, r is equal to 2, and remember, that was the original purpose, to find the period r so that you can then go ahead and find the factors (see Fig. 6.34). In real problems the period will be much longer than two, and correspondingly many more peaks in the QFT and you may need special algorithms to find them efficiently.

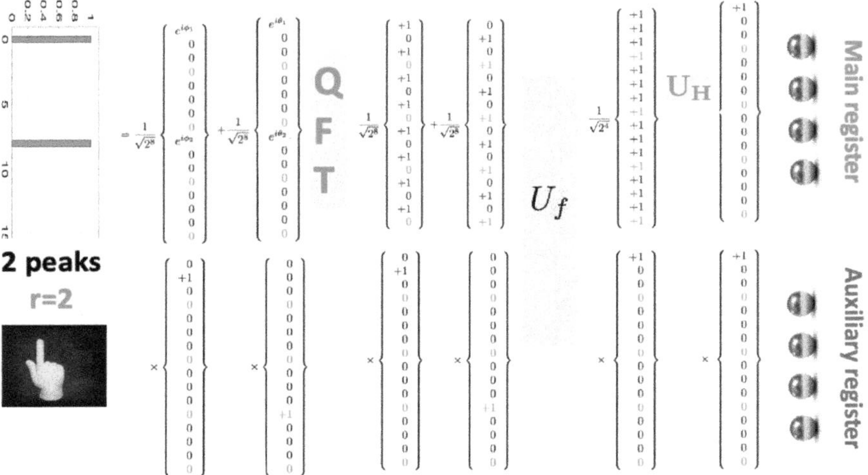

Fig. 6.34 Quantum Fourier Transform.

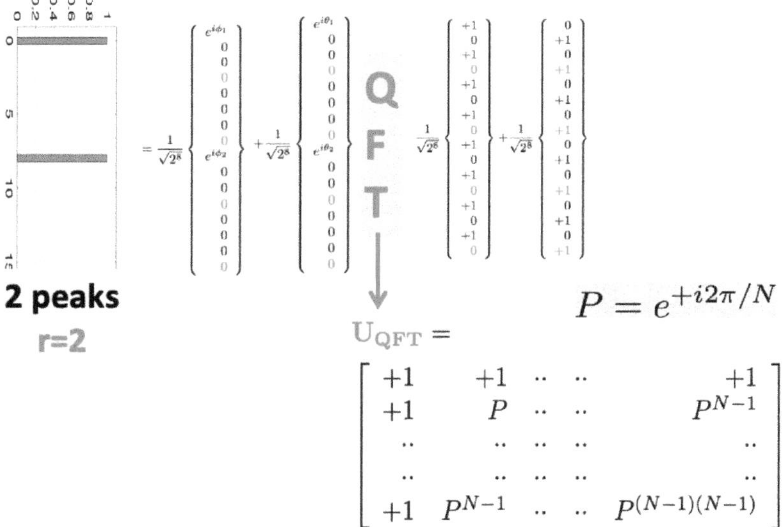

Fig. 6.35 U-matrix for Quantum Fourier Transform.

6.4.2.3 *Fig. 6.35*

Now, what does the *U-matrix* for this Quantum Fourier Transform look like? Well, the basic transformation would look something like this. This is basically the digital Fourier Transform for disrete time samples that you may have seen before. The first column is all 1's. Next one goes 1, P, P^2, etc. The next one goes 1, P^2, P^4, etc, where P is the phase factor $exp(+i2\pi/N)$.

6.4.3 *Fig. 6.36: Summary*

So overall, the picture is something like this. You start with the zero state for both registers $\delta_0 \times \delta_0$, apply the Hadamard to the main register to get $h_0 \times \delta_0$.

Then you apply U_f which anytime there's an x in the main register, associates it with a $f(x)$ in the auxiliary register. giving a sum over r terms, r being the period of $f(x)$: $\sum_{i=0}^{r-1} \psi_i \times \delta_{f(i)}$.

All ψ_i have the same Fourier transform ϕ except for an overall phase factor, so when we apply the QFT to the main register we get $\phi \times \sum_{i=0}^{r-1} \delta_{f(i)}$. Now you look at the main register and count the number of peaks to obtain the period, r.

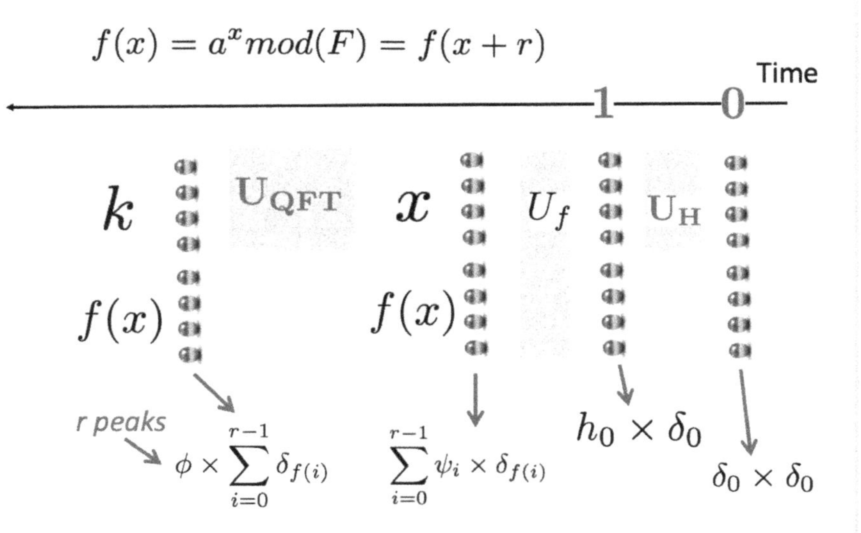

Fig. 6.36 Shor's algorithm.

If this was a course on quantum computing, then the next point we'd be discussing is, how we implement this QFT transformation and this other transformation that I talked about, which takes x and associates an $f(x)$ with the auxiliary register.

So these are things we won't be going into. My main point is to show how these quantum algorithms make use of interference, make use of complex numbers to get peaks in the result, peaks that give you the correct solution in a way that is very different from what you can do with classical circuits.

6.4.4 *Quiz*

6.4.4.1 *Question 1*

The input wavefunction to the U_f gate in Shor's algorithm can be written as $\psi \times A$ which is a Kronecker product of the wavefunction ψ of the main register with that for the auxiliary register, A. After the U_f gate the wavefunction breaks up into r pieces: $\psi_1 \times A_1 + \psi_2 \times A_2 + \cdots + \psi_r \times A_r$.

What is r?[9]

6.4.4.2 *Question 2*

Which register(s) does the quantum Fourier transform (QFT) in Shor's algorithm act on?[10]

[9] r = period of $f(x) = a^x$ mod(F).
[10] Only on the main register, irrespective of the auxiliary register.

6.5 Feynman Paths

This is Lecture 6.5: Watch youtube video

In the last few lectures, we have been talking about gated quantum computing, where the idea is to manipulate the wave function through a sequence of quantum gates and we just discussed two of the celebrated quantum algorithms, which do just that. Now, what we want to do in this lecture is to introduce a different way of looking at what these gates do in terms of what are called Feynman Paths. But instead of looking at specific algorithms, we'll try to illustrate the main point by looking at just the Hadamard gate, the one we introduced Lecture 6.2 and which is used as part of all these algorithms. This illustrates the basic point that we want to get across.

6.5.1 *Figs. 6.37-6.40: Matrix multiplication as a sum of paths*

6.5.1.1 *Fig. 6.37: Hadamard chain*

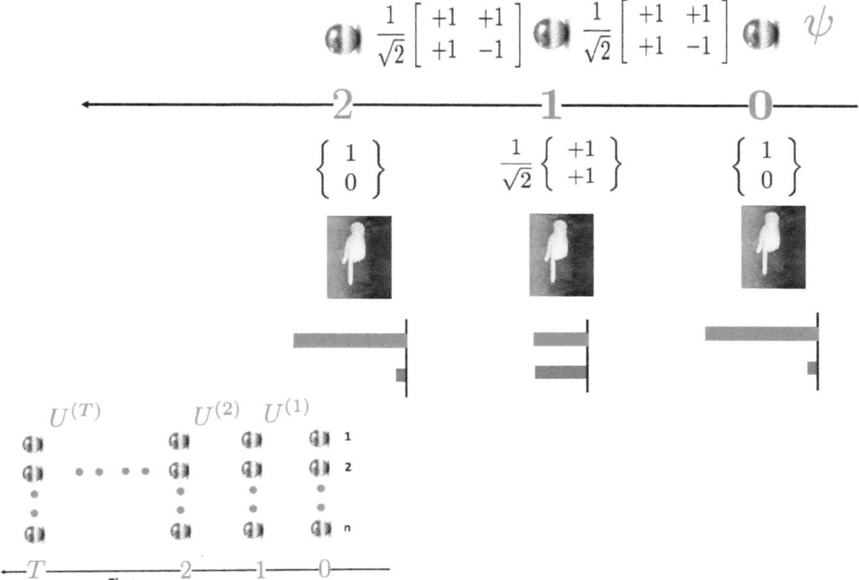

Fig. 6.37 Hadamard gate.

Remember the transformation matrix for a one q-bit Hadamard matrix. The interesting thing is if you start from all up and you apply it once, it spreads it out equally between the up and the down states. Then when you apply it again, it goes back to all up. This spreading and then coming back, that's usually not something you can do with classical systems and that's kind of part of the magic of quantum and comes from this negative sign(s) in the U-matrix. We'll talk more about this.

6.5.1.2 *Fig.* 6.38

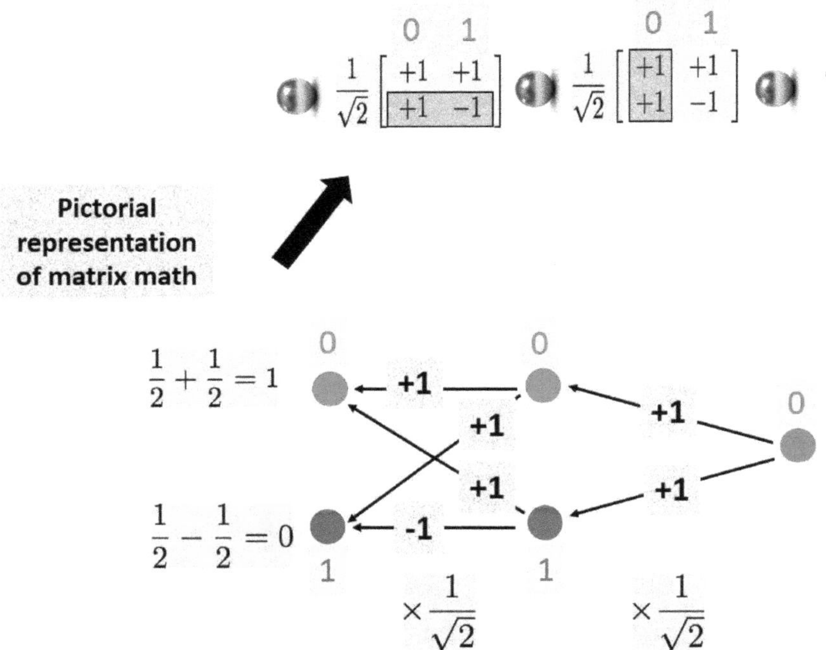

Fig. 6.38 Matrix multiplication as a sum of paths.

Feynman paths give you a different way of looking at it. You could think of it this way, supposing you start with the 0 state initially and we know that after applying this Hadamard gate twice, you get back to 0, and the reason is that if I multiply the two matrices, I get the identity matrix, which takes me back where I started from.

But as we noted in Fig. 4.45 in the classical context, matrix multiplication involves summations like $[AB]_{ij} = \sum_k A_{ik}B_{kj}$ and one can view each term in the summation as the weight of a path that takes you from j to i and the sum over all the paths gives you the final answer.

So you could think of it this way that you went from 0 to 0, but through one of two paths, one path is (000), and the other path is (010). Both have the same amplitude $1/\sqrt{2} \times 1/\sqrt{2}$, that's a 1/2, and you add them up, you get 1.

Now, consider the other outcome, the one that doesn't happen. Here too we have two possible paths (100) and (110) but now the amplitudes are $+1/2$ and $-1/2$ and they cancel out. The negative sign comes from U_{11} which is involved in the path (110), but not in (100). So that's the Feynman path way of thinking, but it is really just a pictorial view of the underlying matrix math.

6.5.1.3 *Fig. 6.39*

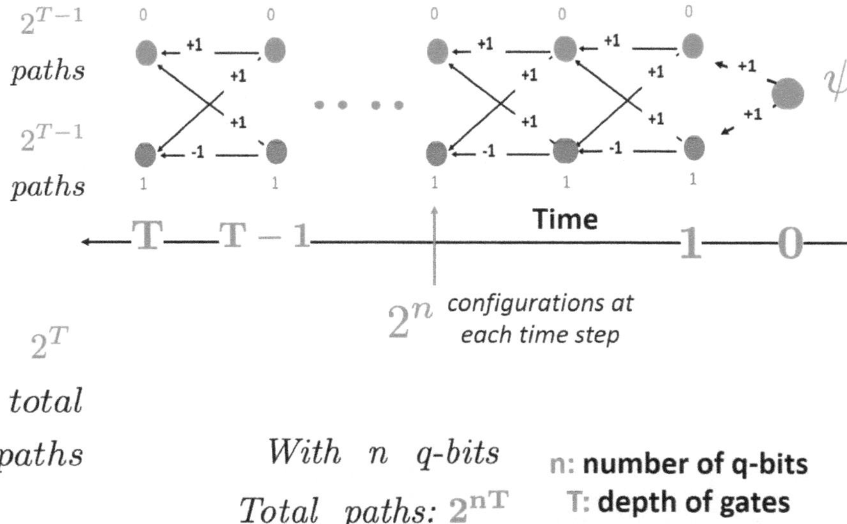

Fig. 6.39 Number of paths increases exponentially with circuit depth.

Now, if you had many of these Hadamard gates, all applied sequentially, at time steps 1, 2, all the way to capital T, then you see we now have lots and lots of paths that can be labeled with binary numbers having $T + 1$ digits. Earlier we had $T = 2$ and so paths were labeled with three digits like (010). So now starting from a particular state, say 0, you have 2^T total paths, half of them 2^{T-1} end up at 0 and the other half at 1.

Now, if you had n q-bits, then there would be 2^n configurations at each time step and the total number of paths would be 2^{nT}. So that's the number that determines how many paths you have: involves both the number n of q-bits and the number of time steps or the depth of the gates, T.

6.5.1.4 *Fig. 6.40: Quantum versus probabilistic circuit*

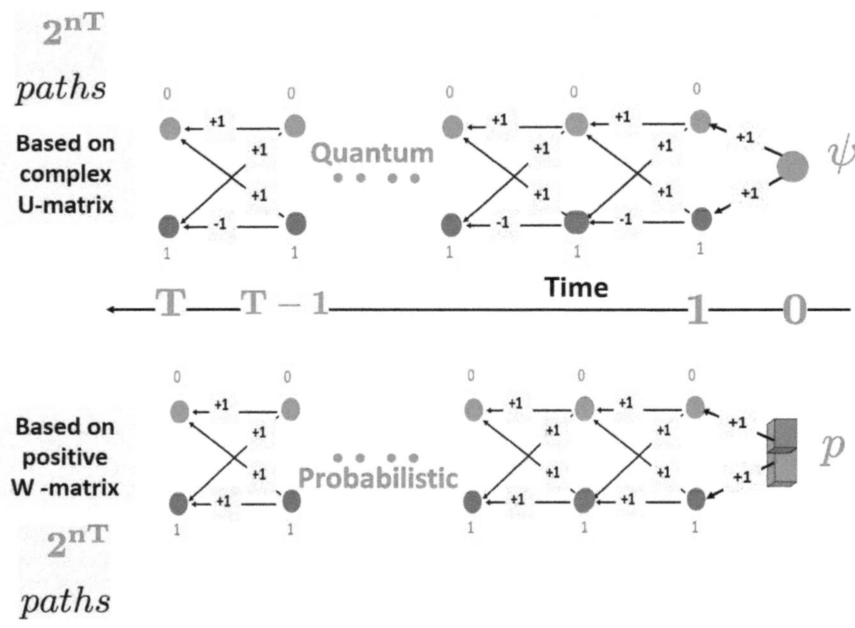

Fig. 6.40 Quantum versus probabilistic circuit.

Now, if you were doing this with a probabilistic circuit, you'd still have the same number of paths. But the difference is that the amplitudes for the paths are determined by the classical transition matrix W which has all positive elements. In the quantum case, that amplitudes are determined by the U matrix where each amplitude is a complex number.

Does that make a difference? Well, not too much if we are just going to multiply the matrices. If we're going to write down matrices and multiply them, then you see, it's not too much more difficult to multiply complex matrices compared to real matrices. It's a little more complicated, but not a whole lot. But in practice, you see, as you scale the problem up, you cannot really afford to write down matrices and multiply them, why? Because the matrices are $2^n \times 2^n$, and as we know, as n goes up, this 2^n just goes up exponentially, and it's very soon it's out of control.

6.5.2 *Fig. 6.41: Quantum Monte Carlo*

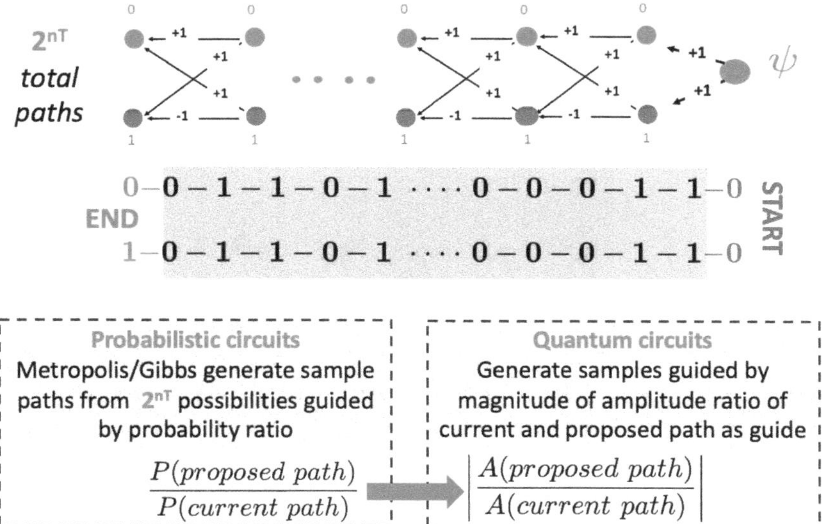

Fig. 6.41 Adapting sampling techniques to quantum circuits.

So what do you do? Well, for practical problems, you use sampling techniques as we discussed in Chapters 3 and 4, which let us operate in nT space and generate samples in the 2^{nT} space. Similarly we could generate sample paths that start with 0 as shown and end on a 0 or a 1. In classical sampling we use some algorithm like Metropolis or Gibbs to select proposals based on the probability ratio of the proposed path and the current path. In quantum sampling we have complex path amplitudes whose squared magnitude gives the probability. We could use the same classical algorithms replacing the probability ratios with the magnitude of amplitude ratios. But we also have to replace ordinary samples with *complex samples* whose phase reflects the *phase of the path amplitudes*. That seems straightforward enough, but replacing positive samples with complex samples is not as innocent as it sounds. It leads to the well-known sign problem associated with Quantum Monte Carlo.

6.5.3 *Fig. 6.42: Sign problem*

Actually our illustrative problem with the Hadamard chain presents an extreme example that clearly shows the difficulty with complex samples. Consider the two sets of paths shown, assuming just one q-bit ($n = 1$), and a depth of $T = 10$. So we have $2^10 = 1024$ paths, 512 of which end up at (0) and the other 512 end up at (1). Interestingly every path has the same magnitude, $(1/\sqrt{2})^{10}$, but some are positive and some are negative. This is because the amplitude of any path is a product of ten elements of the U_H matrix, and all elements of this matrix have the same magnitude $1/\sqrt{2}$.

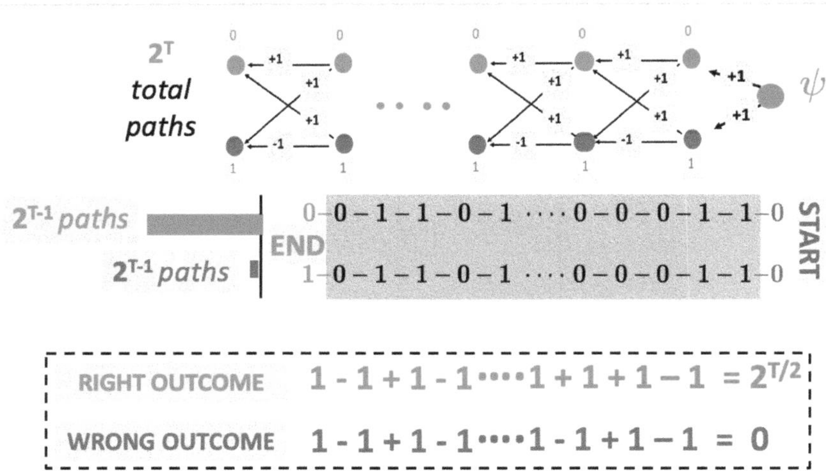

Fig. 6.42 Sign problem.

But if both outputs (0) and (1) have 512 paths leading upto them all having the same magnitude $(1/\sqrt{2})^{10}$, then why do they add up to 1 for one and to 0 for the other? *Answer:* For the wrong output (1), 256 paths are positive, 256 are negative, and they cancel perfectly. For the correct output (0), 272 paths are positive, 240 are negative, giving a a net positive of 32. Since each path has a magnitude $(1/\sqrt{2})^{10} = 1/32$, they add up to 1.

This cancellation of paths makes it much harder to get reliable results, it requires a lot more samples to be able to distinguish between the correct output (0), $272 - 240 = 32$ and the wrong output (1), $256 - 256$. Roughly speaking we could say that the signal to noise ratio is 32/1024. The situation gets worse as the depth gets larger.

In general the signal to noise ratio is $2^{T/2}/2^T = 2^{-T/2}$, and to detect the signal reliably we have to reduce the noise by collecting lots of samples, N_s: $1/\sqrt{N_s} \sim 2^{-T/2} \rightarrow N_s \sim 2^T$. More generally the number of samples $\sim 2^{nT}$. But the point is that sampling is really not getting us any advantage at all. If we are going to collect $\sim 2^{nT}$ samples, we might as well sum all $\sim 2^{nT}$ exactly. The strength of the sampling method lies in being able to get accurate answers with far less samples than the total population of 2^{nT} paths. Because all paths in this problem have the same amplitude (magnitude wise) our method is choosing all paths with equal probability. This amounts to random sampling and we do not get any of the advantages that usually come from classic sampling algorithms like Metropolis or Gibbs.

Now, although we did not discuss it in Chapter 5, the density matrix $\sim e^{-\beta H}$ in adiabatic quantum computing can also be evaluated by sampling Feynman paths, and in that case people make this distinction between stoquastic Hamiltonians and non-stoquastic Hamiltonians. Stoquastic ones are those where all paths have the same sign with no cancellations, and so sampling is very effective, whereas non-stoquastic ones are those that involve path cancellation, with its associated sign problems that we just discussed.

In this chapter we have been focusing on gated quantum computing, which is based on the quantum transition matrix $U = e^{-iH}$ which is almost always non-stoquastic. But the most severe sign problems arise when all elements have the same magnitude like the Hadamard matrix or the *U-matrix* for the quantum Fourier transform (QFT), Fig. ??. Our standard sampling algorithms then lead to essentially random sampling, requiring an enormous number of samples comparable to the total number of paths.

Problems with severe *sign problems* like this are precisely the ones where quantum computers can shine by comparison. In the sampling method, an output that has zero probability, attracts 2^{T-1} samples, which cancel out to give zero. By contrast a q-bit in a quantum computer would know *instinctively* that the net wavefunction for this output is zero, and not a single sample would reach that output.

Of course, that's true only of the ideal quantum computer, the one that's noiseless. In the real world, we have to deal with noise because the quantum computer is in touch with its surroundings, which have noise that destroys the phase and when the phase is destroyed, the samples cannot cancel very effectively and give you nulls. It remains to be seen how much noisy quantum computers can actually help us with problems having sign problems.

6.5.4 *Quiz*

6.5.4.1 *Question 1*

A Hadamard gate $\frac{1}{\sqrt{2}}\begin{bmatrix} 1 & 1 \\ 1 & -1 \end{bmatrix}$ acting 20 times in sequence on a wavefunction $\{0 \quad 1\}^T$ produces the same wavefunction $\{0 \quad 1\}^T$ at the end.

2^{19} Feynman paths lead from the specified initial state $\{0 \quad 1\}^T$ to the final state $\{0 \quad 1\}^T$.
2^{19} Feynman paths also lead from the specified initial state $\{0 \quad 1\}^T$ to the WRONG final state $\{1 \quad 0\}^T$.

Why is the final probability for the wrong state so much smaller than that for the correct state?[11]

6.5.4.2 *Question 2*

A Pauli-X gate $\begin{bmatrix} 0 & 1 \\ 1 & 0 \end{bmatrix}$ acting 20 times in sequence on a wavefunction $\{0 \quad 1\}^T$ produces the same wavefunction $\{0 \quad 1\}^T$ at the end.

[11]Because for the wrong state half the paths have negative amplitudes canceling the other half which have positive amplitudes.

2^{19} Feynman paths lead from the specified initial state $\{0 \quad 1\}^T$ to the final state $\{0 \quad 1\}^T$.
2^{19} Feynman paths also lead from the specified initial state $\{0 \quad 1\}^T$ to the WRONG final state $\{1 \quad 0\}^T$.

Why is the final probability for the wrong state so much smaller tha that for the correct state?[12]

[12]Because for the wrong state all the paths have zero amplitude.

6.6 Fig. 6.43: 5-minute Summary

Watch youtube video, after 2:20

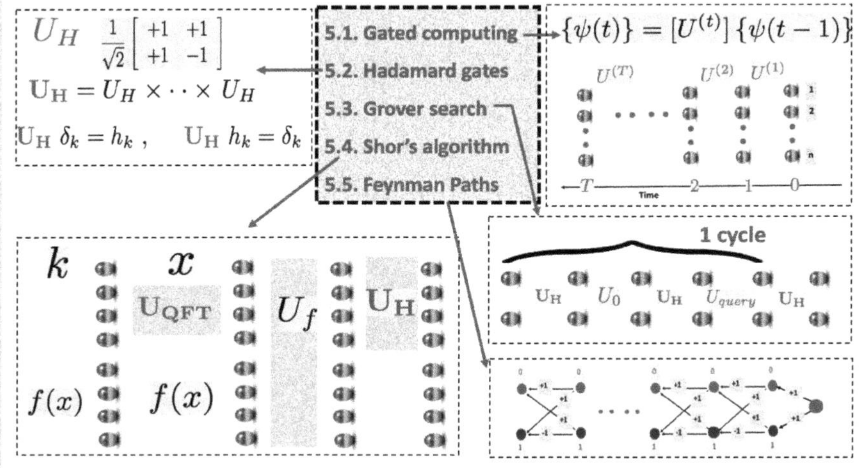

Fig. 6.43 Chapter 6 summary.

In this chapter we transitioned to gated computing involving isolated quantum systems that can be described in terms of its wave function which is transformed in time according to these quantum gates, applied sequentially one after the other. In Lecture 6.1 we introduced the quantum transition matrix U describing this transformation of wavefunctions. It is also the quantum analog of the classical transition matrix W in Chapter 4.

In Lecture 6.2 we introduced the Hadamard gate which is a very useful gate and used in many quantum circuits. It also illustrates the basic magic of quantum circuits, coming from the negative element in U which allows it to do something very remarkable: If you start from a delta function distribution, delta function meaning where all the amplitude is in one particular state and apply a Hadamard gate to it, it spreads out into a distribution where all components are present, but then you apply the Hadamard gate again and you come back to the delta function, this is something that wouldn't happen with probabilistic distributions. Once you have spread out, it will continue spreading.

In Lecture 6.3 and 6.4 we talked about how this Hadamard gate is combined with other ideas in two celebrated quantum algorithms, the Grover's search and Shor's algorithm. Finally, in Lecture 6.5 we talked about this concept of Feynman Paths, how you can think about all these quantum gates, or probabilistic circuits within the same framework. What you get at the end is like a sum of the amplitudes of different paths and the difference between the quantum and the classical is, in the classical case all paths have positive amplitudes whereas in the quantum case they can have negative or even complex amplitudes which can cancel each other out, and because of this "sign problem" the sampling procedure which is so effective with classical system is trickier to implement in the case of quantum systems.

But quantum systems in order to perform their magic require all the phases to be precisely preserved, and in practice you have to deal with noise and control it. At this time there is worldwide effort and research trying to see if we can use noisy quantum systems to solve real world problems more efficiently than their classical counterparts.

Epilogue

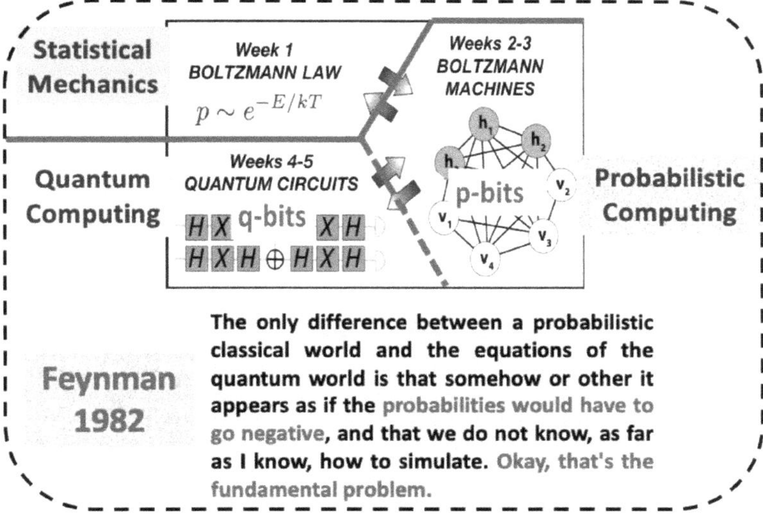

Fig. 6.44 In this course, we've brought together concepts from three very different areas.

I personally was very intrigued by something I had read over 40 years ago. It was a comment by Feynman in a paper that is actually one of the papers that inspired the world of quantum computing. But in that paper before getting to quantum computing, he introduced the idea of a probabilistic computer and he made the point that what really makes the quantum world so different is, it is as if you have negative probabilities, something that's unknown in our everyday classical world. And that is the fundamental difference.

This thought seems to be just as true today as it was 40 years ago, and that is what I've tried to convey in this course using modern examples from machine learning and quantum computing. I was hoping to give you a different perspective, showing the connections between these two different worlds. I hope you find that enjoyable and will have use for it.

But as I mentioned at the outset, this is a work in progress. Hope to have a more complete story next time.

MATLAB Codes

MATLAB code for Figs. 3.36 and 3.37, Lecture 3.3:

```
% Max-cut problem
clear all
rng(1)

N = 6; C = zeros(N); N2 = N/2;
C(1,2) = 12; C(2,1) = C(1,2);
C(1,5) = 3; C(5,1) = C(1,5);
C(3,4) = 6; C(4,3) = C(3,4);
C(2,5) = 5; C(5,2) = C(2,5);
C(3,6) = 8; C(6,3) = C(3,6);
C(4,6) = 14; C(6,4) = C(4,6);

u=ones(N,1);
% % % %      ctr=randperm(N); C=C(ctr,ctr);

X=[0:2^N-1]; Look = 2.^[N-1:-1:0];
I0=1/4; T = 1e6;

K=5*0; % enforcing equal number in each group
M=+1; % +1 for min-cut, -1 for max-cut

w= 2*K - M*4*C; w= w - diag(diag(w));
x = -K*(N-1) + M*C*u + M*C'*u;

% % % % Boltzmann law
    rhos=zeros(N,N); rhom=zeros(N,N); E=zeros(1,2^N);

    for ii= 1:2^N
        n=de2bi(ii-1,N,'left-msb')';
        E(ii) = n' * x + 0.5 * n' * w * n ;
    end
P=exp(-I0*E); P=P./sum(P);

```

```
% % % % Sampling method

n=de2bi(1,N,'left-msb')'; %initial state
for ii=1:T
for jj=randperm(N)

     xx= x(jj) + w(jj,:)*n;
     f=1/(1+exp(I0*xx));
          n(jj)=0;  if f > rand
                       n(jj)=1; end
end
nn(:, ii)=n;
end

D=Look*nn;
PSL=histcounts(D,[0:2^N]);
PSL=PSL./T;

figure(2)
bar(X',[PSL'],0.75)
set(gca,'Fontsize',24)
grid on

figure(20)
PP=P;
PP=reshape(PP,2^N2,2^N2);
bar3(PP,0.25)
set(gca,'xticklabel', dec2bin([0:2^N2-1]) )
set(gca,'xticklabelrotation', -90)
set(gca,'yticklabel', dec2bin([0:2^N2-1]) )
set(gca,'yticklabelrotation', 90)
set(gca,'Fontsize',14)
grid on
```

MATLAB code for Figs. 3.59 and 3.60, Lecture 3.5:

```
%%%% General learning code for Boltzmann machine with hidden units using Boltzmann law
%%%% Jan Kaiser, 6/13/2020

clear all

rng(1)
momentum=0.9*0; epsilon=1e-2; weightcost=1e-4; % learning rate, regularization
NT=1e5; %run time

%%%% Use this to train full adder with no hidden units
Nv = 5; Nh = 0; Nm= Nv + Nh; % visible, hidden
d=zeros(1,2^Nv);     d([0 6 10 13 18 21 25 31]+1)=1; % PDF, full
```

```
    adder

% Nv = 6; Nh = 4; Nm= Nv + Nh; % visible, hidden
% d=zeros(1,2^Nv);     d([5 10 17 24 29 40 48 51 57 62]+1)=1;

df=repelem(d,1,2^Nh);

J=randn(Nm,Nm);J=J-diag(diag(J));J=(J+J')/2; Jinc=zeros(Nm,Nm);
h=zeros(1,Nm); hinc=zeros(1,Nm); tic

for epoch=1:NT

    for ii=0:2^Nm-1
        m=flip(de2bi(ii,Nm))'*2-1; mm(ii+1,:)=m';
        E(ii+1)=-m'*J/2*m-h*m;
    end
    E=E-min(E);
    Pf=exp(-E);Z=sum(Pf); Pf=Pf/Z; % Free phase

    for ii=1:2^Nv  %% artificallly normalize for hidden units
        P0(1+(ii-1)*2^Nh:(ii)*2^Nh)=...
          Pf(1+(ii-1)*2^Nh:(ii)*2^Nh)./sum(Pf(1+(ii-1)*2^Nh:(ii
    )*2^Nh));
    end
    Pc=P0.*df; ZZ=sum(Pc); Pc=Pc/ZZ; % Clamped phase

%%%% correlations
    Corrf=zeros(Nm,Nm); Corrc=zeros(Nm,Nm);
    for ii=1:Nm
        for jj=1:Nm
            Corrf(ii,jj)=sum(mm(:,ii).*mm(:,jj).*Pf',1);
            Corrc(ii,jj)=sum(mm(:,ii).*mm(:,jj).*Pc',1);
        end
    end
    Corrf = Corrf-diag(diag(Corrf));
    Corrc = Corrc-diag(diag(Corrc));

%%%% bias
    hf=Pf*mm; hc=Pc*mm;

%%%% update
    Jinc=epsilon*(Corrc-Corrf-weightcost*J) + momentum*Jinc;
    hinc=epsilon*(hc-hf) + momentum*hinc;

    J=J+Jinc; h=h+hinc;

        Jincrement(epoch)=sum(sum(abs(Jinc)));
        hincrement(epoch)=sum(abs(hinc));   err(epoch)=sum(abs(
    Pf-Pc));

```

```
        if mod(epoch,1e3)==0
            disp(['Learning process: ',num2str(epoch/NT*100),'%
        ',...
            'Time: ', num2str(toc)])
        end

end

save J

    if Nh==0
        Pfv=Pf; Pcv=Pc;
    end

    if Nh~=0
        Pfv=sum(reshape(Pf,2^Nh,2^Nv));
        Pcv=sum(reshape(Pc,2^Nh,2^Nv));
    end

%%
%%%% Plot results
figure(1)
bar([0:2^Nv-1],[Pfv(1:2^Nv)',Pcv(1:2^Nv)'],0.5)
set(gca,'Fontsize',12)
legend('learned distribution','target distribution')
ylabel('PDF')
xlabel('configuration')
```

MATLAB code for Fig. 3.61, Lecture 3.5:

```
% Separating hidden variables
clear all
rng(1)

% 5 10 17 24 29 40 48 51 57 62, 10 peaks
load J % First run previous code with these peaks and save J.
    mat

Nv=6; N=10; u=ones(N,1);
J = -J; h = -h;
w=4*J; % % % % Bipolar to Binary
x=2*h'-J*u-J'*u;

%%%%%%%%%%%%%%%%%%%%%%%%%%%%%%%%%%%%%%%%%%%%%%%%%%%%%%%%%%%%%%%%%%%
I0 = 1/2;
% % % Boltzmann law
for ii= 1:2^N
    n=de2bi(ii-1,N,'left-msb')';
    E(ii) =  n' * x + 0.5 * n' * w * n ;
end
```

```
Emin=min(E);
P=exp(-I0*(E-Emin)); P=P./sum(P);
PP=reshape(P,16,64);

% % Sampling
T = 1e4;
Look = 2.^[N-1:-1:0];

n=de2bi(1,N,'left-msb')'; %initial state
for ii=1:T
for jj=randperm(N)

    xx= x(jj) + w(jj,:)*n;

    f=1/(1+exp(I0*xx));
        n(jj)=0;  if f > rand
                      n(jj)=1; end
end
nn(:, ii)=n;
end

D=Look*nn;

PSL=histcounts(D,[0:2^N]);
PSL=PSL./T;
PPSL=reshape(PSL,16,64);

X=[0:2^Nv-1];

figure(1) % Boltzmann
bar(X',[sum(PP)'],0.75)
set(gca,'Fontsize',24)
grid on
xlim([-1 64])

figure(10) % Boltzmann
bar3(PP,0.25)
set(gca,'XTickLAbel', {0:15} )
set(gca,'xticklabelrotation', 90)
set(gca,'YTickLabel', [0:63] )
set(gca,'yticklabelrotation', 90)
set(gca,'Fontsize',0.1)
grid on
zlim([0 0.1])

figure(2) % Sampling
bar(X',[sum(PPSL)'],0.75)
set(gca,'Fontsize',24)
grid on

```

```
figure(20) % sampling
bar3(PPSL,0.25)
set(gca,'XTickLAbel', {0:15} )
set(gca,'xticklabelrotation', 90)
set(gca,'YTickLabel', [0:63] )
set(gca,'yticklabelrotation', 90)
set(gca,'Fontsize',0.1)
grid on
zlim([0 0.1])
```

MATLAB code for Fig. 5.42, Lecture 5.5:

```
% Max-cut problem Annealing, Classical and quantum
clear all
rng(1)

E0=1; hx=15; % Change these parameters

N2=3;
A=randi(10,N2); A= A-diag(diag(A)); A=A+A';
B=randi(10,N2); B= B-diag(diag(B)); B=B+B';
Z=0*ones(N2,N2);

C = [A Z;Z' B]./2;

    N=length(C); u=ones(N,1);
    ctr=randperm(N); C=C(ctr,ctr);

K=5; % enforcing equal number in each group
M=+1; % +1 for min-cut, -1 for max-cut

X=[0:2^N-1];

w= 2*K - M*4*C; w= w - diag(diag(w));
x = -K*(N-1) + M*C*u + M*C'*u;

    % Bipolar
    J = 0.25 * w;
    h = 0.5*x + 0.125 * w * u + 0.125 * w' * u;

% % % % Quantum

sx=[0 1;1 0]; sy=[0 -1i;+1i 0]; sz=[+1 0;0 -1]; s0=[1 0;0 1];

s1z=kron(sz,kron(s0,kron(s0,kron(s0,kron(s0,s0)))));
s2z=kron(s0,kron(sz,kron(s0,kron(s0,kron(s0,s0)))));
s3z=kron(s0,kron(s0,kron(sz,kron(s0,kron(s0,s0)))));
s4z=kron(s0,kron(s0,kron(s0,kron(sz,kron(s0,s0)))));
s5z=kron(s0,kron(s0,kron(s0,kron(s0,kron(sz,s0)))));
s6z=kron(s0,kron(s0,kron(s0,kron(s0,kron(s0,sz)))));
```

```
s1x=kron(sx,kron(s0,kron(s0,kron(s0,kron(s0,s0)))));
s2x=kron(s0,kron(sx,kron(s0,kron(s0,kron(s0,s0)))));
s3x=kron(s0,kron(s0,kron(sx,kron(s0,kron(s0,s0)))));
s4x=kron(s0,kron(s0,kron(s0,kron(sx,kron(s0,s0)))));
s5x=kron(s0,kron(s0,kron(s0,kron(s0,kron(sx,s0)))));
s6x=kron(s0,kron(s0,kron(s0,kron(s0,kron(s0,sx)))));

H= h(1)*s1z + h(2)*s2z + h(3)*s3z + h(4)*s4z + h(5)*s5z + h(6)*
    s6z...
+ J(1,2)*s1z*s2z + J(1,3)*s1z*s3z + J(1,4)*s1z*s4z + J(1,5)*s1z
    *s5z + J(1,6)*s1z*s6z...
+ J(2,3)*s2z*s3z + J(2,4)*s2z*s4z + J(2,5)*s2z*s5z + J(2,6)*s2z
    *s6z...
+ J(3,4)*s3z*s4z + J(3,5)*s3z*s5z + J(3,6)*s3z*s6z...
+ J(4,5)*s4z*s5z + J(4,6)*s4z*s6z + J(5,6)*s5z*s6z...
+ hx*s1x + hx*s2x + hx *s3x + hx*s4x + hx*s5x + hx*s6x;

rho=expm(-E0*H); rho=rho./trace(rho);

Q=diag(abs(rho));

% % % % Plot

figure(20)
bar(X',[Q],0.5,'r')
set(gca,'Fontsize',16)
grid on
ylim([0 max(Q)+0.005])
legend('quantum model')

% % % % Classical Boltzmann calculation, works only for hx=0
for ii= 1:2^N
    n=de2bi(ii-1,N,'left-msb')';
    E(ii) = n' * x + 0.5 * n' * w * n ;
end
P=exp(-E0*E); P=P./sum(P);

figure(2)
bar(X',[flip(P)'],0.5,'k')
set(gca,'Fontsize',24)
grid on
ylim([0 max(P)+0.005])
legend('classical model')
```

MATLAB code for Fig. 6.22, Lecture 6.3:

```
% Grover search
clear all

n=10; % # of q-bits
N=2^n;  NT=40; % Number of iterations

k=N/2; % Target configuration
R=eye(N); R(k,k)=-1; %U_Q

H=[1 1;1 -1]./sqrt(2); HH=H;
for ii=1:n-1
    HH=kron(HH,H);
end

% Diffusion matrix
DD=-eye(N,N); DD(1,1)=+1; D=HH*DD*HH; % UH * UO * UH

% Alternative expression for diffusion matrix
% D=-eye(N)+(2/N)*ones(N);

psi=ones(N,1)./sqrt(N); % Initial wavefunction created by first Hadamard
phi(:,1) = psi.^2;
for ii=2:NT
    psi=D*R*psi; % Grover iteration
    phi(:,ii)=psi.^2;
end

hold on
h=plot(phi(k,:),'ko-');
set(gca,'fontsize',[20])
xlabel('Number of cycles')
ylabel('Amplitude of target')
grid on
```

MATLAB code for Figs. 6.31 and 6.32, Lecture 6.4:

```
% Factorizing F, by finding the period of a^x mod(F)
clear all

n=4;N=2^n;

a=7; F=15; aa=a;
for ii=0:20
  m(ii+1)= mod(aa, F);
  aa= a*m(ii+1);
end

X=[0:20];
```

```
h=plot(X,m,'r-o');
set(h,'Linewidth',2.0)
set(gca,'fontsize',[32])
grid on

r=4;
[gcd(a^(r/2)-1,F) gcd(a^(r/2)+1,F)]
```

Index

Milton Keynes UK
Ingram Content Group UK Ltd.
UKHW050954190824
447134UK00013B/733